Ethics and Human Rights in a Globalized World

Ethics and Human Rights in a Globalized World

An Interdisciplinary and International Approach

Edited by

Klaus Hoffmann-Holland

Mohr Siebeck

Klaus Hoffmann-Holland is Professor of Criminology and Criminal Law at Freie Universität Berlin.

This publication was funded by the German-Israeli Year of Science and Technology 2008.

ISBN 978-3-16-149992-0

Die Deutsche Nationalbibliothek lists this publication in the Deutsche Nationalbibliographie; detailed bibligraphic data is available in the Internet at *http://dnb.d-nb.de*.

The book was typeset and printed by Gulde-Druck in Tübingen on non-aging paper and bound by Großbuchbinderei Spinner in Otterweier.

Printed in Germany.

Preface

In November 2008, the Freie Universität Berlin together with the Hebrew University of Jerusalem, the resident Minerva Center for Human Rights and the Israel Democracy Institute held the symposium "Ethics and Human Rights in a Globalized World". It was kindly funded by the German Federal Ministry of Education and Research. The event was embedded in the German-Israeli Year of Science and Technology, and aimed at developing sustainable cooperation in human rights research between Berlin and Jerusalem, with a focus on the promotion of young researchers.

Both Germany and Israel have a long tradition of ethics and human rights research. The scientific cooperation between the two countries has, however, usually demonstrated a strong disciplinary focus and has yet to take sufficient advantage of the potential of multidisciplinary approaches. In addition, the German-Israeli cooperation could benefit in the long term through increased networking of already existing thematically similar projects and from resulting synergies. Against this background, the initiative of the Freie Universität Berlin and the Hebrew University of Jerusalem provides the field of German-Israeli human rights research with a common and structured platform for promoting continuing cooperation between the two countries in this area.

The purpose of the cooperation between the two institutions is to develop research structures that pay due attention to the international and interdisciplinary aspects of ethical issues concerning the protection of human rights. To this end, the main focus will be on taking measures that encourage academic exchange between young German and Israeli researchers. Postgraduate students are given the opportunity to benefit from the international cooperation and interdisciplinary-oriented research.

In the name of all the participants in the symposium, I thank the Federal Minister of Education and Research and the Israeli Minister of Science, Culture and Sports for their generous support within the framework of the German-Israeli Year of Science and Technology in 2008.

I also thank my colleagues from the Hebrew University of Jerusalem, Yuval Shany, Mordechai Kremnitzer and Danny Evron, for all their enthusiasm in organizing this symposium. The symposium would also not have been possible without the work of the staff of the Minerva Center for Human Rights, the Israel Democracy Institute and the Freie Universität Berlin, especially Anat

Mishali and Merav Kaddar from the Minerva Center and Hagit Agmon from the Israel Democracy Institute, as well as Matthias Kuder and Kristina Kühl from the Freie Universität Berlin. My thanks go as well to Sr. Katherine Wolff, Sophie Birkner, Matthias Simonis and Jan Storm.

Berlin/London, February 2009 Klaus Hoffmann-Holland

Table of Contents

Chapter II

International Criminal Law

Chapter III

Structures of Implementation of Human Rights in a Globalized World

Chapter IV
Selected Human Rights Aspects

Report on the Discussions

Ethics and Human Rights in a Globalized World

An Interdisciplinary Approach[1]

Klaus Hoffmann-Holland

I. Rights, Wrongs and Ethical Contributions

In his "secular theory of the origins of rights", *Alan Dershowitz* argues that rights neither come from religion, nor nature, nor logic, nor law, but from wrongs (such as the human experience with injustice).[2] An example can be found in the development of international humanitarian law (that is closely linked to human rights law[3]). The milestone of the 1864 Geneva Convention for the Amelioration of the Condition of the Wounded in Armies in the Field, the first general multilateral convention and the root of the Geneva law, is a reaction to the aftermath of the battle of Solferino in 1859, where 38.000 men were lying on the battlefield without sufficient care.[4]

But we can see that human beings faced wrongdoings of all kinds throughout history, and often the result was not a right or its enforcement (and isn't the denial of a right also a wrong?). What was the right or the enforcement of rights after September 11, 2001? The attempt to curtail terrorism very often led to

---

[1] This article is deeply influenced by the discussions, letters and emails before, during and after the symposium "Ethics and Human Rights in a Globalized World" in Jerusalem, an event during the German-Israeli Year of Science and Technology 2008. To name but a few, I have to thank Daniel Bogner, Michael Bongardt, Matthias Kuder, Kristina Kühl and Kristina Roepstorff for many thoughts, perspectives and ideas expressed in this article.

[2] *A. Dershowitz*, Rights from Wrongs – A Secular Theory of the Origins of Rights, New York 2004, pp. 8 f.

[3] *R. Kolb*, The Relationship between International Humanitarian Law and Human Rights Law: A Brief History of the 1948 Universal Declaration of Human Rights and the 1949 Geneva Conventions, International Review of the Red Cross 324 (1998), p. 409; *R. Provost*, International human rights and humanitarian law, 3rd ed. Cambridge 2004; *W. Sandholtz*, Humanitarian Intervention – Global Enforcement of Human Rights?, in: A. Brysk (ed.), Globalization and Human Rights, Berkeley 2002, p. 201.

[4] *J. K. Klefner*, Protection of the Wounded, Sick and Shipwrecked, in: D. Fleck (ed.), The Handbook of International Humanitarian Law, 2nd ed. Oxford 2008, pp. 325 f.

curtailing human rights.[5] We should look again more closely at the example of the battle of Solferino: The initiative of *Henry Dunant*, who was an eye witness of the sufferings of the wounded in the field, was necessary.[6] So it takes more than wrongs to produce rights. The question is: What is the mechanism or context that may transform a wrong to a right? This is a question that cannot be answered within the narrow confines of laws or any other single discipline. The answer can only be found in an interdisciplinary perspective. Different perspectives may help to understand the dimensions of a phenomenon. The importance of perspectives may be demonstrated by an analogy with art. We can compare two paintings, both showing aspects of the battle of Solferino: In his 1863 painting "Napoleon III at the Battle of Solferino", *Jean-Louis-Ernest Meissonier* concentrates on living mounted soldiers in file, showing only little of the disorder. This is one way of looking at the events of Solferino. *Katharina Ziemke*, however, lets us take part in a view that may be closer to what *Dunant* witnessed. In her painting "Solferino", she doesn't show any living soldier, but only blood and dead bodies, most of them torn apart.

Going even further back in the history of international humanitarian law, we can see that ethics and religion influence the basis of rights. The influential treaty "The Art of War" by *Sun Tzu*, written presumably in the 6th century BCE, is inspired by Taoism as a philosophical and religious concept.[7] And even if "there are no universal ethics", as *Micheline Ishay* points out, she starts her history of human rights with "early ethical contributions".[8] Human Rights are (a part of) formalized ethics.

Concentrating on current debates and problems of human rights as liberal, social and moral rights (II.), the example of globalization (III.) shows that the need for an international and systematic interdisciplinary dialogue (IV.) is not sufficient. The awareness of an international and interdisciplinary interaction can affect the debate within jurisprudence and its methodology (V.).

II. Freedom, Social and Moral Rights

Human Rights may be understood as an immediate result of human dignity. They must not be denied on a basis of ethnicity, religion, age or gender, as article

[5] *D. Cole*, Enemy Aliens – Double Standards and Constitutional Freedoms in the War on Terrorism, 2nd ed. New York 2005, p. 57; *R. Foot*, Human rights and counter terrorism in America's Asia policy, Oxford 2004; *J. Strawson*, Law After Ground Zero, Florence 2002.

[6] *J. K. Klefner*, Protection of the Wounded, Sick and Shipwrecked, in: D. Fleck (ed.), The Handbook of International Humanitarian Law, 2nd ed. Oxford 2008, p. 325.

[7] *F. Bouchet-Saulnier*, The Practical Guide to Humanitarian Law, 2d ed. Lanham 2007, p. 212; *T. Hanzhang/R. Wilkinson*, The Art of War – Sunzi Bing Fa, Ware 1998, pp. 16 ff.

[8] *M. R. Ishay*, The History of Human Rights – From Ancient Times to the Globalization Era, Berkeley 2008, p. 16.

1 of the Universal Declaration of Human Rights, adopted and proclaimed by General Assembly resolution 217 A (III) of 10 December 1948, stipulates:

"All human beings are born free and equal in dignity and rights. They are endowed with reason and conscience and should act towards one another in a spirit of brotherhood."

The emphasis on equality as a basis for freedom refers to the dangers to human rights. Human rights neither depend on the acceptance by a state nor on the actions of human beings. They are inalienable, as is stated in the 1776 constitution of Virginia (Bill of Rights), section 1:

"That all men are by nature equally free and independent, and have certain inherent rights, of which, when they enter into a state of society, they cannot, by any compact, deprive or divest their posterity, namely, the enjoyment of life and liberty, with the means of acquiring and possessing property, and pursuing and obtaining happiness and safety."

And again, the emphasis on freedom by nature refers to the fact that states and regulations on the one hand endanger human rights and on the other hand should protect them.

We can distinguish between three generations of human rights:[9] First generation liberal rights (e.g. freedom of speech, religion, freedom from torture), second generation social or collective rights (e.g. right to work, equal payment, a standard of living, right to education, social security, food),[10] and third generation solidarity and developmental human rights (e.g. right to development, right to peace, right to a healthy environment).[11] These generations all refer to particular philosophical, political and sociological backgrounds.[12]

Human Rights may apply to all human beings, but they are endangered differently in differing contexts and for different groups. In *Price v. the United Kingdom*, the European Court of Human Rights considered that to detain a severely disabled person in conditions in which her special needs could not be met (and where "she is dangerously cold, risks developing sores because her bed is too hard or unreachable, and is unable to go to the toilet or keep clean without the greatest of difficulty") constitutes a treatment contrary to Article 3 of the European Convention on Human Rights, which prohibits inhuman or degrading treatment.[13] So the principle of equality as a basis for freedom can, espe-

---

[9] *K. Vasak*, Pour les droits de l'homme de la troisième génération: les droits de la solidarité, Revue de Droits de l'Homme (1979), p. 3.

[10] See articles 23–29 of the Universal Declaration of Human Rights and the 1966 United Nations International Covenant on Economic, Social and Cultural Rights.

[11] *O. C. Ruppel*, Third-generation human rights and the protection of the environment in Namibia, in: N. Horn/A. Bösl (eds.), Human Rights and the Rule of Law in Namibia, Windhoek 2008, pp. 101, 102.

[12] *M. R. Ishay*, The History of Human Rights – From Ancient Times to the Globalization Era, Berkeley 2008, p. 11.

[13] *Price v. the United Kingdom*, 34 EHRR 1285 (2002).

cially in the perspective of social rights, require that someone is treated differently. As pointed out in the separate opinion of Judge *Greve*, "the applicant is different from other people to the extent that treating her like others is not only discrimination but brings about a violation of Article 3".[14] The decision whether a certain condition or circumstance requires different treatment (or under which circumstances treating persons differently in analogous situations is a prohibited discrimination) is a legal one, but it needs awareness of political, social and especially ethical dimensions. In the words of Judge *Greve*:

> "In a civilised country like the United Kingdom, society considers it not only appropriate but a basic humane concern to try to improve and compensate for the disabilities faced by a person in the applicant's situation." [15]

A very special link between ethics and human rights can be seen in the discussion on moral rights. Examples for moral rights are the right to participation, the right to autonomy and self-development, the right to equal respect, the right to security and livelihood, the right to freedom.[16] These moral rights refer directly to ethical foundations.[17]

III. The Example of Globalization

Globalization is an example for the need of an interdisciplinary and international approach in human rights research. When we talk about globalization, we have to distinguish between phenomena that are already global in their origin and phenomena that are local in their origin but spread around the globe, which is characteristic of globalization. So globalization is different from internationalization. It is closer to transnational developments. From this point of view, a "globalized world" is a paradox, as the world is global in its origin, at least from a geographical perspective. But the world we share can be influenced, and sometimes even dominated, by transnational phenomena. Globalization can be defined as

> "the growing interpenetration of states, markets, communications, and ideas across borders".[18]

---

[14] *Price v. the United Kingdom*, 34 EHRR 1285 (2002), sub para. 37.

[15] *Price v. the United Kingdom*, 34 EHRR 1285 (2002), sub para. 37.

[16] *P.H. Werhane*, Persons, rights, and corporations, Englewood Cliffs, 1985, p. 16ff.

[17] See *J. Hinkmann*, Ethik der Menschenrechte – eine Studie zur philosophischen Begründung von Menschenrechten als universalen Normen, Marburg, 2002; *T. Talaulicar*, Unternehmenskodizes: Typen und Normierungsstrategien zur Implementierung einer Unternehmensethik, Wiesbaden 2006, p. 404.

[18] *A. Brysk*, Introduction – Transnational Threats and Opportunities, in: A. Brysk (ed.), Globalization and Human Rights, Berkeley 2002, p. 1.

The impact of globalization is not restricted to a single system or discipline. It can be seen in (information-) technology as well as in the social, cultural, economic, and political system, and it affects the way we talk (and think).[19] *Gopinath* shows that there are varying perspectives on globalization in the different disciplines, when a geographer watches the interaction of places and people, a sociologist defines globalization as the "intensification of worldwide social relations that link distant localities ...", an economist understands it as "the removal of barriers to free trade", and a political theorist highlights the intensification of worldwide social interdependencies and a growing awareness of deepening connections.[20] So the question whether globalization enforces human rights in the world or whether it endangers human rights[21] has to be debated in the different disciplines as well as on an interdisciplinary level. But is an interdisciplinary dialogue about the globalization of human rights[22] possible?

IV. Systematic Interdisciplinary Dialogue

Although human rights are discussed extensively in scientific literature, a systematic interdisciplinary debate covering questions of implementation and enforcement of human rights in conflict and an exchange between different (legal) traditions are lacking. Human rights are a global issue. The realisation of these human rights is sought on a regional, national and international level. The interplay of these various levels can cause difficulties resulting from varying institutional arrangements and the significance of respective specific regional contexts, cultural traditions or thematic experience.

For the success of interdisciplinary exchange, it is useful to start with the practice, method and self-understanding of *one* academic discipline – namely jurisprudence. Introducing the perspectives of additional disciplines can lead to a critical debate on the functional requirements and the paradigmatic understanding of jurisprudence.[23] Therefore, attention has to be paid to the effective

[19] *C. Gopinath*, Globalization – A Multidimensional System, Los Angeles 2008, p. 36; *R. Clark*, Global Awareness – Thinking Systematically about the World, Lanham 2002.

[20] *C. Gopinath*, Globalization – A Multidimensional System, Los Angeles 2008, pp. 7f.

[21] See the contributions in M. Mehra (ed.), Human Rights and Economic Globalisation: Directions for the WTO, Uppsala 1999; *A. Brysk*, Introduction – Transnational Threats and Opportunities, in: A. Brysk (ed.), Globalization and Human Rights, Berkeley 2002, pp. 1, 7, 9.

[22] See *J.-M. Coicaud*, Human Rights in Discourse and Practice – The Quandary of International Justice, in: J.-M. Coicaud, M. W. Doyle, A.-M. Gardner (eds.), The Globalization of Human Rights, Tokyo 2003, pp. 178ff.

[23] Understanding the parallels to other disciplines like theology (hermeneutics, text interpretation, use of sources) can lead to more intellectual richness in jurisprudence, see *G. Samuel*, Is Law Really a Social Science? A View from Comparative Law, Cambridge Law Journal 67 (2008), p. 288.

but often not explicitly addressed presuppositions in the self-understanding of jurisprudence. Such presuppositions can be best demonstrated in terms of specific concepts: What exactly is meant when speaking of "norm-justification", "entitlement to liberty", "consensus" or (legal) "dogma"? From where does the law borrow its categories and from what are they derived?

In this respect, the systematic interdisciplinary dialogue, the starting point of which is the formulation of legal questions, plays a key role in understanding the complex human rights issues that derive from a particularly tense relationship between the different disciplines. Terms of relevance for this topic differ in the various disciplines and various languages. Intercultural and interdisciplinary dialogue will help the participating disciplines to understand each other better and to be mutually supportive in advancing joint research.

In this way, the interdisciplinary approach leads to a deliberate and fundamental debate about scientific paradigmatic functions which could be enlightening not only for jurisprudence but also for the other disciplines involved, which implicitly and repeatedly refer to the law. Differences and parallels in disciplinary approaches should be discussed. An example might be the question whether in jurisprudence "hard cases make bad law" and in philosophy "artificial cases make bad ethics".[24] Internationalism and interdisciplinarity enable an innovative discussion of (classic) areas such as the universality of human rights or the manifestations of individual human rights. Enforcement strategies that support the recognition and realisation of human rights also need to be examined.

The envisaged research focus is, for example, on migration and rights of participation, the relationship between freedom and terror prevention, as well as the responsibility of transnational companies. Due attention has to be paid thereby to the fact that the concepts of "justification", "enforcement" and "tradition" differ in the various disciplines (ethics, law, politics). Even terms such as "violence" or "security" are used and determined differently in the various disciplines. The importance of the use of legal terms with an ethical background cannot be underestimated, as the example of the term "torture" in the current debate about "harsh interrogation tactics" in the so called "war on terror" shows.[25] Each discipline involved adds a specific and indispensable contribution to the common debate. For example, political theory can provide a perspective on the role and function of law in the political-social process, whilst comparative ethics and philosophy can show those aspects that transcend a mere positivist understanding of human rights.

---

[24] *H. Shue*, Torture, Philosophy & Public Affairs 7 (1978), p. 141.

[25] *D.J. Luban*, The War on Terrorism and the End of Human Rights, in: T. Shipka (ed.), Philosophy – Paradox and Discovery, 5th ed. Boston 2004, p. 393; *D. Luban*, Torture and the Professions, Criminal Justice Ethics 26 (2007), p. 59.

The specific cultural contexts not only shape the specific human rights discourse, but pose particular difficulties for the realisation of human rights, for example in terms of religious law or legal pluralism in general. In addition, particular experiences cause a context-specific perspective of universal human rights. The specific narration of suffering is reflected in the thematic prioritisation of individual rights as well as in the thematic focus in a particular cultural context (gender, fragile statehood, terrorism, AIDS, etc.). Therefore, fundamental aspects for the realisation of human rights are reflected in the interplay of the different institutional levels (constitutional level, International Criminal Law, actors beyond the State / Non-State Actors such as NGOs, businesses or the role of the media).

V. The Interdisciplinary Approach and the Methodology of Jurisprudence

The interdisciplinary approach enriches jurisprudential work. Results of interdisciplinary dialogue can influence jurisprudential analysis. An interdisciplinary perspective allows jurisprudence to take into account not only the axioms of its terminology but also the consequences of its actions. In its methods, jurisprudence can and must consider these consequences. A focus on consequences is permissible when applying teleological interpretation. This focus also connects jurisprudence to other disciplines in the interdisciplinary approach.

1. Consequence-Oriented Interpretation

Interpretation focused on consequences can be understood as a means of opening jurisprudence to sociological methods and factors.[26] According to the concept of consequence-oriented interpretation, the social consequences of jurisdiction are to be considered and if necessary have to guide the process of interpretation.[27] However, not the consequences provided by the law itself are the subject matter of the consequence-focused interpretation, but the empirically

[26] See *M. Deckert*, Zur Einführung: Die folgenorientierte Auslegung, Juristische Schulung (1995), p. 480.

[27] *M. Deckert*, Zur Einführung: Die folgenorientierte Auslegung, Juristische Schulung (1995), p. 480; *A. Eser, in*: A. Schönke/H. Schröder, Strafgesetzbuch, 26. Aufl., München 2001, § 1 Rn. 54; *W. Hassemer*, Über die Berücksichtigung von Folgen bei der Auslegung der Strafgesetze, in: N. Horn (ed.), Europäisches Rechtsdenken in Geschichte und Gegenwart, Festschrift für Helmut Coing, Band I, München 1982, pp. 493, 498; *G. Lübbe-Wolff*, Rechtsfolgen und Realfolgen – welche Rolle können Folgenerwägungen in der juristischen Regel- und Begriffsbildung spielen?, Freiburg/München 1981, p. 25; *T. Sambuc*, Folgenerwägungen im Richterrecht, Berlin 1977; *S. Wälde*, Juristische Folgenorientierung, Königstein/Ts. 1979, p. 5.

identifiable social consequences of its application.[28] The loss of employment due to a prison sentence to be served, for instance, would be considered such a consequence.[29] The effect on the design of future demonstrations caused by changes in jurisdiction on coercion (§ 240, I, 2 German Criminal Code [StGB]) – relevant to the freedom of speech – would constitute another example of such consequences, in this case a consequence of adaptation.[30]

2. *Constitutionally Limited Legitimacy of Consequence-Orientation*

The core issue of consequence-oriented interpretation in criminal law is the legitimacy of consequence-orientation, since it is subject to constitutional limitations. According to *Luhmann*, jurisprudence is defined by conditional routines and is to be free of expectations and considerations of consequence. He claims that consequence-orientation is not part of the jurisprudence programme.[31]

Contrary to that assumption, law itself incorporates rules that require jurisprudence to consider consequences. For example, Article 17, para. 1 of the Rome Statute of the International Criminal Court states as an issue of admissibility that the Court shall consider whether, due to a total or substantial collapse or unavailability of its national judicial system, a State is unable to get access to the accused or to gather the necessary evidence and testimony or otherwise unable

[28] *M. Deckert*, Zur Einführung: Die folgenorientierte Auslegung, Juristische Schulung (1995), p. 480; *W. Hassemer*, Über die Berücksichtigung von Folgen bei der Auslegung der Strafgesetze, in: N. Horn (ed.), Europäisches Rechtsdenken in Geschichte und Gegenwart, Festschrift für Helmut Coing, Band I, München 1982, pp. 493, 513; *G. Lübbe-Wolff*, Rechtsfolgen und Realfolgen – welche Rolle können Folgenerwägungen in der juristischen Regel- und Begriffsbildung spielen?, Freiburg/München 1981, p. 25; *H. Rottleuthner*, Zur Methode einer folgenorientierten Rechtsanwendung, in: Wissenschaften und Philosophie als Basis der Jurisprudenz, Beiheft N. F. Nr. 13 des ARSP, Wiesbaden 1980, pp. 97, 107; *T. Sambuc*, Folgenerwägungen im Richterrecht, Berlin 1977, p. 107; *S. Wälde*, Juristische Folgenorientierung, Königstein/Ts. 1979, p. 6; in this respect, *R. Schmitz*, in: Münchner Kommentar zum StGB, 1. Auflage, München 2003, § 1 Rn. 84, is incorrect. He states that consequence-orientation is only applicable when choosing legal consequences, claiming that otherwise issues of a particular case would function as criteria for the interpretation of the elements of a crime. However, the consideration of factual consequences does not just affect singular cases but factors in general issues that are relevant for the interpretation of the elements of a crime, see BVerfGE 45 (Decisions of the Federal Constitutional Court), p. 187 (concerning the interpretation of the elements of murder) and *W. Hassemer*, Über die Berücksichtigung von Folgen bei der Auslegung der Strafgesetze, in: N. Horn (ed.), Europäisches Rechtsdenken in Geschichte und Gegenwart, Festschrift für Helmut Coing, Band I, München 1982, p. 493 (497).

[29] *W. Hassemer*, Über die Berücksichtigung von Folgen bei der Auslegung der Strafgesetze, in: N. Horn (ed.), Europäisches Rechtsdenken in Geschichte und Gegenwart, Festschrift für Helmut Coing, Band I, München 1982, p. 493 (513).

[30] See *M. Deckert*, Zur Einführung: Die folgenorientierte Auslegung, Juristische Schulung (1995), p. 480 (481).

[31] *N. Luhmann*, Funktionale Methode und juristische Entscheidung, Archiv des öffentlichen Rechts (1969), p. 1 (3 f.); *N. Luhmann*, Rechtssystem und Rechtsdogmatik, Stuttgart/Berlin/u. a. 1974, p. 5.

to carry out its proceedings. The consideration of consequences is also implicitly entrusted to jurisprudence by the legislature, for instance in the Rome Statute preamble. Para. 5 of the preamble arranges for a system of "prevention by enforcement",[32] while para. 8 even establishes "non-intervention in internal affairs".[33]

This procedure of considering consequences is particularly frequent in new fields of law[34] and ultimately provides for legal sustainability.[35] Considerations of consequences can also influence the interpretation of elements of a crime in the jurisdiction of the German Federal Constitutional Court (BVerfG). This was the case, for example, in the decision concerning the constitutionality of the life sentence for murder (§ 211 StGB), where the factual consequences for the person concerned were taken into consideration and therefore a restrictive interpretation of the elements of crime was postulated.[36]

Altogether, the consideration of consequences can – contrary to *Luhmann* – be a part of jurisprudence. In modern statute law, which entails the differentiation of a society and its law, jurisprudence must allow for the variety of areas of life. Thus, welfare state concerns must be considered in the application of criminal law, which does not *per se* take precedence.[37] However, this also means that the strict adherence of criminal law to the rule of law has to be maintained. As Article 22 paragraph 2 Rome Statute of the International Criminal Court states,

> "the definition of a crime shall be strictly construed and shall not be extended by analogy. In case of ambiguity, the definition shall be interpreted in favour of the person being investigated, prosecuted or convicted".

Considerations of consequences need to be capable of integration into the complex and diverse system of legal norms. In doing so, both the rule of speciality and the hierarchy of norms have to be taken into account. First and foremost, the statute to be interpreted has to leave a margin for interpretation, especially

---

[32] *O. Triffterer*, in: O. Triffterer (ed.), Commentary on the Rome Statute of the International Criminal Court – observers' notes, article by article, 2. ed. München 2008, preamble Rn. 15.

[33] *M. Bergsmo*, in: Triffterer, Otto (ed.), Commentary on the Rome Statute of the International Criminal Court – observers' notes, article by article , 2. ed. München 2008, preamble Rn. 19.

[34] *M. Deckert*, Zur Einführung: Die folgenorientierte Auslegung, Juristische Schulung (1995), p. 480 (481); *S. Wälde*, Juristische Folgenorientierung, Königstein/Ts. 1979, p. 11.

[35] See *K. F. Gärditz*, Nachhaltigkeit und Völkerrecht, in: W. Kahl (ed.), Nachhaltigkeit als Verbundbegriff, Tübingen 2008, pp. 137 ff.

[36] BVerfGE 45, p. 187 (267); see *W. Hassemer*, Über die Berücksichtigung von Folgen bei der Auslegung der Strafgesetze, in: N. Horn (ed.), Europäisches Rechtsdenken in Geschichte und Gegenwart, Festschrift für Helmut Coing, Band I, München 1982, p. 493 (497).

[37] BVerfG, Neue Juristische Wochenschrift (1977), p. 1489 (1490 f.); *A. Kreuzer*, Beschluß des Bundesverfassungsgerichts über die Beschlagnahme von Klientenakten einer Suchtberatungsstelle mit Anmerkungen und einer Stellungnahme, Suchtgefahren (1978), p. 84 .

considering the wording and the legal context.[38] In addition, the consequence-oriented interpretation has to be in keeping with the particular aim of the statute in order to observe the rule of law and the separation of powers.[39] Therefore, considerations of consequence-orientation have to allow for adjustments to laws of higher and equal rank.

As long as these requirements are met, consequence-oriented interpretation does not constitute a violation of the separation of powers and is thus constitutionally legitimised.

3. Relationship to Teleological Interpretation

However, the relationship between consequence-oriented and teleological interpretation needs to be determined. *Winfried Hassemer*, former vice-president of the Federal Constitutional Court, seeks to delimit teleological from consequence-oriented interpretation by distinguishing between "internal" and "external" consequences, which are both perceived as effects of an interpretation.[40] He claims that internal consequences are effects of one interpretation of a statute on other interpretations of that statute, for example a certain definition of the term "intent" that would have to be considered in future decisions. According to *Hassemer*, these internal consequences are a subject of teleological interpretation.[41] External consequences, on the other hand, are a subject of consequence-oriented interpretation and affect

> "future situations that are expected consequences of a certain interpretation of a statute and are empirically describable."[42]

This distinction unduly narrows the scope of teleological interpretation and does not sufficiently reflect the extent to which consequence-orientation is subject to the rule of law. A methodologically sound, objective teleology must imply that a certain statute is always supposed to formatively fit into an overall legal system. Only in this respect can a statute be seen as a forward-looking and

---

[38] *M. Deckert*, Zur Einführung: Die folgenorientierte Auslegung, Juristische Schulung (1995), p. 480 (483); *H. Rottleuthner*, Zur Methode einer folgenorientierten Rechtsanwendung, in: Wissenschaften und Philosophie als Basis der Jurisprudenz, Beiheft N. F. Nr. 13 des ARSP, Wiesbaden 1980, p. 97 (114 f.); *S. Wälde*, Juristische Folgenorientierung, Königstein/Ts. 1979, p. 96.

[39] See *T. Sambuc*, Folgenerwägungen im Richterrecht, Berlin 1977, p. 111.

[40] *W. Hassemer*, Über die Berücksichtigung von Folgen bei der Auslegung der Strafgesetze, in: N. Horn (ed.), Europäisches Rechtsdenken in Geschichte und Gegenwart, Festschrift für Helmut Coing, Band I, München 1982, p. 493 (513).

[41] *W. Hassemer*, Über die Berücksichtigung von Folgen bei der Auslegung der Strafgesetze, in: N. Horn (ed.), Europäisches Rechtsdenken in Geschichte und Gegenwart, Festschrift für Helmut Coing, Band I, München 1982, p. 493 (512 f.).

[42] *W. Hassemer*, Über die Berücksichtigung von Folgen bei der Auslegung der Strafgesetze, in: N. Horn (ed.), Europäisches Rechtsdenken in Geschichte und Gegenwart, Festschrift für Helmut Coing, Band I, München 1982, p. 493 (513).

reasonable instruction to government bodies. Consequently, the consideration of legal consequences that pertain to a different area of statutes than the one to be interpreted is subject to teleological interpretation. This holds especially true if the consequential future situation is "empirically describable". This is again exemplified by the Federal Constitutional Court jurisdiction on the restrictive interpretation of the elements of murder.[43] This jurisdiction on the one hand concerns empirically describable "external consequences" – the effects of prolonged prison sentences on the person concerned – and considers them within the scope of the constitutional rule of proportionality. On the other hand, this jurisdiction affects other interpretations in terms of "internal consequences". Hence internal and external consequences cannot be strictly assigned to one of the interpretational methods each, but are both a subject of teleological interpretation.

So consequence-orientation can only be perceived as a particular aspect of a comprehensive teleological interpretation. It concerns the part of teleological interpretation that widens the scope of consideration from the statute at hand to the overall system of statutes, including the hierarchy of statutes. Likewise, consequence-orientation as an aspect of the teleological method applies to the empirically verifiable part of consequences.[44] In that, *Hassemer*'s terminological distinction is correct. Additionally, consequence-orientation is only constitutionally legitimised to the extent to which this application of the law is also an application of the statutes and thus follows the aim of the legislator. Consequence-orientation in terms of an application of law that exceeds the aims of the legislator could no longer be considered application of a statute and would constitute independent legislation by the judiciary and therefore a violation of the separation of powers.

Ultimately, consideration of consequences or consequence-orientation has to be understood as a part of teleological interpretation. On this basis, the perspectives of different disciplines can be introduced, even included, in a sustainable jurisprudence.

VI. Outlook

In a globalized world, an interdisciplinary dialogue on ethics and human rights is possible, necessary and fruitful for jurisprudence. Human Rights can be understood as formalized ethics. So ethics can, on the one hand, be a foundation of human rights. They are the framework for a communication of rights.[45] This

---

[43] BVerfGE 45, p. 187 (267).

[44] See *M. Deckert*, Zur Einführung: Die folgenorientierte Auslegung, Juristische Schulung (1995), p. 480 (482).

[45] See *G. Ulrich*, Towards a Theory of Global Ethics in Support of Human Rights, in: W.

communication is the context in which wrongs can be transformed into rights. But ethics, on the other hand, shape "existing" (recognized) human rights as well. Human rights are "ethics in action".[46] The enforcement of human rights, especially in international criminal law, as well as the structures of implementation bring the ideas and principles of rights to life in a globalized world. So we should approach participation rights, social rights and human rights in private as well as in public life from interdisciplinary perspectives.

Benedek/K. de Feyter/F. Marrella (eds.), Economic Globalization and Human Rights, Cambridge 2007, p. 39.

[46] See *D. A. Bell*, Introduction: Reflections on Dialogues between Practitioners and Theorists of Human Rights, in: D. A. Bell/J.-M. Coicaud (eds.), Ethics in Action – The Ethical Challenges of International Human Rights Nongovernmental Organizations, Cambridge 2007, p. 1.

The Role of a Judge in a Democracy[1]

Aharon Barak

I. Introduction

I am not a philosopher. I am not a political scientist. I am a judge – a judge in the highest court of my country's legal system. So I ask myself a question that many supreme court judges – and, in fact, many judges on all courts in modern democracies– ask themselves[2]: what is my role as a judge? Certainly it is my role – and the role of every judge – to decide the dispute before me. Certainly it is my role, as a member of my nation's highest court, to determine the law by which the dispute before me should be decided. But is that all that can be said about my role? Are there criteria for assessing the quality of my work as a judge? What is my role, and do I even have a "role" beyond merely deciding the dispute before me according to the law? These questions occupy me daily as I enter the courtroom and take my seat on the bench.

This question is important not merely to judges who want to assess their performance, but to the system as a whole. The answer determines the criteria for developing the law and provides a basis for formulating a system of interpretation of all legal texts. Establishing criteria for judging judges is particularly important in view of the frequent attempts to dress up political problems in legal garb and place them before the court. *De Tocqueville* characterized this tendency to legalize political questions 170 years ago as unique to the United States[3]. Today, however, this phenomenon is common in modern democracies[4].

---

[1] This article was published in: S. Breitenmoser/B. Ehrenzeller/M. Sassoli/W. Stoffel/B. Wagner Pfeifer (eds.), Human Rights, Democracy and the Rule of Law, pp. 939 ff. (2007) and is partly based on my book The Judge in a Democracy (2006) and on *A. Barak*, Foreword: The Role of a Supreme Court in a Democracy, Harvard Law Review 116 (2002), p. 16.

[2] See *B. McLachlin*, The Charter: A New Role for the Judiciary, Alberta Law Review 29 (1991), p. 540; *M. Kirby*, Judging: Reflections on the Moment of Decision, Australian Bar Review 1 (1999).

[3] See *A. de Tocqueville*, Democracy in America, 1835, H.C. Mansfield and D. Winthrop (eds.), 2000, p. 97.

[4] See *B. McLachlin*, The Role of the Court in the Post-Charter Era: Policy-Maker and Adjudicator, University of New Brunswick Law Journal 39 (1990), p. 38 (49).

How are we judges to deal with political problems that have taken on a legal character?

These questions do not arise in the "easy cases"[5] in which there is only one answer to the legal problem, and the judge has no choice but to choose it. But how am I to decide the "hard cases,"[6] the cases in which the legal problem has more than one legal answer? These are the cases that find their way to the highest court, and I have discretion in resolving them. My decision may be legitimate, but how do I know if it is the proper one? What must I do in order to fulfil my role?

One might try to dismiss my question with the philosophical argument that there are no "hard cases" and that judicial discretion in this sense does not exist. That answer is far from satisfactory. Even Professor *Ronald Dworkin* – proponent of the theory that every legal problem has only one correct answer[7] – merely says that there are better and worse judicial decisions[8]. He propounds a complete theory describing how Judge Hercules should make the better decision in "hard cases".[9] Is Hercules the proper model by which we should judge? Whatever the philosophical answer may be, the reality is that the large majority of judges think, as I do, that in some cases they do have a choice.[10] This thought is not the result of judicial imperialism. It reflects the uncertainty inherent in law. The source of this uncertainty is the uncertainty of language, the limitations of the creator of the legal text, and the uncertainty of interpretive rules.[11] Of course, the power to choose – judicial discretion – is never absolute. It is always subject to procedural limitations (such as fairness) and substantive limitations (such as reasonability, proportionality, coherency, consistency, and rationality). But what should the judge do when the scales are balanced?

Different judges have varying answers to the questions that I am posing.[12] These differences stem from variances in education, personalities, responses to the world around us, and outlooks on the world in which we live. This is only natural. Each judge is a distinct world unto himself, and we would not wish it otherwise. Ideological pluralism, not ideological uniformity, is the hallmark of

---

[5] On easy cases, see: *A. Barak*, Judicial Discretion, New Haven, 1989, pp. 36ff.

[6] See *A. Barak*, Judicial Discretion, 1989, p. 20; see also *T. Bingham*, The Business of Judging: Selected Essays and Speeches, Oxford 2000, p. 35.

[7] See *R. Dworkin*, Taking Rights Seriously, 1977, p. 81; *R. Dworkin*, No Right Answer, New York University Law Review 53 (1978), p. 1.

[8] See *R. Dworkin*, Pragmatism, Right Answers, and True Banality, in: M. Brint/W. Weaver (eds.), Pragmatism in Law and Society, Boulder 1991, p. 359.

[9] On *Dworkin*'s Hercules, see *R. Dworkin*, Law's Empire, Boston 1983, p. 239; on other models, see: R. Badinter/S. Breyer (eds.) Judges in Contemporary Democracy: An International Conversation, New York 2004.

[10] See *A. Paterson*, The Law Lords, Basingstoke 1982, p. 190.

[11] See *A. Barak*, Purposive Interpretation in Law, Princeton 2005, p. 26.

[12] See *T. Bingham*, The Business of Judging: Selected Essays and Speeches, Oxford 2000, p. 35; *J. Steyn*, Democracy Through Law: Selected Speeches and Judgments, Aldershot 2004.

judges in democratic legal systems. Diverse judges reflect – but do not represent – the different opinions that exist in their societies. But I think many of us agree that the question I have posed is central to our function as judges, even if we disagree about its answer. Our judicial policy and our judicial philosophy are fundamental to us, since they guide us in our most difficult hours. Every judge has difficult hours. They mold us and give us self-confidence. They inform us that our strength as judges is in understanding our limitations. They teach us that, more than we have answers to the difficult legal problems that confront us, we have questions regarding the path we should take.

My purpose today is to suggest answers to the questions I have posed. I wish to present my views on the role of a court and its judges in a democracy. My aim is to describe the judicial policy and judicial philosophy that guide me. I do not naïvely claim that my position reflects an absolute truth. Democratic countries differ from one another, and what is good and proper for one may not be good and proper for another[13]. And what is good and proper at one time may not be good and proper, within a given democracy, at another time.

According to my judicial philosophy, a judge in a democracy – especially a judge of a supreme court or constitutional court – has two main roles: bridging the gap between law and society, and protecting the constitution and democracy.

II. Bridging the Gap between Law and Society

The law regulates relationships between people. It prescribes patterns of behaviour. It reflects the values of society. The role of the judge is to understand the purpose of law in society and to help the law achieve its purpose. But the law of a society is a living organism. It is based on a factual and social reality that is constantly changing. Sometimes the change is drastic, sudden, and easily identifiable. Sometimes the change is minor and gradual, and cannot be noticed without the proper distance and perspective. Law's connection to this fluid reality implies that it too is always changing. Sometimes change in law precedes societal change and is even intended to stimulate it. In most cases, however, a change in law is the result of a change in social reality. Indeed, when social reality changes, the law must change too. Just as change in social reality is the law of life,[14] responsiveness to change in social reality is the life of the law.

---

[13] See *R. Gavison*, "The Role of Courts in Rifted Democracies", Israel Law Review 33 (1999), p. 216.

[14] See *W. Rehnquist*, The Changing Role of the Supreme Court, Florida State University Law Review 14, p. 7.

The life of law is not just logic or experience[15]. The life of law is renewal, based on experience and logic, which adapt law to the new social reality. Indeed, there are always changes in law, caused by changes in society. The history of law is also the history of adapting law to life's changing needs. The legislative branch bears the primary role for making conscious changes in law. It has the power to change the legislation which it itself created. It has the power to create new legal tools that can encompass the new social reality and even determine its nature and character. In the field of legislation, the legislature is the senior partner. The role of the judge is secondary and limited.

The need for change presents the judge with a difficult dilemma, because change sometimes harms security, certainty, and stability. The judge must balance the need for change with the need for stability. Professor *Roscoe Pound* expressed this well more than eighty years ago: "Hence all thinking about law has struggled to reconcile the conflicting demands of the need of stability and of the need of change. Law must be stable and yet it cannot stand still".[16] Stability without change is degeneration. Change without stability is anarchy. The role of a judge is to help bridge the gap between the needs of society and law without allowing the legal system to degenerate or collapse into anarchy. The judge must ensure stability with change, and change with stability. Like the eagle in the sky that maintains its stability only when it is moving, so too is the law stable only when it is moving. Achieving this goal is very difficult. The progress of case law throughout history must be cautious. The decision is not between stability and change. It is a question of the speed of the change. The decision is not between rigidity and flexibility. It is a question of the degree of flexibility. The judge must take into account a complex array of considerations. A judge must consider: (1) the coherence of the system in which he operates; (2) the powers and limitations of the judiciary as an institution as defined within that system; and (3) the way in which his role is perceived.[17]

The judge's role is to be the bridge between the law and life. He must not ignore this role. Nevertheless, the public must not expect the judge to bridge every gap between law and life. His discretion is limited. He functions within a given social and legal framework. The court's ability to link life and law is, therefore, limited by its very nature. One should not harbour expectations that cannot possibly be met. On this issue, one should not oscillate between extremes. One must not accept the claim, often raised, that one should not expect the court to make the necessary change in order to bridge the gap between law and life[18]. But at the same time, one cannot accept the claim that the judge is all-

---

[15] For a different approach, see *O. W. Holmes*, The Common Law, 1881, p. 1.

[16] *R. Pound*, Interpretation of Legal History, 1923, p. 1.

[17] For details, see *A. Barak*, Judicial Discretion, New Haven, 1989, p. 113; *A. Barak*, The Judge in a Democracy, Princeton 2006, p. 12.

[18] See *G. N. Rosenberg*, The Hollow Hope, Chicago 1991.

powerful and his will alone determines the existence or non-existence of the change[19]. Reality is infinitely more complex. Sometimes it is possible to bridge the gap between law and life's changing reality through legitimate judicial actions; and at times, such a bridge cannot possibly be constructed. On this matter, like many others, one must be realistic[20] and understand both the judicial power and its limitations.

III. Protecting the Constitution and Democracy

1. The Struggle for Democracy

The second role of the judge in a democracy is to protect the constitution and democracy itself. Legal systems with formal constitutions impose this task on judges, but judges also play this role in legal systems with no formal constitution. Indeed, if we wish to preserve democracy, we cannot take its existence for granted. We must fight for it. This is certainly the case for new democracies, but it is also true of the old and well-established ones. The assumption that "it cannot happen to us" can no longer be accepted. Anything can happen. If democracy was perverted and destroyed in the Germany of Kant, Beethoven, and Goethe, it can happen anywhere. If we do not protect democracy, democracy will not protect us. I do not know whether the judges in Germany could have prevented Hitler from coming to power in the 1930s. But I do know that a lesson of the Holocaust and of the Second World War is the need to enact democratic constitutions and ensure that they are put into effect by judges whose main task is to protect democracy. It was this awareness that, in the post-World War II era, helped promote the idea of judicial review of legislative action and made human rights central.[21] It led to the recognition of defensive democracy and even militant democracy.[22] And it shaped my belief that the main role of the judge in a democracy is to maintain and protect the constitution and democracy. As I noted in one of my opinions[23]:

"The struggle for the law is unceasing. The need to watch over the rule of law exists at all times. Trees that we have nurtured for many years may be uprooted with one stroke of

[19] As claimed by many of the Critical Legal Studies scholars. See *G. Peller*, The Metaphysics of American Law, California Law Review 73 (1985), p. 1151.

[20] See *M. Kozlowski*, The Myth of the Imperial Judiciary: Why The Rights is Wrong About the Courts, New York 2003.

[21] See *M. Cappelletti*, Judicial Review in the Contemporary World, Indianapolis 1971, p. 45; D. Greenberg et al. (eds.), Constitutionalism and Democracy: Transitions in the Contemporary World, Oxford 1993; C. N. Tate/T. Vallinder (eds.), The Global Expansion of Judicial Power, New York 1995.

[22] See A. Sajo (ed.), A Militant Democracy, Utrecht 2004.

[23] H. C. 5364/94 Velner v. Chairman of Israeli Labor Party, 49(1) P. D., p. 758 (808).

the axe. We must never relax the protection of the rule of law. All of us – all branches of government, all parties and factions, all institutions – must protect our young democracy. This protective role is conferred on the judiciary as a whole, and on the Supreme Court in particular. Once again we, the judges of this generation, are charged with watching over our basic values and protecting them against those who challenge them."

The protection of democracy is, I believe, a priority for many judges in modern democracies. Legal scholars often explain this phenomenon as an increase in judicial power relative to other powers in society.[24] This change, however, is merely a side effect. The purpose of this modern development is not to increase the power of the court in a democracy, but rather to increase the protection of democracy and human rights. An increase in judicial power is an inevitable result, because judicial power is one of many factors in the democratic balance.

Each branch of the government must protect the constitution and democracy. And every judge in the state, particularly the judges of the supreme court, must also give effect to democracy. They must educate the people in the democratic spirit, because judges are also educators. To do so, judges must educate the public about the law and the role of the judiciary. In this regard, a court should function as an educational institution whose judges are teachers participating, as *Eugene Rostow* puts it, "in a vital national seminar".[25]

2. *The Essence of Democracy*

What is democracy? According to my approach, democracy is a rich and complex normative concept.[26] It rests on two bases. The first is the sovereignty of the people. This sovereignty is exercised in free elections, held on a regular basis, in which the people chooses its representatives, who in turn represent its views. This aspect of democracy is manifested in majority rule and in the centrality of the legislative body through which the people's representatives act. This is a formal aspect of democracy.

The second aspect of democracy is reflected in the rule of values (other than the value of majority rule) which characterizes democracy. The most important of these values are separation of powers, the rule of law, judicial independence, human rights, and basic principles which reflect yet other values (such as morality and justice), social objectives (such as the public peace and security) and appropriate ways of behaviour (reasonableness, proportionality and good faith). This aspect of democracy is the rule of democratic values. This is a substantive aspect of democracy.

---

[24] See *R. Hirsch*, Towards Juristocracy: The Origins and Consequences of the New Constitutionalism, Boston 2004.

[25] *E. Rostow*, The Democratic Character of Judicial Review, Harvard Law Review 66 (1952), p. 193 (208).

[26] *C. S. Nino*, The Constitution of Deliberative Democracy, New Haven 1996, p. 8.

Both aspects – the formal and the substantive – are necessary for democracy.[27] A regime in which the people are not sovereign, and the legislative and executive branches do not represent it, is not a democratic regime. A regime devoid of the separation of powers, the rule of law, the independence of judges, human rights and fundamental values reflecting ethical values, social objectives, and appropriate ways of behaviour, is not a democratic regime. Indeed, a regime in which the majority denies the minority of human rights is not a democratic regime.

Democracy's world is rich and multifaceted. Democracy should not be viewed from a one-dimensional vantage point. Democracy is multidimensional. It is based both on the centrality of laws and on democratic values, and, in their centre – human rights. Indeed, democracy is based on every individual's enjoyment of rights, of which even the majority can not deny him simply because the power of the majority is in its hands[28]. Democracy has its own internal morality, without which the regime is no longer democratic.

Democracy, then, is based on the simultaneous existence of both the rule of the majority and the rule of values which characterize democracy. This dual nature should not lead to the assumption that any flaw in one of these aspects denies the regime its democratic character. We are dealing with a spectrum of situations, which runs from the minimal existence of the different aspects which ensure the existence of a democratic regime to the maximal existence of those aspects. Therefore, there are 'better' and 'stronger' democracies, and 'worse' and 'weaker' democracies. There are "soft" democracies and "militant" democracies. However, there is a certain minimum which must be maintained, without which a regime is no longer democratic. A delicate balance must be kept, therefore, between the two aspects of democracy, in a way that protects the nucleus of each one of its aspects. This balance will be based, inherently, upon the restrictions placed both on majority rule and on the rule of fundamental values of democracy.

IV. Preconditions for Realizing the Judicial Role

The realization of those two roles by the judge requires the existence of some preconditions. These preconditions vary among democracies, but three are common to all democratic systems of law: (1) judicial impartiality and objectivity, (2) decisions within the social consensus; and (3) public confidence in the judiciary. For all three, we must ensure not only that they are upheld, which is the main point, but also that the public recognizes that they are upheld.

---

27 See *R. Post*, Democracy, Popular Sovereignty, and Judicial Review, California Law Review 86 (1998), p. 429.

28 See *R. Dworkin*, A Bill of Rights for Britain, London 1990, p. 35.

1. *Judicial Impartiality and Objectivity*

The judge must realize his role in a democracy impartially and objectively. Impartiality means that the judge treats the parties before him equally, providing them with an equal opportunity to make their respective cases, and is seen to treat the parties so. Impartiality means the judge has no personal stake in the outcome. Absence of bias is essential to the judicial process. With impartiality comes objectivity.[29] It means making judicial decisions on the basis of considerations that are external to the judge and that may even conflict with his personal views. Judges must look for the accepted values of society, even if they are not their values. They must express what is regarded as moral and just by the society in which they operate, even if it is not moral and just in their subjective views[30]. When judges consider the weight of different values, they must do so according to the fundamental views of the society in which they live, not according to their own personal fundamental views.

This objectivity makes strenuous demands, requiring the judge to take moral stock of himself. The judge must be aware that he may have values that lack general acceptance and that his personal opinions may be exceptional and unusual[31]. The judge must be capable of looking at himself from the outside and of analyzing, criticizing, and controlling himself. A judge who thinks that he knows all, and that his opinions are right and proper to the exclusion of all else, cannot properly fulfil his role.

The judge is a product of his times, living in and shaped by a given society in a given era. The purpose of objectivity is not to sever the judge from his environment. Rather, its purpose is to allow him to ascertain properly the fundamental principles of his time. The purpose of objectivity is not to rid a judge of his past, his education, his experience, his belief, or his values. Its purpose is to encourage the judge to make use of all of these personal characteristics to reflect the fundamental values of the society as faithfully as possible. A person who is appointed as a judge is neither required nor able to change his skin. The judge must develop sensitivity to the dignity of his office and to the restraints that it imposes. As the ancient Jewish text reminds judges: "Do you imagine that I offer you rulership? It is slavery that I give you."[32] The judge must display the self-criticism and humility that will prevent him from identifying himself with everything good and praiseworthy. A judge must display the self control that will allow him to distinguish between personal feelings and national aspirations. A judge must display intellectual modesty.

---

[29] On objectivity in law, see *K. Greanawalt*, Law and Objectivity, Oxford 1992; *N. Stavropoulous*, Objectivity in Law, Oxford 1996.

[30] See *B. Cardozo*, The Nature of the Judicial Process, New Haven 1921, p. 89.

[31] See H.C. 693/91, Efrat v. Dir. of Population Register, 47(1) P.D., p. 749 (781).

[32] Babylonian Talmud, Horayot 10a-b.

The objectivity required of a judge is difficult to attain. Even when we look at ourselves from the outside, we do so with our own eyes[33]. Nonetheless, my judicial experience tells me that objectivity is possible. A judge does not operate in a vacuum. A judge is a part of society, and society influences the judge. The judge is influenced by the intellectual movements and the legal thinking that prevail. A judge is always part of the people. It may be true that the judge sometimes sits in an ivory tower, though my ivory tower is located in the hills of Jerusalem and not on Mount Olympus in Greece. The judge progresses with the history of the people. All of these elements contribute to the judge's objective perspective.

Moreover, the judge acts within the limits of a court. He lives within a judicial tradition. The same spark of wisdom passes from one generation of judges to the next. This wisdom is mostly unwritten, but it penetrates little by little into the judge's consciousness and makes his thinking more objective. The judge is part of a legal system that establishes a framework for the factors that a judge may and may not consider. The heavier the weight of the system, the greater the objectification of the judicial process.

When judges give expression to the fundamental values of the system, they give expression to the values that, in their eyes, seem proper and basic. Some subjectification of this process is inevitable. Complete objectivity is unattainable. The personal aspect of a judge is always present, and his life experience neither disappears nor can disappear. We would not want it to, because in these situations, it is the judge's personality that finds expression – the same personality that underwent, and passed, the judicial nomination process. We need not, however, go from extreme to extreme. Rejecting complete objectivity does not require us to embrace complete subjectivity. There is a third way, reflected in acknowledging the importance and centrality of judicial objectivity while recognizing unreservedly that it can never fully be achieved. It is enough for a judge to make an honest attempt to objectify his exercise of discretion, recognizing that it cannot be done in every circumstance.

2. *Social Consensus*

As a rule, I have always tried to carry out my role as a judge within the framework of social consensus, to the extent that data exist about it. The judge should generally not be the flag-bearer of a new social consensus. As a rule, judges should reflect values and principles that exist in their system, rather than create them. Justice *Traynor* rightly stated: "The very responsibilities of a judge as an arbiter disqualify him as a crusader".[34]

---

[33] See *B. Cardozo*, The Nature of the Judicial Process, New Haven 1921, p. 13.

[34] See *R. Traynor*, The Limits of Judicial Creativity, Hastings Law Journal 29 (1978), p. 1025 (1030).

Nevertheless, there are cases – and they must naturally be few – in which the judge carries out his role properly by ignoring the prevalent social consensus and becoming a flag-bearer of a new social consensus. Consider the case of *Brown v. Board of Education*[35].I do not know what the consensus was in the United States just before the Supreme Court's decision in *Brown*, but in my opinion, the Court at that time fulfilled its role, even if it ruled against the then-prevailing consensus. Naturally, a court will not retain public confidence if it announces a new *Brown* twice every week. Similarly, a court will lose public confidence if it misses an opportunity like *Brown* when faced with it. In the final analysis, everything is a question of degree.

The consensus within which judges usually ought to operate should be a consensus grounded in the fundamental values of the legal system. Judges should not act according to a consensus formed by transient trends that are inconsistent with the society's fundamental values. Judges' social framework must be central and basic, not temporary and fleeting. When society is not being true to itself, judges are not required to give expression to its passing trends. They must stand firm against these trends, while giving expression to the social consensus that reflects their society's fundamental principles and tenets.

3. Public Confidence

An essential condition for realizing the judicial role is public confidence in the judge. This means confidence in judicial independence, fairness, and impartiality. It means public confidence in the ethical standards of the judge. It means public confidence that judges are not interested parties to the legal struggle, and that they are not fighting for their own power, but to protect the constitution and democracy. It means public confidence that the judge does not express his own personal views, but rather the fundamental beliefs of the nation. Indeed, the judge has neither sword nor purse[36]. All he has is the public's confidence in him. This fact means that the public recognizes the legitimacy of judicial decisions, even if it disagrees with their content.

The precondition of "public confidence" runs the risk of being misunderstood. The need to ensure public confidence does not mean the need to ensure popularity. Public confidence does not mean following popular trends or public opinion polls. Public confidence does not mean accountability to the public in the way that the executive and the legislature are accountable. Public confidence does not mean pleasing the public; public confidence does not mean ruling contrary to the law or contrary to the judge's conscience to bring about a result that the public desires. On the contrary, public confidence means ruling according

---

[35] Brown v Board of Education, 347 U.S. 483 (1954).

[36] See *A. Hamilton*, Federalist No. 78, (1788). Also see the opinion of Judge *Frankfurter* in Baker v. Carr, 369 U.S. 186, 267 (1961).

to the law and according to the judge's conscience, whatever the attitude of the public may be. Public confidence means giving expression to history, not to hysteria. Public confidence is ensured by the recognition that the judge is doing justice within the framework of the law. Judges must act in a manner that preserves public confidence in them. They must understand that judging is not merely a job but a way of life. It is a way of life that does not include the pursuit of material wealth or publicity; it is a way of life based on spiritual wealth; it is a way of life that includes an objective and impartial search for truth. It is not fiat, but reason; not mastery, but modesty; not strength, but compassion; not riches, but reputation; not an attempt to please everyone but a firm insistence on values and principles; not surrender to or compromise with interest groups but insistence on upholding the law; not making decisions according to temporary whims but progressing consistently on the basis of deeply held beliefs and fundamental values. Admittedly, judging is a way of life that involves some degree of seclusion, abstention from social and political struggles, restriction on the freedom of expression and the freedom to respond, and a large amount of isolation and internalization. But judging is emphatically not a way of life that involves a withdrawal from society. There should be no wall between the judge and the society in which the judge operates. The judge is a part of the people. If this view of the judicial role is adopted by judges, we can hope that the public will have and maintain confidence in the judiciary. In this respect, I wish to note several judicial traits that can help the public maintain confidence in its judges.

First, the judge ought to be aware of his power and his limits. A judge has great power in a democracy. Like all power, judicial power can be abused. The judge ought to recognize that his power is limited to realizing the proper judicial role. From my experience, I know that it takes considerable time for a new judge to learn his role on a court. Naturally, the judge knows the law and the power it grants to the judge, but he must also learn the limits imposed on him as a judge; he must know that power should not be abused, and that a judge cannot obtain everything he wants.

Second, a judge must recognize his mistakes. Like all mortals, judges err. A judge must admit this. I hope that if we admit our mistakes as judges, we will strengthen public confidence in the judiciary.

Third, in our writing and our thinking, judges must display modesty and an absence of arrogance. Statements such as those of Chief Justice *Hughes* that "we are under a Constitution, but the Constitution is what the judges say it is"[37] are not merely incorrect but also arrogant.

Fourth, judges should be honest. If they create new law, they should say so. They should not hide behind the rhetoric that judges declare what the law is but

---

[37] *C. E. Hughes*, Speech at Elmira (3 May 1907), in: D.J. Danelski/J.S. Tulchin (eds.), The Autobiographical Notes of Charles Evans Hughes, Boston 1973, p. 144.

do not make it. Judges make law, and the public should know that they do. The public has the right to know that we make law and how we do it; the public should not be deceived. Public confidence in the judiciary increases when the public is told the truth.

V. *The Means*

1. *The Legitimacy of the Means*

What are the means a judge can use in order to fulfil his role? What are his tools? Of course, the means of realizing the judicial role must be legitimate. The principle of the rule of law applies first and foremost to judges themselves, who do not share the legislature's freedom in creating new tools. The bricks with which we build our structures are limited. Our power to realize our role depends on our ability to design new structures with the same old bricks or to create new bricks. Sometimes we succeed in creating new "tools." Here the genius of law is evident. But such "inventions" are few. Usually we return to the old tools, and use them to resolve new situations. Let me mention six tools used by judges. They are not the only ones, but they are the most important in my eyes.

2. *Interpretation*

Interpretation, by which I mean rational activity giving meaning to a legal text[38], is both the primary task and the most important tool of a court. Interpretation derives the legal meaning from the text. Put another way, interpretation constitutes a process whereby the legal meaning of a text is "extracted" from its semantic meaning. The interpreter translates "human" language into "legal" language. He changes "static law" into "dynamic law" by transforming a linguistic text into a legal norm.

Many aspire in vain to uncover what the legal meaning of a text "truly" is. This is a fruitless search: a text has no "true" meaning. We do not have the ability to compare the meaning of a text before and after its interpretation, through focus on its "true" meaning. There is no pre-interpretive understanding of a text, for we can only access and understand it through an interpretive process. Only different interpretations of a given text can be compared. The most to which we can aspire is the "proper" meaning, not the "true" meaning.

The key question is, what is the "proper" system of interpretation? There are indeed many systems of interpretation. Legal history is the history of the rise and fall of different systems of legal interpretation. All interpretive systems

---

[38] On interpretation in law and its theories, see *A. Barak*, Purposive Interpretation in Law, Princeton 2005.

struggle with the limitations of language and generalizations. All interpretive systems must resolve the relationship between text and context; between the "word" (*verba*) of the text and its "spirit" (*voluntas*). All interpretive systems must adopt a position on the relationship between the real and hypothetical intention of the author; between the author's "declared" intent, which is learned from the text, and his "real" intent, which is learned from the text and from sources outside the text. How can we determine the proper system of interpretation?

In answering this question, we should realize that a proper theory of interpretation should aim to such meaning that bridges the gap between law and life, and protects the constitution and democracy. Indeed the bridging of the gap between law and life and the protection of the constitution and democracy is not just the outcome of the interpretive theory. It is the underlying goal of the interpretive theory itself. We judges should shape our interpretation rules so as to achieve the two-fold goals imposed upon us.

3. *The Development of the Common Law*

Judges not only interpret statutes created by the legislature; they also create law outside such statutes. This applies to all legal systems. There is no judging without creation of law. It is most strongly manifested in common law systems[39]. The common law is judge-made law. It has been created by judges for hundreds of years. "The history of the common law is a history of continuous, gradual development over a period of many centuries."[40] The common law may develop and provide new solutions to new problems without the need for any legislative authorization. A judge's power to create the common law is inherent to a common law legal system. English judges have done so for almost a thousand years; that is what judges do in the United States, Canada, Australia, India, Israel and the other common law countries.

In exercising authority to develop the common law, judges should fulfil their role: they should bridge the gap between law and life; they should protect the constitution and its values. This is the theory of the common law in a nutshell. This is how it is integrated into law, as a primary limb of the body politic. The common law like judicial interpretation is a primary tool in realizing the judicial role. It is an important tool. Its latent potential to change and rejuvenate facilitates the law's adaptation to changing social needs. Its characteristic sensitivity to fundamental values and fundamental perspectives guarantees appropriate protection for the constitution and its values.

---

[39] On common law systems, see *K. Llewellyn*, The Common Law Tradition, Boston 1960; *M. A. Eisenberg*, The Nature of the Common Law, Boston 1988.

[40] *Lord Goff*, Judges, Jurist and Legislature, The Denning Law Journal (1987), p. 79 (80).

4. *Balancing and Weighing*

The *third* most important tool for a judge to realize his role is balancing and weighing[41]. Balancing and weighing, themselves metaphors, reflect the need to decide a conflict between values and principles that are accepted in the legal system.[42] The result of the balance is important both to the development of common law and to the determination of the objective purpose in a legal text (such as statutes and constitutions). The concept of balancing recognizes that fundamental principles may conflict with one another, and that the proper resolution of this conflict lies not in the elimination of the inferior value but in determining the proper boundary between the conflicting values. Similarly, the concept of "balance" reflects the recognition that fundamental principles have "weight" and that it is possible to classify them according to their relative social importance. The act of "weighing" is merely a normative act designed to give the principles their proper place in the law[43]. By using balancing and by preferring it upon categorization, the judge has at his disposal the most important tool – except interpretation – for realizing his role.

5. *Non-Justiciability or "Political Questions"*

A *fourth* tool that judges use to fulfil their role in a democracy is determining justiciability. That is, judges identify those issues about which they ought not make a decision, leaving that decision to other branches of the state[44]. The more non-justiciability is expanded, the less opportunity judges have for bridging law and society and for protecting the constitution and democracy. Given these consequences, I regard the doctrine of non-justiciability or "political questions" with considerable wariness. I prefer insofar as possible to examine an argument on its merits. In many cases where some of my colleagues have dismissed claims on the grounds of non-justiciability, I dismissed them on the grounds that the disputed action was legal and therefore that the claim should be dismissed on the merits because of lack of cause of action[45]. My approach does not assume that the court is always the best institution to resolve disputes; indeed, I accept

---

41 See *F. Coffin*, Judicial Balancing: The Protean Scale of Justice, New York University Law Review 63 (1988), p. 16; *K. Sullivan*, Post-Liberal Judging: The Role of Categorization and Balancing, University of Colorado Law Review 63 (1992), p. 293.

42 See *R. Alexy*, A Theory of Constitutional Rights, trans. J. Rivers, Oxford 2002, p. 100.

43 See *R. Pound*, A Survey of Social Interests, Harvard Law Review 57 (1943), p. 1.

44 See *Y. S. Zemach*, Political Questions in the Courts: A Judicial Function in Democracies-Israel and the United States, Detroit 1976; *G. Marshall*, Justiciability, in: A. Guest (ed.), Oxford Essays in Jurisprudence, Oxford 1961, p. 269; *T. Koopmans*, Courts and Political Institutions: A Comparative View, Cambridge 2003, p. 98; *L. Sossin*, Boundaries of Judicial Review: The Law of Justiciability in Canada, Toronto 1999.

45 See *L. Henkin*, Is There a 'Political Question Doctrine', Yale Law Journal 85 (1976), p. 597; *Radish*, Judicial Review and the 'Political Question', Northwestern University Law Review 79 (1984–1985), p. 1031.

that certain disputes are best decided elsewhere. However, the court should not abdicate its role in a democracy merely because it is uncomfortable or fears tension with the other branches of the state. This tension not only fails to justify dismissing claims, but is even desirable on occasion. It is because of this tension that the freedom of the individual is guaranteed. True, the "passive virtues" that Professor *Alexander Bickel* advocates so persuasively[46] do have great force. Like everything, though, their power is relative and must be balanced with their significant shortcomings.[47] Overall, the benefit gained from a broad doctrine of non-justiciability is significantly smaller than the benefit gained from a narrow one.

6. *Standing*

The *fifth* tool judges use in order to fulfil their role in a democracy in shaping the rules of standing. These are the rules by which the judge decides who can apply to the court in a public law complaint. The issue of standing appears too many to be marginal in public law. This is certainly the case if one adopts the view that only a person who has experienced an injury in fact possesses standing. But if we liberalize the tests for standing, we will usher in a new era for judicial decision-making whose ramifications are far greater than the issue of standing itself. This is the case because liberal rules of standing enable courts to hear matters that ordinarily would not find their way before a court.

How a judge applies the rules of standing is a litmus test for determining his approach to his judicial role. A judge who regards his role as deciding a dispute between persons with rights – and no more – will tend to emphasize the need for an injury in fact. By contrast, a judge who regards his judicial role as bridging the gap between law and society and protecting democracy will tend to expand the rules of standing. My approach is that the role of a court in a democracy is not restricted to adjudicating disputes in which parties claim that their personal rights have been violated. I believe that my role as a judge is to bridge the gap between law and society and to protect democracy. It follows that I also favour expanding the rules of standing and releasing them from the requirement of an injury in fact. The Supreme Court of Israel has adopted this approach. Gradually, at first in minority opinions of justices in the 1960s and 1970s, and thereafter as a majority, the Court has adopted the view that when the claim alleges a major violation of the rule of law (in its broad sense), every person in Israel has legal standing to sue. Fears that the court would be "flooded" with frivolous lawsuits have proven groundless. In practice, it is primarily citizen watchdog groups and human rights organizations that have exploited

---

[46] See *A. M. Bickel*, The Least Dangerous Branch, New Haven 1962.

[47] See *G. Gunther*, The Subtle Vices of the 'Passive Virtues' – A Comment on Principle and Expediency in Judicial Review, Columbia Law Review 64 (1964), p. 1.

this provision. I think that, overall, the outcome has been positive. I was happy to learn that the Republic of South Africa adopted a similar solution in its Constitution[48]. Like the Israeli Supreme Court, the Supreme Court of India has reached a similar result by adopting a liberal standing doctrine[49]. Other common law systems are moving towards liberalizing their standing requirements.

7. Comparative Law

I have found comparative law to be of great assistance in realizing my role as a judge.[50] The case law of the courts of the United States, Australia, Canada, United Kingdom, and Germany have helped me significantly in finding the right path to follow. Indeed, comparing oneself to others allows for greater self-knowledge. With comparative law, the judge expands the horizon and the interpretive field of vision. Comparative law enriches the options available to us. In different legal systems, similar legal institutions often fulfil corresponding roles, and similar legal problems (like hate speech, privacy, and now the fight against terrorism) arise. To the extent that these similarities exist, comparative law becomes an important tool with which judges fulfil their role in a democracy ("microcomparison").[51] Moreover, because many of the basic principles of democracy are common to democratic countries, there is good reason to compare them ("macrocomparison").[52] Indeed, different democratic legal systems often encounter similar problems. Examining a foreign solution may help a judge choose the best local solution. This usefulness applies both to the development of the common law and to the interpretation of legal texts.

Naturally, one must approach comparative law cautiously, remaining cognizant of its limitations. Comparative law is not merely the comparison of laws. A useful comparison can exist only if the legal systems have a common ideological basis. The judge must be sensitive to the uniqueness of each legal system. Nonetheless, when the judge is convinced that the relative social, historical, and religious circumstances create a common ideological basis, it is possible to refer to a foreign legal system for a source of comparison and inspiration. Indeed, the importance of comparative law lies in extending the judge's horizons. Comparative law awakens judges to the potential latent in their own legal systems. It

[48] The Constitution of the Republic of South Africa 1996, sec. 38.

[49] See *J. Cassels*, Judicial Activism and Public Interest Litigation in India: Attempting the Impossible, American Journal of Comparative Law (1989), p. 495.

[50] See *B. Markesinis/J. Fedtke*, The Judge as Comparatist, Tulane Law Review 80 (2005), p. 11.

[51] See *K. Zweigert/H. Kotz*, Introduction to Comparative Law, vol. 1, trans. T. Weir, 2nd ed., Oxford 1987, p. 3.

[52] See *K. Zweigert/H. Kotz*, Introduction to Comparative Law, vol. 1, trans. T. Weir, 2nd ed., Oxford 1987, pp. 4 ff.

informs judges about the successes and failures that may result from adopting a particular legal solution. It refers judges to the relationship between a solution to the legal problem before them and other legal problems. Thus, comparative law acts as an experienced friend. Of course, there is no obligation to refer to comparative law. Additionally, even when comparative law is consulted, the final decision must always be "local." The benefit of comparative law is in expanding judicial thinking about the possible arguments, legal trends, and decision-making structures available.

Comparative law is a tool that aids in constitutional and statutory interpretation. This assistance may work on three levels. The *first* concerns interpretive theory. Comparative law helps the judge better understand the role of interpretation and the role of the judge therein. To exemplify the point, consider the interpretative status of the intent of the creator in understanding constitutions and statutes. Before judges decide their own position on the issue, they would do well to consider how other legal systems treat the question. The *second* level on which judges rely on comparative law is connected with democracy's fundamental values. Democracies share common fundamental values. Democracy must infringe on certain fundamental values in order to maintain others. It is important for judges to know how foreign law treats this question and what techniques it uses. Does it employ a technique of balancing or of categorization? Why is one technique preferred over another? Every legal system grapples with the issue of constitutional limitations on human rights. What are these limitations, and what technique was used to reach them? What are the remedies for violating an unlawful order, and how can they be determined? The *third* level of aid provided by comparative law concerns the solutions it offers to specific situations: how protected is racist speech? Is affirmative action recognized? How does the foreign system deal with terrorism? Of course, the resolution of these issues is intrinsically local. However, in different legal systems, they have a common core, in that they reflect the problems of democracy and the complexity of human relations. Again, I do not advocate adopting the foreign arrangement. It is never binding. I just advocate an open approach, one which recognizes that for all our singularity, we are not alone. That recognition will enrich our own legal systems, if we take the trouble to understand how others respond in situations similar to those we encounter.

8. *A Good Philosophy*

I will conclude my discussion of the tools for realizing the judicial role with an important tool: a good philosophy. Maybe philosophy ought not to be called a tool in the hands of a judge. My intention is merely to say that the most practical instrument for a judge is good philosophy. I am referring to several types of philosophy: philosophy of life, philosophy of law, philosophy of judging. A full discussion of this complex subject is outside the scope of this lecture, but I would like to make three points.

First, I consider it essential that a supreme court judge in a democracy have the tools to allow him to understand the philosophical discourse. Through it, he may participate in the search for truth, while understanding the limits of the human mind, and the complexity of humankind. Many judges, including myself, are frustrated philosophers because they have not been given the opportunity to participate in this rich dialogue.

Second, from the outset of our studies in law school until the end of our professional lives, we are exposed to various philosophical approaches to the law: positivism, naturalism, realism, legal process, critical legal studies, law and sociology, law and economics, feminism, and others.[53] I have found these theories to be of great interest, for each has an element of truth. Nonetheless, human experience is too rich to allow it to be imprisoned in only one legal theory[54]. Indeed, in my view, only by considering all the theories, while giving each of them the proper weight, will it be possible to understand the law and the role of the judge. Law is a tool that is intended to realize social goals. There is no consensus about the content of these goals, which is why it is necessary to find a balance among the various theories *inter se*. Some will regard the eclectic approach as an attempt to avoid a coherent legal theory. There will doubtless be others who regard the eclectic approach as an independent legal theory in itself. Whatever the case, each judge should adopt for himself a position on these questions. It will serve him as a tool for realizing his judicial role.

Third, in fulfilling his judicial role, a judge would do well to formulate for himself a judicial philosophy. A judge should be aware of his own judicial policy. Most of us have one, but only a few of us think about it and consciously formulate it. I have tried to put to you my judicial philosophy. It is an important tool with which I realize my judicial role.

VI. Final Remarks

I tried to summarize some aspects of my judicial philosophy as to the role of a judge in a democracy. I do realize that such a philosophy has its critics. It may and does sharpen the natural tension between the judiciary and the other two branches of government. It may affect the confidence of the public in the judiciary. It may be labelled as "activist" in some aspects. It clearly has its disadvantages. It may not fit some democracies. It may not fit us in years to come. I do, however, believe that it is the proper judicial philosophy for our democracy in

[53] See *B. Bix*, Jurisprudence: Theory and Context, 4th ed., London 2006.
[54] See *E. Patterson*, Jurisprudence: Men and Ideas of the Law, Brooklyn 1953, p. 556.

our times. One should not forget that a large part of Israel's population immigrated to Israel from the Near East and from Eastern Europe – places where there are no democratic traditions. Democracy is thus young in Israel. Furthermore, because of English influences, many view democracy in formal terms. Parliament, for them, is omnipotence. Furthermore, for a variety of reasons, the concept of "it is not done" is not a central part of governing in Israel. Israel lacks a rigid constitutional framework. Basic structures and concepts can be changed by bare majorities. The protection of those structures and concepts needs judges who see their role as protectors of our constitution and democracy.

Human rights in Israel until 1992 were largely the creation of the courts. Since 1992 they are embodied in two basic laws. The Supreme Court interpreted those basic laws to mean that the courts have review power of the constitutionality of these laws.[55] The Parliament and the Executive branch are following this decision. In order to properly fulfil such power, one needs a judicial philosophy that views the protection of human rights as a major role of the judges. Such philosophy is especially important when a country is under security risks. The political non-accountability of Israeli judges makes us fit to protect human rights against excessive demands of security. And so we decided that interrogators cannot use torture in order to protect us against a "ticking bomb" situation;[56] that the security fence, in some parts, is illegal,[57] and that the use of protected persons under belligerent occupation in a zone of combat is prohibited even under consent.[58] Israel is a militant democracy. In order to be militant and still be a democracy, Israel needs judges that do believe that the protection of Israel's democracy is their main task.

Does all this affect the confidence of the people in the judges? I don't know. Polls of Israeli public opinion show that judges in Israel have a very high rate of confidence. It may of course change. I do believe that at this stage of our national development we need judges with a strong commitment to democracy and its protection. In better times, things may, and probably will, change.

I regard myself as a judge who is sensitive to his role in a democracy. I take seriously the tasks imposed upon me – bridging the gap between law and society and protecting the constitution and democracy. Despite frequent criticism – and it frequently descends to personal attacks and threats of violence – I have continued on this path in the twenty- eight years I am on the Court. I hope that by doing so, I am serving my legal system properly. Indeed, as judges in our countries' highest courts, we must continue on our paths according to our con-

---

[55] See CA 6821/92 United Mizrahi Ltd. v. Migdal Cooperative Village, 49 (4) P.D., p. 221.

[56] See H.C. 5100/94, Pub. Comm. Against Torture in Isr. v. Gov't of Israel, 53(4) P.D., p. 817.

[57] See H.C. 2056/04 Beit Sourik Village Counsel v. Gov't of Israel; H.C. 7957/04 Mara'abe v. Prime Minister of Israel.

[58] See H.C. 3799/02 Adalah v. GOC Central Command, IDF.

sciences. A heavy responsibility rests on our shoulders. But even in hard times, we must remain true to ourselves. As a judge, I do not have a political platform. I am not a political person. Right and left, religious and secular, rich and poor, man and woman, disabled and non-disabled – all are equal in my eyes. All are human beings, created in the image of the Creator. I will protect the human dignity of each. I do not aspire to power. I do not seek to rule. I am aware of the chains that bind me as a judge and as the President of the Supreme Court. I have repeatedly emphasized the rule of the law and not the rule of the judge. I am aware of the importance of the other branches of government – the legislative and executive.

I view my office as a mission. Judging is not a job. It is a way of life. I expressed those ideas in an opinion considering whether extraordinary methods of interrogation may be used on a terrorist in a "ticking bomb" situation[59]:

> "Deciding these applications has been difficult for us. True, from the legal perspective, the road before us is smooth. We are, however, part of Israeli society. We know its problems and we live its history. We are not in an ivory tower. We live the life of this country. We are aware of the harsh reality of terrorism in which we are, at times, immersed. The fear that our ruling will prevent us from properly dealing with terrorists troubles us. But we are judges. We demand that others act according to the law. This is also the demand that we make of ourselves. When we sit at trial, we stand on trial."

[59] See H.C. 5100/94, Pub. Comm. Against Torture in Isr. v. Gov't of Israel, 53(4) P.D. p. 817 (845).

Chapter I

Ideas about the Foundation of Human Rights and the Communication of Human Rights

"The German's Village"

Boualem Sansal and the Entanglement of History and Experience

Daniel Bogner

It is by no means a new thesis that human rights have to do with human experience. Nonetheless, I shall use this thesis as the basis of my lecture, because even though it is emphasized time and again that human rights proceed from concrete experiences of suffering, injustice and violence, it nonetheless is not clear exactly how the two – historical, contingent experience and the current validity claim of human rights today – are related. I would like to contribute to the clarification of this question and will do so by means of a literary example. This is a contemporary novel, a work by the Algerian writer Boualem Sansal with the title, "The German's Village. Or the Schiller Brothers' Diaries", which appeared at the beginning of 2008. But before speaking about the book itself, I would like to briefly outline a conceptual framework within which my reading of the text could have its place.[1]

What exactly do human rights have to do with experience? First of all, it is helpful to differentiate between historical origins and the validity claim. No one would argue with the statement that the struggles for independence with their experiences of suffering in early modern times such as those in England or the United States of America, but also the French Revolution, were decisive in formulating human rights.[2] But what about their validity claim today: is the experiential level equally necessary now?

My thesis is: Yes, it is, but in order to be able to bring out the meaning of historical experiences for considering the validity claim of human rights, a careful *hermeneutic of experiences* is necessary, a context-based interpretation of their meaning. Historical experiences are never transmitted directly and immediately; rather, they are passed on into the present as symbols. They can only

[1] I would like to dedicate this text to Mordechai Kremnitzer. His remarks helped me to understand better what I am talking about.

[2] *H. Bielefeldt*, Philosophie der Menschenrechte, Grundlagen eines weltweiten Freiheitsethos, Darmstadt 1998, pp. 230ff.

be caught symbolically, which is to say by means of fictional or documentary texts that are locked up in archives or available through modern forms of electronic communication, and then they must be interpreted. Only when they have been interpreted does it becomes clear whether anything and if so what can be said regarding a possible normative content in those experiences. A hermeneutic of experience must determine in which direction, with which meaning and effect, and perhaps at what price such evidence can make a statement. The goal of such an interpretation is to ascertain how the experiences might resonate in the present and thereby reveal their significance in the search for meaning and norm.[3] I begin not by asking about the philosophical foundations of the norm, but rather with a broader perspective: I am interested in the validity of the norm.

My working hypothesis is as follows: it is not possible to speak of the validity of human rights without addressing the possibility of implementing these rights. What is of interest is the legal practice of human rights. The term "validity claim" could then be understood as two-sided: as valid positive law on the one hand, but on the other hand also as the adopted and implemented acceptance of human rights on the political and societal level. Dealing with legal practice places one in the field of historical contingency.[4] The obvious thing to do then is to survey experiences, since communicated experiences can be important indicators for the realm of legal reality, for the existing possibilities but also the limits of a human rights ethos.

So much for now as regards my methodological background. I would like to provide an example and a starting point for examining such realms of experience by using a literary work by *Boualem Sansal*, "The German's Village".[5] What is the book about? The text weaves together the diaries of two Algerian brothers who grow up in Paris. As children, the two were brought by their parents to live with an uncle in France, because of its better social opportunities and in order to escape the civil war at home. The older of the two, Rahel, manages to climb the social ladder and has a good position in a successful business. The younger of the two, Malrich, is a child of the Parisian *banlieue* and is sur-

[3] The point is to be able to measure how experiences can become the starting point for the formation and validity of norms. It goes without saying that the function which experience then takes on will be very different depending on the philosophical orientation. In some cases, experience is the starting point, reinforcement or springboard, in other cases, it is the reason, the point of adhesion or the source of the acceptance of a norm. Idealistic and transcendental philosophical ways of thinking are secondary to phenomenological or pragmatic ways. No decision should be made in this matter.

[4] Concerning the paradigm of "contingency" in history and social sciences, see: *W. Knöbl*, Die Kontingenz der Moderne, Wege in Europa, Asien und Amerika, Frankfurt 2007, p. 361; *M. Makropoulos*, Kontingenz, Aspekte einer theoretischen Semantik der Morderne, Archives Européennes de Sociologie 45 (2004), pp. 369–399.

[5] *B. Sansal*, Le village de l'Allemand, Ou le journal des frères Schiller, Paris 2008, p. 264.

prised time and again at how bad life can be for the socially disadvantaged of the milieu, at the government's retreat from the problematic quarters surrounding Paris, and at friends who are torn between Islamism and traditional morals.

Rahel, the older brother, commits suicide in the mid-1990's, and the book begins with the handing over of his personal items to his younger brother Malrich. One of the items Malrich finds is Rahel's diary, in which he depicts his path to suicide. Malrich keeps a diary of his own, in which he reflects upon his brother's ideas. These diaries show two very different ways of dealing with the same fate. The brothers both knew that their father, Hans Schiller, originally came from Germany. One day, Rahel learns of an appalling massacre led by the Islamic terror group GIA (Islamist Armed Group) who, on the back of secular society, fought a dreadful civil war against the armed forces of the Algerian State in the 1990's. The terrorists have all but leveled the village of the brothers' family, murdering most of its population. Among the victims are also the parents of Malrich and Rahel. Driven by the memory of his parents, Rahel sets out for the small village in remote Algeria. There his father is still revered as a *sheikh*, a wise old man and benefactor, a village elder and astute administrator, and not without reason. He had fought as a "*Mujahid*" with the FLN (*Front de la Libération National*/Algerian National Liberation Front) in the Algerian War of Independence (1954–1962) in which the Algerians liberated themselves from French colonial rule. At this point, the story makes an about face. The father had worked as a military advisor for the Algerian "revolution", selling the knowledge he had acquired in a completely different context during the Nazi regime, as a German SS-officer in the "*Totenkopf*" division in the concentration camps of World War II.

This is a major blow to Rahel. He begins to research his father's past across the whole of Europe and discovers the singularity of the crimes he had committed. The knowledge drives Rahel mad. He asks himself if guilt can be inherited. In the end he takes his own life and bequeaths his diary to his brother Malrich so that he too may learn the truth about their parents. However, Malrich deals with this knowledge in a completely different way. When confronted with the "talibanization" of his Paris neighborhood, he cannot avoid making comparisons between Nazism and Islamism. He is told that such a comparison could get him into trouble, but he uses it nonetheless as a source for his daily struggle to survive in the *banlieue*.

So much about this exciting book's story. Even though it is a work of fiction, as the author himself emphasizes, there is a real historical background, at least for the character of the father, from which *Sansal* draws. In fact the book is electrifying because it is based on real current and historical tensions. Most interesting for my reading of the text is the question of how it is received. How might the book be understood? What effect can it have? How will these effects differ depending on the national context to which the book is speaking?

Brought out by the French publisher *Gallimard* in France, the effects of the book vary. Malrich's unsparing critique of the politics of the French Republic regarding troubled quarters in the big cities reverberates loudest of all. It is the perspective of an insider who believes in the blessings of a republic with its promises of human rights and of equal treatment and equal rights for all who decide to belong to the Republic. Malrich's voice reminds the French Republic of its unredeemed promises, its faults and failures. Many of the immigrants who have meanwhile become French citizens and who have been and continue to be discriminated against and excluded, have Algerian roots. *Sansal's* work links the glaring problems of French immigration policy with the historical legacy of the Algerian war. And this war continues to be a wound in France's political identity. In 1962, demoralized and defeated people left North African soil at de Gaulle's behest, accepting the necessity but going against the whole desire of their heart. The Algerian mercenary troops who had fought for the *Grande Nation* and against their compatriots were left behind, helpless and betrayed. War crimes such as torture, extra-judicial executions and enforced disappearances have never been processed. So *Sansal* reminds the reader that the past and the present are interconnected and that the suppression of yesterday leads to failures today.

The character of the former SS officer Hans Schiller, who has become a military advisor to the FLN, can make an ambivalent impression: When the insurgents go so far as to cooperate with the Nazi criminals, are not the repression of the Algerian independence movement and the colonial war legitimized retroactively to some extent? At least, reading the book in a French nationalist perspective may lead to the conclusion that the charges against the French war practices no longer weigh so heavily, nor are they so scathing.[6]

So much for the book's possible resonance in France. And what about Algeria, the author's home country? There, it was not even permitted to publish the book. In fact, since 2005 none of *Sansal's* books have been allowed in Algeria, because the former regime led by the Liberation Front (FLN) accuses the author of violating the "holy values of the revolution". Unlike many other authors who emigrated, *Sansal*, who until a few years ago held a high position in the Algerian government's administration, decided to remain in Algeria. What does the book say to Algerians who manage to read it via the French edition or otherwise? It could blow great holes into the prescribed Algerian way of reading national history, which is to say, the iconography of the victorious fight against the French and the resulting eternal legitimation of the corrupt FLN independence party, which hinders the processing of its own war crimes. Just as Rahel

---

[6] An overview of the various debates about the meaning of the Algerian war is given by *F. Renken*, Frankreich im Schatten des Algerienkriegs, Die Fünfte Republik und die Erinnerung an den letzten großen Kolonialkonflikt, Göttingen 2006, p. 569 ff.

seeks assistance from the authorities in his demand for an investigation of the terrorist acts of the GIA in his parents' village and never receives an answer, so it is to the present day for many Algerians with their government. To Algerians, *Sansal's* book must sound like a long overdue indictment of the regime, in whose view the population is made up of subordinates rather than citizens. And it is like a bomb exploding when an Arab writer tells his own people in which dark corners the FLN acquired its military know-how. An Algerian-Arab taboo is broken in the novel when an Algerian talks to his compatriots about the Shoah. *Sansal* names and addresses openly the mixture of indifference, doubt and blatant negation in Algeria where this chapter of history is concerned.[7]

And finally, how might Germans experience the book and its themes? I am not sure. Is it primarily a feeling of trepidation, of embarrassment because *Sansal* compares Nazism with Islamism? In the text, Malrich says: "When I see what the Islamic fundamentalists are doing here in France and elsewhere, I say to myself that some day when they are in power, they will be worse than the Nazis." Does that not simply invite things to be relativized, perhaps even German history? Or is it a blank check to throw fundamentalist Islamism and Islam into the same pot and deny Muslim's ability for democracy? Is *Sansal's* book embarrassing because it shows with what sympathy Nazism was accepted in parts of the Arab world? *Sansal* shows that not only the "New Left" of West Germany supported the FLN in its movement for emancipation, a support that was declared to be "morally good", but that the FLN also received concrete military advice from a completely different tradition. All this may come to mind when one looks at the story through a German lens.

I would like to mention another even more fundamental point, which accounts for the explosive force of the book. *Boualem Sansal* shows that the acceptance and validity of human rights, which in Germany are often taken for granted as the basis for civilization and considered to be eternally valid, are actually not that "normal". *Sansal* recalls the real historic process and the struggle with which human rights are always associated. Without those struggles, they would not exist as laws. In breaking one or more of his country's taboos as the first Algerian writer to openly take a stand regarding anti-Semitism,[8] denouncing the totalitarianism of his country's regime, its corruption and misuse of

[7] *Sansal* was one of the few Arabic writers who did not boycott the meeting at the Paris *Salon du Livre* in March 2008 because Israel was the guest country.

[8] "There was complete silence regarding the Shoah in Algeria, when not presented as a shabby Jewish invention. This shocked me. To this day no film or documentary on this topic has been shown on Algerian television. Never has a responsible person said a word nor an intellectual written about this theme. This is incomprehensible because we have made national awareness the alpha and omega as a result of our drama during the Algerian war. I think we should also have been interested in the dramas that have affected other peoples around the world." *Boualem Sansal* in an interview in: Le Nouvel Observateur, accessible under: http://bibliobs.nouvelobs.com/print/2505 (accessed 25 February 2009).

power, *Sansal* puts himself and his writing career at risk. He reminds us that human rights require courage and are not a gift from heaven, but always have to be fought for anew within the social process. Even if the process of legally regulating human rights has begun, one may not succumb to the illusion that the struggle for them has ended. History does not repeat itself, but because human rights are always a matter of the individual's powerlessness in the face of external forces, human rights standards are always threatened. Their acceptance must always be won anew, which at some point is then reflected in legislation. And the spiral continues.

At the end of my examination of the various resonances in how the book is received, I would like to return to the methods of which I spoke at the beginning of my deliberations. Having attempted to look at the way French, Algerian and German readers might experience the book, one could ask: "How might it be received for example in Israel, among Palestinians – or elsewhere?"

When I read *Sansal's* book for the first time, I was moved by the unrelenting openness with which the author depicts his characters' thoughts, feelings and intentions. Although the book deals with a particular segment of history, I was certain that he was alluding to and giving voice to experiences beyond the events depicted. After I had introduced my interpretation of *Sansal's* book in Jerusalem in the autumn of 2008, a German-born Israeli whose parents had emigrated to Israel with him in the late 1940's, came to me and told me something he had remembered as he listened. One of the earliest childhood photos in his family album showed him being held by a woman who had taken care of him during the first months of his life when his mother had been ill. This woman was a close friend of his mother and probably a trusted family friend. In the course of American military investigations in Germany after the war, it was revealed that the woman's husband was hoarding goods stolen from Jewish Germans. He was a staunch Nazi, who adhered to the Nazi racial ideology and who had become rich at the cost of Jews whilst his wife had lovingly cared for their Jewish neighbours' baby.

What are the consequences of knowing this aspect of one's childhood? Is there "guilt" – some form of dark inheritance – from the past that carries over into the present? Or rather, does this glimpse into the past open one's eyes to the fact that human beings are individuals who live in the present with their own very personal world, past and history. And that may lead to a growth in the moral responsibility to treat oneself and the other as equals – so a path between that of Rahel and of Malrich, one which offers a third alternative not explicitly found in *Sansal's* book, but which would form a convincing sequel.

The interpretation of such realms of experience is incomplete and shows the degree to which the setting of standards for human life depends on historical experiences. These vary widely and need not be defined according to national criteria. For into the wine of the universal validity of human rights is poured the water of the historical relativity of their acceptance and reception. But this interpretation opens up an enormous potential: the tremendous opportunity found in carefully addressing such experiences in order to release their supportive strength for the validity claim of human rights. Contingent, which is to say contextual and situational human experiences within a specific period of time could serve as powerful reinforcements to such validity claims. In this perspective, the role of history, the past, what has been lived is always double. As the philosopher *Paul Ricoeur* pointed out: precisely the "unredeemed promises of the past"[9] must be investigated in the hermeneutical process, and then they can be politically relevant in shaping the present. In this way, human experiences can reveal a fictitious visionary potential. The politics of human rights cannot succeed without such fiction.

---

[9] *P. Ricœur*, Die Rätsel der Vergangenheit, Erinnern – Vergessen – Verzeihen, Göttingen, 4th ed., 2004 (1998), p. 64 (Essener Kulturwissenschaftliche Vorträge 2).

The Struggle over Human Rights in Mexico[1]

Markus-Michael Müller

Looking at Latin America from the vantage point of human rights confronts the spectator with a somehow ambivalent picture. On the one hand, Latin America actively contributed to the development of human rights as a normative universalizing principle of the modern political imaginary. From *Bartolomé de las Casas'* manifestoes for the human rights of the "New World's" indigenous peoples in the 16th century to the triumph of liberal thought in the late 18th century and the inclusion of the idea of human rights in the republican constitutions; from the expansion of the idea of human rights to the realm of social rights in the 1917 Mexican constitution to the formulation of the first models upon which the 1948 Universal Declaration of Human Rights was drafted; from the "invention" of the category of "disappeared persons" to the establishment of truth commissions in the region, by way of an interdependent transfer process, Latin America has contributed substantially to our contemporary understanding of human rights.[2] On the other hand, however, the historical experience of most of the Latin American countries has a darker side, characterized by a long tradition of human rights negations and violations. These stretch from *Bartolomé de las Casas'* initial position to replace native forced labourers with African slaves to the unfulfilled promises of 19th century liberalism, whereby despite the constitutional guarantees of human rights, citizenship and democracy, the dominant elites perpetuated the colonial social order by rejecting "all assertions of equality between themselves and the subaltern groups over which they ruled".[3] And they continued from the eruptions of political violence to military dicta-

[1] Research for this article was conducted within the Project C3 "Public Security as Governance? Policing in Transitional and Developing Countries" located at the Research Center (SFB) 700: "Governance in Areas of Limited Statehood – New Modes of Governance?", funded by the German Research Foundation (DFG).

[2] For an excellent overview on Latin America's unique human rights tradition and contributions, see *P. G. Garozza*, From Conquest to Constitutions: Retrieving a Latin American Tradition of the Idea of Human Rights, Human Rights Quarterly 25 (2003), pp. 281 ff. and his article "They are our brothers, and Christ gave his life for them", The Catholic Tradition and the Idea of Human Rights in Latin America, Logos 4 (2003), pp. 82 ff.

[3] *D. Nugent*, State and Shadow State in Northern Peru *circa* 1900: Illegal Political Net-

torship under bureaucratic authoritarian regimes and more contemporary manifestations of human rights violations in the aftermath of the so-called democratic transitions – most of all related to the contemporary security crisis and the "(un)rule of law".[4] In Latin America, the concrete implementation and practice of human rights have been in danger ever since.

This brief appraisal immediately raises the question of how one can account for this paradox? Aware of the fact that space is limited, I cannot present an all-encompassing answer to this question, the aim of this article is of a rather modest nature. By limiting myself to a detailed reconstruction of the question and problems of human rights in Mexico, the case I know best, I will try to demonstrate that when addressing the question of the paradox development of human rights in Latin America, it is important to be sensitive to "the limits of legal language"[5] and to move beyond a mere legal conception of human rights by tracing their development within the realm of the political. Therefore, the main argument of this article is primarily a methodological one. By focussing on the development of human rights in Mexico, the article will show that an understanding of the concrete development of human rights within a particular empirical setting accounts for the enabling and limiting structures of the respective political order in which this development is embedded. Such a focus helps us to understand the differences and contradictions that are inherent to the always contingent and tension-ridden relationship that exists between the abstract idea of human rights as a universalizing principle and more concrete, path-dependent manifestations of human rights practices and struggles.

On this background, my contribution will be organized as follows: First, I will present an overview of the development of human rights in Mexico in the 20th century, highlighting the structural features of the local political system which limited and in practice negated the existence of human rights, as well as the struggles of various protagonists in overcoming this situation. Second, by drawing on empirical research done in Mexico City, I will indicate the contemporary challenges and problems faced by human rights activists as regards one of the most critical areas of Mexico's contemporary human rights agenda: the question of public security and law enforcement. This section will demonstrate how the long shadow of past (in)experiences with human rights in Mexico is seriously challenging the possibilities for protecting human rights in the country's contemporary political order. Finally, I will relate these empirical observa-

works and the Problem of State Boundaries, in: J. McC. Heyman (ed.), States and Illegal Practices, Oxford 1999, p. 71.

[4] This term is borrowed from J. E. Mendez/G. A. O'Donnell/P. S. de M. S. Pinheiro (eds.), The (Un)Rule of Law and the Underprivileged in Latin America, Notre Dame 1999.

[5] *C. Hastrup*, Representing the Common Good: The Limits of Legal Language, in: R. A. Wilson/J. P. Mitchell (eds.), Human Rights in Global Perspective. Anthropological studies of Rights, Claims and Entitlements, London 2003, pp. 16ff.

tions to a more general theoretical question concerning the potential universal character of human rights and its relationship to what I shall call the political space of modernity and its plural and always path-dependent unfolding.

I. Human Rights in Post-Revolutionary Mexico

The most important event of Mexico's entry into the 20th century was the Mexican Revolution, the first successful social revolution of the 20th century.[6] One of the most significant documents, reflecting the efforts and visions of the victorious forces for the foundation of a new social and political order, as well as their concerns for human rights in Mexico, was the Constitution of 1917. Whereas an official and explicit commitment to the issue of human rights was also present in the "liberal" constitution of 1857, this matter remained a dead letter during the liberal oligarchic regime of Porfirio Díaz (1876–1911). The revolutionary constitution of 1917 gave the human rights issue in Mexico a new quality, converting them into real constitutional guarantees.[7] However, and this is important for my purpose, a particular and at first sight extremely progressive feature of the constitution seriously affected the importance given to human rights guarantees. This was its strong emphasis on social rights and the related constitutional emphasis on an active, interventionist role of the state in guaranteeing their efficiency. Because of the importance given to *collective* social rights, in practice individual guarantees and human rights were legally overpowered by the social rights and their safeguarding through the Mexican state. Whereas classic liberal ideas of human rights are based on the idea that the individual as a human being possesses certain inalienable rights that are to be protected from the state, the Mexican Constitution with its emphasis on the protection of social rights turned this understanding upside down. By stating the importance of collective social rights for the new political order, it provided the post-revolutionary state with substantial constitutional powers to intervene permanently in the realm of individual rights on behalf of the less privileged collectivities such as workers or peasants.[8] However, this overemphasis on so-

[6] The political process of the Mexican Revolution spanned a period of more than thirty years. The first revolutionary confrontations began in 1910. During 1917 and 1920, the armed confrontations came to an end, the post-revolutionary Mexican constitution was written, and the corresponding political regime came into being. The revolutionary process finally ended during the consolidation of the regime under the presidency of Lázaro Cárdenas (1940). On the Mexican Revolution see *F.-X. Guerra*, México: del Antiguo Régimen a la Revolución, 2 Volumes, Mexico City 1992; *A. Knight*, The Mexican Revolution, 2 Volumes, Cambridge 1986; *H. W. Tobler*, Die Mexikanische Revolution, Frankfurt am Main 1992.

[7] On the constitutional development of human rights in Mexico, see *R. Lara Ponte*, Los Derechos Humanos en el Constitucionalismo Méxicano, Mexico City 1997.

[8] *D. Boris*, Mexiko im Umbruch. Modellfall einer gescheiterten Entwicklungsstrategie, Darmstadt 1996, pp. 7ff.

cial rights is only one factor in explaining the marginality and inefficiency of human rights in post-revolutionary Mexico. Another and more important factor which contributed to this marginality resides in the fact that these rights are embedded in the political structures of Mexico's post-revolutionary political system.

In fact, despite official commitments and declarations concerning the importance of social and human rights, both sets of rights as truly impersonal and enforceable *legal rights* were practically absent within Mexico's post-revolutionary political system. This was due most of all to the absence of a state as an impersonal power[9] and to the related consequences for the formation of the Mexican legal system. Since the beginning, the Mexican legal system was most of all a project of the elite which never became anchored in the daily lives of the majority of the local population.[10] This mismatch continued to exist after the Mexican Revolution. Despite a nearly fetish-like production of legal documents, in practice, one particular component of the Mexican "unrule of law" consisted in the transformation of law and rights into a medium of political negotiation, a practice, which was at the heart of the post-revolutionary political system, centred around the one-party rule of the Partido Revolucionario Institucional (Institutional Revolutionary Party, PRI). Because law and rights were embedded in the corporatist and patron-client structures of the post-revolutionary regime, rights and the law did not operate as impersonal mediums of social regulation. Instead, the Mexican "legal" system and the "rights" it guaranteed functioned as a medium of informal political bargaining, negotiation and for political mobilization and interpellation for the political elites.[11] In this context and despite official claims, like in most other Latin American countries, "law" and legal "rights" (including human rights) served primarily as a medium through which obedience to the dominant political order was negotiated constantly and mostly informally.[12]

I would suggest that this de facto absence of an impersonal legal system and of rights, including human rights, is the main factor for understanding the relative insignificance and marginality of human rights in the Mexican political

[9] *M.-M. Müller*, Raum, Herrschaft und die Produktion von (Un-)Sicherheit in Mexiko, in: S. de la Rosa/U. Höppner/M. Kötter (eds.): Transdisziplinäre Governanceforschung. Gemeinsam hinter den Staat blicken, Baden-Baden 2008, pp. 58 ff.

[10] *S. López-Ayllón/H. Fix-Fierro*, Tan cerca, tan lejos. Estado de derecho y cambio jurídico en México (1970–1999), Boletín Méxicano de Derecho 97 (2000), p. 161.

[11] *M. Braig/M.-M. Müller*, Das politische System Mexikos, in: S. Rinke/K. Stüwe (eds.): Die politischen Systeme in Nord- und Lateinamerika, Wiesbaden 2008, pp. 409 f.; *M. Braig*, Zwischen Menschenrechten und Rechtstaatlichkeit. Zivile Frauenorganisationen und Demokratisierung des Staates in Lateinamerika, in: M. Gräser et al. (eds.), Staat, Nation und Demokratie. Festschrift für Hans-Jürgen Puhle, Göttingen 2001, pp. 141.

[12] On this topic, see *P. Waldmann*, Nachahmung mit begrenztem Erfolg. Zur Transformation des europäischen Staatsmodells in Lateinamerika, in: W. Höpken/M. Riekenberg (eds.), Politische und ethnische Gewalt in Südosteuropa und Lateinamerika, Köln 2001, pp. 19 ff.

imaginary during most of the 20th century. Based on their daily experience of the absence of law and rights as impersonal and empowering aspects of the local political order, the local population did not develop a positive and affirmative image of legal subjectivity. As a consequence, legal rights, including human rights, did not rank high on the citizen's political agenda. This became particularly evident in the reaction against the Mexican version of a dirty war. In countries like Brazil or Argentina, the experience of military rule under bureaucratic authoritarian regimes stimulated the growth of civic associations whose activities positively shaped the processes of democratic transitions in the respective countries. But Mexico's experience with political state repression and human rights violations, committed by the police, military and secret police, culminating in the dirty war of the 1970s, did not stimulate a similar outcome. Although notwithstanding its comparable "soft" character, the local version of a dirty war produced serious human rights violations,[13] political activists and civil society actors avoided addressing them as a human rights issue. In addition to the negative experience and practical inoperativeness of the Mexican legal system, which stemmed from the characteristics mentioned above, another aspect was crucial in this regard.

As *Sergio Aguayo*[14] pointed out, the marginalization of the topic of human rights during this period can be traced back to the concerns of most Mexican political activists, that by taking up the issue of human rights in their own country, they would open the door for a massive political intervention from the United States where, during the Carter administration, the promotion of human rights issues became central in US foreign policy issue. Therefore, by joining the call for foreign "non-intervention" into domestic political issues, the victims of the human rights violations joined a somehow paradoxical coalition with their oppressors and opted not to voice their suffering in the language of human rights. Instead, most of them sought other, frequently violent, means to challenge the existing political order of PRI one-party rule and its acts of political repression.

However, despite this widely shared scepticism as regards the topic of human rights in Mexico, it cannot be denied that first important steps towards a positive embedding of the idea of human rights in post-revolutionary Mexico were taken in the 1970's. This decade not only witnessed a first comprehensive report by Amnesty International on human rights violations.[15] The 1970's also produced the first formation of civic associations which addressed human rights

---

[13] *C. Doyle*, La "diplomacia tranquila" de estados unidos, in Proceso 1384 (2003), pp. 20ff.

[14] *S. Aguayo*, Seguridad nacional y derechos humanos en México, Revista Mexicana de Ciencias Políticas y Sociales, 170 (1997), pp. 82f.

[15] *L. Martínez Zuñiga/N. S. Rodley*, Violación de derechos humanos en México?, Universitas 49 (1975), pp. 131ff.

violations committed by the Mexican state. The most important organization in this respect is the EUREKA! Committee, formed in 1977 by *Rosario Ybarra de la Piedra*, mother of a "disappeared" son, who with other friends and relatives of imprisoned or disappeared persons, campaigned against the state's human rights violations and arbitrary detentions of political activists by military and police forces. During the 1980's, the growth of such associations was met by state repression leading to imprisonment and the death of human rights activists. Despite such acts of repression from state authorities, this decade witnessed a substantial growth in the number of civic associations addressing human rights violations by the Mexican state against social and political movements, as well as the problem of Central American refugees searching for asylum in Mexico. During this decade, many important (and still active) human right organizations were founded, frequently with a strong Catholic background, including for example the *Centro de Derechos Humanos Fray Francisco de Vitoria* (Fray Francisco de Vitoria Human Rights Centre), founded in 1984; the *Centro de Derechos Humanos "Miguel Agustín Pro Juárez"* (Miguel Augustín Pro Juárez Human Rights Centre), founded in 1988; or the *Centro de Derechos Humanos de Fray Bartalomé de las Casas* (Fray Bartalomé de las Casas Human Rights Centre), founded in 1989.

However, the growth and consolidation of human rights activism throughout the 1980's was triggered by a particular political conjuncture, which created a historically unparalleled opportunity structure for such developments. Five factors were crucial in this regard.[16] First of all, the political events since the Tlateloclco massacre in 1968[17] stimulated a growing political opposition, which directly sought to challenge the existing political system under PRI dominance. This political climate received further stimuli from the political repression during the dirty war of the 1970's and early 1980's, as well as from the revolutionary movements in Central America. Second, these developments were strengthened by the 1982 economic crisis. With limited financial resources to deal with the crisis through an expansion of government spending and substantial social dislocations, the PRI could not control the resentment of a growing number of Mexicans. Furthermore, the crisis provoked a serious social breakdown that was reflected in increasing crime rates on the one hand, and on the other hand, greater human rights violations as a result of police responses to that crisis. Third, the gradual political opening of the regime since the 1980's gave oppositional political actors more space for political articulation outside the established channels of the PRI party structure, enabling them to address topics

[16] See *E. L. Cleary*, Human rights organizations in Mexico: Growth in turbulence, Journal of Church & State, 37 (1995), pp. 793 ff.

[17] On 2 October 1968, military and police agents killed hundreds of protesters, predominantly students participating in the local students movement on the Plaza de Tlatelolco in Mexico City.

which were previously considered to be taboo. Fourth, the earthquake that shook Mexico City on September 19, 1985, and the inefficient state response to the disaster led to a (re)vitalization of urban social movements in Mexico City, which was identified by many commentators as the birth of civil society in Mexico City. These commentators saw it as such, because the civic activism in the aftermath of the natural disaster consolidated into a strong network of neighbourhood organizations which played a crucial role in future transformations of the Mexican political system. Fifth, these developments were accompanied by a growing academic interest in issues of human rights violations. An emblematic expression of this development was the publication in 1988 of the *First Report on Democracy*. The book, edited by the nationally renowned intellectual and former director of the Autonomous National University of Mexico (UNAM), Marcos Pablo Gonzalez Casanova, included a chapter written by *Miguel Concha*, which gave a detailed empirical account of fifteen years of human rights violations in Mexico and formed the empirical core of this publication, contributing to the national and international attention that this publication received.

The next important developments, which increasingly linked such civic activities to issues of public (in)security and rule of law, occurred in the 1990's. Once again this was due to a particular political conjuncture, overdetermined by the impact of economic liberalization around the NAFTA integration process. Because of the manifold human rights violations observed in Mexico and because of the high level of impunity and tolerance given to such acts, Mexican politicians faced growing criticism and pressure from US politicians and international NGOs, such as the important report in 1990 "*Human Rights in Mexico: A Politics of Impunity*" by Americas Watch. The same year, *Norma Corona*, a political activist who documented police abuses, was assassinated -a case which received wide international media coverage- and the Inter-American Commission on Human Rights (IAHCR) declared that Mexico had violated substantial political rights during various state-level and municipal elections in the 1980's. As an immediate reaction to such criticisms, in June 1990 the then-president Carlos Salinas de Gortari created by a presidential decree the National Human Rights Commission (CNDH). First located at the Ministry of the Interior, through a constitutional reform and the passing of the *Ley de la Comisión Nacional de Derechos Humanos* (Law of the National Human Rights Commission), the CNDH in 1992 received a legal status making it independent of the Ministry of the Interior.[18] Within the context of a growing international awareness of the human rights situation in Mexico, this decision, followed in the following years by the creation of a state-level human rights commission,

[18] Human Rights Watch, Mexico's National Human Rights Commission: A Critical Assessment, New York 2008.

led to a substantial opening of discursive and institutional spaces for human rights-related topics and encouraged the work of the local NGO community.

Without going into detail, we can conclude that the NAFTA integration process had two important consequences for the development of civic activism in Mexico. First, these developments and the repressive responses of the Mexican state to the Chiapas uprising in 1994 produced a greater international scrutiny and sensitivity for Mexican politics and the local human rights situation. This in turn led the Mexican government in its desire to be acknowledged as a thoroughly modern and democratic country, to officially recognize the role of NGOs and the importance of human rights issues. Second, many Mexican NGOs perceived the NAFTA process as an opportunity to search for partnerships with US-based civic organizations, a fact which contributed to a growth of civic organizations in Mexico throughout the 1990's.

In addition, in recent years the dramatic deterioration of the public security situation since the 1994 economic crisis and the growing relevance and visibility of drug trafficking in Mexico linked issues of human rights abuses by state authorities (most of all the police) to general questions of public security and the quality of the rule of law in Mexico. In such a context, since the late 1990's new civic organizations explicitly addressing issues of public insecurity and police inefficiency -and relating them to wider human rights issues- have been founded, in part directly by crime victims or their relatives. Through their personal encounters with the local police and justice institutions, these people had become aware of the inefficiencies in the local administration of justice and decided to confront these problems through the foundation or the financing of civic organizations targeting these issues. In addition, a growing number of academics discovered the importance of these topics and their practical relevance. This stimulated the active participation of academics inside civic organizations, as well as the founding of civic organizations through academics. Finally, a growing number of "traditional" human rights NGOs increasingly gave questions around public security and a central place on their agenda. This more security-related development within the contemporary field of human rights activism in Mexico will be the focus of analysis in the following section.

II. The Impact and Problems of Contemporary Human Rights Activism in Mexico: The case of Public Security

At the end of the previous section, I highlighted the central place questions of public security and law enforcement occupy in Mexico's contemporary human rights environment. Although it would be far beyond the scope of this article to present an exhaustive account of this topic, a few remarks seem necessary in order to give the reader who is unfamiliar with the Mexican context a brief insight into what specifically is going wrong in the realm of Mexico's law enforcement efforts and how this affects the quality of human rights.[19]

There is common agreement among researchers dealing with the local problems of insecurity that the immediate aftermath of the 1994 economic crisis brought a significant increase in the officially reported number of crimes, mostly as regards robbery and theft, during the period between 1994 and 1997 (in particular 1995–1997). Although, at least according to official data, crime rates have declined since the late 1990's, they are still high compared to the historical experience of criminality in post-revolutionary Mexico. The most prominent contemporary manifestations of these developments can be identified in the still unresolved feminicide in Ciudad Júarez or the violent confrontations between competing drug cartels and the Mexican state. Their brutality and the number of casualties has been rising ever since the declaration of war against drug trafficking by *Felipe Calderón* in December 2007. Whereas in 2006 there were 2.120 reported drug-related killings, this number increased to 2.280 in 2007; during the first five months of 2008, the death toll reached 1.245, and as this article was being written, no change for the better was in sight.

In addition to the massive loss of human life, another result of this declaration of war was massive military involvement and related human rights violations in the campaign against drug trafficking. This accelerated the already existing tendency towards a militarization of Mexican law enforcement measures. Despite the impressive fact that there are more than 1.000 different police units with approximately 410.000 policemen and – women operating in the country -which, if we calculate with a population of 103.263.388 people makes one police officer for every 251 inhabitants – their overall contribution to an improvement of the local security environment is more than doubtful. The main reasons for this can be identified in general problems of the local police apparatuses. These can be summed up in the lack of adequate human resources and training, high turnover rates, a lack of vocational ethics, deficient and outdated equipment, low salaries, police corruption, the absence of a clear normative framework of action, and the frequently direct participation of police officers in organized (and unorganized) crime, violence and human rights violations. However, not just the police apparatus but the whole system of administration of justice contributes at least in part to the current security problems. Indeed, the situation within the Mexican justice system does not look very promising. Research on this topic identified certain structural deficiencies, including a lack of professional-

[19] For detailed accounts on this issue, see for example *D. E. Davis*, Undermining the Rule of Law: Democratization and the Dark Side of Police Reform in Mexico, Latin American Politics & Society 48 (2006), pp. 55 ff.; *J. Bailey/J. Chabat* (eds.), Transnational Crime and Public Security. Challenges to Mexico and the United States, San Diego 2002; *W. A. Cornelius/D. A. Shirk* (eds.), Reforming the Administration of Justice in Mexico, Notre Dame 2007.

ism, incoherence, arbitrary detentions, torture, corruption and bribery. These not only impede an efficient and impartial handling of the presented cases, but frequently tend to legalize violations of basic rights committed by law enforcement officers against presumed criminals.[20]

This sad state of affairs has given rise to a wide range of pressure groups and human rights bodies focussing on human rights violations committed by Mexico's law enforcement agencies. Many if not most of these organizations are operating from Mexico City. During my fieldwork in Mexico City, I was able to identify 23 NGOs explicitly struggling for an improvement of the local security situation and the protection of human rights in Mexico. These organizations' activities covered a wide range, from the publication of reports and statistics to discursive interventions in public debate, the organization of workshops and conferences on related issues, and legal action against the violation of human rights by institutions administering justice.

In my interviews and conversations[21] with members of local human rights NGOs that focus on the promotion of an policing approach based on human rights, I was surprised to realize that, when asked how they perceived the impact of their work, most interviewees were highly sceptical about their achievements. Although most of them were more or less content with their personal achievements and those of their organizations, it was a commonly shared perception that despite such advances, the overall impact of civic associations on the local security and human rights situation was relatively weak. Although a growth of civic organizations addressing topics of human rights violations, public security and the rule of law can be noted, public authorities are more committed to address these topics in close collaboration with civil society organizations, and more international funding is being given for civic activities in Mexico. Nevertheless, all partners agreed that these factors did not bring about a substantial improvement in either the local human rights situation or in the quality of the rule of law and of public security in Mexico. In fact, many people even argued that despite an impressive opening of discursive and institutional spaces for publicly addressing such topics, the human rights situation under the first two democratic governments has been even worse than in the previous decades of PRI-rule.

A first set of problems contributing to this outcome is related to the internal dynamics of the local civil society. Many with whom I spoke complained about

---

[20] *Miguel Augustín Pro Júarez Human Rights Center/Lawyers Commitee For Human Rights*, Legalized Injustice. Mexican Criminal Procedure and Human Rights, New York 2001; *G. Zepeda Lecuona*, Crimen sin castigo. Procuración de justicia penal y ministerio público en México, Mexico City 2005.

[21] The information summarized on the following pages draws on fourteen in-depth interviews and eight informal and formal conversations with members of different human rights NGOs conducted in Mexico City between May and July 2007.

the general weakness of the local civil society. Despite the recent democratic opening of the local political system, there seems to be a relatively weak tradition of organized civic activism that is independent of state and party structures in Mexico. This is closely related to the structure of corporatism and clientelism during the PRI regime as described in the preceding section; at that time, many civic organizations were directly financed by state institutions, and they acted on the basis of a "hidden agenda", which in many cases served particular political (and financial) goals, often to the benefit of the dominant party. These practices have had a negative impact on the credibility and legitimacy of civic associations and NGOs and impeded their becoming deeply embedded in Mexican society. Because of this, it can be assumed that many Mexicans who are not directly engaged in or affected by political and social struggles have no particular knowledge of or sympathy for such organizations, nor do they perceive them as relevant protagonists in the resolution of the country's security problems.

Whereas the weakness of the local civil society affects the entire spectrum of civic organizations in Mexico, this problem seems to be even more acute when it comes to the human rights issue, the rule of law and public security. Members of the local human rights community were frequently worried about the still small number of civic organizations focussing on these questions. Because of this, many local NGO members feared that due to the perceived severity of the current security situation, and the great popular support for politics of "being tough on crime", which involve a rather lax adherence to the law and a small preoccupation of human rights issues by the public security forces, local human rights NGOs cannot serve as an efficient counterweight and effectively challenge this trend.

A second set of problems that emerged in these interviews was the question of the lack of professionalism of many human rights organizations operating in this field. One manifestation of this is the recruitment of personnel in local NGOs. It is said to be frequently based on personal relationships and (sometimes) not on the particular qualifications of the persons employed. When it came to professionalism, many interview partners also complained about the lack of an "integral" or "complex" vision of the local security problems by parts of the local NGO community. Some organizations were criticized for their exclusive focus on one-dimensional strategies in confronting the large and complex problem of human rights abuses and public security. These strategies included a nearly exclusive focus on the collection of statistical data or other predominantly "academic" activities. In contrast, organizations dedicated precisely to such issues complained about the mere "protest attitude" of their counterparts, who were said to emphasize action over analysis. These criticisms should be taken seriously, as they indicate tensions and conflicting perspectives inside the local human rights NGO community. Despite the fact that all interviewees mentioned that their organizations closely collaborate with other organizations in this area, some people (most of all but not exclusively those belonging to smaller organizations) openly acknowledged that they are in the unpleasant situation of open competition with other organizations. This can give rise to situations in which "strategic" information, for example new funding possibilities, is not passed on to other organizations or is passed on with delays in order to gain a competitive advantage.

It turned out that the strong dependence on external funds is a crucial factor in this regard. As most local NGOs are aware of the historically grounded negative perception that can arise from close collaboration with public authorities in Mexico, they prefer to maintain a certain distance to these, most of all in matters of financial support. This in turn implies that they depend on other sources of income. Because most NGOs cannot cover their overall expenditures through donations, they are interested in obtaining financial resources, mainly from international donor organizations or philanthropic foundations, including amongst others, the World Bank, the European Commission, the MacArthur Foundation, the Tinker Foundation, the William and Flora Hewlett Foundation, the Open Society Institute, the Ford Foundation, the Friedrich Ebert Stiftung, or the National Endowment for Democracy. We can assume that the resources provided by these have been and still are an essential factor in the growth of the local NGO community over the past decade.[22]

Where this is concerned, it is interesting to point out that this development was not welcomed by all interviewees. For example, two of the NGO members I interviewed described this development as the externally financed "constitution of an NGO market in Mexico", where it was expected "that you can make a lot of money"; and another NGO member characterized the director of his organization as an "entrepreneur" (empresario), because of his outstanding ability to "sell" the projects of his NGO and the related allocation of international funding. The constant growth of the local NGO community fuelled competition over these funds among the newcomers to the local NGO community. This problem was further aggravated by recent changes in the priorities of important donors, most of all in US-American foundations. It was said that after 9/11 many of these institutions re-directed a large part of their resources towards regions affected by the new US national security agenda, which further increased the competition over the available sources of income.

This dependence on the allocation of external resources indicates two sets of problems. First, it raises the question to what extent the funding agencies' policies influence the activities, strategies and projects developed by the local

[22] See *R. Stanley/R. Figari-Layus/M. M. Müller*, Transnational Actors in the Governance of Urban Security: Buenos Aires and the Federal District of Mexico, unpublished manuscript, Berlin, 2009.

NGOs. Second, it demonstrates the structural vulnerability of a local NGO community, which, because of the particular political legacy analyzed above, is dependent mainly on financial support from international funding agencies. As the latter's availability and volume are closely related to the priorities of the funding agencies, a thematic or geographical shift in their funding agenda can provoke negative effects on the NGOs activities and their capacity for improving the local security and human rights environment.

However, questions concerning the problems of cooperation between local NGOs do not arise only out of the competition between local NGOs over financial resources. Another factor affecting collaboration within the local NGO community is closely related to the historical development of the latter. Some NGOs emerged out of political and/or social movements, or their foundation was closely linked to a particular social movement. This implies that they bring a heritage and specific memory of past ideological and political struggles into their organizations. This in turn can sometimes overshadow the quality of collaboration between various organizations or between particular members within a given NGO (not to mention public authorities) who come from a different ideological background or political position.

Despite these problems and limitations of organized civic activism in Mexico City, the positive impact of these organizations on the local human rights and public security agenda should not be underestimated. The quality and quantity of Mexican civic activism in the field of human rights and public security still needs to be substantially strengthened and to become more embedded in local society. Nevertheless, I am convinced that the local security and human rights situation would be worse without the courage and commitment of these organizations and the people involved in this struggle. In addition, the interview material clearly indicates that the most serious problems limiting the impact of the local NGO community on improving the human rights and public security situation do not stem from the internal problems of the local NGO community, but from the obstacles posed by the Mexican state.

The relationship between local NGOs and public authorities (politicians, members of the police and judiciary) in Mexico is shaped not only and probably not predominantly by a particular NGO's ability to mobilize people, but by the social and political capital which a particular NGO represents for the political elites. As one interviewee put it:

> "Well, what I'm trying to say is that the differences between the NGOs and their different profiles affect their access to the public authorities. For example, for an organization of indigenous people from Chiapas, it will be very difficult to gain access to the President, because they are living in different worlds, in very distant worlds. On the other hand, an organization of wealthy people, dedicating their work to street children, will, with a very high probability, get this access, no?" (Interview June 14, 2007).

This quotation clearly demonstrates the importance of the socio-economic and political capital associated with a particular NGO (as well as the members who make it up) and the issues it addresses. The less conflictive the issue is, and the more "prestigious" the respective NGO in the eyes of the political authorities, the higher the probability that public authorities will *talk* to the organization. However, talk does not necessarily imply neither responsiveness or concrete actions on the part of the local authorities. Most interviewed NGO members expressed a certain degree of frustration as regards the willingness of local politicians and of members of the institutions of the administration of justice to implement their promises made to civic organizations. This was explained 1) with the authoritarian heritage of the Mexican political system, whereby politicians were not accustomed to being accountable to accountable to social actors; 2) political loyalties among members of the political elite and the upper echelons of the security forces that guarantee a certain degree of impunity to the members of their institutions; 3) structural deficiencies in the Mexican legal system. Faced with this situation, some local NGOs dedicated fighting human rights violations committed by police institutions even appealed to international courts such as the Inter-American Court of Human-Rights, in order to put pressure on Mexican politicians to act. Such strategies have been called "boomerang effect", because domestic NGOs bypass their state and go directly to international actors and institutions, thus attempting to put pressure on their states from the outside.[23] However, even this strategy is no guarantee that the Mexican political and justice system will react positively. The following lengthy citation from an interview with a member of a local NGO that focuses on legal action against human rights abuses gives us an appropriate insight into the magnitude of obstacles to such processes of implementing international human rights standards in Mexico.

"What is true is that the state listens to you, but it does not comply. In Mexico there is no legal system which would apply international [human rights M.M.] recommendations or decisions to the national level. This means that it [the international human rights system M.M.] only serves as a medium for political pressure. Unfortunately in our legal environment, there exists no possibility of applying international criteria to concrete legal cases. Despite the fact that our constitution gives international treaties the status of supreme laws, there are no institutional juridical mechanisms which permit the direct application of a decision of, let's say the UN Committee against Torture in the case of *Atenco*.[24] There is no respective legal system or the judge is not obliged to apply these

---

[23] *M. Keck/K. Sikkink*, Activists beyond Borders: Advocacy Networks in International Politics, Ithaca 1998, p. 12.

[24] On 2 and 3 May 2006 during a police operation against social protestors in the municipalities of San Salvador de Atenco and Texoco, nearly 200 people suffered serious human rights violations by police officers, including sexual abuses committed against 45 women. On this topic, see ProDh/INSYDE, De Atenco a la reforma policial democrática. Una mirada propositiva en clave de reforma policial democrática y derechos humanos, Mexico City 2007.

recommendations. And on the other hand, although international human right treaties have the character of supreme laws, it is certain that the judges, that all the jurisdictional personnel neither has the capacity to adopt them, nor knows something about these treaties. (...) Another problem consists in the fact that even the litigation lawyers don't know exactly the contents of these international human rights treaties. (...) The possibility to sanction high ranking police personnel when they or the officers under their command commit human rights violations is confronted with serious structural problems. First, the Mexican justice system. Here, first of all the public prosecutor (*ministerio público*) has to prove the subjective responsibility and the type of offence. Although a woman, like in the case of Atenco, could state that: I was violated so and so, but I cannot identify the aggressor because they covered my eyes and I was in a dark bus. Nevertheless, I know that these 20 men were in the bus. Who of them violated me, well I don't know, but it is certain that other testimonies support my declaration, but due to the fact that I could not identify my aggressor, this declaration will not be processed. What I am trying to explain is that whenever there is no individual responsibility with first-name and last-name, judicial sanctions will not be applied. Now, in the estimated case that the victim recognized her aggressor, let's say the police agent Juan Pérez, as long as he does not testify that he received an order from his superiors to violate that woman in this particular moment, there is no legal responsibility for his superiors, and when there is no legal responsibility, there is also no political responsibility. Because in order to sanction a governor or a police chief of whom we know that he gave the orders for this operation, you need a political judgement (*juicio político*) from the legislative power of the respective state or from the federal level. But, for sure, this guy has his godfathers (*compadres*) among the deputies, and they won't prosecute him. So, there is no way, definitely no way to sanction neither high ranking police officers, nor the responsible politicians" (Interview July 2, 2007).

To overcome such problems, local NGOs try to develop alternative strategies for gaining access to public authorities. Such strategies are most often centred on the establishment of good personal contacts – some interviewees referred to them as "friendship" – with key persons in the respective institutions. Another option for local NGOs to improve their access to local institutions as well as the latter's responsiveness, is the strategy of "luring" institutional personnel by presenting collaboration with NGOs as useful for their future (political) career. As one interviewee put it:

"You have to understand that politicians have their own agenda. You have to look where points of convergence are and these have to be taken up" (Interview July 16, 2007).

The previous observations showed the variety of difficulties with which local civic organizations for an improvement of the local human rights and public security situation are confronted in their struggle. The legacy of the PRI regime, a personalistic political culture, the weakness of the local civil society and its internal dynamics, as well as dependence on external funding have placed serious constraints on the impact of organized civic on the overall improvement of the local security situation. However, as I already mentioned, in spite of these limitations, local civil society has played and will continue to play a crucial role in the overall struggle for a rule of law and an equitable provision of security as a true public good. In fact, in spite of the problems mentioned above, in the face of the present "war" against drug trafficking and the growing militarization of Mexico's law enforcement agencies and strategies, the importance of organized civic activism as an essential counterweight to such developments should not be underestimated. On this background, I will now try to relate these empirical observations to a more general theoretical question concerning the potential universal character of human rights.

III. Some Concluding Reflections on the Universal Character of Human Rights from the Vantage Point of Latin America

In his book, *The Europeanization of the World. On the Origins of Human Rights and Democracy*, the historian John M. Headley presents a passionate manifesto for the "unique gifts" which Western, or more precisely European, civilization bequeathed to the world. He is convinced that there is something like "a unique combination of exceptional elements, intellectual and religious, present in the inception of Western development", which contributed to a unique Western "universalizing principle directed toward the construction of humanity as idea and fact".[25] With respect to the growing sensibility for post-colonial research in our contemporary academic world, such a view seems somehow outdated. Already in 1959, in a post-colonial gesture *avant la lettre*, the French philosopher Louis Althusser argued that what has been enthusiastically called "the rise of the West"[26] was not the result of a somehow endogenous development, but rather of Europe's encounter(s) with other parts of the world.[27] And these encounters which were constitutive for our understanding of modernity, were also characterized by a dark side, reflected in violence, unequal relations of power, brutal domination and exploitation – including the realms of knowledge and science themselves. On this background, *Walter Mignolo*, writing from the perspective of Latin American post-colonial scholarship and its commitment to a decolonial move within our conception of modernity, recently said:

"The decolonial shift is of the essence if we would stop seeing 'modernity' as a goal rather than seeing it as a European construction of history in Europe's own interests. Dialogue can only take place once 'modernity' is decolonized and dispossessed of its mythical march towards the future. I am not defending 'despotism' of any kind, Orien-

[25] *J. M. Headley*. The Europeanization of the World. On the Origins of Human Rights and Democracy, Princeton 2008, p. 65.

[26] *W. McNeil*, The Rise of The West: A History of the Human Community, Chicago 1992.

[27] *L. Althusser*, Montesquieu, la politique et l'histoire, Paris 1959 [1992], pp. 13f.

tal or Occidental. I am just saying that 'dialogue' can only take place when the 'monologue' of one civilization (Western) is no longer enforced."[28]

What does all this have to do with the question of human right? A lot, I think. Not only because the inherently (modern) Western idea of a particular human community (including the human rights issue) is frequently at the heart of such monologues which narrate affirmative stories about the rise of the West. But also because the Western idea of human rights itself as enshrined in documents like the *Universal* Declaration of Human Rights holds a not unproblematic claim towards universalization. As *Mark A. Goodale* recently argued, this universalizing claim is based on a fundamental "trick". By assuming that all human beings are essentially equal and the same, and by deducing certain inalienable rights from this sameness, a universal understanding of human rights asserts a first and founding principle which is improvable – at least through empirical evidence. This implies that the idea of human rights is obtained through inherently deductive thinking. Its legitimacy is based on a set of unproven principles: the idea of a common humanity as a moral (and not only biological) quality, the assumption that this entails a specific normative framework, and the assertion that this normative framework is expressed through rights. One important consequence of this deductive operation is the simple fact that the resulting global and, in its abstract sense, universalizing idea of human rights somehow "seduces" us to think that "human rights practices do – or should – unfold at a much broader scale than they in fact do"[29].

This mismatch between the abstract idea of human rights and their concrete actuality brings us back, I think, to the question of modernity and its plural or "multiple" unfolding,[30] which challenges such linear triumphalist interpretations of the uniqueness of Western ideas of modernity and human rights. As *Teresa Caldeira*, writing from the perspective of a Brazilian social scientist argued, "(b)ecause these notions are formulated on the basis of a specific Western European or American experience, to apply them directly to a country like Brazil results only in seeing it as a failed or incomplete modernity." Against this background, she suggests "that different societies have diverse ways of engaging the elements generally available in a common repertoire of modernity to create their specific nations, citizenries and democracies"[31] – and one should add: ideas and practices of human rights.

[28] *W. D. Mignolo*, The Idea of Latin America, Malden 2005, p. xix.

[29] *M. Goodale*, Locating Rights, Envisioning Law Between the Global and the Local, in: M. Goodale/S. E. Merry (eds.). The Practice of Human Rights. Tracking Law Between the Global and the Local, Cambridge 2007, pp. 10f.

[30] On the notion of "multiple modernities", see *S. N. Eisenstedt* (ed.), Multiple Modernities, New Brunswick 2002.

[31] *T. P. R. Caldeira*, City of Walls. Crime, Segregation, and Citizenship in Sao Paulo, Berkely 2000, p. 340.

I totally agree with this perspective and I am convinced that it would be misleading to interpret this understanding of a different modernity as a plea for cultural relativism. Rather, in the remaining paragraphs I will argue that it is the context depended unfolding of what can be termed "political space of modernity" which determines the way such a "common repertoire of modernity" develops. That development is what is decisive for the degree of distance between the universal idea of human rights and their existence within a particular empirical setting.

To begin with this exploration, I have chosen a particular historical moment that is characterized by a concrete empirical setting and a specific temporality. This historical moment is the French Revolution in 1789. Although it may seem somehow contradictory first to argue against a triumphalist interpretation of the gifts of the West and then to select precisely such a Western context as the starting point for my argument, I am convinced that from an analytical and explicitly non-normative and affirmative point of view, this event condensed in a nutshell the basic and decisive features for both the political formulation of the idea of human rights as a universalizing principle and the possibilities for making this ideal real. Indeed, it can be argued that the central place which the topic of human rights occupied in this process is the concrete expression of the foundation of new, modern, political order and of its claim to universality that emerged in this particular conjuncture. But what are the particular features of this conjuncture and of the related emergence of a new political space that is condensed and reflected in the idea and declaration of human rights?

First of all, as *Marcel Gauchet*[32] has convincingly argued in his reading of the 1789 Declaration of Human Rights, the French Revolution and the Declaration brought about a new understanding of the state as an "impersonal power"[33] and as a founding principle of a new political order. This "revolutionary" understanding of the state implied a rupture with all prevailing conceptions of state power, in which the latter was understood to be the organizing principle of as society made up of mediating corporations. Instead, this new understanding converted the state into an instance which constitutes its society through the construction of social relationships among the atomized individually which are its *citizens*.[34] This point already indicates the second feature of the political space of modernity as reflected in the 1789 Declaration: the idea of individual legal subjects who, freed from the bonds of particular mediating powers, form the centre and only source of political legitimacy for the new political order. This new political order, this new, modern understanding of the political, is the

32 *M. Gauchet*, Die Erklärung der Menschenrechte. Die Debatte um die bürgerlichen Freiheiten 1789, Reinbek 1981, pp. 117ff.

33 See in particular *H. Gerstenberger*, Impersonal Power. History and Theory of the Bourgeois State, Leiden 2007.

34 *P. Rosanvallon*, Der Staat in Frankreich. Von 1789 bis heute, Münster 2000, pp. 68f.

"society of individuals", and the Declaration is its "birth certificate".[35] Indeed, the Declaration represents a fundamental and foundational "mutation of the symbolic order",[36] because it instituted

"a society without a body, as a society which undermines the representation of an organic totality (...) the disappearance of natural determination, which was once linked to the person of the prince or to the existence of a nobility, leads to the emergence of a purely social society in which the people, the nation and the state take on the status of universal entities, and in which any individual or group can be accorded the same status"[37].

In this respect, the Declaration institutes society "as the association of free and equal human beings"[38]. This dimension of the political space of modernity as reflected in the Declaration is linked to the third constitutive feature of this new political space, which is the entry of the masses into the realm of the political. Not only the immediate revolutionary process as such was, as *Antonio Negri* states, "the time of the masses"[39]. The entire Declaration is a document which *tendentially*[40] institutes the masses as legitimate political subjects and protagonists. This coincides with the breakthrough of the new political logic of hegemony,[41] in which political domination is not based primarily on the coercive capacities of the rulers, but on the active consent of the population over which domination is exercised[42].

In sum, I would like to suggest that the concrete unfolding of these constitutive features of the political space of modernity is decisive for the degree of convergence or divergence between the idea and practice of human rights. This unfolding is contingent upon the particular social, cultural and political characteristics of the respective society. In fact, when we confront this brief and highly stylized model of the political space of modernity with the reflection on the state of human rights in Mexico presented above, we can understand the local marginality of human rights and the obstacles encountered by human rights activists as reflections of a particular configuration of the political space of mo-

---

35 *M. Guachet*, Die Erklärung der Menschenrechte. Die Debatte um die bürgerlichen Freiheiten 1789, Reinbek 1981, p. 109.

36 *C. Lefort*, Democracy and Political Theory, Cambridge 1988, p. 16.

37 *C. Lefort*, Democracy and Political Theory, Cambridge 1988, pp. 17f.

38 *C. Lefort*, Menschenrechte und Politik, in: U. Rödel (ed.), Autonome Gesellschaft und libertäre Demokratie, Frankfurt am Main 1990, p. 260.

39 *A. Negri*, Insurgencies. Constituent Power and the Modern State, Minneapolis 1992, p. 193.

40 This tendential character was most obvious in the exclusion of women as equal political subjects.

41 *E. Laclau/C. Mouffe*, Hegemony and Socialist Strategy, 2nd edition, London 2002, pp. 149ff.

42 The term hegemony as used in this context is taken from Antonio Gramsci. The most comprehensive account of Gramsci's conception of hegemony can still be found in *C. Buci-Glucksmann*, Gramsci and the State, London 1980.

dernity. This particular configuration is characterized by the absence of the state as an impersonal power, the permanently negotiated character of the local political order, the absence of widespread experiences with notions and practices of individual legal subjectivity, and the fragmented unfolding of hegemony as a logic structuring the local political order.[43]

Against this background, two final remarks, or better, suggestions are necessary. First, we should be cautious in our interpretation of this outcome and not read it as another case of "failed" or "deficient" development in the so-called Global South. Rather, we should try to separate normativity from analysis and first seek to understand the particular unfolding of this political space of and the related impact on the human rights issue in its own right. Such an endeavour helps us to understand the particularity of local developments without making our own expectations the single and exclusive point of reference and the measure for "success". Rather, such an attempt stresses the irreducible character of local human rights interpretations, which are based on "personal biographies, community histories, and on expressions of power relations between groups". Their "relationship to formal, legal versions has to be discovered, not assumed"[44]. Second, and this brings normativity back into the argument, even when the Mexican development of the political space of modernity provided serious structural obstacles for narrowing the gap between the idea and the practice of human rights – a gap which exists to varying degrees in every country around the world, as we should keep in mind – local appropriations of the idea of human rights and growing attempts, however limited, to make this idea practical, can be found. We should remember that structures are dynamic condensations of social relations and constellations of force that can be modified by political struggles. In particular, Mexico's struggle over human rights is a powerful and important aspect of the current political conjuncture and of its potential for overcoming the ambivalent legacy of 71 years of one-party rule and post-revolutionary state formation.

[43] On the fragmented character of hegemony in Mexico, see *W. Roseberry*, Hegemony and the Language of Contention, in: G.M. Joseph/D. Nugent (eds.), Everyday Forms of State Formation. Revolution and the Negotiation of Rule in Mexico, Ithaca 1994, pp. 355 ff.; *A. A. Alonso*, The Effects of Truth: Re-Presentation of the Past and the Imagining of Community, Journal of Historical Sociology 1 (1988), pp. 58 ff.

[44] *R. A. Wilson*, Human Rights, Culture, Context: An Introduction, in: R. A. Wilson (ed.), Human Rights, Culture & Context. Anthropological Perspectives, London 1997, p. 12.

New Media, New Opportunities?

Technology and Human Rights Organizations in a Digital Globalized World

Hadas Eyal

I. Introduction

In the political communication arena, where various groups send and receive messages intended to influence the political process, human rights organizations (HROs) challenge governmental institutions to endorse their version of a better society and a better world. A major turf upon which this political exchange takes place is the mass media.

Reciprocal communication between the political system and the public is passed through the media and projected in a way that shapes and defines the public agenda on issues such as national priorities, policy, values, decision making, range of legitimate ideas, resource allocation etc. Whether consciously or unconsciously, journalists paint a picture of the desired political and cultural norms and values that are important to society.[1] Media coverage is therefore crucial for HROs and it is an inseparable component of their struggle for political power.[2]

Mass media is motivated first and foremost by making mass profits. *Wolfsfeld*[3] pinpointed four selection criteria that media outlets adopt in order to select commercially wise news items: drama, immediacy, simplicity and patriotic ethnocentric feelings. New media information and communication technologies have the potential to supply mainstream mass media with the type of sensational and commercial content it thrives on, such as visual images of drama and conflict. But unfortunately, media preference for story simplicity and an ethnocentric viewpoint can sometimes stand in stark conflict with human rights issues in many ways – human rights can be complex, multifaceted and laden with

---

[1] *H.J. Gans*, Deciding What's News, Evanston 1979/2004.

[2] *W.A. Gamson/G. Wolfsfeld*, Movements and media as interacting systems, Annals of American Academy of Political and Social Science 582 (1993), pp. 114–125.

[3] *G. Wolfsfeld*, Media and the Path to Peace, Cambridge 2004.

legal aspects under international law. Although creative use of new media technologies may get HROs into the news under certain circumstances, the quality of the coverage they get may be out of their control.

What exactly are these new media information and communication technologies? The enticing and alluring promise of 'new' refers to digital audio-visual media that evolve from the convergence of computer technology, telecommunications, and traditional media, such as the internet, hand-held video cameras, video phones, portable computers, etc.[4].

Communication scholars are sceptical about the extent of technology's revolutionizing potential, and do not see new media completely replacing mainstream media any time soon.[5] They do agree however that technology, for better or worse, has changed news reporting by making the news more immediate, live, unfiltered, more independently event-driven and less institutionally-spun, and more accessible, global, interactive, rich, contextualized, comprehensive, customized, flexible, post-modern and ubiquitous; but they question whether most audiences ultimately get more of the same commercialized drama, sensationalization, simplification and other distortions and biases that characterize mainstream mass media.

The literature on movements and the media tends to either lump all movements into a general 'social movement' category or focus on one issue (e.g., anti-globalization, national liberation, women's rights and even terrorism) or on a particular case study. Furthermore, precious little has been written specifically about media coverage of human rights and with the exception of one journal article,[6] nothing was found about mass media and organizations defined as HROs (such as Amnesty International, Human Rights Watch, Witness, or Human Rights First).

In addition to the external functions of transmitting and conveying organization messages to various audiences, new media technologies have important internal organization functions such as recruitment, formation of a collective

---

[4] *J. V. Pavlik*, New Media and News: Implications for the future of journalism, New Media & Society 1 (1999), no. 1, pp. 54–59.

[5] *S. Barnett*, New media, old problems; new technology and the political process, European Journal of Communication 12 (1997), no. 2, pp. 193–218; *L. W. Bennett/R. G. Lawrence/S. Livingston*, None dare call it torture: Indexing and the limits of press independence in the Abu Ghraib scandal, Journal of Communication 56 (2006), no. 3, pp. 467–485; *S. Cottle*, Mediatized conflict, Maidenhead 2006; *J. Curran*, Global Journalism: a case study of the Internet, in: N. Couldry/J. Curran (eds.), Contesting media power: Alternative media in a networked world, Lanham 2003, pp. 227–241; *S. Livingston/W. L. Bennett*, Gatekeeping, indexing and live-event news: Is technology altering the construction of news?, Political Communication, 20 (2003), pp. 363–380; *W. van de Donk/B. D. Loader/P. G. Nixon/D. Rucht*, Introduction: Social movements and ICTs, in: W. van de Donk/B. D. Loader/P. G. Nixon/D. Rucht (eds.), Cyberprotest: New media, citizens and social movements, London 2004, pp. 1–25.

[6] *R. Ramos/J. Ron/O. N. T. Thoms*, Shaping the Northern media's human rights coverage, 1986–2000, Journal of Peace Research 44 (2007), no. 4, pp. 385–406.

identity, fundraising, mobilization and interactivity.[7] This project therefore, seeks to examine the relationship between the characteristics of different-issue HROs and their use of new media technologies to internally recruit and mobilize and to externally exploit the media to promote their message. This will be done by listening to the views and voices of professionals with first hand, practical, operational experience: organization staff, mainstream and new media journalists and editors.

To begin with, their insights will be used to gauge the advantages of using new media technologies for internal organization purposes and to explore the reasons that limit willingness and capability of an organization to invest in internet applications and successfully use them for recruitment, mobilization and interactive network building. The next objective is to evaluate how new media technologies have changed the ability of these organizations to successfully influence the quantity and quality of the mass media coverage they manage to get.

II. Theoretical Background

1. Political Communication as a Contest Arena

Garber defines the political communication field as the space in which all political messages that are intended to impact directly or indirectly on the political process are formulated, sent, received and processed.[8] This space includes actors, issues and initiatives that compete for public attention and public resources.

> "The key element is that the message has a significant political effect on the thinking, beliefs and behaviours of individuals, groups, institutions and whole societies and the environments in which they exist."[9]

McNair[10] adds the concepts of purposefulness and intentionality to the definition of political communication: all *purposeful* communication from, to and about any political actor with the intention of achieving specific political goals. A political actor, according to *Wolfsfeld/ Sheafer*,[11] is any individual, group or institution that strives to shape political policy.

---

[7] *P. van Aelst/S. Walgrave*, New Media New Movements? The role of the internet in shaping the 'anti-globalization' movement, in: W. van de Donk/B. D. Loader/P.G Nixon/D. Rucht (eds.), Cyberprotest: New media, citizens and social movements, London 2004, pp. 97–122.

[8] *D. A. Graber*, Political communication faces the 21st century, Journal of Communication 55 (2005), pp. 479–507.

[9] *D. A. Graber*, Political Communication: Scope, progress, promise, in A. W. Finifter (ed.), Political Science: The state of the discipline, Washington (D. C.) 1993, pp. 305–332.

[10] *B. McNair*, An introduction to political communication, London/New York 2007.

[11] *G. Wolfsfeld/T. Sheafer*, Competing actors and the construction of political news: The contest over waves in Israel, Political Communication 23 (2006), pp. 333–345.

The political communication field is often likened to a contest arena, complete with turf, game rules, winners, losers and prizes.[12] In essence, mass media are the major turf upon which political communication is contested, but it is not a simple inanimate plot of sod, nor is it a merely neutral pipeline or hose used to disseminate messages. Rather, the media is a selective system that transforms these messages to fit its commercial needs and by its nature does not equally favour all political actors and all issues.[13]

The term 'mediatisation' of modern democracy was coined by *Mazzoleni/Schultz*[14] to describe the intrusion of mass media work routines upon the political process by shaping the public agenda and public discourse. Although most mass media outlets do not have specific political goals and this imposition is actually an unintended consequence of the media,[15] it is nonetheless real and has real-world effects.

Wolfsfeld's political contest model[16] explains the role of the news media in political processes using six principles: the political process influences the media more than the other way around; the influence of the media on political processes is a cycle initiated by changes in the political sphere (P) that effect the way the media acts (M), causing a further change in the political sphere (P); control over the political environment is a key variable in understanding quantity and quality of media coverage; the role of the media in political processes dynamically changes over time and circumstances; the media modifies its role according to the ebb and flow in the balances of power and dependency that determine the rules of the media game – who will win access and which meaning frame will be chosen; and finally, although political authorities have an inherent advantage over challengers in terms of quantity and quality of media exposure, challengers are able to penetrate the media and exploit it to their political advantage. Obviously, social movements in general and human rights organizations in particular are assigned the role of challengers in this competitive arena equation.

---

[12] *T.E. Cook*, The news media as a political institution: Looking backward and looking forward, Political Communication 23 (2006), pp. 159–171; *G. Mazzoleni/W. Schultz*, 'Mediatization' of politics: A challenge for democracy?, Political Communication 16 (1999), no. 3 pp. 247–262; *G. Wolfsfeld*, Media and political conflict: News from the Middle East, Cambridge 1997.

[13] *T.E. Cook*, The news media as a political institution: Looking backward and looking forward, Political Communication 23 (2006), pp. 159–171.

[14] *G. Mazzoleni/W. Schultz*, 'Mediatization' of politics: A challenge for democracy?, Political Communication 16 (1999), no. 3, pp. 247–262.

[15] *G. Wolfsfeld*, Media and the Path to Peace, Cambridge 2004.

[16] *G. Wolfsfeld*, Media and political conflict: News from the Middle East, Cambridge 1997; *G. Wolfsfeld*, Media and the Path to Peace, Cambridge 2004.

2. *Social Movements and Mainstream Mass Media – Quantity and Quality of News Coverage*

Social movements, the challengers of the political communication arena, depend on the media for their existence,[17] and the competition for media attention is, or should be, an inseparable component of their struggle for political power.[18] When a news item is handed to a journalist, it is compared with the existing supply of meaning frames in terms of compatibility, competing conceptions and potential for new alternatives. Social conflict frames usually revolve around inequality versus law and order. Thus, the more a message resonates in terms of current and local culture, political atmosphere and media requirements for a good story, the better the chance that journalists will adopt it.[19]

The quantity and quality of news coverage are the end products of the intricate interactions between organizational, media, political and cultural variables.[20] Quantity is a straightforward item count. As previously mentioned, profit-driven media selection criteria favours items that are dramatic, simple, ethnocentrically-centred and those that require immediate reporting.[21] The magnitude of consumer exposure, type of target audience, emphasis on the visual and an entertainment focus are media characteristics that affect the quality of news coverage of social movements.[22]

Quality, on the other hand, refers to content, to the way the media frames and presents the issue. *Entman* defines the framing process as

> "selecting and highlighting some facets of events or issues, and making connections among them so as to promote a particular interpretation, evaluation or solution".[23]

The more frames are congruent with public sentiment – the more consensus they rally, the more they are ambiguous – the more they are susceptible to con-

---

[17] *W. A. Gamson/G. Wolfsfeld*, Movements and media as interacting systems, Annals of American Academy of Political and Social Science 582 (1993), pp. 114–125.

[18] *G. Wolfsfeld*, Media and political conflict: News from the Middle East, Cambridge 1997.

[19] *L. W. Bennett*, Toward a theory of press-state relations, Journal of communication 40 (1990), no. 2 pp. 103–125.

[20] *L. W. Bennett*, Toward a theory of press-state relations, Journal of communication 40 (1990), no. 2 pp. 103–125; *R. Bray*, Spin works!: A media guidebook for communicating values and shaping public opinion, San Francisco 2000; *Cottle*, Mediatized conflict, Maidenhead 2006; *R. M. Entman*, Projections of Power, Chicago 2004; *W. A. Gamson/G. Wolfsfeld*, Movements and media as interacting systems, Annals of American Academy of Political and Social Science 582 (1993), pp. 114–125; *T. Gitlin*, The whole world is watching: Mass media in the making and unmaking of the new left; Berkeley 2003; *S. Livingston/W. L. Bennett*, Gatekeeping, indexing and live-event news: Is technology altering the construction of news?, Political Communication 20 (2003), pp. 363–380.

[21] *G. Wolsfeld*, Media and the Path to Peace, Cambridge 2004.

[22] *W. A. Gamson/G. Wolfsfeld*, Movements and media as interacting systems, Annals of American Academy of Political and Social Science 582 (1993), pp. 114–125.

[23] *R. M. Entman*, Projections of Power, Chicago 2004.

test, and when frames are incongruent with public sentiment, they are completely blocked from public discourse. *Iyengar*[24] has found that political issues in the media are invariably presented either in an episodic frame which focuses on specific events and particular cases, or in a thematic frame which places political issues and events in a more general context. Episodic frames are a better fit to media requirements – personal drama is simple, tugs at emotions, and produces "good television". In contrast, thematic frames are complex, lengthy, in-depth, abstract and could be rather dull. An important component of a frame is the attribution of responsibility. Episodic frames attribute responsibility for creating the problem and solving it on the *individual*, while thematic frames hold *public forces, institutions and authorities* responsible.

Although no group has complete control over the amount of media exposure or way the media will frame its message, measures can be taken to maximize favourable coverage.[25] Organizations can improve their chances of successfully broadcasting their message and productively campaigning for constructive policy change if they are professionally organized (leadership, division of labour, etc.), the more financial and information resources they own, when they adopt a positive ideological stance regarding the centrality of mass communication to achieving organization, and provided the issues they represent are culturally and politically congruent.[26]

As for the media, the general rule of thumb is that profit considerations trump other journalistic values even when they attempt to construct news stories that resonate culturally.[27] While the message of advocate-organizations carries ideological intentions, the media message has a short-term commercial purpose: to interpret and package an item into the easiest story for the audience to understand and want to see/read.

Simply put,

> "the more closely the concerns and values of social movements coincide with the concerns and values of elites in politics and the media, the more likely they are to become incorporated into the prevailing news frames".[28]

---

[24] *S. Iyengar*, Is anyone responsible? How television frames political issues, Chicago 1991.

[25] *W. A. Gamson/G. Wolfsfeld*, Movements and media as interacting systems, Annals of American Academy of Political and Social Science 582 (1993), pp. 114–125.

[26] *R. M. Entman*, Projections of Power, Chicago 2004; *W. A. Gamson/G. Wolfsfeld*, Movements and media as interacting systems, Annals of American Academy of Political and Social Science 582 (1993), pp. 114–125; *S. Livingston/W. L. Bennett*, Gatekeeping, indexing and live-event news: Is technology altering the construction of news?, Political Communication, 20 (2003), pp. 363–380.

[27] *W. A. Gamson/G. Wolfsfeld*, Movements and media as interacting systems, Annals of American Academy of Political and Social Science 582 (1993), pp. 114–125.

[28] *T. Gitlin*, The whole world is watching: Mass media in the making and unmaking of the new left, Berkeley 2003.

Cultural and media resonance is a dynamic feature, but the effort to pin it down is worthwhile because choice of frame can influence policy and allocation of public resources.

3. *Research on Human Rights Organizations*

Very little has been written on the topic of *media coverage of human rights*, and with the exception of one study by *Ramos/Ron/Thoms*,[29] a literature search found mostly anecdotal inferences on the relationship between *media of any sort and HROs* like Amnesty International, Human Rights Watch, Witness, and Human Rights First.

By and large, studies on human rights and media coverage focused on media production and do not include an organizational perspective. These studies examined media coverage as a consequence of a variety of independent variables such as access to media, freedom of press, trade openness, foreign investment, conflict intensity, military expenditures, level of democracy, population size, and economic development;[30] item sources;[31] and types of human rights (personal, civil and political rights vs. economic, social, cultural and collective rights), geographical regions most likely to be reported, and breadth of coverage.[32] *Metzl*[33] inventoried how NGOs, governments and the United Nations can use information technology systems to promote human rights by listing advantages, potential dangers (for example: saturation and public numbness caused by excess coverage of atrocities, and use of technology to violate human rights by using it for surveillance and oppression) and suggesting strategies (such as forming strategic alliances with governments and global industries, and rethinking organizational goals and budget priorities). Others[34] reported straightforward numbers of items on human rights in the printed press and/or on television.

---

[29] *R. Ramos/J. Ron/O. N. T. Thoms*, Shaping the Northern media's human rights coverage, 1986–2000, Journal of Peace Research 44 (2007), no. 4, pp. 385–406.

[30] *C. Apodaca*, The whole world could be watching: Human rights and the media, Journal of Human Rights 6 (2007), pp. 147–164.

[31] *T. Joseph*, Kashmir, human rights and the Indian press, Contemporary South Asia 9 (2000), no. 1, pp. 41–45.

[32] *S. M. Caliendo/M. P Gibney/A. Payne*, All the news that's fit to print? New York Times coverage of human rights violations, Harvard International Journal of Press/Politics 4 (1999), no. 4 pp. 48–69; *D. P. Fan/J. Ostini*, Human rights media coverage in Chinese East Asia, Annals of American Academy of Political and Social Science 566 (1999), pp. 93–107; *J. S. Ovsiovitch*, News coverage of human rights, Political Research Quarterly 46 (1993), no. 3, pp. 671–89.

[33] *J. F. Metzl*, Information technology and human rights, Human Rights Quarterly 18 (1996), no. 4, pp. 705–746.

[34] *A. E. Geyer/R. Y. Shapiro*, Human Rights, Public Opinion Quarterly 52 (1988), p. 386–398; *K. J. Pritchard*, Human rights: A decent respect for public opinion, Human Rights Quarterly 13 (1991), pp. 123–142.

One study stands out in terms of topic, scope and methodology. Titled 'Shaping the Northern media's human rights coverage, 1986–2000', this project by *Ramos/Ron/Thoms*[35] explored the factors which influenced *international* exposure of events and abuses in explicit human rights terms as expressed by quantity of news items in one northern newspaper and one magazine. They also examined the circumstances under which HROs have the most effective impact. The number of stories in "The Economist" and "Newsweek" were regressed on indicators of civil and political rights, civil society, Northern aid, economic development, military size, population size, and number of Amnesty press releases. The data was organized by country and year. Results showed that "The Economist" and "Newsweek" reported human rights abuses more frequently when they occur in countries characterized by repressive regimes, greater per capita wealth, large populations and higher Amnesty advocacy attention. Less significant effects were found for variables of political openness, number of battle-deaths, and civil societies. Another finding revealed that Amnesty press releases had a larger impact when the country reported did not usually get much media attention.

While the *Ramos/Ron/Thoms* study does stand out, there is no mention of the advent and revolutionizing impact of new communication technologies such as the internet, mobile video cameras and compact satellite hook-up equipment on international media reporting during the time period covered . Data graphs show sharp increases beginning 1996 in the number of human rights items and in the number of countries reported – from less than 10 countries covered by "Newsweek" in 1996 to over 35 by 1998, and from approximately 35 countries covered by "The Economist" in 1996 to almost 50 by 2000 – but there is no mention of the possible contribution of new media technologies to this amplification, although the timelines match. This 2007 study was preceded by an earlier project by *Ron/Ramos/Rodgers*[36] which investigated the factors that affect the volume of country reporting by Amnesty International (number of reports and press releases). Here as well, the new media revolution was ignored.

Clearly, the academic foundations on the topic of media and human rights at this point are not very solid. Can this project use the more established body of research on media and social movements as its theoretical background?

Marmura quotes political sociologist *Mario Diani*, who defines a social movement as a

[35] *R. Ramos/J. Ron/O. N. T. Thoms*, Shaping the Northern media's human rights coverage, 1986–2000, Journal of Peace Research 44 (2007), no. 4, pp. 385–406.

[36] *J. Ron/R. Ramos/K. Rodgers*, Transnational information politics: NGO human rights reporting, 1986–2000, International Studies Quarterly 49 (2005), pp. 557–587.

"network of informal interactions between a plurality of individuals, groups and/or organizations engaged in a political or cultural conflict on the basis of a shared collective identity".[37]

Van Aelst/Walgrave[38] built upon previous theories to compile four elements that define a social movement: a shared definition of the problem as a basis for a collective identity, mobilization of people to join and participate in action to achieve social and political change within a network of organizations. The HROs chosen for this study all fit these definitions of a social movement and will be considered as such, allowing the knowledge base on social movements and mass media to apply.

The advent of new media technologies such as the internet, laptop computers and videophones altered the relationship between HROs and the media by serving as catalysts for a chain reaction that begins with gaining mainstream mass media coverage and continues with shaping public opinion, rousing authorities to respond, and setting policy change in motion.

4. New Media

The singular noun 'new media' has a misleading face-value appearance of simplicity. Far from representing a single element or a simple concept, the term 'new media' encompasses tools, systems, practices and routines that have evolved from the convergence of computer technology, telecommunications and traditional media, creating new digital audio-visual media that transformed work in other media.[39]

Hand-held video cameras, cellular video phones, portable computers, fibre-optic broadband internet, and live satellite feeds are examples of new media tools that not only transformed journalists as well as chance passer-bys into

---

[37] *S. Marmura*, A net advantage? The internet, grassroots activism and American Middle-Eastern Policy, New Media & Society 10 (2008), no. 2, pp. 247–271 (249).

[38] *P. van Aelst/S. Walgrave*, New Media New Movements? The role of the internet in shaping the 'anti-globalization' movement, in: W. van de Donk/B. D. Loader/P.G Nixon/D. Rucht (eds.), Cyberprotest: New media, citizens and social movements, London 2004, pp. 97–122.

[39] *M. Deuze*, The web and its journalisms: Considering the consequences of different types of news media online, New Media & Society 5 (2003), no. 2, pp. 203–230; *T. Flew*, New Media: An Introduction, Oxford 2002; *M. Lister/J. Dovey/S. Giddings/I. Grant/K. Kelly*, New media: a critical introduction. London & New York 2003; *.R. Rice*, Artifacts and paradoxes in new media, New media & Society 1 (1999), no. 1, pp. 24–32; *E. Siapera*, From couch potatoes to cybernauts? The expanding notion of the audience on TV channels' websites, New Media & Society 6 (2004), no. 2 pp. 155–172; *J. B. Singer*, The political j-blogger: 'Normalizing' a new media form to fit old norms and practices, Journalism 6 (2005), no. 2, pp. 173–198; *N. Thurman*, Forums for citizen journalists? Adoption of user generated content initiatives by online news media, New Media & Society 10 (2008), no. 1, pp. 139–157; *G. D. M. Ursell*, Dumbing down or shaping up? New technologies, new media, new journalism, Journalism 2 (2001), no. 2, pp. 175–196.

fully functioning 24/7 mobile newsrooms,[40] but also shifted personal and social experiences of time, space and place; created new visual and textual experiences; introduced new computer-mediated forms of interaction; formed new habits of media use and reception; and transformed the media industry, culture, economy, ownership, control, regulation and rules of access.[41]

Several key terms are used to define, describe and discuss new media technologies: convergence, digitality, interactivity, dispersal, hypertextuality, and virtuality.[42] Each of these concepts is the topic of multidisciplinary theories and research. Following are a few sentences on each.

Convergence is a three-levelled process that combines four sectors – computing, telecommunications, information and media. On the functional level, all forms of technology become dependent on one another and are diffused together, beginning at the production stage through distribution and ending with consumer use. The second level – industry convergence – is manifested by takeovers, mergers and strategic alliances that consolidate the synergy between the four sectors mentioned above. Convergent products and services is the third level of this process and refers to customized media services that take advantage of the networked broadband infrastructure, digital capabilities and interactivity innovations to form such amenities as personalized cable packages, web-games, 3D virtual worlds such as 'Second Life', and on line shopping – to name just a few.[43]

Digitalization involves turning physical properties of input (text, audio, visual) into numerical data that can be easily manipulated by computer software, compressed, stored and quickly accessed.[44]

Moving to the next new media key term, interactivity bestows media users with freedom of choice, active control over media consumption, the power to intervene and to generate content, and the ability to send feedback to media producers – click a choice, vote by SMS, create a website, respond to a news ar-

---

40 *P. L. Dooley/P. Grosswiler*, "Turf wars": Journalists, New Media and the Struggle for control of political news, Harvard International Journal of Press/Politics 2 (1997), no. 3, pp. 31–51.

41 *M. Lister/J. Dovey/S. Giddings/I. Grant/K. Kelly*, New media: a critical introduction, London & New York 2003.

42 *T. Flew*, New Media: An Introduction, Oxford 2002; *M. Lister/J. Dovey/S. Giddings/I. Grant/K. Kelly*, New media: a critical introduction. London & New York 2003; *J. V. Pavlik*, New Media and News: Implications for the future of journalism, New media & Society 1 (1999), no. 1, pp. 54–59.

43 *T. Flew*, New Media: An Introduction, Oxford 2002.

44 *J. E. Newhagen/S. Rafaeli*, Why communication researchers should study the internet: A dialogue, Journal of communication 46 (1996), no. 1, pp. 4–13. Downloaded from: http://jcmc.indiana.edu/vol1/issue4/rafaeli.html; *J. B. Walther/G. Gay/J. T Hancock*, How do communication and technology researchers study the internet?, Journal of Communication, 55 (2005), no. 3, pp. 632–657; *I. Weber/V. Evans*, Constructing the meaning of digital television in Britain, the United States and Australia, New Media and Society 4 (2002), no. 4, pp. 435–456.

ticle, play a game with a friend on another continent and so on.[45] Interactivity is also the perceived simulation of interpersonal exchange and refers to all forms of synchronous (e.g. chat) and asynchronous (e.g. email) reciprocal audio-visual computer-mediated single-to-single, single-to-many, many-to-single and many-to-many communication.[46]

Another characteristic that distinguishes new media from old media is dispersal. It refers to the decentralization of production and distribution of media (as opposed to centralized production), to the degree of individual customization (as opposed to uniformity) and to its omnipresence.[47]

Two additional new-media features remain on the list. Hypertext is a form of software writing 'above the text' that forms links to other texts, an address-network of sorts, a navigational tool for a web map. And finally, virtuality describes a graphic, computed, digital world that gives the feeling of being in the real world.[48]

Amazingly, the new media revolution in modern democracies took all but a decade or so to accomplish, to the point that it is embedded and indispensable throughout every aspect of life.[49] What then happened to the 'old media'? They did not, of course, roll over and die. On the whole, old media adapted, adjusted and joined the digital transformation – albeit to varying degrees across the myriad of features – blurring the lines between the two.

5. *New Media and Social Movements/HROs*

a) *Movements' Internal Functions of Recruitment and Mobilization*

Digital new media technologies on the whole, and the internet specifically, are perfectly tailored for the needs of social movements in terms of both internal

---

[45] *M. Deuze*, The web and its journalisms: Considering the consequences of different types of news media online, New Media & Society 5 (2003), no. 2, pp. 203–230; *M. Lister/J. Dovey/S. Giddings/I. Grant/K. Kelly*, New media: a critical introduction. London & New York 2003; *J. E. Newhagen/S. Rafaeli*, Why communication researchers should study the internet: A dialogue, Journal of communication 46 (1996), no. 1, pp. 4–13. Downloaded from: http://jcmc.indiana.edu/vol1/issue4/rafaeli.html; *E. R. Rice*, Artefacts and paradoxes in new media, New media & Society 1 (1999), no. 1, pp. 24–32.

[46] *S. Kiousis*, Interactivity: a concept explication, New Media and Society 4 (2002), no. 3, pp. 355–383; *J. B. Walther/G. Gay/J. T. Hancock*, How do communication and technology researchers study the internet?, Journal of Communication 55 (2005), no. 3, pp. 632–657.

[47] *M. Lister/J. Dovey/S. Giddings/I. Grant/K. Kelly*, New media: a critical introduction. London & New York 2003.

[48] *M. Lister/J. Dovey/S. Giddings/I. Grant/K. Kelly*, New media: a critical introduction. London & New York 2003; *J. B. Walther/G. Gay/J. T. Hancock*, How do communication and technology researchers study the internet?, Journal of Communication 55 (2005), no. 3, pp. 632–657.

[49] *L. Lievrouw*, What's changed about new media? Introduction to the fifth anniversary issue of New Media & Society, New Media & Society 6 (2004), no. 1, pp. 9–15; *L. Rainie/P. Bell*, The numbers that count, New Media & Society 6 (2004), no. 1, pp. 44–54.

functions of recruitment and mobilization, because they are inexpensive, immediate, interactive, accessible, flexible, decentralized, unregulated, uncontrolled, unrestricted, uncensored, global, infinitely spacious and multimedia-enabled.[50] To varying degrees of sophistication, web sites, e-mail, chat rooms, e-groups, forums, and social networks are employed for a long list of internal organization purposes: recruitment; mobilization; planning; coordination; networking; fund raising; inspiration; publication of archive material, success stories and testimonials; and creation, reinforcement and preservation of a common identity for scattered members.[51]

Bennett[52] explored the ways in which digital communication networks changed the political game in favour of resource-poor players. Beyond creating networks and coordinating action, he concludes, digital hyper-linked communication, the redundancy of communication channels, and the ability of new media technologies to alter information flows through mass media, enables campaigns to sustain a permanent public presence and facilitates the formation of global strategic political relations between activists, opponents, and spectator publics.

A list of limitations that temper the enthusiasm over the abilities of new media technologies was gathered by *Galili-Zucker*.[53] These include the difficulty of mobilizing the public to leave their desks and take part in real action, the fact that new media does not replace mainstream media, a reality that the quantity of information does not necessarily assure its quality, and the observation that the gap between the public sphere and official political institutions remains large world-wide.

---

[50] *L. W. Bennett*, New media power: The internet and global activism, in: N. Couldry/J. Curran (eds.), Contesting media power: Alternative media in a networked world, Lanham 2003, pp. 17–37; *J. P. Biddix/H. W. Park*, Online networks of student protest: The case of the living wage campaign, New Media & Society 10 (2008), no. 6, pp. 871–891; *B. Cammaerts*, Media and communication strategies of globalized activists: beyond media-centric thinking, in: B. Cammaerts/N. Carpentier (eds.), Reclaiming the media: Communication rights and expanding democratic media roles, Bristol 2006, pp. 265–288; *J. Curran*, Global Journalism: a case study of the Internet, in: N. Couldry/J. Curran (eds.), Contesting media power: Alternative media in a networked world, Lanham 2003, pp. 227–241; *J. F. Metzl*, Information technology and human rights, Human Rights Quarterly 18 (1996), no. 4, pp. 705–746; *P. van Aelst/S. Walgrave*, New Media New Movements? The role of the internet in shaping the 'anti-globalization' movement, in: W. van de Donk/B. D. Loader/P. G. Nixon/D. Rucht (eds.), Cyberprotest: New media, citizens and social movements, London 2004, pp. 97–122; *G. Weimann*, Terror on the Internet: The new arena, the new challenge, Washington (D. C.) 2006.

[51] *G. Weimann*, Terror on the Internet: The new arena, the new challenge, Washington (D. C.) 2006. Although Weimann studied and wrote on the way terrorist organizations use the internet, his observations are applicable to all social movements that use this tool.

[52] *L. W. Bennett*, Communicating global activism: strengths and vulnerabilities of networked politics, in: W. van de Donk/B. D. Loader/P. G Nixon/D. Rucht (eds.), Cyberprotest: New media, citizens and social movements, London 2004, pp. 123–146.

[53] *O. Galili-Zucker*, Contemporary communication politics (Part 1): Online citizenship in an era of new media, Tel Aviv 2008 (in Hebrew).

Do new media technologies mark a dawn of a new day for social movements and HROs in terms of recruitment and mobilization? Are they a dud? Or are they something in the middle? Results from three sample studies that challenged the real-world abilities of the theoretical benefits of new media for internal organization functions, present a mix of validated expectations and disappointingly unfulfilled potential. Interestingly, all three examples (the best found) targeted anti-globalization movements.

Wall[54] studied the task of creating, reinforcing and maintaining a common organization identity by analyzing three email lists used in the Seattle World Trade Organization protests of November 1999 in terms of their contribution to the expression of collective identities online. Results indicated that although each list used at least one of three key processes to form collective identity, overall, none of the lists was entirely successful in doing so. In short, although email was helpful in organization and education within the movement, the full potential in this case was not realized.

Capling/Nossal[55] compared the role of the internet in spurring participation in two protests. The internet successfully moved bulks of information to large numbers of people in distant locations at the cost of the computer and modem, but it failed to mobilize people to physically show up. Despite the theoretical assumption regarding the death of distance in the age of the internet, the authors conclude that geographic distance remained a significant factor in the ability of organizations to mobilize supporters to take action.

Last in this sample, Van *Aelst/Walgrave*[56] analyzed anti-globalization websites looking for evidence that these organizations use the internet to form a basis for collective identity, to actually mobilize supporters and to network with different organizations. Although they were unable to attribute the success of the anti-globalization movement to technological evolution, all 17 websites scored well on each article of the coding scheme.

Internal functions, however important, are not sufficient if an organization wishes to shape social priorities. Optimally, internal functions boost external media exposure goals, which in turn bolster favourable public opinion policy change.

---

[54] *M. A. Wall*, Social Movements and email: Expressions of online identity in the globalization protests. New Media and Society 9 (2007), no. 2, pp. 258–277.

[55] *A. Capling/K. Richard-Nossal*, Death of distance or tyranny of distance? The internet, deterriotorialization and the anti-globalization movement in Australia, The Pacific Review 14 (2001), no. 3, pp. 443–465.

[56] *P. van Aelst/S. Walgrave*, New Media New Movements? The role of the internet in shaping the 'anti-globalization' movement, in: W. van de Donk/B. D. Loader/P. G Nixon/D. Rucht (eds.), Cyberprotest: New media, citizens and social movements, London 2004, pp. 97–122.

b) Movements' External Functions – New Media Exposure and Mainstream Media Exposure

The assessment of media exposure requires two perspectives – that of the organization vying for media coverage, and that of the media channels that either grant entrance or reject the attempt. New communication technologies provide both sides with opportunities and prospects never before possible.

To begin with, the internet has a synergetic quality that creates a new media ecology offering more political opportunities for dissenting voices than in the past, and it constructs a horizontal communicative network that widens the communications environment by disrupting the top-down traditional communication flow.[57] Websites, blogs and alternative media sites, offer important means of news reporting as well as of individual and collective expression.[58] These are, in effect, private, unmediated broadcast channels with a *permanent* updated campaign display and a *long term* archive.[59] Consequently, social movements increasingly see themselves as content providers and news sources that can push their ideological agendas directly to the public and into mainstream media.[60]

From another angle, thanks to increasingly available and affordable technology such as video cameras, cellular videophones and personal computers with editing software, and due to the universality of emotional and empathetic reactions to visual images, organizations worldwide gradually began to make more

[57] *S. Cottle*, Mediatized conflict, Maidenhead 2006.

[58] *L. W. Bennett*, Communicating global activism: strengths and vulnerabilities of networked politics, in: W. van de Donk/B. D. Loader/P. G. Nixon/D. Rucht (eds.), Cyberprotest: New media, citizens and social movements, London 2004, pp. 123–146; *R. E. Howard-Hassmann*, The second great transformation: Human rights leapfrogging in the era of globalization, Human Rights Quarterly 27 (2005), pp. 1–40; *R. Kahn/D. Kellner*, New media and internet activism: From the 'Battle in Seattle' to blogging, New Media & Society 6(1) (2004), pp. 87–95; *D. Lipinski/G. Neddenriep*, Using "new" media to get "old" media coverage: how members of congress utilize their websites to court journalists, Harvard International Journal of Press/Politics 9 (2004), no. 1, pp. 7–21.

S. Marmura, A net advantage? The internet, grassroots activism and American Middle-Eastern Policy, New Media & Society 10 (2008), no. 2, pp. 247–271; *S. Marmura*, A net advantage? The internet, grassroots activism and American Middle-Eastern Policy, New Media & Society 10 (2008), no. 2 pp. 247–271; *J. B. Singer*, The political j-blogger: 'Normalizing' a new media form to fit old norms and practices, Journalism 6 (2005), no. 2, pp. 173–198.

[59] *L. W. Bennett*, Communicating global activism: strengths and vulnerabilities of networked politics, in: W. van de Donk/B. D. Loader/P. G. Nixon/D. Rucht (eds.), Cyberprotest: New media, citizens and social movements, London 2004, pp. 123–146; *J. F. Metzl*, Information technology and human rights, Human Rights Quarterly 18 (1996), no. 4, pp. 705–746; *W. van de Donk/B. D. Loader/P. G. Nixon/D. Rucht*, Introduction: Social movements and ICTs, in: W. van de Donk/B. D. Loader/P. G. Nixon/D. Rucht (eds.), Cyberprotest: New media, citizens and social movements, London 2004, pp. 1–25.

[60] *J. V. Pavlik*, New Media and News: Implications for the future of journalism, New media & Society 1 (1999), no. 1, pp. 54–59.

and more use of video to "make a better world".[61] "See it, film it, change it" is the tagline used by 'Witness', an organization dedicated to human rights video advocacy and video training as a complementary tool to other forms of advocacy. Thus and so, social organizations now have the ability to independently create and distribute dramatic visual images that are production assets for mainstream media.

Meanwhile, back at the news room, competing media channels of all types are constantly on the prowl for new material to satisfy their 24/7 audiences. In the search for news items and stories, some journalists actively seek ideas from source websites, blogs and chat forums, catching circulating information that would not otherwise have penetrated the mainstream gatekeepers.[62]

Bennett[63] identifies four possible ideal-types of such mainstream gatekeepers, each characterized by a specific corresponding filtering criterion: personal judgment of the reporter (reporter ideal), organizational news-gathering routines (organizational ideal), profit calculations (economic ideal) and considerations of immediacy (technological ideal). Political status is an additional filtering criterion taken from *Wolfsfeld*[64] and relates to the degree to which the media considers the organization a legitimate political player and judges its demands to be within the limits of public and political consensus. Theoretically then, organizations that are able to meet as many of these filter criteria as possible, have a better chance of promoting their message in the mass media and campaigning for change.

Pavlik[65] talks about the way new media technologies caused a fundamental transformation in journalism, possibly no less revolutionary than the penny press at the time. This transformation forced professionals and news corporations to adjust to the rules of the new, converged, digital, interactive, dispersed, and virtual media environment. While the change improved journalism in many ways, the new reality in which literally anyone with a computer and internet connection is a potential global publisher, threatens its most fundamental values and standards of source verification, authenticity of content, accuracy and truth.

---

[61] *S. Gregory*, Introduction, in: S. Gregory/G. Caldwell/R. Avni/T. Harding (eds.), Video for change: A guide for advocacy and activism, London 2005, p. xii-xvii.

[62] *S. Livingston/W. L. Bennett*, Gatekeeping, indexing and live-event news: Is technology altering the construction of news?, Political Communication 20 (2003), pp. 363–380; *M. Messner/M. W. Distaso*, The source cycle: How traditional media and weblogs use each other as sources, Journalism Studies 9 (2008), no. 3, pp. 447–463; *J. V. Pavlik*, New Media and News: Implications for the future of journalism, New media & Society 1 (1999), no. 1, pp. 54–59.

[63] *L. W. Bennett*, New media power: The internet and global activism, in: N. Couldry/J. Curran (eds.), Contesting media power: Alternative media in a networked world, Lanham 2003, pp. 17–37.

[64] *G. Wolfsfeld*, Media and political conflict: News from the Middle East, Cambridge 1997; *G. Wolfsfeld*, Media and the Path to Peace, Cambridge 2004.

[65] *J. V. Pavlik*, New Media and News: Implications for the future of journalism, New Media & Society 1(1) (1999), pp. 54–59.

A few words should be said about the reality of the internet being as open and accessible to inaccurate unreliable information as it is to credible dependable information, and as inexpensive and available to terrorist organization as it is to peace movements. *Ayers*[66] describes how the global internet-driven riot against the OECD Multilateral Agreement on Investment (MAI) successfully toppled the treaty after three years of invested negotiations between the most powerful nations in the world by using information that was mostly made up of fears, opinions and information that was impossible to corroborate.

Although social conflicts are not determined by the media alone, new communication technologies have the potential to act as catalysts for global media coverage, public opinion, official response and policy change. A good example of this point, and the only one of its kind that surfaced in the literature search for this project, is the case-study analysis by *Cardoso/Neto*[67] on new media reporting of the pro-East Timor movement in Portugal in 1999. The campaign for a sovereign East Timor took advantage of all that new communication technologies had to offer: a smuggled video tape showing a massacre of native Maubere-Portugese people by Indonesian soldiers; Timorese information websites hosted in Ireland; attacks on Indonesian networks by 'Portuguese Hackers Against Indonesia'; web-based organization and mobilization of simultaneous protests in four continents; over 190,000 emails and faxes sent to President Clinton and other decision makers in the US and Europe; and online polls. Although it was clearly one piece in a much larger cultural, political, military and economic picture, new communication technologies may have helped in balancing this uneven conflict.

III. Research Questions and Expectations

This Israeli-based study is designed as a pilot project towards an international research project. Four research questions are asked in order to explore the way organization staff and journalists perceive the impact of new communication technologies on the success of HROs to recruit, to mobilize and to promote their message in the mass media.

As challengers in the political communication arena, mass media exposure is a crucial integral component of HROs' struggle for political power.[68] In theory,

[66] *J. M. Ayers*, From the streets to the internet: The cyber-diffusion of contention, Annals of the American Academy of Political and Social Science 556 (1999), pp. 132–143.

[67] *G. Cardoso/P. P. Neto*, Mass media driven mobilization and online protest: ITCs and the pro-East Timor movement in Portugal, in: W. van de Donk/B. D. Loader/P. G. Nixon/D. Rucht (eds.), Cyberprotest: New media, citizens and social movements, London 2004, pp. 147–163.

[68] *G. Wolfsfeld*, Media and political conflict: News from the Middle East, Cambridge 1997.

the internet appears perfectly tailored for internal recruitment and mobilization needs of organizations compared to the more traditional methods.[69] A good recent example is President elect *Barack Obama*, who used the internet brilliantly and creatively to sell his inspiring story. Internal mobilization and recruitment of social movements include the following elements: establishment of a shared definition of the problem as a basis for a collective identity; mobilization of people to join and participate in action to achieve social and political goals; creation and maintenance of links to a network of organizations.[70] Hence the first research question is:

Research question #1: What do Israeli HRO staff perceive to be the major advantages of the internet as a tool to internally recruit and mobilize as compared to the more traditional methods?

Shifting from internal functions to external functions, it is expected that HROs that independently create production assets upon which the media thrives, can increase the quantity of their media exposure. *Livingston/Bennett*[71] speculate that the more the organization-produced media content meets four journalistic decision-making norms and practices, the better their chances to gain media coverage: personal judgment of the reporter, news gathering routines of the media outlet, economic pressures and constraints of the medium corporation, and media technologies that define space and time limits in news gathering (immediacy, access, etc.). Political status is an additional filtering criterion taken from *Wolfsfeld*[72] and refers to the degree to which the media considers the organization a legitimate political player and judges its demands to be within the limits of public and political consensus. The second research question is meant to check these expectations:

---

[69] *S. Barnett*, New media, old problems; new technology and the political process, European journal of Communication 12 (1997), no. 2, pp. 193–218; *L. W. Bennett*, New media power: The internet and global activism, in: N. Couldry/J. Curran (eds.), Contesting media power: Alternative media in a networked world, Lanham 2003, pp. 17–37; *J. Curran*, Global Journalism: a case study of the Internet, in: N. Couldry/J. Curran (eds.), Contesting media power: Alternative media in a networked world, Lanham 2003, pp. 227–241; *P. van Aelst/S. Walgrave*, New Media New Movements? The role of the internet in shaping the 'anti-globalization' movement, in: W. van de Donk/B. D. Loader/P. G. Nixon/D. Rucht (eds.), Cyberprotest: New media, citizens and social movements, London 2004, pp. 97–122; *G. Weimann*, Terror on the Internet: The new arena, the new challenge, Washington (D. C.) 2006.

[70] *P. van Aelst/S. Walgrave*, New Media New Movements? The role of the internet in shaping the 'anti-globalization' movement, in: W. van de Donk/B.D. Loader/P.G. Nixon/D. Rucht (eds.), Cyberprotest: New media, citizens and social movements, London 2004, pp. 97–122.

[71] *S. Livingston/W. L. Bennett*, Gatekeeping, indexing and live-event news: Is technology altering the construction of news?, Political Communication 20 (2003), pp. 363–380.

[72] *G. Wolfsfeld*, Media and political conflict: News from the Middle East, Cambridge 1997; *G. Wolfsfeld*, Media and the Path to Peace, Cambridge 2004.

Research question #2: How do Israeli HRO staff and media journalists perceive the way new media technologies changed the *quantity* of media coverage that human rights organizations succeed in gaining?

The quality of media coverage is determined by the extent to which the media tells the story the way the organization would like it to be told. Using *Iyengar's* theory,[73] it is assumed that organizations will improve their chances of controlling the media meaning frame the more they are able to use new technologies to dictate procedural frames (placing the problem in a general context and holding authorities responsible to correct it) rather than the more prevalent episodic frames (focusing on specific events and particular cases that attribute responsibility to individuals) of traditional media. The next question is therefore:

Research question #3: In which ways do Israeli HRO leaders believe that new media technologies have influenced the *quality* of the news coverage their organization and causes receive?

Based on *Gamson/Wolfsfeld's*[74] organizational characteristics, it is expected that organizations that use the internet to their advantage will differ from organizations that do not in the following ways: leadership motivation and willingness; culture and professional division of labour; organization resources; organization goals; and whether there is an agreed stance towards using (or not using) mainstream and new media technologies to promote the organization's message and goals. The fourth research question is therefore:

Research question #4: What factors limit the willingness and capability of Israeli HROs to exploit new media applications?

IV. Summary

This project has not been completed at the time this book goes to press. Here, I have provided the theoretical background and research questions, and I hope to have an opportunity to share the results in the near future.

The new media technology train has not only left the station, it has passed the point of no return. Deciphering and mapping its constantly changing tracks and dynamic junctions with HROs and mainstream media will not only contribute to filling the current theoretical lacuna, but will also provide practical insights that could favourably influence the trajectory of human rights advocacy campaigns.

---

[73] S. *Iyengar*, Is anyone responsible? How television frames political issues, Chicago 1991.

[74] *W.A. Gamson/G. Wolfsfeld*, Movements and media as interacting systems, Annals of American Academy of Political and Social Science 582 (1993), pp. 114–125.

How to Multiply the Notion?

Human Rights Education a Global Responsibility![1]

Claudia Mahler

The 60th anniversary of the UNIVERSAL Declaration of Human Rights (UDHR) was celebrated in different ways. Conferences, workshops, papers and anthologies praised the start of human rights through this prominent document. I am convinced that the celebrations were acknowledged in some newspapers and people might have read about it. But what do people really connect with human rights? "Human rights" seem to be a couple of words without any real meaning or a clear message. What is the whole idea behind them? Many people connect human rights with something good, without further genuine values. A couple of years ago a survey in Germany showed that people have tremendous difficulty in naming specific human rights. On average, the interviewees knew 2.5 rights, which is not really much when keeping in mind that the UDHR has 30 articles.[2] This example shows that there is a lack of knowledge and a lack of awareness that every individual is entitled to human rights because of their human dignity and humanness.

Another very prominent document was also highly celebrated this year: the Vienna Declaration and Programme of Action, which expresses the outcome of

[1] Many conclusions in this paper are based on outcomes of the research project "Teaching Human Rights Education in Europe", which was kindly financed from 2003–2007 by the Volkswagen Stiftung. This project analysed human rights education efforts, programmes, school curricula and cases in various countries during the UN Decade for Human Rights Education. The project had an interdisciplinary setting (international law, political science and social anthropology) and was conducted by three scholars with a specialization in human rights. For further information see *C. Mahler/A. Mihr /R. Toivanen* (eds.), The United Nations Decade for Human Rights and the Inclusion of National Minorities, Frankfurt a.M. 2009.

[2] Cf. among others *G. Sommer*, Die Menschenrechts-Charta der Vereinten Nationen – Kenntnisse, Einstellungen sowie Präsentation in deutschen Prinmedien, in: G. Sommer/J. Stellmacher/U. Wagner (eds.), Menschenrechte und Frieden – Aktuelle Beiträge und Debatten, Marburg 1999, p. 49; for further information on the studies, cf. *L. Müller/B. Weyand*, Wirkung von Menschenrechtsbildung – Ergebnis empirischer Forschung in Deutschland, in: C. Mahler/A. Mihr (eds.), Menschenrechtsbildung, Wiesbaden 2004, p. 279.

the 1993 World Conference on Human Rights. The experiences discussed in Vienna also showed very clearly that human rights education (HRE) is an unfulfilled obligation both then and now. In 1993, almost all UN member states agreed on the Vienna Declaration and expressed their support of human rights education in a world-wide appeal calling upon state environments to give space to the increasing number of centers for human rights education. This was seen as one of many steps in convincing the states to fulfill their obligation of spreading the human rights message.[3]

The World Conference on Human Rights reaffirms that States are duty-bound, as stipulated in the Universal Declaration of Human Rights and the International Covenant on Economic, Social and Cultural Rights and in other international human rights instruments, to ensure that education is aimed at strengthening the respect of human rights and fundamental freedoms. The World Conference on Human Rights emphasizes the importance of incorporating the subject of human rights education programmes and calls upon States to do so. Education should promote understanding, tolerance, peace and friendly relations between the nations and all racial or religious groups and encourage the development of United Nations activities in pursuance of these objectives. Therefore, education on human rights and the dissemination of proper information, both theoretical and practical, play an important role in the promotion and respect of human rights with regard to all individuals without distinction of any kind such as race, sex, language or religion, and this should be integrated in the education policies at the national as well as international levels. The World Conference on Human Rights notes that resource constraints and institutional inadequacies may impede the immediate realization of these objectives.[4]

To show the importance of the Vienna Declaration and its goals, the Republic of Austria celebrated its 15th anniversary with a follow-up conference, "Global Standards – Local Action", which dealt with one very prominent topic that was discussed in a workshop dealing with how the delegates can further human rights education in the next period and what was done during the last 15 years. Representatives of governmental and non governmental organizations and scholars from all over the globe spoke of their best projects. But the conference came to the conclusion that much needs to be done and that everybody therefore needs to focus their daily tasks on finding the perfect channels for spreading the human rights message so as to include human rights in the daily lives of the people.

How can we further human rights and what is human rights education about? The main goal of HRE is to effectively teach respect for and knowledge of human rights for all people. In addition, HRE strives to promote learning about the practice of human rights, which should be an accessible part of the educa-

---

[3] *E. Klein/C. Menke* (eds.), Universalität – Schutzmechanismen – Diskriminierungsverbot. 15 Jahre Wiener Weltmenschenrechtskonferenz, Berlin 2008.

[4] Vienna Declaration and Programme of Action, UN Doc A/CONF.157/23, Pt I, para 33, 1993.

tion of all members of society.[5] Article 26 of the UDHR is one benchmark, believing that education can strengthen respect for human rights by promoting the understanding of differences and fostering tolerance.[6] The content of HRE is based on the objective of transferring knowledge, raising awareness and building skills in order to establish a 'culture' where human rights are understood, respected and defended.[7] By ratifying international treaties or agreeing on international declarations, states have accepted legal obligations to make HRE available for all people living under the state's jurisdiction. As a member of international treaties, each state has the duty to endorse legislation and to take other measures to fulfill its commitments for implementing HRE.[8]

HRE means many things. One of the ideas is to provide information on human rights so that people can stand up for their rights and protect the rights of others. Yet, they can do that only if they know what human rights are in the broad sense and what human rights consist of substantively.

But where can people receive HRE and what is included in the training? These seem to be the major questions when focusing on HRE in practice. HRE can be promoted in the formal, informal and non-formal educational sectors.[9] Accordingly, the content may vary, since the needs and contexts of the groups receiving HRE are different.[10] One very important aspect of these needs and contexts involves improving ethnic relations within states.

---

[5] *J.-B. Marie*, Human Rights Education. A Fundamental Resource in the Prevention of Violations, in: L.-A. Sicilianos (ed.), The Prevention of Human Rights Violations: Contribution on the Occasion of the Twentieth Anniversary of the Marangopoulos Foundation for Human Rights (MFHR), Athens/The Hague 2001, p. 269 (269).

[6] See Article 26 UDHR. For background information see *R. P. Claude*, The Right to Education and Human Rights Education, 2 *SUR* (2005), pp. 37–59 (p. 38).

[7] *M. Nowak*, The Right to Education, in: A. Eide/C. Krause/A. Rosas (eds.), Economic, Social and Cultural Rights. A Textbook, Dordrecht 2001, p. 245 (p. 246); Human Security Network (ed.), Understanding Human Rights: Manual on Human Rights Education, Graz 2003, pp. 14–16.

[8] *L. Henkin*, The Age of Rights, New York 1999.

[9] See also the interesting categorization by L. Müller, which is based on empirical findings: "explicit HRE", "implicit HRE" and "education with a human rights approach", in: *L. Müller*, Menschenrechtserziehung an Schule und Hochschule, Arbeitsgemeinschaft Menschenrechte Universität Trier, Occasional Paper No. 6, Trier 2002, pp. 7–9.

[10] For many of these, see *S. Spiliopoulou Akermark*, Education and Human Rights: Kind Intentions and Brutal Reality, in: C. Mahler/A. Mihr/R. Toivanen (eds.), The United Nations Decade for Human Rights Education and the Inclusion of National Minorities, Frankfurt a. M. 2009.

The Right to Human Rights Education (HRE)

The right to education is mentioned in many international treaties.[11] It consists of a variety of aspects of education and academic freedom. Education is, on the one hand, a requirement for the use of human rights and, on the other hand, it is a method for strengthening human rights.[12] Many human rights can only be exercised with a minimum level of education. Respect for and acceptance of human rights comprises one critical goal of education, namely seeking to foster a human rights culture through HRE.[13]

The right to HRE on a universal level is stated most prominently in Article 26(2) of the Universal Declaration of Human Rights (UDHR):

> Education shall be directed to the full development of the human personality and to the strengthening of respect for human rights and fundamental freedoms. It shall promote understanding, tolerance and friendship among all nations, racial or religious groups, and shall further the activities of the United Nations for the maintenance of peace.[14]

International Documents Referring to Human Rights Education

Several international treaties that include HRE in their specific articles or general comments make up part of the interpretation of the treaties' norms. These international treaties demonstrate the vast range of applicability of HRE to a variety of social actors, professions and specific groups. Some conventions outline the means of achieving the goals of HRE while others set forth the expected impact of HRE on society at large. These conventions are united by the common goal of promoting and achieving respect for human rights.

Contrary to the assumption that education primarily takes place in formal educational settings (schools), several UN treaties mention HRE in connection with professional training sessions. For example, the Convention Against Torture and Other Cruel, Inhumane and Degrading Treatment or Punishment (CAT) states in Article 10(1) that:

---

[11] For further information, see *K.D. Beiter*, The Protection of the Right to Education by International Law: Including a Systematic Analysis of Article 13 of the International Covenant on Economic, Social and Cultural Rights, Leiden/Boston 2006.

[12] *R.K.M. Smith*, International Human Rights, Oxford 2005, p. 310.

[13] *M. Nowak*, The Right to Education, in: A. Eide/C. Krause/A. Rosas (eds.), Economic, Social and Cultural Rights. A Textbook, Dordrecht 2001, p. 245 (245).

[14] Article 26(2), Universal Declaration of Human Rights, adopted and proclaimed by General Assembly Resolution 217 A (III) of 10 December 1948, available at http://www.un.org/Overview/rights.html (accessed 20 February 2009).

Each State party shall ensure that education and information regarding the prohibition against torture are fully included in the training of law enforcement personnel, civil or military, medical personnel, public officials and other persons who may be involved in the custody, interrogation or treatment of any individual subjected to any form of arrest, detention or imprisonment.[15]

This excerpt demonstrates that even though the term "human rights education" is not explicitly present in the article, the goal of HRE is nonetheless implied.

On a similar line, incorporating HRE into state policy means not only training specific professionals but also making information regarding human rights available and accessible to everybody. The Committee on Human Rights (HRC), which is the treaty body of the International Covenant on Civil and Political Rights (ICCPR),[16] included in its early General Comment No. 3 a description of the content of Article 2 of the Covenant:

In this connection, it is very important that individuals should know what their rights under the Covenant (and the Optional Protocol, as the case may be) are and also that all administrative and judicial authorities should be aware of the obligations which the State party has assumed under the Covenant. To this end, the Covenant should be publicized in all official languages of the State and steps should be taken to familiarize the authorities concerned with its contents as part of their training. It is desirable also to give publicity to the State party's cooperation with the Committee.[17]

Other treaties focus less on the specific means of implementing HRE and more on the possible outcome of such education. The International Convention on the Elimination of All Forms of Discrimination (CERD) promotes HRE as an effective means to prevent discrimination. Article 7 reads:

States parties undertake to adopt immediate and effective measures, particularly in the fields of teaching, education, culture and information, with a view to combating prejudices which lead to racial discrimination and to promote understanding, tolerance and friendship among nations and racial or ethnic groups, as well as to propagating the purposes and principles of the Charter of the United Nations, the Universal Declaration of Human Rights, the United Nations Declaration on the Elimination of All Forms of Racial Discrimination, and this Convention.[18]

---

[15] Article 10(1), Convention Against Torture and Other Cruel Inhuman or Degrading Treatment or Punishment, adopted and opened for signature, ratification and accession by General Assembly Resolution 39/46 of 10 December 1984, entry into force 26 June 1987, in accordance with Article 27(1), available at: http://www.ohchr.org/english/law/pdf/cat.pdf; CAT/C, available at: http://www.ohchr.org/english/bodies/cat/index.htm (accessed 20 February 2009).

[16] International Covenant on Civil and Political Rights, adopted and opened for signature, ratification and accession by General Assembly Resolution 2200A (XXI) of 16 December 1966, entry into force 23 March 1976, in accordance with Article 49, available at: http://www.ohchr.org/english/law/pdf/ccpr.pdf; HRC, available at: http://www.ohchr.org/english/bodies/hrc/index.htm (accessed 20 February 2009).

[17] HRC, General Comment No. 3, "Implementation at the National Level (Article 2)", dated 29 July 1981 (Thirteenth session).

[18] Article 7, Convention on the Elimination of All Forms of Discrimination against Wom-

The International Covenant on Economic and Social and Cultural Rights (CESCR)[19] includes in its Article 13(1) a formulation similar to Article 26(2) of the UDHR but with additional references to human dignity, participation in free society and ethnic groups.[20]

Certain conventions incorporate HRE provisions that make particular reference to the protection of gender equality. According to Article 10(c) of the Convention on the Elimination of all Forms of Discrimination Against Women (CEDAW), the state parties shall implement

"the elimination of any stereotyped concept of the roles of men and women at all levels and in all forms of education by encouraging coeducation and other types of education which will help to achieve this aim and, in particular, by the revision of textbooks and school programmes and the adaptation of teaching methods".[21]

This paragraph states not only the goal of HRE in abolishing stereotypical gender roles, but also provides for concrete steps as to how this can be achieved. Furthermore, the Committee on the Elimination of all Forms of Discrimination against Women adopted General Recommendation No. 19 on violence against women, which calls for

"preventive measures, including public information and education programmes to change attitudes concerning the roles and status of women".[22]

Lastly, there are articles in place to promote HRE in the classroom itself. Article 29(1) of the Convention on the Rights of the Child (CRC)[23] describes how chil-

---

en, adopted and opened for signature, ratification and accession by General Assembly Resolution 34/180 of 18 December 1979, entry into force 3 September 1981, in accordance with Article 27(1), available at: http://www.unhchr.ch/html/menu3/b/e1cedaw.htm (accessed 20 February 2009).

[19] International Covenant on Economic, Social and Cultural Rights, adopted and opened for signature, ratification and accession by General Assembly Resolution 2200A (XXI) of 16 December 1966, entry into force 3 January 1976, in accordance with Article 27, available at http://www.ohchr.org/english/law/pdf/cescr.pdf; CESCR/C, available at: http://www.ohchr.org/english/bodies/cescr/ (accessed 20 February 2009).

[20] *J. Delbrück*, The Right to Education as an International Human Right, 35 *GYIL* (1992), p. 92 (100).

[21] Convention on the Elimination of all Forms of Discrimination against Women, adopted and opened for signature, ratification and accession by General Assembly Resolution 34/180 of 18 December 1979, entry into force 3 September 1981, in accordance with Article 27(1), available at: http://www.ohchr.org/english/law/pdf/cedaw.pdf; CEDAW/C, available at: http://www.un.org/womenwatch/daw/cedaw/committee.htm (accessed 20 February 2009).

[22] CEDAW/C, General Recommendation No. 19, A/47/38, dated 29 January 1992 (Eleventh session), p. 1, Para. 24(t), available at: http://www.un.org/womenwatch/daw/cedaw/recommendations/recomm.htm#recom19 (accessed 20 February 2009).

[23] Convention on the Rights of the Child, adopted and opened for signature, ratification and accession by General Assembly Resolution 44/25 of 20 November 1989, entry into force 2 September 1990, in accordance with Article 49, available at: http://www.ohchr.org/english/law/pdf/crc.pdf; CRC/C, available at: http://www.ohchr.org/english/bodies/crc/ (accessed 20 February 2009).

dren should be educated. As stated in Lit. B of Article 29(1) CRC, "the development of respect for human rights and fundamental freedoms" should be part of the educational curriculum.[24] Consistent with Lit. D of Article 29(1) CRC, education should include

> "the preparation of the child for a responsible life in a free society, in the spirit of understanding, peace, tolerance, equality of sexes, and friendship among all peoples, ethnic, national and religious groups and persons of indigenous origin".[25]

Article 17 of the CRC on the role and function of the mass media is also significant.

As has been demonstrated through the excerpts from the UN Documents, HRE is not really a new concept. Moreover, the idea of HRE is included in many documents that are aimed at the protection of human rights, and certain treaties include the protection of vulnerable groups like ethnic/national minorities. Those documents have been ratified by many member states of the UN.

Human rights have also received attention at the regional level. Standard-setting activities were developed by regional organisations. Most prominent major human rights treaties were adopted under the auspices of the Council of Europe. There is a wide range of interesting documents referring to HRE treaties on the regional level.[26]

International human rights standards have changed the relationship between governments and individuals and made national authorities much more responsible. The value of setting standards is undeniable; at the same time, the creation of standards has generated new challenges. Some rights overlap and duplicate one another, and very often these duplicated standards offer different forms and degrees of protection. This bears the risk of ineffective protection when states find it too burdensome to cooperate with all the different monitoring mechanisms in order to show their compliance. In addition, the implementation of existing standards needs to be improved, because in some countries human rights standards are still not fully implemented despite incorporation.[27]

---

[24] Article 29(1), Convention on the Rights of the Child, available at: http://www.ohchr.org/english/law/pdf/crc.pdf, p. 9 (accessed 20 February 2009).

[25] Article 29(1), Convention on the Rights of the Child, available at: http://www.ohchr.org/english/law/pdf/crc.pdf, p. 9 (accessed 20 February 2009).

[26] For further information see *G. Alfredsson*, The Right to Human Rights Education, in: A. Eide/C. Krause/A. Rosas (eds.), Economic, Social and Cultural Right, Dordrecht 2001, p. 273.

[27] International Human Rights Council on Human Rights Policy (ed.), Human Rights Standards: Learning from Experience, Geneva 2006, p. 3.

The UN Decade for Human Rights Education 1995–2004

In 1993, at the World Conference on Human Rights in Vienna, more than 150 states declared that states should

"include human rights, humanitarian law, democracy and rule of law as subjects in the curricula of all learning institutions in formal and non-formal settings".[28]

In 1994, the UN Decade for Human Rights Education was proclaimed.[29] In December 1994, the General Assembly gave common approval to the proposal that this ten-year period should focus on facilitating the distribution of relevant information so as to increase knowledge of human rights as stated in the UDHR. During the decade, issues regarding the promotion and further development of human rights values were to be raised. Furthermore, by intensifying HRE, special attention was to be given to the protection of human rights, wherever and whenever human rights abuses occurred. The concept of HRE takes into account the diverse segments of society as target groups, such as children, indigenous peoples, minorities and disabled persons.[30]

The decade sought generally to promote a human rights culture. In order to support the aim of the decade, all actors were to provide public information. The guiding principles of the campaign sought a comprehensive approach to education on human rights, including civil, cultural, economic, political and social rights, as well as an effort to recognize the indivisibility and interdependence of all rights.

The "International Plan of Action for the Decade" initiated the assessment of needs and a formulation of effective strategies. It was decided that comprehensive, effective and sustainable educational programmes at the local, national, regional and international levels should be developed and strengthened.[31] Important themes that should be highlighted in HRE activities are

"the human rights of women, children, the elderly, minorities, refugees, indigenous peoples, persons in extreme poverty, persons with HIV infection or AIDS and other vulnerable groups".[32]

---

[28] Vienna Declaration and Programme of Action, adopted by the World Conference on Human Rights in Vienna on 25 June 1993, A/CONF.157/23, Part II, Para. 79, available at: http://www.ohchr.org/english/law/pdf/vienna.pdf (accessed 20 February 2009).

[29] United Nations Decade for Human Rights Education, adopted and proclaimed by General Assembly Resolution 1994/184 of 23 December 1994, A/RES/49/184, dated 6 March 1995.

[30] A/RES/49/184, dated 6 March 1995, available at: http://www.unhchr.ch/pdf/lessonslife3_E.pdf, pp. 1–4 (p. 2) (accessed 20 February 2009).

[31] See *V. Lehnhart*, Pädagogik der Menschenrechte, Leverkusen 2003, pp. 89–95.

[32] Aktionsplan der Vereinten Nationen für die UN-Dekade der Menschenrechtsbildung, 1995–2004; UN-Doc.-No.: A/51/506/Add.1, dated 12 December 1996.

The state parties should coordinate the development of effective materials, strengthen the role and capacity of the mass media and facilitate the global dissemination of the UDHR.

UNESCO, as an experienced organization in the field of education and human rights, cooperated with the Office of the High Commissioner for Human Rights (OHCHR) to implement the Plan of Action. According to the High Commissioner, the proclamation of the Decade for Human Rights Education makes it clear that the education in and of human rights is a right in itself.[33] The High Commissioner was given the responsibility of coordinating relevant UN education and public information programmes in the field of human rights.[34]

In 1998, the UN High Commissioner for Human Rights, *Mary Robinson*, indicated that HRE is her highest priority. She stated that "this empowerment can also make a critical contribution to the prevention of human rights violations".[35] To help states to prepare the implementation of HRE, the OHCHR published "Guidelines for National Plans of Action for Human Rights Education". The OHCHR was also responsible for monitoring and following the progress of the UN Decade for Human Rights Education.

In 2000, the OHCHR and UNESCO initiated a mid-term evaluation of the Decade for Human Rights Education. The results were very depressing. The OHCHR received almost no information about the state parties' efforts to promote or implement the decade's policies in their countries. At the end of 2004, almost none of the governments had implemented HRE in their national school curricula.[36] Very few state parties had established some kind of a National Action Plan for Human Rights Education. In spite of all the efforts that had been put into making it successful, at the end of the decade a number of critical voices expressed their disappointment.[37]

---

[33] *M. Robinson*, Foreword, in: United Nations, United Nations Decade for Human Rights Education (1995–2004): Lessons for Life, Series on the United Nations Decade for Human Rights Education, No. 1, New York 1998, iii.

[34] High Commissioner for the Promotion and Protection of all Human Rights, adopted by the General Assembly with Resolution 48/141 of 20 December 1993.

[35] *M. Robinson*, Foreword in: United Nations, United Nations Decade for Human Rights Education (1995–2004): Lessons for Life, Series on the United Nations Decade for Human Rights Education, No. 1, New York, 1998, iii.

[36] United Nations, "General Assembly Proclaims World Programme for Human Rights Education, Stressing its Importance to Realization of all Fundamental Freedoms, Assembly President Jean Ping (Gabon) Says Effective Human Rights Education Remains Best Prerequisite for Achievement of Peaceful World", GA/10317, United Nations Press Release of 10 December 2004.

[37] See *L. Müller*, Menschenrechtsbildung in Deutschland. Ziele, Erfolge, Perspektiven, in: G. Sommer/J. Stellmacher/U. Wagner (eds.), Menschenrechte und Frieden, Marburg 1999, p. 349; *N. Rosemann*, Die Rechtlichen Grundlagen von Menschenrechtserziehung, Zeitschrift für internationale Bildungsforschung und Entwicklungspädagogik 25 (2002), no. 4, p. 22 (25).

In April 2004, the "Follow-up to the United Nations Decade on Human Rights Education Resolution of the Commission on Human Rights" (204/71) was accepted. It says that the commission considered reports dealing with the achievements and shortcomings of the decade as well as suggestions for a follow-up procedure or the declaration of a new decade. There is a need to maintain a global framework for the promotion of HRE.

Several follow-up procedures were discussed. One of the preferred options called for another decade following the first one on HRE. However, a number of experts agreed that a decade is not the best way to affect the situation. Other experts proposed that the time had come to draft a Convention on Human Rights Education.[38] In April 2004, the Human Rights Commission of the UN Economic and Social Council proclaimed a World Programme for Human Rights Education. On July 14th 2005, the UN General Assembly adopted the revised Draft Plan of Action[39] in its resolution on the World Programme for Human Rights Education (53/312). The definition of HRE is almost the same as for the Decade on Human Rights Education.[40]

States do not always live up to the obligations they accept by ratifying international statements. This is very true both for the right to education and for the right to HRE. The right to education includes a minimum level of education for all people, which is an important criterion for other human rights. Yet, it has been made clear by all of the international treaty bodies that the right to education is not being fulfilled in the cases of some vulnerable and marginalized groups such as minorities.[41] This means that many marginalized groups are not afforded the same opportunities to determine their own future, and that they have no way of securing the enjoyment of their human rights due to their lack of knowledge.

---

[38] This proposal was made in March 2004 at the OSCE/ODIHR supplementary meeting on Human Rights Education in Vienna, see: Final Report of 4 May 2004, available at: http://www.osce.org/documents/odihr/2004/05/2864_en.pdf (accessed 20 February 2009).

[39] Revised Draft Plan of Action for the First Phase (2005–2007) of the World Programme for Human Rights Education, adopted by the General Assembly, A/59/525.Rev.1, dated 2 March 2005, available at: http://www.ohchr.org/english/issues/education/docs/A.59.525.Rev.1.pdf (accessed 20 February 2009).

[40] See Revised Draft Plan of Action for the First Phase (2005–2007) of the World Programme for Human Rights Education, adopted by the General Assembly, A/59/525.Rev.1, dated 2 March 2005, available at: http://www.ohchr.org/english/issues/education/docs/A.59.525.Rev.1.pdf, at Para. 3(d): "The enabling of all persons to participate effectively in a free *and democratic* society *governed by the rule of law*; (*e*) *The building of maintenance of peace; (f) the promotion of people-centred sustainable development and social justice*", available at: http://www.ohchr.org/english/issues/education/docs/A.59.525.Rev.1.pdf (accessed 20 February 2009), at 3, emphasis added.

[41] E.g. Roma children are very often excluded from the school system because they are sent to special schools. For further information see *I. Stern/J. Luptakova*, Human Rights Education and Roma in Slovakia, in: The United Nations Decade for Human Rights Education and the Inclusion of National Minorities, Frankfurt a.M. 2009, p. 171 (173).

Whilst HRE is already included in many human rights treaties, the preceding analysis implies that a failure to include HRE in human rights treaties is not the reason why member states seem to be unaware of HRE's methods and concepts. It is also apparent that the treaty bodies have focused their efforts on initiating more human rights training for specific groups in order to raise awareness of the diversity of the population and its special needs. The experts have sometimes mentioned the UN Decade on Human Rights Education in their recommendations to the state parties to point out their support of the decade's goals. It can be seen from the recommendations that their efforts to strengthen HRE training for law enforcement officers, other authorities and teachers increased in the last years of the decade.

The Active Groups

The active protagonists in most countries are NGOs and governmental representatives, but more often members of NGOs are the main educators, who promote their training programmes on human rights on the national level.[42] It can also be said that there were no initiatives taken by governments. Instead, the governments' very practical approach was to find NGOs, give them financial support, and promote their ideas, which included the development of their own programmes and projects.[43] By critical observation, one can imagine that it was the easiest way to give only the money to non-governmental organizations. The activities of the NGOs cannot really be seen as the fulfillment of the states' obligations. But this outsourcing mentality can be found in other fields as well. In the mid-term evaluation, some state parties even showed the decade programmes of NGOs as their national activities.[44]

As has already been said, states agreed to be part of the Decade on Human Rights Education, but during that decade, most of them failed to agree on a national plan of action, to change the national school curriculum or to implement human rights education programmes in all necessary parts of the administration. Some states, for example, started their activities after the decade had ended, and developed a national working group with many active partners on the national level. For instance, Slovakia started a working group with representatives from the ministry of education, the pedagogical administration, NGOs and the pedagogical colleges to work on a plan for the implementation of human rights education.

[42] *C. Mahler/A. Mihr/R. Toivanen*, Teaching Human Rights in Europe and its Role for Minorities, in: M. Brosig (ed.), Human Rights in Europe, Frankfurt a. M. 2006, p. 169.

[43] *F. Tibbitts*, Menschenrechtsbildung und der NGO Sektor in: C. Mahler/A. Mihr, Menschenrechtsbildung, Wiesbaden 2004, p. 149.

[44] Germany, for example, reported the activities of the Bertelsmann Foundation.

We have to keep in mind that the implementation of human rights education in national school curricula can only occur when the state itself is interested in furthering human rights on the national level. If there is no real commitment, the state can be very creative in finding ways which can be seen in the end as a waste of time, or it can generally ignore the overall idea.

Finland, for example, integrated human rights as a fundamental value into the national curricula. Human rights as a fundamental value would be a challenge for every teacher, because such a value is a mainstream idea that can be found in all subjects. Even though representatives of the national board of education were sure that the Finnish teachers would include human rights, they had no idea what was taught by whom.[45] They would also not have known which books the teachers would use in their classes, and it was therefore useless to show that human rights are included in various books. Another factor which was not integrated in the overall ideas was that many teachers would lack a basic knowledge of human rights. This is because human rights were not taught at universities in the past, and nowadays only a handful of universities include human rights for teacher training. Therefore it can also not be said that all the younger teachers would know how to integrate human rights into their subject.

These are some basic observations why human rights education has not been fully implemented in the national curricula, especially in the case of Finland.

But as already discussed, human rights education should not only be taught to children during their time at school. There are many aspects of life in which human rights are badly needed.

One group which is mentioned very often are the law enforcement officials. This particular group includes human rights training for police officers, prison guards and people in similar positions. The Council of Europe has been very active, especially in the training of police forces.[46] But it can also be said that a high number of people in law enforcement have not had a chance to be part of human rights training sessions. Therefore the international monitoring bodies and the creators of the training try to involve officials on the national level, in order to make human rights training available for a broader range of people, which until the present seems necessary.

Another group which is also very much in the focus of educators are teachers of all subjects who would need training in order to have a realistic chance of including human rights as a fundamental value on a daily basis in their subjects.

---

[45] This lack of knowledge was also critizied by the Committe of the Rights of the Child in its Concluding Observation, UN Doc CRC/C/15/Add.272, 20 October 2005.

[46] *C. Mahler*, Menschenrechtsbildungsprogramme im Bereich des Europarates, in: C. Mahler/A. Mihr (eds.), Menschenrechtsbildung Bilanz und Perspektiven, Wiesbaden 2004, p. 105 (110).

In a globalized world, networks including different NGOs, governments and international organisations are needed in order to cope with human rights in the new dimension of cultural globalisation.[47] Human rights education is part of the globalized world and tries to combat the possible negative effects of the market globalization. The human rights movement can be described as a constraining power that tries to help regulate the extensive general trend towards globalization, to strengthen its message as a universal one, so as to get a chance to be heard as well in a globalized world.[48]

How to Multiply the Notion?

We have seen that the obligation to implement human rights education exists because of various commitments. This is true on the international, universal level, because governments have ratified international human rights treaties and are obliged to implement these rights on the national level. The international monitoring bodies have shown in many reports that the practical impact on the national level has many gaps. The states parties are obliged to bridge these gaps by means of national action. The same is true for the regional level, especially in Europe, where the Council of Europe was quite active in the field. A new participant has been observed. The EU with its new fundamental rights agency was very energetic in finding its place in the field of human rights. The latest development was the employment of a human rights education coordinator, which might be very helpful in combining the different initiatives in the European Union and in the nation states.

Even though there have been several international gatherings, manifesting that human rights education is very important might be a means to calm some of the distrust that is arising because of terrorist attacks and other national crises. It has been obvious that the implementation and furthering of human rights education has not been a political priority for governments over the last decades. One reason why governments might not be keen to further human rights education might be the fear that people with knowledge regarding human rights might force the state into action. Civil society with a human rights background can be a very active watchdog, and it can be seen that this approach is not popular with governments. It might be discovered that various obligations have not been fulfilled.

---

[47] *D. Suarez/F. Ramirez*, Human rights and citizenship: the emergence of human rights education, CDDRL Working Paper No. 2, 2004.

[48] *R. Toivanen*, Education on Human Rights – a Method for Including Global Critical Thinking, in: T. Kaivola/M. Melen Passo (eds.), Education for Global Responsibility, Helsinki 2007, p. 33 (35).

So we can come to the conclusion that it would be a big step if human rights education could find its way to the political agenda on the national level. If this step were taken, it would be easy to set up a working group, whose main task would be to create a national action plan on human rights education. With the strategies worked out in a national action plan with representatives from more or less all the active groups, it would not be too hard to implement two or three different ways of furthering human rights education. One of the obligations already agreed upon in the Vienna Declaration was the implementation of human rights in the national curricula. But as we have already seen, hardly any state party has integrated human rights into the national curricula with all the necessary actions such as teacher training on human rights, additional information in regular school books or special activities/ programmes, so as to create a durable approach for implementing a human rights culture in the daily life of schools at all levels.

Various countries have begun to implement human rights in the national school curriculum, using different methods and strategies, but this has also shown that official changes need additional efforts to implement human rights in practice. For example, human rights are part of the Armenian national school curriculum and special books were printed to include human rights in regular teaching. But the setting in the classrooms and the teaching methods for human rights were not adapted, and we have therefore seen and heard that small children recited the Articles of the UDHR by heart, but hadn't a clue as to the meaning behind the article. This example shows clearly that it is not enough to integrate human rights into the national school curriculum, change the books and start to teach human rights in regular classes. Pedagogical staff badly needs to have a chance to learn the skills for teaching themes and issues of human rights and to connect these with real examples from daily life. The articles of the UDHR are useless if they are not filled with examples to tackle the emotional side, so as to understand the universal values of human rights.

This also seems to be the right place to say that there exist perfect materials on how to teach students about human rights. The materials are adapted to different age groups and some national books have taken the history and diversity of the country's population into account. Most of these materials have been edited by NGOs with support from supranational organisations on the regional level, such as the Council of Europe or the EU, and on the universal level, special organisations of the UN like UNDP or UNESCO. Governments and private donors and foundations have also supported the different initiatives. But as can be observed in all areas of education, in practice, many books do not get the money for updating or evaluation, and this can mean a loss of resources. Other very professionally edited materials are only available in English and therefore cannot be a useful tool for small initiatives or for people without international networking.

The use of the internet has furthered the networking process of NGOs and educators from all over the world. Many fora have been established and networks like the Human Rights Education Associates (HREA) or the Human Rights Education Consortium have a very active exchange through their websites, newsletters and mailing lists. These global networks have a broad dimension of cooperation.

We have seen that it is not that easy to include human rights in the national curricula, and it is almost too late to prepare the teachers through human rights education teaching skills to make this dream come true. But there are also many other groups of professionals who would need an awareness of human rights for their daily work, e.g. lawyers, judges, law enforcement staff, governmental clerks in many fields.

I have shown that human rights education has been a low-ranking theme on the political agenda; but we must also keep in mind that human rights are not a topic which generates high interest for instance for law students, e.g. in Germany. Many of the students can pass their exams without any particular knowledge of human rights. Some students said that they never really heard about the UN human rights system; the Council of Europe has a better chance of being heard of, but there is still a long way to go before being able to say that the procedures are well known. This is also true for many other countries, where you can pass the law exams without any knowledge of human rights, even though most people would agree that human rights seem to be a part of law.

Even though these facts are well known, nobody seems to care, so long as there are specialized lawyers. But as regards other countries, the EU and the Council of Europe started some human rights teaching programmes for judges and lawyers, focusing in particular on the states of the former Soviet Union and the EU's new member countries. One way to spread the message would be to ensure that professional groups needing an awareness of human rights get a basic knowledge of human rights during their university education, and that they receive further training if there appear to be practical gaps which need to be bridged in order to have a human rights approach in their jobs.

Some professional groups would need special skills and knowledge because they have to deal with vulnerable groups. Such groups would include e.g. migrants or minorities, who have their own cultural background and history and might not understand the mainstream ways of how the administration works or how to deal with the health care system or insurance agencies; these groups would appreciate it if governmental clerks had special knowledge. It might be helpful to have a human rights understanding and special knowledge of the cultural diversities of the people living together in the country when dealing for example with social benefits for foreigners or migrants. Examples from Slovakia showed quite impressively that police treated members of the Roma community more violently and very rudely compared to the majority population. The explanation for this was that every Slovak policeman knows implicitly or explicitly that Roma are more violent and criminal than the Slovak population. Because of the racist attitudes in the police forces, Slovak policemen got special training on human rights and minorities. The training was a joint programme from NGOs and official trainers of the police and military forces. Similar programmes were conducted in many countries in Europe,[49] most of them with the goal of preventing discrimination and racism.[50]

In pursuing the question of how to multiply the notion, it must be noted that many parts of a country's population get their information from the media. If the media are the main source of information, that means that programme managers and journalists are one professional group which needs to have a basic understanding of human rights. Or to make it more practical: they should take into account that their reports bear special weight on how the majority population might think or consider other groups. Some surveys exist on how the media mention e.g. minority groups. Headlines which only illustrate the stealing Roma, the Russian mafia, etc. describe the marginalized groups only with negative associations, which in turn can lead to further discriminatory opinions in the majority population without their knowing the particular background of the stories or the real people. Journalists really need to keep in mind that their wording and personal views might have another outcome than that intended.

Another goal seems to be to exchange short-time projects for longer lasting programmes, which are financed for longer periods and can show a stable outcome with a realistic impact on particular groups. This impact cannot be measured easily, and it would therefore not be a waste of money to evaluate pilot projects, so as to invest only in implementing realistic programmes with a positive outcome. If for example the states would agree to give NGOs financial support over a longer period, it would not be a real problem if the governments tried to outsource the implementation of human rights education in the nonformal sector. The formal sector needs the state party commitment because NGOs cannot implement human rights education in the national school curriculum. Civil society can be one part of a working group, e.g. for a national action plan, but the government needs to focus on durable changes in the school curricula and on corresponding needs of the teachers so they can fill the curriculum with real life in relation to human rights.

It would be important that the human rights education programmes be evaluated and that those which correspond with the goals get long-term financial support, because as we all know, to change people's minds might take a long

[49] *N. Weiß*, Polizei für interkulturelle Verständigung in Brandenburg (PiViB) – Ein Praxisbeispiel, in: C. Mahler/A. Mihr (eds.), Menschenrechtsbildung, Wiesbaden 2004, p. 255.

[50] *N. Rosemann*, Menschenrechtsbildung als Prävention gegen Rassismus und Diskriminierung, in: C. Mahler/A. Mihr (eds.), Menschenrechtsbildung, Wiesbaden 2004, p. 206 (214).

time, even decades. Therefore the states should give the educators, who are very often small NGOs, the assurance that their work on the grassroots level will be financed over a longer period of time. It would help the educators to focus on their pedagogical strategies and improvement if they do not have to apply for new financial support, which is very time-consuming.

Recommendation for More Research

During the work on our project,[51] it was obvious that research on human rights education programmes or projects is very rare. We came across several evaluations made of a small number of programmes and projects. The reason why nobody seems to care about the outcome of project programmes through evaluation seems to be that many donors believe that the money is needed more for teaching. This might be true at first glance, but when observed over a longer period of time, one would agree that it would not be a waste of money to show which programmes or projects achieved which goals. It would be good to know which aspects have been successful in fulfilling their goals, and because of this knowledge, the projects or programmes could be adapted and made more effective in the next round. In my opinion, this would be a big step, if we keep in mind that the overall idea is to spread the message of human rights so as to bring about a human rights culture. Therefore I would recommend launching more research to find out which strategies and pedagogical tools are valuable in changing people's minds. It would be constructive to have more information on the influence of media and how we can use these to spread the human rights message.

Conclusion

The first step seems to be lobbying the governments to help human rights education to be given space on the political agenda. After achieving this first goal, we should have a look at the kind of programmes that ought to be implemented and which additional or parallel strategies might be ways of fulfilling the major purpose.

There have been many effective programmes and projects to promote human rights, but it has also been noted that the active protagonists in society need to work together with the government in order to have a long lasting approach in view of changing awareness of human rights in society. To further the cooperation between the different partners on the governmental and the non-govern-

[51] For forther information see fn. 1.

mental side, coordinators should be established. This is already true for some states, where for example the national human rights institutions take care of the networking on the national level. But these activities can be coordinated in a much livelier way in order to further cooperation between the different educators and to show overlapping performances. This would also help to work on quality standards by actively meeting on the national level.

Programmes over a long period of time are needed and should be implemented to further human rights. The more popular short-term projects should only be launched as pilots and should change to a long-term programme after a positive evaluation; the others that could not match the goals need to be changed or should be stopped in consideration of the best investment of the financial resources.

It should be stressed that human rights teaching and research makes a real difference in practice, and this is why investment in research and teaching is beneficial. Human rights education should be furthered in many ways, because we are still a long way from all people knowing their own rights and being able to live in states with a human rights culture.

Chapter II

International Criminal Law

The International Criminal Law Regime and International Human Rights Law

Theoretical and Empirical Explorations

Salif Nimaga

I. Introduction

No one would doubt that relationships between international human rights law and international criminal law exist. To systematize them is, however, not an easy task. Taken by themselves, most of these relationships are discussed in great detail; yet, a good overview is surprisingly hard to find.[1] A reason for this might lie in the fact that many different scientific disciplines are called upon to provide a satisfactory answer and interdisciplinarity is an aspect in the study of international criminal law that needs to be further developed. The following analysis from an interdisciplinary perspective is an attempt to provide a synoptic overview of possible links between international criminal law and international human rights law.

A first approach to the question regarding the relationship between international criminal law and international human rights law is to look at definitions of these terms. The term international criminal law can be used in many ways, but for this analysis should be understood as "a body of rules designed both to proscribe categories of conduct (war crimes, crimes against humanity, genocide,

[1] Textbooks on international criminal law do not provide satisfactory answers to the question, e.g. *A. Cassese*, International Criminal Law, 2nd ed., Oxford 2008 and *K. Ambos*, Internationales Strafrecht. Strafanwendungsrecht – Völkerstrafrecht – Europäisches Strafrecht, München 2006. *C. de Than/E. Shorts*, International Criminal Law and Human Rights, London 2003 (pp. 12–13) is overly general. *G. Werle*, Principles of International Criminal Law, The Hague 2005 (pp. 39ff.) dedicates a section to the problem and *R. Cryer/H. Friman/D. Robinson/E. Wilmshurst*, An Introduction to International Criminal Law and Procedure, Cambridge 2007 (pp. 9–11) contains a very good summary addressing the most relevant points. Even articles explicitly dedicated to the question fail to reveal the complexity of these relationships, see e.g. *S. Parmentier/E. G. M. Weitekamp*, Introduction. On the Double Relationship of Crime and Human Rights, in: S. Parmentier/E. G. M. Weitekamp (eds.), Crime and Human Rights, Oxford, Amsterdam, San Diego 2007, p. 1 and *G. Werle*, Menschenrechtsschutz durch Völkerstrafrecht, ZStW 109 (1997), p. 808.

torture, aggression, terrorism) and to make those persons who engage in such conduct criminally liable".[2] Unlike other branches of public international law that only recognize violations by States, international criminal law creates *individual* criminal responsibility for violations of international law. The sources of international criminal law are international treaty law and to a large extent also customary international law. Major institutions in the application of international criminal law at the international level were the International Military Tribunal at Nuremberg (IMT) and the International Military Tribunal for the Far East (IMTFE) after World War II, the UN *ad hoc* tribunals, created in the 1990s, namely the International Criminal Tribunal for the former Yugoslavia (ICTY) and the International Criminal Tribunal for Rwanda (ICTR), and the (permanent) International Criminal Court (ICC).[3] A new development are internationalized or so-called 'hybrid' tribunals, that are characterized by national as well as international elements and which have been created for Sierra Leone, East Timor, Kosovo, Cambodia and recently for Lebanon.[4]

Human rights are "those liberties, immunities, and benefits which, by accepted contemporary values, all human beings should be able to claim 'as of right' of the society in which they live".[5] International human rights law in the traditional sense creates international obligations upon States in regard to these rights, thus restricting the authority of sovereign State power.[6] Central instruments are the UN Declaration of Human Rights, the International Convention on Political and Civil Rights (ICCPR), the International Convention on Economic and Social Rights and regional treaties such as the European and Inter-American Conventions on Human Rights, the African Charter on Human and People's Rights etc. It also includes the abundant case law of international bodies such as the European Court of Human Rights (ECHR), the Inter-American Court of Human Rights (IACHR) and the UN Human Rights Committee.

---

[2] This is the definition given by *A. Cassese*, International Criminal Law, 2nd ed., Oxford 2008 (p. 3). Different meanings of the term international criminal law were already explored by *G. Schwarzenberger*, The Problem of an International Criminal Law, Current Legal Problems 3 (1950), p. 263.

[3] For a historical overview, see *A. Cassese*, From Nuremberg to Rome. International Military Tribunals to the International Criminal Court, in: *A. Cassese/P. Gaeta/J. R. W. D. Jones* (eds.), The Rome Statute of the International Criminal Court. A Commentary, Vol. I, Oxford 2002, p. 3.

[4] Compare the contributions to *C. P. R. Romano/A. Nollkaemper/J. K. Kleffner* (eds.), Internationalized Criminal Courts and Tribunals. Sierra Leone, East Timor, Kosovo and Cambodia, Oxford 2004.

[5] *L. Henkin*, Human Rights, in: *R. Bernhardt* (ed.), Encyclopedia of Public International Law, Vol. II, Amsterdam 1992, p. 886.

[6] This definition is traditional in the sense that it does not reflect if and how *non-State* actors can also be bound by human rights norms. A knowledgeable introduction to this topic can be found in *Bühring's* contribution to this collection; for a more detailed analysis, see *A. Clapham*, Human Rights Obligations of Non-State Actors, Oxford 2006 and the contributions to *P. Alston* (ed.), Non-State Actors and Human Rights, Oxford 2005.

A third relevant term is international humanitarian law. It is often used synonymously with the term "laws of war" or the Latin term "*ius in bello*", i.e. the rules governing the conduct of armed conflicts. In fact, international humanitarian law is a narrower term because it only refers to the laws of war that concern the protection of individuals, civilian or military, during armed conflicts, as specified for example in the Four Geneva Conventions of 1949 with the Additional Protocols of 1977. This focus of international humanitarian law leads to the inclusion of relevant parts of international human rights law.[7] Art. 1 of the Statutes of the ICTY and the ICTR refer to this concept and grant these tribunals "the power to prosecute persons responsible for serious violations of international humanitarian law".

These definitions facilitate a distinction between these areas of law at a conceptual level. In concrete situations, for instance, during so-called humanitarian interventions, it might not always be clear which body of law dominates the reactions to such complex emergencies, as a process of convergence of these areas of law has been observed for quite some time, which undercuts the clarity the definitions seemingly suggest.[8] Art. 1 of the Statutes of the ICTY and the ICTR can be seen as an example of this convergence. In the following exploration I will focus on the relationships between human rights law and international criminal law.

II. Theoretical Aspects of the Analysis

This section consists of three parts. In the first, I will present a model developed by *Bassiouni* to characterize different stages in the development of international human rights norms that will provide an instructive point of departure for the following analysis. The second part introduces a socio-legal framework by *Geiger* to facilitate a distinction between the enforcement and the protection of human rights. Finally, I will show how the model presented in the first part can and should be extended.

---

[7] In this sense, *K.J. Partsch*, Humanitarian Law and Armed Conflict, in: *R. Bernhardt* (ed.), Encyclopedia of Public International Law, Vol. II, Amsterdam 1992, p. 933.

[8] For an early account regarding the convergence of human rights law and international humanitarian law, see *A. Eide*, The Laws of War and Human Rights. Differences and Convergences, in: C. Swinarski (ed.), Studies and Essays on International Humanitarian Law and Red Cross Principles in Honour of Jean Pictet, Geneva 1984, p. 675. Later evaluations include *T. Meron*, The Convergence between Human Rights and Humanitarian Law, in: *D. Warner* (ed.), Human Rights and Humanitarian Law. The Quest for Universality, The Hague 1997, p. 97; *J. Dugard*, Bridging the Gap Between Human Rights and Humanitarian Law. The Punishment of Offenders, International Review of the Red Cross 324 (1998), p. 445; *D. O'Donnell*, Trends in the Application of International Humanitarian Law by United Nations Human Rights Mechanisms, International Review of the Red Cross 324 (1998), p. 481.

1. *Bassiouni's Model of Norm Development in International Human Rights Law*

Bassiouni distinguishes the following stages in the development of international human rights norms:

"Stage 1 – *The Enunciative Stage* – The emergence and shaping of internationally perceived shared values through intellectual and social processes.
Stage 2 – *The Declarative Stage* – The declaration of certain identified human interests or rights in an international document or instrument.
Stage 3 – *The Prescriptive Stage* – The articulation of these human rights in some prescriptive form in an international instrument (general or specific) generated by an international body; or the elaboration of specific normative prescriptions in binding international conventions.
Stage 4 – *The Enforcement Stage* – The search for, or development of, modalities of enforcement.
Stage 5 – *The Criminalization Stage* – The development of international penal proscriptions.[9]"

This attempt of an abstract description of norm generating processes in the area of international human rights law clarifies that criminal sanctions are a means of enforcement that enters only at the latest stage of the development. The model should not be understood in the sense that every human right that does not reach this last stage is only incompletely realized: not all provisions of human rights law reach this last stage, nor are they necessarily supposed to do so. For *Bassiouni* the insight into the inadequacy of other enforcement mechanisms is the central reason to resort to the *ultima ratio* application of criminal sanctions. However, the significance of the right sought to be protected is, contrary to his position, not without influence on the estimation whether or not to resort to criminal sanctions. The *ultima ratio* nature of criminal sanctions also requires that the infringement of the rights of the perpetrator in the sanctioning process is legitimized by the gravity of his/her offence, which in turn is based, *inter alia*, on the significance of the human right that is violated.[10]

With these clarifications in mind, we can reach a first conclusion about the relationship between international criminal law and human rights law in terms of their content: almost every international crime is a violation of fundamental human rights, but not every violation of human rights entails direct criminal responsibility. The reason for this is that human rights create obligations prima-

[9] This quote is from *M. C. Bassiouni*, International Criminal Law and Human Rights, in: M.C. Bassiouni (ed.), International Criminal Law. Vol. 1: Crimes, 1st ed., New York 1986, p. 15 (16). The following discussion refers to comments on p. 17.

[10] A second aspect, albeit without further relevance to the following analysis, pertains to the observation that a specific human rights norm does not need to go through all the stages successively but under certain circumstances may take several steps at the same time, e.g. when its specific formulation coincides with the institutionalization of enforcement mechanisms.

rily upon States and it is up to them to decide how to ensure respect of these obligations by their own agents.[11] On the one hand, this is a descriptive account that achieves an analytical reconstruction of the norm generation process in the field of international human rights law. At the same time, this description includes the claim that a higher stage in the development equals a higher degree of protection. One version of this claim is a central theme in the literature regarding the relationship between international criminal law and international human rights law: international human rights law is an infringement on the sovereignty of States that is further intensified through the criminalization of certain human rights violations.[12]

2. *Geiger's Concept of Social Validity*

To evaluate the assumption that a higher degree of protection of human rights is achieved by the criminalization of certain human rights violations, I will use an observation by legal sociologist *Theodor Geiger* (1891–1952).[13] *Geiger* pointed out that a norm can have two different effects: the norm can either be followed or behaviour in violation of the norm can be sanctioned.[14] Taken together, these effects make up the validity of a norm (*Verbindlichkeit*). A norm is ineffective or invalid insofar violations of the norm remain unsanctioned. In this understanding, validity is not determined in a purely legal sense, but on the ground of empirical observations. Therefore, one might consider it to be some sort of social validity. Given *Geiger's* predilection for the formulaic language of natural sciences, he measured social validity in per cent, adding the number of cases of conform behaviour and the number of sanctions for deviant behaviour, dividing this sum by the total number of cases.

Applying these general remarks to the concrete example of human rights norms, this means that these norms can become effective by being followed by

---

[11] This is also the conclusion of *R. Cryer/H. Friman/D. Robinson/E. Wilmshurst*, An Introduction to International Criminal Law and Procedure, Cambridge 2007 (pp. 10f.).

[12] For a detailed analysis, see *F. Neubacher*, Kriminologische Grundlagen einer internationalen Strafgerichtsbarkeit. Politische Ideen- und Dogmengeschichte, kriminalwissenschaftliche Legitimation und strafrechtliche Perspektiven, Tübingen 2005.

[13] Geiger was born in Germany and emigrated to Denmark in 1933. He published in German and Danish and he has not received the status of a 'classic' in the Anglo-Saxon tradition of the sociology of law. On his life and work, see the contributions in *S. Bachmann* (ed.), Theodor Geiger: Soziologe in einer Zeit "zwischen Pathos und Nüchternheit". Beiträge zu Leben und Werk, Berlin 1995.

[14] *T. Geiger*, Vorstudien zu einer Soziologie des Rechts, 2nd ed., Neuwied am Rhein, Berlin 1970 [1947], p. 70. His formulation is as follows: "Die Wirkung der Norm ist damit disjunktiv bestimmt. Sie besteht *entweder* in Realisierung des Normkerns *oder* in abweichendem Gebaren mit sozialer Reaktion als Folge. *v* dagegen, der Begriff der Verbindlichkeit, ist nicht disjunktiv, sondern einheitlich bestimmt. *v* ist nämlich nicht entweder das eine oder das andere, sondern Inhalt der *v* ist *das Entweder-Oder*, d.h., *die Alternative selbst*, welcher AA [die Normadressaten] gegenüberstehen." (emphasis in the original)

persons and entities to whom they are addressed and through sanctions of human rights violations. Let us consider three hypothetical constellations in regard to the prohibition of torture:

- 100 cases, in which torture does not occur;[15]
- 50 cases, in which torture does not occur and 50 cases, in which it occurs, and the violators are punished for their behaviour;
- 100 cases in which torture occurs, and all the violators are punished.

Although these constellations vary greatly, on the basis of *Geiger's* distinction, the social validity of the prohibition of torture is always the same, namely 100%. In the first case, there was no specific form of enforcement necessary to reach this result. In the second case, however, sanctioning of violations contributed to 50% and in the third case even to 100% to the social validity of the norm. The degree of protection the prohibition of torture can grant in these cases is inverse to the degree of enforcement necessary to produce social validity: there are no victims in the first case, 50 victims in the second and 100 in the third. Therefore one must conclude that the mere possibility of a sanction does not *prima facie* contribute to the protection of the human right norm, as the harm might have already been caused.[16]

With this in mind, we shall return to *Bassiouni's* description of the norm development process in order to clarify the relationship between human rights and international criminal law. The introduction of the possibility of criminal sanctions at the fifth stage can increase the degree of social validity in cases where human rights norms have been violated. In terms of protection, the honest answer to the victims of human rights violations must be that the normative power of the prohibitions, even when they include the concept of individual criminal responsibility, was obviously too weak to prevent victimisation. The harm cannot be undone. In these cases, the only way to achieve a higher degree of social validity is to engage in a sanctioning process. This can be considered to be the added bonus of reaching the last stage of the development as described by *Bassiouni*.

One could argue that sanctions are not specific to the fifth stage, as at the fourth stage other, non-criminal, sanctions might be provided. Indeed, in his analysis *Geiger* does not distinguish between different types of sanctions and their adequacy in relation to the violation. From this perspective, one might

[15] For the sake of argument, let us assume one can provide a satisfying answer to the question of what constitutes one case of non-occurrence of torture.

[16] On the basis of numerous accounts, both in legal sociology as well as in legal philosophy, one could talk about the protection of the norm itself from the erosion through constantly ignoring violations against it. This aspect is addressed, for example, in *Durkheim's* sociology of crimes, compare e.g. *S. Nimaga*, An International *Conscience Collective*? A Durkheimian Analysis of International Criminal Law, International Criminal Law Review 7 (2007), p. 561 (579f.).

consider it irrelevant which kind of negative sanction a norm violation entails. Criminal sanctions for fundamental human rights violations usually lead to the deprivation of liberty in the form of prison sentences, as the death penalty is not provided for in the current international criminal justice system. This is the harshest form of intervention of organized and legitimate political power into the life of the individual. In this regard the enforcement of criminal sentences not only adds quantitatively to the social validity of the norm by providing another punishment mechanism, but also qualitatively by choosing the harshest sanction available. Based on the equation that the higher a certain value is regarded the more severe the sanctions for its violation and vice versa, this qualitative element points to the symbolic effects of criminal law.[17]

3. *The Protection of Human Rights through Punishment*

The earlier remark that the mere punishment of human rights violations does not contribute to the protection of human rights needs to be qualified in two regards. First, we have to include the fact that the act of punishing itself can contribute to the protection of human rights. Further, the integration of a temporal perspective reveals that the punishment might not only be aimed at human rights violations that have already occurred, but also at the prevention of future breaches of these norms. This second aspect will be discussed in the following section dealing with empirical aspects.

The first observation is that punishment for certain human rights violations has become mandatory: The sanctioning process is no longer considered to be merely directed at past violations; rather, the failure to provide adequate accountability mechanisms is considered to be in itself a violation of human rights norms.[18] The reason for this development is the realization that the systematic refusal by States to investigate and sanction human rights violations leads to a perpetuation and intensification of the harm done to the victims and their immediate surroundings.[19] This syndrome is usually summarized under the head-

---

[17] As described above, *Bassiouni* does not consider the symbolic value of punishment as the motor for norm development. A sophisticated version of a symbolic theory of international criminal law is provided by *D. M. Amann*, Group Mentality, Expressivism, and Genocide, International Criminal Law Review 2 (2002), p. 93 (117 ff.).

[18] For a thorough discussion of the obligations of States to prosecute gross human rights violations, compare *D. F. Orentlicher*, Settling Accounts. The Duty to Prosecute Human Rights Violations of a Prior Regime, Yale Law Journal 100 (1991), p. 2537.

[19] The empirical aspects of this argument relate to the question, what the denial of punishment of the perpetrators of international crimes implies for the surviving victims of these crimes. See, for example, *J. O'Connell*, Gambling with Psyche. Does Prosecuting Human Rights Violators Console Their Victims? Harvard International Law Journal 46 (2005), p. 295.

ing of impunity and has attracted scholarly attention particularly with regard to Latin America.[20]

Exemplary is the Velásquez-Rodríguez-Case, as decided by the Inter-American Court for Human Rights. This case concerned the arrest, torture, and execution of the Honduran student activist *Angel Manfredo Velásquez Rodríguez* by the Honduran military, which occurred in violation of the Inter-American Convention of Human Rights, namely the rights to life, to humane treatment and to personal liberty. The Court therefore established Honduras' responsibility for violating these substantive rights. It went further, however and stated that Honduras had also breached the general obligation of Article 1(1) of the Convention, which establishes a more general obligation to ensure these rights:

> "The State has a legal duty to take reasonable steps to prevent human rights violations and to use the means at its disposal to carry out a serious investigation of violations committed within its jurisdiction, to identify those responsible, to impose the appropriate punishment and to ensure the victim adequate compensation".[21]

Three aspects will be considered in the interpretation of this decision. First, we have to ask whether the protection from torture is supplemented by an independent right to accountability. This conclusion would be a misinterpretation of the judgment, which does not proclaim an isolated human right of the victim to the punishment of those who violated human rights norms. Thus, the victim does not gain an additional human right; rather, the existing right is more broadly interpreted to include a protection from situations where perpetrators act with impunity. Speaking in terms of *Bassiouni's* model of norm development, there is not a circularity with the formation of a new human right to be free from impunity that can go through the five stages mentioned above. More precisely, we witness a sixth stage in the development of human rights norms, which turns the criminalization of the fifth stage from an optional into an obligatory reaction.

Secondly, it is important to realize that the judgment refers to a variety of reactions that include serious investigations, sanctioning of those responsible and adequate compensation of the victims. While not interchangeable, the focus can be on one or two of these measures. Thus, criminal sanctions are not the

---

[20] For a detailed analysis of the concept of impunity, compare *N. Roht-Arriaza* (ed.), Impunity and Human Rights in International Law and Practice, New York, Oxford 1995 and *K. Ambos*, Straflosigkeit von Menschenrechtsverletzungen. Zur "impunidad" in südamerikanischen Ländern aus völkerrechtlicher Sicht, Freiburg i. Br. 1997. See also the UN Commission on Human Rights' "Set of Principles for the Protection and Promotion of Human Rights through Action to Combat Impunity", as updated 8 February 2005 (E/CN.4/2005/102/Add.1).

[21] *Velásquez Rodríguez*, IACHR, 29 July 1988, para. 174.

only form of accountability for the perpetrators[22] and neither are they the only form of relief provided to the victims of gross human rights violations.[23]

The last point takes up an earlier observation and combines it with the two preceding points. As mentioned above, not all human rights will necessarily go through all stages of development, because particularly the criminalization stage as an *ultima ratio* reaction will be reserved for extreme cases of human rights violations. Given the availability of other forms of accountability and the fact that there is no isolated human right to punishment of human rights violations, it is obvious that the obligatory criminal punishment of human rights violators will be reserved for the most severe violations of the most fundamental human rights norms.

III. Empirical Aspects Regarding the Prevention of International Crimes

In the preceding analysis, the protection of human rights, particularly those of the victims, occurs *ipso iure* through the application of international criminal law norms. Whether the international criminal justice system contributes to the prevention of human rights violations in the form of international core crimes such as genocide, crimes against humanity and war crimes is an empirical question. The link between international criminal law and international human rights law can in this instance only be made if social scientific research can demonstrate that the prosecution of these crimes does contribute to their non-recurrence.

In conceptual terms, the prevention of international crimes and the corresponding human rights violations by means of international criminal law can take three major forms, which will be evaluated separately. They are (1.) prevention on the basis of consequentialist theories of (international) criminal law, (2.) prevention through influencing the criminogenic context of collective violence, and (3.) prevention through the swift prosecution of inchoate offences

1. Consequentialist Theories of (International) Criminal Law

Consequentialist or utilitarian theories of criminal law propose that punishment does not occur (primarily) in reaction to the violation of the norm in the

---

[22] This variety of reactions to grave human rights violations has been highlighted particularly in the literature on transitional justice. For an introduction, see N.J. Kritz (ed.), Transitional Justice. How Emerging Democracies Reckon with Former Regimes, Washington, DC 1995.

[23] For a detailed analysis, see *C. Tomuschat*, Reparation for Victims of Grave Human Rights Violations, Tulane Journal of International and Comparative Law 10 (2002), p. 157.

past but in order to prevent future offences.[24] The ICTY stated that it considered deterrence to be one of the main purposes relevant to the imposition of sentences before the International Tribunal.[25] The concept of deterrence is based on the assumption that fear of punishment will contribute to the prevention of crimes in the future. It can take the form of specific deterrence, aiming at reducing recidivism among perpetrators on the basis of their experience with the criminal justice system, and general deterrence, which aims at reducing criminality among potential perpetrators in the society at large.[26]

Another assumption is that the criminal justice system can prevent crimes not only by assuring that 'crime does not pay', but also by instilling aversions to the behaviour prohibited by law. This concept of norm-stabilization and norm-internalization as a contribution to the prevention of crime is also considered to be of fundamental importance, particularly in an emerging field such as international criminal law.[27] An illustration of this assumption is provided by the following quote:

"The Trial Chamber [of the ICTY] is further of the view that another relevant sentencing purpose is to show the people not only of the former Yugoslavia, but the world in general, that there is no impunity for these types of crimes. This should be done in order to strengthen the resolve of all involved not to allow crimes against international humanitarian law to be committed as well as to create trust in and respect for the developing system of international criminal justice."[28]

The concept of rehabilitation, i.e. the treatment of offenders with the goal of enabling them to lead their future lives without resorting to criminal behaviour, is only marginal in international criminal law, particularly insofar as leaders of

---

[24] Compare *M.J. Aukerman*, Extraordinary Evil, Ordinary Crime. A Framework for Understanding Transitional Justice, Harvard Human Rights Journal 15 (2002), p. 39; *D. Wippman*, Exaggerating the ICC, in: *J. Harrington/M. Milde/R. Vernon* (eds.), Bringing Power to Justice? The Prospects of the International Criminal Court, Montreal 2006, p. 99 (108ff.); *L.E. Fletcher/H.M. Weinstein*, Violence and Social Repair. Rethinking the Contribution of Justice to Reconciliation, Human Rights Quarterly 24 (2002), p. 573 (589ff.); *I. Tallgren*, The Sense and Sensibility of International Criminal Law, European Journal of International Law 13 (2002), p. 561.

[25] Pros. v. *Kupreškić et al*, ICTY, TC II, 14 January 2000 (IT-95–16-T), para. 848.

[26] The relevance of the approach of deterrence for international criminal law is discussed by *D. Wippman*, Atrocities, Deterrence, and the Limits of International Justice, Fordham International Law Journal 23 (1999), p. 473.

[27] A good overview is provided by *R.D. Sloane*, The Expressive Capacity of International Punishment. The Limits of the National Law Analogy and the Potential of International Criminal Law, Stanford Journal of International Law 43 (2007), p. 39 (75ff.) and *D.M. Amann*, Group Mentality, Expressivism, and Genocide, International Criminal Law Review 2 (2002), p. 93. The didactic element of trials is highlighted by *M.J. Osiel*, Mass Atrocity, Collective Memory, and the Law, New Brunswick 1997.

[28] Pros. v. *Kupreškić et al*, ICTY, TC II, 14 January 2000 (IT-95-16-T), para. 848.

collective violence are concerned, while incapacitation seems to play a more important role.[29]

The empirical assessment of these general assumptions of the effects of criminal law is difficult, to say the least. Therefore, criminological research at the national level has moved away from these fundamental questions to evaluating more concrete measures of crime prevention.[30] The current stage of development of the international criminal justice system does not allow for focusing on such concrete measures of crime prevention, simply because this requires the existence of highly diverse sanctions and sanctioning mechanisms and institutions that we simply do not find at the international level. There, punishment regularly occurs in form of prison sentences handed down by permanent or *ad hoc* international criminal courts and so-called hybrid tribunals.

To assess these basic questions regarding the consequentialist approaches to international criminal law is also fraught with more general methodological problems. In evaluation research, experiments are considered the pre-eminent research design to test causal hypotheses inherent in the assumption of the preventive capacities of criminal law.[31] However, experimental research-designs are no option in the area of international criminal law. Randomization which characterizes true experimental designs cannot be applied in this area, as the gravity of crimes forbids a decision based on chance. Quasi-experimental designs, sometimes called natural experiments, are problematic as well, because the contexts for which international criminal courts and tribunals have been created differ widely. Finally, research designs using statistical tools will at this point hardly yield significant results, as the number of cases in which the international criminal justice system has become active is still considerably small. All this makes it virtually impossible to infer that particular developments, in our case the degree to which crimes do recur, were caused by the prosecution of international crimes or the lack thereof.

Given these methodological problems, evaluating the consequentialist approaches to international criminal law might benefit from an indirect approach.[32] I conceptualize these approaches as dependent on a psychological influence on (potential) perpetrators. Using a utilitarian psychological model of explaining or predicting norm-conform and deviant behaviour, the potential success of

---

[29] *J. Elster*, Retribution, in: J. Elster (ed.), Retribution and Reparation in the Transition to Democracy, Cambridge 2006, p. 33.

[30] Compare L.W. Sherman/D.P. Farrington/B.C. Welsh/D.L. MacKenzie (eds.), Evidence-Based Crime Prevention, London, New York 2002.

[31] On impact assessment, see *P. H. Rossi/ M. W. Lipsey /H. E. Freeman*, Evaluation. A Systematic Approach, 7th ed., Thousand Oaks 2004 (chs. 8–9).

[32] This is one of the central arguments of my dissertation thesis on the effects of international criminal law, which I will not be able to further discuss here, due to the restrictions of this paper.

achieving this influence can be assessed.[33] I consider international crimes to be phenomena of macrocriminality that have to be carefully distinguished from ordinary crime due to their collective nature.[34] Therefore, the model has to be adapted to account for these differences. Socio-psychological research on the actors of collective violence is especially helpful in characterizing the particularities of the perpetration of international crimes.[35] On this basis, I come to the conclusion that the expectations regarding the preventive function of international criminal law need to be moderated, as sanctions of international criminal law are uncertain, distant and comparatively mild compared to the influences and sanctions (potential) perpetrators have to expect from their immediate surroundings.[36] Given this situation, consequentialist approaches to international criminal law seem to fare even worse than their counterparts in the national context.

2. *The Criminogenic Context of Collective Violence*

Preventing future human rights violations by means of international criminal justice is not restricted to consequentialist theories in the way they have just been described. Rather than influencing the (potential) perpetrators, it is expected that the international criminal justice system can positively influence the contexts that foster collective violence and the perpetration of international crimes. The foundation of this argument is the realization that international crimes are committed primarily during armed conflicts, both international and non-international in character. "No Justice, No Peace" is the slogan that became emblematic for the contribution that international criminal courts might provide to peace processes in post-conflict societies in particular and to international peace in general. If we look at the *ad hoc* tribunals created through UN Security Council resolutions, this contribution becomes even the basis for the legitimacy of these tribunals, as they were created with the powers vested in the Security Council by Chapter VII of the UN-Charter dealing with threats to

---

[33] This model was developed by *A. Diekmann*, Die Befolgung von Gesetzen. Empirische Untersuchungen zu einer rechtssoziologischen Theorie, Berlin 1980.

[34] The concept of macrocriminality was established by the German criminologist *Herbert Jäger*; for an introduction, see *H. Jäger*, Makrokriminalität. Studien zur Kriminologie kollektiver Gewalt, Frankfurt a.M. 1989.

[35] In German, see the excellent study by *H. Welzer*, Täter. Wie aus ganz normalen Menschen Massenmörder werden, Frankfurt a.M. 2005. In English, see *D. Chirot/ C.R. McCauley*, Why Not Kill Them All? The Logic and Prevention of Mass Political Murder, Princeton, Oxford 2006; *J. Waller*, Becoming Evil. How Ordinary People Commit Genocide and Mass Killing, New York 2002.

[36] With a different methodological approach, similar results are presented by *J. Ku/J. Nzelibe*, Do International Criminal Tribunals Deter or Exacerbate Humanitarian Atrocities?, Hofstra University School of Law, Legal Studies Research Paper No. 06–22 <http://ssrn.com/abstract=931567>.

international peace and security.[37] Often this argument is linked to the necessity of a wider reconstruction of post-conflict societies under the aegis of rule of law, democracy and human rights, thus alluding to the democratic peace theory.[38]

In short, in order to make the connection between international criminal law and the protection of human rights, we have to asses empirically the contribution of the international criminal justice system to peace and democratization processes in post-conflict societies. This is no easy task. In analogy to the challenges of documenting the impact of international criminal law with regard to consequentialist approaches, similar methodological problems arise here, namely the unfeasibility of (quasi-)experimental research designs and the lack of significant quantitative research due to small case numbers. Another problem is that trials by international criminal courts are never the only intervention in post-conflict societies. Therefore it is difficult to isolate analytically the effects of the international criminal justice system from other peace-building and democratisation mechanisms that are applied simultaneously or successively.[39]

Given this absence of data conforming to the highest standards of empirical research, the interpretation and evaluation of the impact of the international criminal justice regime differ widely: While some shout "no peace without justice", others speak of "peace vs. justice".[40] This controversy cannot possibly be resolved within the confines of this article. Still, I want to make three brief comments. Some of the controversy can be diminished by specifying a time frame, as most can agree that possible detrimental effects of criminal trials on peace processes are more likely to occur in the short than in the long run.[41] Another

---

[37] There is a vast literature on this subject. The presentations at the War Crimes Research Symposium "The Role of Justice in Building Peace", as published in the Case Western Reserve Journal of International Law 35/2 (2003) are a good introduction. Compare also *P.R. Williams/M.P. Scharf*, Peace with Justice? War Crimes and Accountability in the Former Yugoslavia, Lanham 2002, pp. 11–22. An example of a very critical position is the article by *J. Snyder/L. Vinjamuri*, Trials and Errors. Principle and Pragmatism in Strategies of International Justice, International Security 28 (2003), p. 5.

[38] An introduction to the democratic peace theory is provided by *B. Russett*, Grasping the Democratic Peace, Princeton 1993, and the contributions to *M.E. Brown/S.M. Lynn-Jones/S.E. Miller* (eds.), Debating the Democratic Peace, Cambridge 1996.

[39] The multitude of options policy-makers face is exemplified by *D. Bloomfield/T. Barnes/L. Huyse* (eds.), Reconciliation after Violent Conflict. A Handbook, Stockholm 2003.

[40] The same position is formulated by *I. Tallgren*, The Sense and Sensibility of International Criminal Law, European Journal of International Law 13 (2002), p. 561 (592): "A supplementary argument often reiterated in support of international criminal justice is that of 'no peace without justice'. [...] Such broad arguments are impossible to verify by any empirical means. [...] It seems to be the case that this slogan is only as valid as any other slogan, such as 'peace without justice and 'justice without peace'." Very critical: *J. Snyder/L. Vinjamuri*, Trials and Errors. Principle and Pragmatism in Strategies of International Justice, International Security 28 (2003), p. 5.

[41] This temporal aspect is highlighted by *P.H. Baker*, Conflict Resolution Versus Democratic Governance. Divergent Paths to Peace?, in: *C. Crocker/F.O. Hampson* (eds.), Manag-

aspect that unnecessarily magnifies the differences between the positions is the multitude of meanings associated with the word 'peace'. In the tradition of *Galtung*, one should differentiate between negative peace, characterized by the mere absence of physical violence, and positive peace, which in addition requires the absence of structural and cultural violence.[42] A third concept of peace could be added, based on the German notion of *Rechtsfrieden* or 'peace through law', which is already achieved when the resolution of a conflict can no longer be questioned within the legal system.[43] When put in ascending order – peace through law, negative peace, positive peace –, there should also be consensus that the ability of (international) criminal law to achieve or contribute to these stages decreases as we go along.

However, I also consider problematic that international criminal justice is too often seen as possessing essential traits. In explaining my unease with the current situation, a reference to a distinction by *Mani* is helpful.[44] She distinguishes between three dimensions of justice in post-conflict peacebuilding. First, 'legal justice' or the rule of law needs to be addressed, due to the lack of operative structures after a period of institutionalized repression by the State. In reference to *Aristotle*, she further distinguishes between rectificatory and distributive justice. In order to achieve rectificatory justice, remedies for injustices inflicted upon people need to be provided, in particular by punishing those responsible for international crimes and other human rights violations. Distributive justice aims at reducing inequalities between individuals and groups, which are both a root cause and a result of the conflict, by resorting to mechanisms such as restitution and (foreign) aid.

The stress on the retributive elements of (international) criminal law prevents the appreciation of its versatility. Hybrid or internationalized criminal courts play a direct part in establishing the rule of law in the countries affected by international crimes. International criminal courts punish violations of international criminal law, but while doing so, they also contribute to establishing a historical record.[45] Finally, mechanisms to provide restitution to victims can be incorporated in international criminal proceedings.[46] These examples shall suf-

---

ing Global Chaos. Sources of and Responses to International Conflict, Washington, DC 1996, p. 563.

[42] See *J. Galtung*, Violence, Peace and Peace Research, Journal of Peace Research 6 (1969), p. 167.

[43] The consequences of this approach are well demonstrated by *N. Luhmann*, Legitimation durch Verfahren, Neuwied 1969.

[44] The following description is based on *R. Mani*, Beyond Retribution. Seeking Justice in the Shadows of War, Cambridge 2002 (esp. pp. 3–11).

[45] On the latter aspect, see *R.A. Wilson*, Judging History. The Historical Record of the International Criminal Tribunal for the Former Yugoslavia, Human Rights Quarterly 27 (2005), p. 908.

[46] Compare Art. 75 ICC-Statute.

fice to demonstrate that international criminal justice is not reduced to the aspect of rectificatory justice. Instead of essentializing international criminal justice, one should rather ask two questions: first, which results are to be achieved and second, if and how the necessary mechanisms can be incorporated into the international criminal justice system.[47] Such a project depends on more reliable data on the effects of international criminal justice. Until then, the question whether the prosecution of international crimes contributes to more peace and thus to the non-recurrence of gross human rights violations will remain open.

3. *Criminalization and Prosecution of Inchoate Offences*

Inchoate or 'just begun' crimes describe punishable behaviour preparatory to otherwise prohibited offences that are not completed themselves.[48] The criminalization of inchoate offences is focused on acts that already contain an attack on the protected interest but fall short of a complete realization of the crime in all its severity. Still, the danger of these acts is considered to be sufficiently grave to merit criminalization. In principle, the advantage of this form of criminalization is that it allows action by criminal law agencies before (more) serious damage has been caused. Therefore, swift prosecution of inchoate offences in the area of international criminal law is one form of prevention of gross human rights violations.

Illustrative in this regard is an examination of the Genocide Convention. Although the full title of this convention refers to the prevention and punishment of genocide, a study of the text reveals that the drafters relied primarily on a concept of prevention *through* punishment.[49] Art. 4(3) of the ICTY-Statute and Art. 2(3) of the ICTR-Statute, for example, are based on Art. 3 of the Genocide Convention and include in lit. (c) the inchoate crime of direct and public incitement to commit genocide. As the ICTR pointed out, direct and public incitement to commit genocide is punishable whether or not the crime of genocide has been carried out.[50] Thus, a swift prosecution of this inchoate crime is a preventive measure that could stop further acts of genocide before one life has been

---

[47] This does not mean that the whole panoply of peace-building mechanisms could or should be incorporated into the international criminal justice regime. An eloquent critique of such a one-size-fits-all approach is presented by *M.A. Drumbl*, Atrocity, Punishment, and International Law, Cambridge 2007. However, a more nuanced approach to the possibilities in the concrete organisation of international criminal proceedings is called for. Beginnings of such an enterprise are presented by *M. Findlay/R. Henham*, Transforming International Criminal Justice. Retributive and Restorative Justice in the Trial Process, Cullompton 2005.

[48] For a discussion of inchoate offences in international criminal law, see *A. Cassese*, International Criminal Law, 2nd ed., Oxford 2008, pp. 219ff.

[49] More detailed, *W.A. Schabas*, Genocide in International Law. The Crime of Crimes, Cambridge 2000 (ch. 10).

[50] This issue is discussed at length in *Pros. v. Akayesu*, ICTR, TC I, 2 September 1998 (ICTR-96-4-T), paras. 549ff.

taken. In short, the criminalization and prosecution of inchoate offences is, in theory, a tool for the prevention of human rights violations by means of international criminal law.

Looking at the realities of the international criminal law regime should dampen the expectations concerning this possibility of prevention. The problem in empirical terms is the relative immobility of the international criminal justice system. The time span from an initial investigation until a conviction is rather long, and the same applies to the more relevant time span between the beginning of an investigation to the issuing of an arrest warrant and its execution. These characteristics of the judicial process obviously run contrary to prevention through the criminalization of inchoate offences. Given the current state, effective prosecution does not occur at a time when the perpetration of international crimes is still in the inchoate phase.

The practice of international criminal law has further shown that this form of criminalization was only prosecuted once the plans for genocide had been carried out. In these instances, the criminalization of inchoate offences, such as direct and public incitement to commit genocide, may allow for a more comprehensive prosecution, as the causal nexus to the completed crime does not need to be proven. In those instances, the gain in possible prevention is, however, negligible.

The development of these aspects under the jurisdiction of the ICC will have to be closely monitored. Thus far, the trend is that cases before the ICC do not move forward very quickly. Another aspect specific to the ICC is the principle of complementarity.[51] In order to exercise its complementary jurisdiction, the Court will have to wait in order to determine whether or not a State is "unwilling or unable" to genuinely investigate or prosecute a case in the sense required by Art. 17 ICC-Statute. The result is a further extension of proceedings with its detrimental effect on preventing that inchoate crimes reach their completion.

With these sceptical remarks, we can leave the aspect of prevention of gross human rights violations by means of international criminal law. Before we move on, the crime of direct and public incitement to commit genocide can serve to highlight yet another aspect of the relationship between international criminal law and international human rights law. Interpreting the scope of public and direct incitement is characterized by striking a balance between the risk inherent in the concrete urge to commit genocide as it is communicated to a large public and the human right of freedom of expression, a fundamental human right as recognized in Art. 19 of both the ICCPR and the Universal Declaration of Human Rights. The most prominent case in this regard was the so-called

---

[51] Compare *J. T. Holmes*, Complementarity. National Courts *versus* the ICC, in: A. Cassese/P. Gaeta/J. R. W. D. Jones (eds.), The Rome Statute of The International Criminal Court. A Commentary, Vol. I, Oxford 2002, p. 667.

media trial before the ICTR, which concerned three accused who were central figures in the broadcasting station *Radio Televison Libre des Mille Collines* and the propaganda newspaper *Kangura*.[52] This case highlights the fine line that delineates behaviour that is a legitimate and protected exercise of human rights and behaviour that is a violation of international criminal law. This example of an infringement of international human rights norms on the interpretation of norms of international criminal law serves as a good transition to the following section, which focuses on the human rights of perpetrators.

IV. Human Rights of the Perpetrator

The guarantees of due process and fair trial are likely to be the area of human rights law with the greatest relevance to the daily work of any international criminal court. In many regards, the international criminal procedural law is challenged with finding a balance between the necessity to create an effective sanctioning mechanism while respecting the human rights of the perpetrators during all stages of the sanctioning process, namely in their position as suspects, accused and convicted.[53]

International human rights law exerts great influence on criminal procedure of national jurisdictions.[54] International criminal courts and tribunals are, however, not parties to the relevant human rights treaties. Nevertheless, their normative foundations, such as the Statutes and Rules of Procedures and Evidence, are heavily influenced by the guarantees provided by these instruments; particularly Art. 14 ICCPR has served as a model.[55] Like every ordinary criminal, the perpetrators of international crimes therefore have the right to a "fair and public hearing by a competent, independent and impartial tribunal established by law" and are presumed innocent until proved guilty in a fair and expeditious trial.[56] Apart from specific guarantees, Art. 21(3) ICC-Statute even goes further

---

[52] See *Pros. v. Nahimana et al*, ICTR, TC I, 3 December 2003 (ICTR-99–52-T). An introduction to this problem with particular reference to the media trial is provided by *T. Salomon*, Freedom of Speech v Hate Speech. The Jurisdiction of 'Direct and Public Incitement to Commit Genocide', in: R. Henham/P. Behrens (eds.), The Criminal Law of Genocide. International, Comparative and Contextual Aspects, Aldershot 2007, p. 141.

[53] See *C. J. M. Safferling*, Towards an International Criminal Procedure, Oxford 2001.

[54] For an extensive documentation, see *S. Trechsel*, Human Rights in Criminal Proceedings, Oxford 2005.

[55] See the more detailed analysis by *E. Møse*, Impact of Human Rights Conventions on the Two *Ad Hoc* Tribunals, in: M. Bergsmo (ed.), Human Rights and Criminal Justice for the Downtrodden. Essays in Honour of Asbjørn Eide, Leiden, Boston 2003, p. 179. Relevant norms were collected by *M. C. Bassiouni*, The Protection of Human Rights in the Administration of Criminal Justice. A Compendium of United Nations Norms and Standards, Irvington-on-Hudson 1994.

[56] The most exhaustive discussion of human rights aspects in international criminal pro-

and requires that the "application and interpretation of law pursuant to this article must be consistent with internationally recognized human rights" in general.

But international human rights law not only had an impact on the norm creation process of international criminal law. The jurisprudence of international criminal tribunals contains numerous references to the decisions of human rights bodies, such as the ECHR, and frequently adopts them to the unique characteristics of international proceedings.[57]

It is interesting to see that comparable human rights as regards the participation of victims in international criminal proceedings do not exist. International human rights norms in relation to victims primarily focus on their access to justice and various forms of restitution or reparation as already discussed. This does not mean that victims do not have any rights in international criminal proceedings. On the contrary, with the Statute of the ICC the position of victims has been considerably extended.[58] However, these rights to participate do not seem to be safeguarded by international human rights norms. With the observation that the expansion of the role of victims in the proceedings before the ICC can to a large extent be attributed to pressure exerted by non-governmental organisations in the negotiation process of the Rome Statute, we turn to the last section of this article.

V. The Human Rights Community and International Criminal Law

The discussion of the relationship between international criminal law and international human rights law would be incomplete without an analysis of the contributions that human rights organizations made in the long and difficult process of the institutionalization of international criminal tribunals and courts. As this topic cannot be discussed here in its entirety, a brief analysis on the work of the Coalition for an International Criminal Court (CICC) and its influence on the negotiations of the ICC-Statute at the Diplomatic Conference in

---

ceedings is contained in *S. Zappalà*, Human Rights in International Criminal Proceedings, Oxford 2003.

[57] Compare *A. Cassese*, The Influence of the European Court of Human Rights on International Criminal Tribunals. Some Methodological Remarks, in: M. Bergsmo (ed.), Human Rights and Criminal Justice for the Downtrodden. Essays in Honour of Asbjørn Eide, Leiden, Boston 2003, p. 19.

[58] See Art. 68 ICC-Statute and the commentary by *C. Jorda/J. de Hemptinne*, The Participation of Victims in International Criminal Proceedings, in: A. Cassese/P. Gaeta/J. R. W. D. Jones (eds.), The Rome Statute of The International Criminal Court. A Commentary, Vol. II, Oxford 2002, p. 1382.

Rome (16 June – 17 July 1998) will allow me to highlight some of the most important aspects of this relationship.

The CICC was founded on 10 February 1995. *William Pace* of the New York-based organisation World Federalist Movement became the coordinator, and the NGO he was heading functioned as the secretariat. Initially a small network of NGOs and international law experts, membership increased significantly and by the time of the Rome Conference more than 800 organisations formed part of the network; in June 2000 it had passed the number of 1,000. Interestingly, the accreditation of the NGOs was handled by the CICC itself. This mandate was interpreted widely by *Pace* and because of this self-regulation process, unprecedented in the preparation of multilateral treaties, almost all NGOs that were willing and able to send delegates to Rome were allowed to do so. The final number of NGOs represented at the Diplomatic Conference was 236. Seen as a block, the CICC thus contributed the biggest delegation to the Rome Conference, and outnumbered even the largest State delegations.[59]

This introduction is only a very general description of NGO-participation in the preparation of the Rome Statute. In order to specify the particular contribution of the human rights community, a classification of the NGOs is indispensable (see Fig. 1).

According to this overview, about a third of the NGOs are focused on human rights questions. In interpreting these numbers, two aspects need to be taken into consideration. First, it is important to note that the percentages refer to the number of NGOs and not the number of NGO-delegates, an important difference because the category of human rights organisations comprises organisations such as Amnesty International, Human Rights Watch, the Lawyers Committee for Human Rights, the Féderation Internationale des Ligues de Droits de l'Homme and the International Commission of Jurists, which all sent large teams of representatives to Rome and played a predominant role among the NGOs. The other equally important aspect is that the categories are not mutually exclusive; rather, they identify the NGOs' thematic focus. This becomes clear when one looks at particular groups, such as Equality Now or the Women's Caucus for Gender Justice that can easily be connected to human rights issues of gender equality, the vocal anti-abortion and pro-family groups that take a specific stance on the human right to life, or groups such as the International Committee of the Red Cross which is subsumed under the heading of

[59] I rely heavily on the excellent description by *M. Glasius*, The International Criminal Court. A Global Civil Society Achievement, London 2006 (pp. 22ff.). Other relevant accounts are by *W. R. Pace/J. Schense*, The Role of Non-Governmental Organizations, in: *A. Cassese/P. Gaeta/J. R. W. D. Jones* (eds.), The Rome Statute of The International Criminal Court. A Commentary, Vol. I, Oxford 2002, p. 105; *F. Benedetti/J. Washburn*, Drafting the International Court Treaty. Two Years to Rome and an Afterword on the Rome Diplomatic Conference, Global Governance 5 (1999), p. 1.

global governance and is a paradigmatic case of the merging of international human rights law and international humanitarian law discussed earlier. In summary, while not all the NGOs represented in Rome have their roots in the human rights community, for the majority this characterization is nevertheless appropriate.

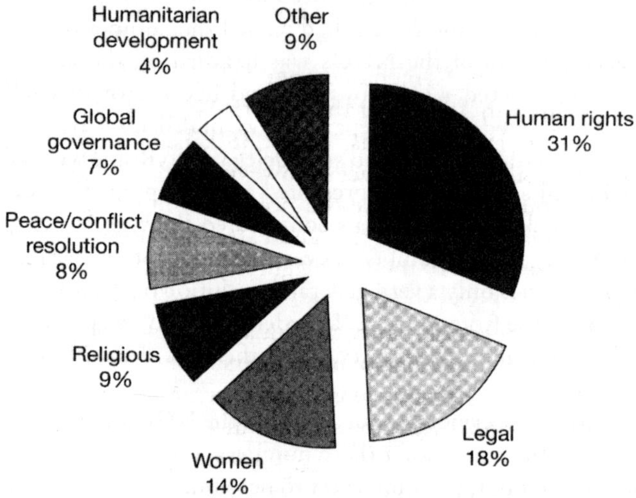

Fig. 1: Functional representation of the NGOs accredited to participate in the negotiations of the Rome Statute[60]

Obviously, the activities of human rights organizations did not end once the treaty for the creation of the International Criminal Court was signed. In many countries there have been successful attempts by these organizations to accelerate the ratification process.[61] Finally, the ICC-Statute itself provides several possibilities for participation of human rights organizations. Art. 15(2) ICC-Statute, for example, clarifies that the Prosecutor in his *proprio motu* investigations may rely on "additional information from States, organs of the United Nations, intergovernmental or non-governmental organizations". Art. 44(4) ICC-Statute includes the provision that the court may, in exceptional circumstances, employ gratis personnel offered by various sides, including NGOs.

---

[60] *M. Glasius*, The International Criminal Court. A Global Civil Society Achievement, London 2006, p. 31.

[61] See *M. J. Struett*, The Politics of Constructing the International Criminal Court. NGOs, Discourse and Agency, New York 2008, ch. 7.

VI. *Conclusion*

To end, let me summarize the multiple relationships between international human rights law and the international criminal justice system by roughly differentiating between the stages of norm formation and norm application during the sanctioning process.

At the level of norm formation, we can first observe an interplay between international human rights norms and the concept of individual criminal responsibility: the heightened value of certain human rights guarantees leads to the criminalization of their violation; at the same time, the *ultima ratio* function of criminal law has the symbolic effect that this criminalization leads to a consolidation of the specific value accorded to these human rights guarantees. The criminalization of gross human rights violations at the international level is also relevant in ensuring victims' rights to the access to justice.

With regard to substantive provisions of international criminal law, we have encountered an example of the moderating effect of the freedom of expression on interpreting the proscription of public and direct incitement to commit genocide. With regard to procedural norms, we have seen how Art. 14 ICCPR served as a model for a concretization of fair trial elements in the Statutes and Rules of Procedure and Evidence of international criminal courts and tribunals.

In terms of the actors in the norm generating processes, the participation of the human rights community in the negotiation of the Rome Statute was highlighted.

Finally, the prevention of gross human rights violations as proposed by consequentialist approaches can in theory occur already subsequently to the formulation of prohibitions of international criminal law as such. This relates to the aspects of general deterrence and norm-stabilization and -internalization. Empirical research at the level of national criminal law, however, has demonstrated that these preventive effects are difficult to document. They also seem to be tied less to the existence of criminal proscriptions as such than to the effectiveness of the criminal justice system, namely the perceived probability of detection and gravity of the punishment, thus pointing to the importance of the sanctioning stage.

At the stage of the sanctioning process, these preventive effects are joined by the possibility of specific deterrence, incapacitation and rehabilitation as potential factors for reducing the recurrence of international crimes and the accompanying gross human rights violations. Despite the difficulty of empirical research in this area, expectations for the success of the international criminal justice system should remain rather low. The same applies to the swift prosecution of inchoate crimes as a means of preventing further and more severe violations. The capacities of international criminal law to contribute to peace-building in post-conflict societies, thus environments conducive to the emergence of collective violence, need yet to be further elaborated and documented by means of the social sciences.

Obviously, the sanctioning process is the stage at which the human rights of the accused to a fair and expeditious trial must pass the test of praxis, while the victims' rights to participation in the proceedings do not seem to have an equivalent in international human rights norms.

Introduction to the Procedure of the International Criminal Court

War Crimes in Darfur

Birte Brodkorb

I. Introduction

The International Criminal Court (ICC) in The Hague began its work in 2003, five years after the international community agreed on the implementation of the Court in Rome in July 1998. In contrast to war crimes tribunals such as Nuremberg, Tokyo, Rwanda or the former Yugoslavia, the ICC is the first permanent court with the authority to prosecute individuals for large-scale atrocities. The Court's aim, as stated in the preamble of the Rome Statute, is that 'the most serious crimes of concern to the international community as a whole must not go unpunished and that their effective prosecution must be ensured'[1].

108 states are members of the Court, meaning they have signed and ratified the legal framework of the institution, the 'Rome Statute'. Further 40 states have signed but not ratified the treaty, of which some have indicated that they do not intend to ratify the treaty. Among them are the United States of America an the republic of Sudan[2].

II. The Situation in Darfur

Sudan has been suffering from civil wars ever since its independence from colonialism in 1956. The recent crisis in Darfur, a region in the South of Sudan, had started at the beginning of 1990 and turned into war in 2003, when ethnic tensions in the region escalated.

---

[1] Rome Statute, Preamble para. 4, http://www2.icc-cpi.int/NR/rdonlyres/EA9AEFF7–5752–4F84-BE94–0A655EB30E16/0/Rome_Statute_English.pdf (accessed 9 February 2009).

[2] *E. Rubin*, New York Times Magazine, 2 April 2006, II.

Before granting independence to Sudan, colonial ruler Britain assigned indirect domination to the few elite Arabic tribes in Sudan, in an attempt to exert better control over the enormous territory. After Sudan's sovereignty, those tribes maintained power. They were supported by Libya's leader Muammar Al-Gaddafi, who propagated the cultural supremacy of the Arabic groups over the 'zurqa' ('blacks')[3], thereby causing clashes of the different ethnic groups.

The main trigger for the recent conflict was the dispute over the distribution of scarce resources, mainly water[4]. Arab nomads had moved southwards with their livestock to land mainly occupied by Black African farming communities in search for water and farmland[5]. Black African minority movements accused the Arab government in the capital Khartoum of neglecting the Darfur region and oppressing Non-Arabs.

In response to the uprising of Darfurians, the government of Sudan supported an Arab militia known as the 'Janjaweed', which translates as 'man' or 'devil on horseback'[6]. The Janjaweed spread terror among the non-Arab population by committing mass killings, looting, and systematic rape; they burned down whole villages, driving the surviving inhabitants to flee to refugee camps, where the persecution often continued.

All this was done with the approval of the Sudanese government, which used the militia as their principal counter-insurgency ground force in Darfur against ethnic groups such as the Fur, Zaghawa and Massalit[7] and which denied access to the refugee camps by international human aid organisations[8]. By the summer of 2004, between 50,000 and 100,000 people had been killed and more than 2 million had been driven from their homes, causing a major humanitarian crisis in the region[9].

The attacks against the civilians keep continuing until today.

---

[3] *W. Hinsch/D. Janssen*, Menschenrechte militärisch schützen, Bundeszentrale für politische Bildung, Bonn 2006, p. 206.

[4] Which some believe is a consequence of the desertification due to climate change, see *Ban Ki Moon*, A Climate Culprit In Darfur, Washington Post, Saturday, 16 June 2007, http://www.washingtonpost.com/wp-dyn/content/article/2007/06/15/AR2007061501857.html; http://www.reliefweb.int/library/documents/2005/ici-sub-25feb.pdf.

[5] *J. Flint/A. de Waal*, 'Darfur: A New History of a Long War', Zed Books, London/New York, 2008, pp. 1–8.

[6] *E. Rubin*, New York Times Magazine, 2 April 2006 III.

[7] http://www.hrw.org/legacy/english/docs/2004/07/19/darfur9096.htm.

[8] *W. Hinsch/D. Janssen*, Menschenrechte militärisch schützen, Bundeszentrale für politische Bildung, Bonn 2006, p. 209.

[9] UN News Centre, http://www.un.org/apps/news/story.asp?NewsID=19948&Cr=sudan&Cr1=; for the newest numbers: http://www.cnn.com/2008/WORLD/africa/04/22/darfur.holmes/index.html?eref=rss_topstories; *W. Hinsch/D. Janssen*, Menschenrechte militärisch schützen, Bundeszentrale für politische Bildung, Bonn 2006, p. 201.

III. Reaction of the International Community

In March 2005, more then two years after the war in Darfur had begun to rage, the crisis and the atrocities occurring in the region, reached the attention of the international community. But even though politicians and activists have been spotlighting the genocide unfolding in Darfur, military actions where launched only reluctantly as the Western attention was drawn on the war in Iraq[10]. The United Nations were unable to reach an agreement on a military intervention in the region. UN Resolutions 1556, 1564 and 1574 from 2004, which called on the government in Karthoum to halt the atrocities, disarm the militia, arrest the war criminals and to allow access of aid-organisations to refugee camps, where disregarded by Karthoum[11].

In July 2004, the African Union (AU) had sent troops into Sudan. But the force comprised only 7000 men, whose mandate was restricted to the monitoring of a ceasefire, not for peacekeeping. AU soldiers often had to observe the attacks committed by militias and were, unable to intervene, as they neither had the mandate nor the means to react.

IV. Triggering Proceedings at the ICC

As the international community was unable to stabilize peace in the region, the workup of the conflict was left to the judiciary.

With Resolution 1593 the United Nations Security Council formally referred the situation within Sudan to the prosecutor of the International Criminal Court. The resolution affirmed that justice and accountability were crucial to establishing lasting peace and security in Darfur[12].

A referral by the UN Security Council is one of three ways a 'situation' may reach the ICC. The ways which will induce the beginning of proceedings at the Court are called "trigger mechanisms". These trigger mechanisms play an important role in ensuring the neutrality of the ICC as an institution. The objectivity of the ICC is one difference to ad hoc tribunals, such as Nuremberg, Rwanda or Yugoslavia, which are implemented according to political need.

---

[10] *W. Hinsch/D. Janssen*, Menschenrechte militärisch schützen, Bundeszentrale für politische Bildung, Bonn 2006, p. 210.

[11] http://www.un.org/News/Press/docs/2004/sc8050.doc.htm (accessed 8 February 2009), http://daccessdds.un.org/doc/UNDOC/GEN/N04/364/95/PDF/N0436495.pdf?OpenElement (accessed 8 February 2009), resolutions 1556, 1564, 1574: http://www.un.org/Docs/sc/unsc_resolutions04.html (accessed 8 February2009), http://daccessdds.un.org/doc/UNDOC/GEN/N04/446/02/PDF/N0444602.pdf?OpenElement (accessed 8 February 2009).

[12] http://daccessdds.un.org/doc/UNDOC/GEN/N05/292/73/PDF/N0529273.pdf?OpenElement (accessed 8 February 2009).

Whether this neutrality is achieved remains to be seen. Critics have referred to the ICC as International Court of Africa, since the only pending situations referred to the Court so far are located on the African continent: Democratic Republic of Congo, Central African Republic, Uganda and Sudan[13].

The three mechanisms triggering an investigation by the Office of the Prosecutor (OTP) of the ICC are listed in article 13 of the Rome Statute (RS): Firstly, a 'situation' may be referred to the Court by a member state (article 13 (a) RS). This was the case in Uganda, in which the government asked the ICC to investigate crimes committed by the Lord's Resistance Army, which committed crimes against civilians in the course of achieving the establishment of a state based on the Ten Commandments and Acholi tradition.

Secondly, proceedings may be initiated by the prosecutor himself (article 13 (c) RS). The prosecutor has so far not availed himself of this method. There is much uncertainty as to the criteria by which the OTP will open investigations on a situation. So far, the only factor applied by the OTP has been the number of victims, thus the quantity of crimes committed.

Finally, as was the case with the Darfur crisis, a 'situation' may be referred to the ICC by the UN Security Council (article 13 (b) RS).

At this point it is to be noted, that in all three varieties, not just one case is referred to the ICC, but always an overall political 'situation'. Referring a whole situation to the court and not a *'case'*, is a mechanism to prevent a misuse of the Court's power so that the ICC does not take on proceedings against political opponents only[14].

Once a situation is referred to the ICC, the court has to examine, whether the situation comes under its jurisdiction.

According to article 5 of the Rome Statute, the court grants jurisdiction over the "most serious crimes of concern to the international community as a whole". Four groups of crimes are, so far, considered as "most serious": the crime of genocide, crimes against humanity, war crimes and the crime of aggression. The statute defines each of these crimes except the last mentioned. The Court will not exercise its jurisdiction over the crime of aggression until the member states have agreed on a definition of the crime and set out the conditions under which it may be prosecuted[15]. It is expected that the working group will come up with a definition by May 2009[16].

---

[13] http://www.icc-cpi.int/Menus/ICC?lan=en-GB (accessed 10 February 2009).

[14] http://www.hrr-strafrecht.de/hrr/archiv/08-08/index.php?sz=9#_ftn13; *K. Ambos*, Internationales Strafrecht, § 8, Rn. 10; *C. Kreß*, in Grützner/Pötz, Internationaler Rechtshilfeverkehr in Strafsachen: Die für die Rechtsbeziehungen der Bundesrepublik Deutschland mit dem Ausland in Strafsachen maßgeblichen Bestimmungen, 2nd edition, 60. Nachlieferung (2003), Vor III 26, Rdn. 18; *S. Fernández de Gurmendi*, in: Lee, The International Criminal Court, 175, 180.

[15] United Nations Department of Public Information, December 2002.

[16] http://www.icc-cpi.int/Menus/ASP/Special+Working+Group+on+Aggression/(accessed 10 February 2009).

V. The Suspects

When the Security Council formally referred the situation in Darfur to the prosecutor of the International Criminal Court, it did neither mention any definite crimes nor specific suspects[17]. The investigation was left to the Office of the Prosecutor.

On his request, the pre trial chamber of the ICC issued arrest warrants against former Minister of State for the Interior, *Ahmad Harun*[18], and Janjaweed militia leader, *Ali Kushayb*[19], for crimes against humanity and war crimes in April 2007[20].

Ahmad Harun served as Sudan's Minister of State for the Interior from April 2003 to September 2005. During this time, he coordinated various government bodies in Darfur, including the police, the armed forces, the National Security and Intelligence Service, as well as the Janjaweed militia[21]. It is alleged that *Harun* recruited, funded and armed the Janjaweed, and incited attacks against civilian populations[22].

Today, *Harun* continues to serve as Sudan's Minister of State for Humanitarian Affairs. Ironically, in September 2007, he was appointed to lead a commission whose mandate includes investigating human rights violations in Darfur[23].

The second suspect, *Ali Kushayb*, was commander of the Janjaweed-militia in Sudan since mid 2003. Kushayb is accused by the OTP of having committed crimes against civilians in Darfur by ordering killings, rapes and lootings during the years 2003 and 2004[24].

According to Sudanese authorities *Ali Kushayb* has been arrested in Karthoum for the infringement of Sudanese law which does not include charges of genocide, war crimes or crimes against humanity[25]. However, it is uncertain where

---

[17] UN Press Release SC/8351, Mar. 31, 2005.

[18] http://www.icc-cpi.int/library/cases/ICC-02-05-01-07-2_English.pdf

[19] http://www.icc-cpi.int/library/cases/ICC-02-05-01-07-3_English.pdf

[20] Statement by Mr. *Luis Moreno Ocampo*, Prosecutor of the International Criminal Court, to the United Nations Security Council pursuant to UNSCR 1593 (2005), International Criminal Court, 5 June 2008; Summary of the Case, http://www.icc-cpi.int/library/organs/otp/ICC-OTP-Summary-20081704-ENG.pdf.

[21] International Criminal Court, Warrant of arrest for Ahmad Harun, 27 April 2007.

[22] International Criminal Court, Prosecutor's Application under Article 58(7); *J. Fisher*: ICC claims further isolate Sudan, BBC News, 27 February 2007.

[23] http://www.wantedforwarcrimes.org/index.php/Ahmad-Harun; Prosecutor's Application for Warrant of Arrest under Article 58 Against Omar Hassan Ahmad Al Bashir, II.b, p. 9; http://www.icc-cpi.int/library/organs/otp/ICC-OTP-Summary-20081704-ENG.pdf.

[24] "International Criminal Court names first Darfur war crimes suspects", CRIN.org. Child Rights Information Network (27 February 2007).

[25] http://news.bbc.co.uk/2/hi/africa/7666921.stm.

Mr. *Kushayb* is being kept and whether or not he will be turned in to the International Criminal Court[26].

The third man that may face charges by the ICC is *Omar al-Bashir. Al-Bashir* is president of Sudan since he took power in a coup in 1989 as colonel in the Sudanese army.

On July 14, 2008, the Chief Prosecutor of the International Criminal Court, *Luis Moreno-Ocampo*, filed charges against *Al-Bashir* for the crimes of genocide, crimes against humanity and war crimes committed since 2003 until July 2008 in Darfur[27]. An official warrant of arrest was requested on February 4, 2009. The evidence was submitted to the Pre-trial chamber which has to decide whether to issue an arrest warrant in the coming months. The question whether the ICC will issue an arrest warrant is now pending. The Pre-trial chamber is expected to come to a decision in February 2009[28]. If formally indicted, *Al-Bashir* would become the first incumbent head of state charged by the ICC[29].

It is possible that an arrest warrant for the president of Sudan could prevent further attacks on the 2.5 million refugees by the Arab militia, the Janjaweed, whose actions are, until now, supported by the government.

VI. Personal Responsibility – Mens Rea

According to article 25, para. 2 and 3 of the Rome Statute, a person shall be individually responsible and liable for punishment. The prosecutor must demonstrate criminal responsibility in the indictment.

The warrant of arrest for the former commander of the Janjaweed-militia, *Ali Kushayb*, as issued by the pre-trial chamber discloses 51 counts, which all attest either his own involvement in the crimes or his direct orders to commit them[30]. Thus, the requirement of personal criminal responsibility according to article 25 (3) (a) and (b) is satisfied.

For government officials *Harun* and incumbent president *Al-Bashir*, proving individual responsibility will take more reasoning. The arrest warrant for

[26] The New York Times, Sudan Arrests Militia Chief Facing Trial; BBC, 13 October 2008, http://news.bbc.co.uk/2/hi/africa/7666921.stm.

[27] Prosecutor's Application for Warrant of Arrest under Article 58 Against Omar Hassan Ahmad Al Bashir, http://www.icc-cpi.int/library/organs/otp/ICC-OTP-Summary-2008 1704-ENG.pdf.

[28] http: // www. mg. co. za / article / 2009–02–06-sudan-warns-icc-against-albashir-arrest (accessed 10 February 2009)

[29] "Bashir move bold but problematic", BBC News (accessed 14 July 2008).

[30] http://www.icc-cpi.int/Menus/ICC/Situations+and+Cases/Situations/Situation+ICC+0205/Related+Cases/ICC+0205+0107/Court+Records/Chambers/Pre+Trial+Chamber+I/WARRANT+OF+ARREST+FOR+ALI+KUSHAYB.htm (accessed 8 February 2009).

Harun states his accountability according to article 25 (3) (b) and (d) RS, as there are 'reasonable grounds to believe that *Ahmad Harun*, by virtue of his [...] position, had knowledge of the crimes committed against the civilian population and of the methods used by the Militia/Janjaweed' and that by his public speeches, he 'personally encouraged the commission of such illegal acts'.[31]

In his arrest warrant request for *Al-Bashir*, the ICC-Prosecutor does not allege that the president carried out the charged crimes physically or directly. The crimes were rather committed through indirect action by members of the state apparatus, the army and the militia.[32]

The government of Sudan denies any responsibility for the barbarity of the Janjaweed overall. It refers to the ancient tribal conflict between nomadic Arabs and African farmers in Darfur and it claims inability to control the militias.[33] Only last week, the Sudanese government had warned that 'it would use "all options" available if the International Criminal Court (ICC) were to issue an international arrest warrant for President *Omar al-Bashir*'.[34]

The ICC Prosecution presented evidence showing that *Al-Bashir* 'masterminded and implemented a plan to destroy in substantial part the Fur, Masalit and Zaghawa groups, on account of their ethnicity' and thus, to commit genocide.[35]

Without the support of the government, the militia would under no circumstances have been able to engage in such an extent in the terror campaign. Not only was there no official attempt to stop the militia and no aid from the government for the victims, but humanitarian assistance from NGOs and the international community was deliberately blocked.

Moreover, the government allowed the attacks against those people who had sought shelter in refugee camps to continue.[36] The government used the attacks on the civilian population as part of a governmental policy of counterinsurgency. Instead of directly targeting the rebels in Darfur, the government of Sudan deployed militias which would overtly terrorise and demoralise the civilian population of Darfur. The strategy was to pit tribes against tribes, without hav-

---

[31] http://www.icc-cpi.int/iccdocs/doc/doc279813.PDF (accessed 8 February 2009).

[32] Prosecutor's Application for Warrant of Arrest under Article 58 Against Omar Hassan Ahmad Al Bashir, http://www.icc-cpi.int/library/organs/otp/ICC-OTP-Summary-20081704-ENG.pdf.

[33] *E. Rubin*, New York Times Magazine, 2 April 2006, III.

[34] http://www.mg.co.za/article/2009–02–06-sudan-warns-icc-against-albashir-arrest.

[35] http://www.icc-cpi.int/menus/icc/situations%20and%20cases/situations/situation%20icc%200205/press%20releases/a (accessed 6 February 2009).

[36] Prosecutor's Application for Warrant of Arrest under Article 58 Against Omar Hassan Ahmad Al Bashir, II.b, p. 5, 6; http://www.icc-cpi.int/library/organs/otp/ICC-OTP-Summary-20081704-ENG.pdf (accessed 19 October 2008).

ing to take any responsibility for the crimes that the militias were committing.[37]

The Sudanese government controlled the militia completely and actively contributed to the attacks.[38] The pattern, in which the attacks were performed, demonstrates that the militia operated jointly with the Sudanese Army[39] and hence were supported by Khartoum:[40]

Before attacking a village, the Janjaweed were provided by the Sudanese military with ammunition;[41] the army provided logistical support. The armed forces singled out villages and towns inhabited mainly by members of the targeted groups. They would surround the place with trucks and land cruisers in cooperation with the Janjaweed, arriving on camels or on horseback.[42]

The Sudanese Air Force would then drop bombs on the village so that Janjaweed ground forces could then enter the village and attack the civilian inhabitants, who were not part of the rebel groups. The attacks in Darfur were directed against unarmed civilian targets. The Janjaweed would kill men, children, elderly and women and commit mass rapes. They would leave the village looted and burned.[43]

As President of Sudan and as Commander in Chief of the Armed Forces, *Omar Al- Bashir* had sovereign control over the state's authority. The government of Sudan recruited, armed and refused to disarm the Janjaweed. As head of the government, *Al-Bashir* had knowledge of the looting of villages, and the torture, rape, killings and persecution of innocent civilians by the Janjaweed. The government controlled and directed the perpetrators by covering up their actions systematically using the state-controlled media, giving false official

[37] Prosecutor's Application for Warrant of Arrest under Article 58 Against Omar Hassan Ahmad Al Bashir, III., http://www.icc-cpi.int/library/organs/otp/ICC-OTP-Summary-20081704-ENG.pdf; *W. Hinsch/D. Janssen*, Menschenrechte militärisch schützen, Bundeszentrale für politische Bildung, Bonn 2006, p. 215.

[38] Report of the International Commission of Inquiry on Darfur to the United Nations Secretary-General, 25 January 2005, para. 551 ff., http://www.un.org/News/dh/sudan/com_inq_darfur.pdf.

[39] http://www.zeit.de/online/2008/30/voelkerrecht-diktatoren, *W. Hinsch/D. Janssen*, Menschenrechte militärisch schützen, Bundeszentrale für politische Bildung, Bonn 2006, p. 216.

[40] Prosecutor's Application for Warrant of Arrest under Article 58 Against Omar Hassan Ahmad Al Bashir, III. b, http://www.icc-cpi.int/library/organs/otp/ICC-OTP-Summary-20081704-ENG.pdf.

[41] *E. Rubin*, New York Times Magazine, 2 April 2006, VI.

[42] Prosecutor's Application for Warrant of Arrest under Article 58 Against Omar Hassan Ahmad Al Bashir, III.b, http://www.icc-cpi.int/library/organs/otp/ICC-OTP-Summary-20081704-ENG.pdf (accessed 19 October 2008).

[43] Prosecutor's Application for Warrant of Arrest under Article 58 Against Omar Hassan Ahmad Al Bashir, III.b, http://www.icc-cpi.int/library/organs/otp/ICC-OTP-Summary-20081704-ENG.pdf (accessed 19 October 2008).

statements, denying the events in Darfur and by providing the essential means for the attacks.

Involving the whole state apparatus to perform the crimes, including the armed forces, the intelligence service as well as the justice system, which deliberately failed to prosecute the perpetrators, is enough evidence to prove the planning of the crimes and the individual responsibility of the accused.[44]

VII. ICC Jurisdiction over Darfur?

The Sudanese government in Khartoum contends that the ICC has no jurisdiction to try Sudanese citizens and that it will not hand the accused over to the Court.

Certainly, the Court does not have the universal jurisdiction which was originally proposed during the negotiations that led to the Rome Statute. This proposal was defeated mainly due to the opposition from the United States[45], who feared that US soldiers participating in peacekeeping operations might be charged for their actions by the Court[46].

Compromising, the Court's jurisdiction is based on the principles of territoriality (article 12 (2) (a) RS), active personality (article 12 (2) (b) RS) and complementary (article 17 RS).

Active personality and territoriality imply that the Court may exercise its jurisdiction only in cases where the accused is a citizen of a member state or where the alleged crime took place on the territory of a member state. Given these premises, the ICC would not have jurisdiction over the accused as Sudan is not a member state of the ICC.

However, according to article 13 (b) of the Rome Statute, the ICC has jurisdiction over any state, including non-member states, if a situation is referred to the Court by the United Nations Security Council, as was the case with Sudan[47]. This power granted to the Security Council to intervene into internal affairs of non-member states is not a novelty in international law. According to article 41 of the UN Charter, the Security Council is even provided the power to implement whole new tribunals without consent of the affected state[48].

---

[44] Prosecutor's Application for Warrant of Arrest under Article 58 Against Omar Hassan Ahmad Al Bashir, II.b, p. 7; http://www.icc-cpi.int/library/organs/otp/ICC-OTP-Summary-20081704-ENG.pdf (accessed 19 October 2008).

[45] International Criminal Court, Assembly of States Parties, Accessed 2 October 2008.

[46] *M. Zwanenburg*, The Statute for an International Criminal Court and the United States: Peace Without Justice?, Leiden Journal of International Law (1999), pp. 1–7, *journals.cambridge.org/production/action/cjoGetFulltext?fulltextid=207682.*

[47] UN Resolution 1593/2005 from March 2005.

[48] ICTY Appeals Chamber, Tadic decision, 2. 10. 1995, para. 32–38, http://www.un.org./

Furthermore, the ICC is intended as a court of last resort. In contrast to ad-hoc tribunals, the ICC can exercise its jurisdiction only if national courts are unwilling or unable to investigate or prosecute the crimes *(article 17 RS)*. According to the Non-bis-in-idem paradigm prevailing in international criminal law, the Court does not have jurisdiction over a person, who has already been tried for the offence by another court *(article 20 (3) RS)*.

Primary responsibility to investigate and punish crimes is hence left to individual states, unless the state's prosecution is seriously inadequate.

The government of Sudan declared that the ICC investigation is unnecessary, as Sudanese courts are conducting their own investigations and prosecutions for crimes that may have occurred in Darfur. Immediately after *Moreno-Ocampo* declared in June 2005 that the people he was likely to investigate would not face justice in Sudanese courts, *Al-Bashir*'s ministry of justice announced the creation of the Darfur Special Criminal Court[49].

However, according to a report of the UN Special correspondent on the situation of human rights in Sudan (*Simar Samar*), the criminal prosecution of the crimes within Sudan is incomplete. Not a single person has been convicted of rape in Darfur[50]. Investigations in cases that were brought up against Janjaweed or defence forces were dropped[51]. So far, sentences were passed only in minor, insignificant cases, such as for stealing of sheep[52]. It is noteworthy that Sudanese courts have, instead, convicted several pilots, who *refused* to fly bombing missions over Darfur. The man who decides, which cases will go to the Darfur Special Criminal Court is the prosecutor of South Darfur, *Mauwia Abdullah Ahmed*, who is a member of one of Darfur's Arab tribes.

The prosecution of war crimes and the severe human rights violations within Sudan is far from sufficient. The central function of the established Darfur Special Court is to give the illusion of investigations of the crimes and thus to prevent the prosecution of members of the government by the ICC.

At the present stage, the criminal responsibility of the incumbent head of state, *Omar al-Bashir*, and his minister *Ahmed Harun* is neither being prosecuted nor investigated by Sudanese officials[53]. The charges made by the Court's Office of the Prosecutor may however contribute to initiate a peace process by the Sudanese government. As it rejects the ICC it might strive to promote a

---

icty/tadic/appeal/decision-e/51002.htm; also: *K. Ambos*, NJW 1998, p. 3743 (3744); *B. Hecker*, Europäisches Strafrecht, 2nd edition (2007), § 2, Rn. 88.

[49] *E. Rubin*, New York Times Magazine, 2 April 2006.

[50] *E. Rubin*, New York Times Magazine, 2 April 2006, III.

[51] *E. Rubin*, New York Times Magazine, 2 April 2006, III.

[52] *E. Rubin*, New York Times Magazine, 2 April 2006, IV.

[53] Prosecutor's Application for Warrant of Arrest under Article 58 Against Omar Hassan Ahmad Al Bashir, II, http://www.icc-cpi.int/library/organs/otp/ICC-OTP-Summary-20081704-ENG.pdf.

proper internal resolving of the crisis by national courts so as to prevent the case including the suspects being brought to The Hague.

VIII. Further Proceedings

The prosecutor will formally indict the accused, if there are enough grounds for suspicion, and correspondingly open preliminary proceedings.

Subsequently, the Pre-Trial Chamber (PTC) will initiate investigations, however, only to a limited extent, as the Rome Statute is based on the idea of the adversarial procedure of the Common law system, where the prosecution and the defence are facing each other as opponents and each have to present evidence (see article 61 RS and rules 22 and 111 to 216, Rules of Procedure and Evidence[54]).

In the event that the accused surrenders to the Court, the Pre Trial Chamber will hold a hearing. If the PTC finds that there is sufficient evidence, it will confirm the charges made by the prosecutor and commit the person to the Trial Chamber (articles 60, 61 RS). The Trial Chamber will then start the trial against the accused, which is held in public. According to article 63 Rome Statute, a trial may not take place in absence of the accused.

The Pre-Trial-Chamber issues an arrest warrant, if there are reasonable grounds to believe that the person has committed a crime within the jurisdiction of the Court and an arrest warrant is necessary (article 58 RS). If the arrest warrants against *Harun* and *Kushayb* are executed, the suspects could be brought to the UN-detention centre, in Scheveningen, The Hague.

In the case of *Omar al-Bashir* the decision, of the Pre-Trial Chamber, whether to issue an arrest warrant against the president, has yet to be made. In the case of *Harun* and *Kushayb*, arrest warrants have been issued. However, Sudan has not surrendered the suspects to the Court.

The ICC does not have its own police in order to arrest suspects and accused partied, but has to rely on the cooperation of the state in which it is investigating or where the suspect resides.

The Pre-Trial-Chamber may transmit a request for arrest and surrender to the state in which the accused party is believed to sojourn (articles 89, 91 RS). However, since two of their state officials are charged by the ICC, the Sudanese government rejects its jurisdiction. Thus it is unlikely it will surrender the suspects.

---

[54] http://www2.icc-cpi.int/NR/rdonlyres/F1E0AC1C-A3F3-4A3C-B9A7-B3E8B115E886/140164/Rules_of_procedure_and_Evidence_English.pdf (accessed 8 February 2009)

Sudan's refusal to cooperate with the Court also makes a gathering of evidence almost impossible. The investigators cannot gather any forensic evidence from the crime scenes. They are restricted to the collection of written material and other documents, with a focus on investigating witness testimonies[55]. And, as the security of the victims and their families who are serving as witnesses is at risk, no investigations take place in Darfur. All hearings take place outside of Sudan[56].

IX. The ratio of Justice and Peace – Suspension and Deferral of Proceedings

The prosecutor may refrain from initiating an investigation, if it would not serve "the interests of justice" (Article 53 I lit. c RS). For this decision, the prosecutor takes into account the gravity of the crime on the one hand and the interest of the victim on the other hand. It is possible that the safety of victims who may give testimony is endangered because of insecure conditions within the state where the crime was committed. The prosecutor has to use his discretion in favour of the witnesses' safety, if no measures of protection provide adequate security.

The Rome Statute does not envisage the principle of mandatory prosecution (principle of legality), as prevailing in the Civil Law system. However, the ICC follows the general paradigm, that the most severe infringements of human rights must be prosecuted by the Court, given its jurisdiction. Article 53 I RS provides an exception to this rule[57]. However, the pre-trial chamber may overrule the decision of the prosecutor and obligate him/her to begin investigating.

The main purpose of the International Criminal Court is the provision of justice as a key factor for peace. Therefore, procedures that would form an obstacle to peace or a peace process are to be avoided. Article 16 RS empowers the UN Security Council to defer an ongoing ICC-prosecution for one year, if it imposes a threat or breach of peace according to chapter VII of the UN Charter. This could be the case, for example, if the judicial prosecution of a conflict runs counter to a peace- or reconciliation process.

This arrangement gives a political institution enormous power over the Court. But it is legitimized by the very function of the Security Council according to Article 24 UN Charter, being the main body to maintain global peace.

For Darfur, such a Security Council resolution would be appropriate, if the prosecution of *Kushayb*, *Harun* and *Al-Bashir* were to impede efforts within

---

[55] *E. Rubin*, New York Times Magazine, 2 April 2006, II.

[56] *Moreno-Ocampo* in: Berliner Zeitung, 1 June 2006.

[57] *A. Nguyen*, Online Zeitschrift für höchstrichterliche Rechtsprechung in Strafsachen (HRRS), 8/2008. pp. 372, 373.

Sudan to resolve the conflict. However, as in Sudan no reconciliation processes are taking place at present a deferral-resolution is unlikely.

The option of a deferral-resolution may, however, be used by the Security Council as a political means to increase pressure on the Sudanese government to cooperate with the United Nations/ African Union Hybrid Mission in Darfur (UNAMID). The suspension of the ICC-investigations could be offered in return[58].

However, given that the Security Council has already decided in favour of a criminal prosecution of those responsible and therefore negated a threat to peace by referring the situation to the ICC, and due to the crimes against human rights that have already been committed, this approach seems rather unlikely.

X. Sentencing

If a trial against the suspects *Harun*, *Kushayb* and eventually *Al-Bashir* takes place it is likely that they would face a sentence.

The Rome Statute adheres to the classic retributive forms of sanctions, based on the philosophy of punishment. In case of a conviction, article 77 of the Rome Statute provides the Court with the power to impose a prison sentence for up to 30 years as well as, in restricted circumstances, a life sentence. But the sentence may also be a fine or the forfeiture of any profits that the accused has gained from the crime[59].

Unfortunately, the Statute does not envisage any types of restorative reactions to crime alternative to punishment such as of reconciliation or compensation. Such measures would enable the parties of conflict to initiate a dialogue and are more likely to promote a peace process than are retributive forms of punishment.

XI. Conclusion

The ICC's investigation against *Kushayb*, *Harun* and *Al-Bashir* is fulfilling the goal of the International Criminal Court as to prosecute and punish the most serious crimes of concern to the international community.

---

[58] *A. Nguyen*, Online Zeitschrift für höchstrichterliche Rechtsprechung in Strafsachen (HRRS), 8/2008. p. 376.

[59] For details, see Rules 145–148 ICC Rules of Procedure and Evidence, http://www2.icc-cpi.int/NR/rdonlyres/F1E0AC1C-A3F3-4A3C-B9A7-B3E8B115E886/140164/Rules_of_procedure_and_Evidence_English.pdf (accessed 9 February 2009).

However, the indictment of Sudanese officials by the ICC in 2007 was highly disputed internationally. The targeted population of Darfur as well as Human Rights organisations are supporting the engagement of the ICC as a means to halt the continuing violence in the region[60]. On the other hand UN officials, such as UN General Secretary *Ban Ki Moon*, as well as other politicians were concerned that the security of the joint peacekeeping forces (UNAMID) might be endangered by legal prosecutions of Sudanese government members. Accordingly, the announcement of the arrest warrants against *Harun* and *Kushayb* in 2007 was followed by attacks on UN troops in Sudan.

In November 2008, the ICC-prosecutor presented evidence against rebel commanders for their alleged responsibility for crimes committed against African Union peacekeepers in Darfur on 29th September 2007[61].

Notwithstanding the concerns for security, the official prosecution of the crimes is a basic prerequisite for enduring peace in the conflict region Darfur. If those responsible for the atrocities are not held accountable, the violence will continue. The government of Sudan is fighting a proxy-war on its own behalf, using the engrained conflict between ethnic groups in Darfur allowing and supporting severe human rights violations. As a result of the announced indictment by the ICC's Office of the Prosecutor, the government in Khartoum is now in the limelight of the international community.

In that sense, the referral to the ICC is a decisive measure to halt the continuing violation of human rights in Sudan, the more so as the international community was not able or willing to launch military interventions. Although for many victims the attention of the international community comes too late, the prosecution may yet contribute to put an end to the attacks against civilians, the more so as the international community was not able or willing to launch military interventions.

But first and foremost, the recognition by the International Criminal Court of the crimes that have been committed against the people of Darfur shows respect for those whose human rights have been and continue to be violated. Tribute is paid to the victims if the perpetrators of these crimes are brought to account at fair trials. And worldwide confidence is promoted in the fact that there is an international institution that condemns severe human rights violations.

If the ICC cannot bring peace, at least it can provide justice.

---

[60] Amnesty International press release July 2008, http://www.amnesty.org/en/for-media/press-releases/sudan-international-criminal-court-important-step-20080714; *E. Rubin*, New York Times Magazine, 2 April 2006, VII with further reference.

[61] http://www.icc-cpi.int/press/pressreleases/447.html.

The Rights of the Accused in International Criminal Proceedings

The Choice of a Procedural Model According to the Specific Requirements of International Law

Elisa Hoven

I. Introduction

"The ICTY is, in certain respects, comparable to a military tribunal, which often has limited rights of due process and more lenient rules of evidence."[1]

This controversial statement, through which the International Criminal Tribunal for the Former Yugoslavia (ICTY) sought to define its function, illustrates the problematic nature of the protection of human rights in the course of international legal procedures. The guarantee of a fair trial and the extent of the defendants' rights have not yet been determined on an international level. Should, according to the statement of the ICTY, lower standards really be applied to proceedings at international tribunals? Due to the severity of the violations of international law, the public often shows little understanding of the need for a fair trial. It seems to contradict the human sense of justice that defendants want the principles of human rights to be respected, since they themselves refuted their validity during their term of office. Considering the ICTY's comments and the reservations on the part of the public, the following question should be put forward: why is it important that defendants be treated fairly in international tribunals? The answer can be found in the very nature of international trials. These serve the purpose of sanctioning exceedingly severe crimes against humanity and punishing breaches of international law. Justice can only truly triumph over injustice if legal premises are not dispensed with, even when judging the most severe crimes. If criminal proceedings should serve the purpose of uncovering fundamental ethical principles, they in turn should fulfil the strict

---

[1] *Tadic* (IT-94-1), Decision on the Prosecutor's Motion Requesting Measures for Victims and Witnesses, 10 August 1995, Para. 28.

criteria of human dignity and fairness. The often contested legitimacy of international tribunals judging international crimes against peace and human rights can only be justified, if the tribunals themselves manifest the highest standards to be expected from a State under the rule of law. This notion also formed the basis for the development of the Rome Statute for the International Criminal Court in The Hague. This court should especially strive to guarantee the basic principles of a fair trial. Using the example of its first trial, we shall see later whether it was able to achieve this. So far, the defendant's rights have been determined on a national level; the recent development of an international jurisdiction however has transformed them into an international concern. The impacts of globalisation have made the concept of human rights well-known worldwide. They have also strengthened awareness of the need for an international community in order to effectively sanction international crime. Advancing globalisation gave rise to international cooperation, which in turn enabled the creation of international tribunals in which proceedings against individuals could be carried out on the basis of individual criminal responsibility. Until recently, mainly States could be subjected to international law; now it can also be applied to individuals. The question regarding the rights to which a defendant is entitled in the course of a criminal procedure now has to be settled on an international level. The development of international law requires that the scale and scope of guarantees of legal proceedings and of the defendant's legal protection be universally defined. The particularities of international law have to be taken into consideration whilst elaborating internationally valid rights of defence. Criminal prosecution on an international level entails certain problematic aspects, which do not exist on a national level.

II. Particularities in International Criminal Law

1. Complexity of the Juridical System

One major problematic aspect of international criminal law is the normative nature of its foundations. The defendant's rights are elaborated individually in the Statutes of the respective courts. The actual tribunal determines how the statute is implemented. This can either occur through a resolution of the Security Council or an international agreement. Both, however, require the cooperation between several countries. Thus the creation of the ICC obliged 160 countries to find consensus in the choice of its legal basis. The countries' representatives were accustomed to different legal traditions and thus showed differing approaches in defining international trial law. Anglo-American common law and continental civil law in particular manifest many dissimilarities and had to be reconciled in the form of the ICC statute. This attempt to combine heterogeneous elements has greatly shaped the statute: it is therefore often referred to as a "compromise solution"[2].

The difficult and non-uniform interaction of the different elements having to do with rights, justifies the complexity of international law regarding criminal procedure. The absence of a generally valid standard and congruent procedural maxims make the work more difficult for the organs involved.

The complicated procedural law makes self-defence nearly impossible, since an effective defence of legal positions requires comprehensive legal advice.

In the case of Erdemovic, the problem of the juridical system for the accused became clear. Erdemovic pleaded guilty before the Trial Chamber of the ICTY and after the acknowledgment of his confession, was condemned to 10 years detention[3]. The Appeals Chamber of the Court stated that the accused was not sufficiently informed about the consequences of the process. Erdemovic had pleaded guilty because his defender had promised him a clear reduction of punishment. His lawyer, who came from a continental-European juridical system, did not have sufficient knowledge of the procedural consequences of a guilty plea[4]. It was even difficult for a defender to grasp the different rules of procedure and the legal consequences thereof. Based on this case, there are two possible starting points for improving international criminal procedure. On the one hand, the demand for international unity and consistent procedural law finds support. On the other hand, it becomes clear that the protection of the accused's interests should not be left only to the defence. In view of the complexity of the legal bases, it would be good to extend the responsibility for the legal rights of the accused to the other organs involved.

The compromise between common law and civil law leads to a further problem in the criminal procedure regarding individuals. The connection between the diverging elements also affects the conception and task perception of judges and State lawyers. Since no juridical system has been consistently realized, the organs involved frequently exercise rights and obligations which work against their goals. Their self-understanding is not clearly defined internationally and is therefore guided by national origins.

"[T]here is a strong likelihood that each judge will tend to be guided by his or her own legal experience, and that the procedure of different chambers will actually vary as a result. The disadvantages and potential unfairness, which this may create, weighs particularly heavily on the defendant"[5].

---

[2] *T. Wilhelmini*, Die Verfahrensordnung des Internationalen Strafgerichtshofs – Modell eines universalen Strafverfahrensrechts?, IRP 24 (2004), p. 7 (44).

[3] *ICTY Erdemovic* (IT-96–22-T), Sentencing Judgement, 29 November 1996.

[4] *ICTY Erdemovic* (IT-96–22-A), Judgement, 7 October 1997.

[5] *J. Borek*, The proposed International Criminal Court, in: P. Cullen/W. Gilmore (eds.), Crime sans frontiers: International and European Legal Approaches, Edinburgh 1998, p. 79.

The complexity of the international law of criminal procedure, which connects continental-European and Anglo-American elements in different ways, can lead to uncertainties when looking at the rights of the accused and the role of the organs involved.

2. *Equality of Arms in Gathering Evidence*

A further problem, especially in international criminal procedure, is the lack of equality of arms among the parties as regards proof gathering.

The courts often hold trials outside of the country in which a crime was committed. The distance between the court and the site of the crime can significantly decrease the accessibility of witnesses and complicate access to important evidence. As internal conflicts often play an important role in such cases, the respective national legal systems are often very fragile. This weakness can lead to the retention or even the destruction of important documents. Investigators are thus very dependant on various forms of cooperation between countries. The defence does not dispose of the necessary financial means and personnel to be able to conduct adequate investigations. The prosecution authorities, however, investigate over a period of several months or even years and have so-called "field offices" at their disposal. They are able to admit prosecution witnesses into witness protection programmes and can hold out the prospect of compensation. The defence lacks the necessary financial means and sufficient employees to be able to conduct similar investigations. One also has to consider the fact that, compared to public prosecutors, lawyers do not have a diplomatic status, which would considerably facilitate the essential cooperation in the country in which the crime was committed. In view of the guarantee of a fair trial, these discrepancies represent an offence against the principle of equality of arms. This principle implies that the accused may not be put at a serious procedural disadvantage with respect to the prosecution. In national law, one of the main consequences deriving from this notion is that the accused must have the right to examine the evidence gathered by the prosecution in support of the charges. In international law, the principle of equality of arms must go further. A fair trial must ensure that both parties have the same opportunities to obtain evidence.

3. *The case of Thomas Lubanga as an Example for Specific Problems in International Criminal Law*

The specific problems regarding the rights of the accused in international criminal proceedings can be illustrated by means of the example of the *Thomas Lubanga* case. In this case, both the complexity of the legal order and the difficulty in collecting proof endangered the guarantee of a fair procedure.

a) *Facts of the Case*

Thomas Lubanga was the president of the Union of Congolese Patriots (UPC), a militia group acting in the north-eastern region of the Democratic Republic of Congo that has been implicated in many serious abuses including ethnic massacres, torture, and rape. As the ICC's first defendant, *Lubanga* was charged with the war crimes of enlisting and conscripting children under the age of 15 years as soldiers and using them to actively participate in hostilities. He was arrested in the Congo on those charges and brought into ICC custody in March 2006. The trial against *Lubanga* should have begun this year on June 23rd and play a pioneering role as the court's first trial.

However, the following problem occurred: in the course of his enquiries, the prosecutor received more than 200 documents with potentially exculpatory information. This information had been confidentially given to him and he was therefore not permitted to pass on the documents. Hence the prosecutor was confronted with two contradictory obligations. Under the provision of article 54(3)(e) of the Rome Statute, the prosecution can agree to receive documents or information on a confidential basis, but "solely for the purpose of generating new evidence." This confidential information is supposed to be a "springboard" for the prosecution to collect new evidence in its investigations that can be used at trial.

On the other hand, 67 II ICC-Statute obliges the prosecutor to disclose all exculpatory evidence to the defence. The obligatory disclosure on the part of the prosecutor was defined by the ICC to ensure that the principle of equality of arms be respected in spite of the different conditions of the prosecution and defence. If the prosecutor is able to investigate evidence under better conditions, he must be obliged to disclose his findings to the defence. Considering this background, the contradiction becomes apparent: on the one hand, the prosecutor is not allowed to disclose confidential information; on the other hand, he is obliged to disclose all information to the defence.

b) *The ICC's Decision*

Can equality of arms be guaranteed, if more than 200 potentially exculpatory documents cannot be passed on by the prosecutor due to their confidentiality?

The judges of the Trial Chamber responded negatively to this question and unanimously decided to "stay" the proceedings against *Lubanga*, thus suspending the International Criminal Court's (ICC) first-ever trial[6]. In its decision, the Trial Chamber criticized the prosecution's "excessive use" of article 54(3)(e) in collecting information in its investigations. According to the judges, "the right to a fair trial includes an entitlement to disclosure of exculpatory materi-

---

[6] ICC Trial Chamber, The Prosecutor v. Thomas Lubanga (ICC-01/04-01-06/1401), 13th June 2008.

al". As the prosecutor was not able to disclose the documents to the defence, the trial was temporarily closed until, after long negotiations, a compromise was reached:

The prosecutor is obliged to provide the court with all of the relevant potentially exculpatory documents. In order to assist the Chamber in its review of the documents, the Chamber ordered the prosecution to file with the Registry copies of the documents which cannot be disclosed directly to the defence. These are to be highlighted so as to reveal the particular passages which the prosecution believes may have exculpatory value, and each passage is to be accompanied by a short explanation saying why it may have an exculpatory effect or may assist the defence in other ways. At this point the Court has to assume the responsibilities of the defence and sift through the exculpatory material.

c) Conclusion

The *Thomas Lubanga* case shows that the preservation of the defendant's rights is indeed of great importance in the ICC's jurisdiction. The Court has found a solution, which strives to find a compromise between the guarantee of a fair trial and the actual conducting of an international criminal proceeding. Nevertheless the regulation considerably restricts the rights of the defence. Lawyers are not able to plan their defence themselves, as they must rely on the work carried out by the Court. The ability to design their own strategies and to conduct further investigations based on the documents has been taken away from them. Even though the ICC has given proof of great awareness as regards a fair trial, the causes of difficulties in creating a fair trial lie deeper. The defendant's rights have to be backed by material guarantees and organisational structures. Especially the difficulty in collecting evidence on an international scale and the inconsistent function of the prosecutor prove to be problematic. Both lead to difficulties in the defence of the accused. To solve this problem, two measures must be taken. Firstly, existing norms have to be interpreted and applied, as the ICC did in the *Lubanga* case, whilst protecting the defendant's rights as far as possible. If one wishes to go a step further and also implement the concept of due process, the procedural law governing international tribunals has to be changed fundamentally.

III. Suggestions in View of the Organizational Arrangement

1. Applicable Procedural Law

The *Lubanga* case showed that a substantial problem of the international criminal procedure lies in the arrangement of process rights and obligations. At the same time it became clear that a significant imbalance exists between prosecution and defence, which requires a new weighting of the way the task is perceived. On this background, existing rules of procedure (in view of their connection) are to be examined in view of continental European and Anglo-American elements. Based on the specific problems regarding international criminal law, a suggestion to change the process system is to be developed.

a) Past Legal Situation

A comparison of the normative bases of international tribunals shows that so far no unified international law of criminal procedure could be developed. Courts are not bound to a standardized procedure; rather, they foresee different process procedures where content and structure are concerned. Since there is no common standard on an international level for the definition of obligatory conditions, tribunal rules of procedure are based on the national juridical systems of the States involved. The influence of diverging basic assumptions in national legal systems as regards international criminal proceedings manifests the difference between their normative and structural starting points.

aa) Diverging Principles in Common Law and Civil Law. Anglo-American common law and continental European civil law are based on diverse and opposing starting points for the guarantee of a fair procedure. A substantial difference in the process models exists already in their formal organization as adversarial or inquisitive procedures. The negotiations in the common law system are led as party processes between the prosecutor and the defence. While the judge in this procedure takes on to a large extent a positive role, obtaining evidence and process organization are excluded from the parties' tasks.

In the process of procedure guidance, prosecution and defence face each other antagonistically and to a certain extent deny negotiations as legal process "opponents".[7] The functions of judge and prosecutor in the inquisitive procedure of civil law deviate substantially from the stated principles in common law. The prosecutor is not just a party in the procedure, but is obligated as a neutral authority to be objective and honest. His investigation serves to independently clarify circumstances and not only to incriminate the accused.

The duties of the judge are also extended by the continental European rights. While in the common law system, the court makes its decision based solely on the proof and argumentations presented by the parties, the judge in civil law is officially obligated to independently clarify circumstances.[8] The court's connection to the investigative principle represents an important conceptual differ-

---

[7] *T. Wilhelmini*, Die Verfahrensordnung des Internationalen Strafgerichtshofs – Modell eines universalen Strafverfahrensrechts?, IRP 24 (2004), p. 7 (11).

[8] *T. Wilhelmini*, Die Verfahrensordnung des Internationalen Strafgerichtshofs – Modell eines universalen Strafverfahrensrechts?, IRP 24 (2004), p. 7 (23).

ence to the Anglo-American legal order, which crucially affects the organization of procedure. In view of the judge's passive role in common law, the expiration of the procedure is in principle incumbent on the parties through the designation and questioning of witnesses. Cross examination is the central way of processing, whereby the procedures are navigated by means of a clear process. Civil law does not have such a procedural structure, but instead transfers the main negotiation and the hearing of evidence to the judge. The questioning of witnesses and experts is done in co-operation with the parties; however, in its actual order it stands according to the discretion of the court.

This short representation has shown that the common law and civil law juridical systems contain fundamental differences as to the functions of the involved and the general order of operation. In view of these important divergences, the question arises, how a connection between the conflicting process orders at the level of criminal law regarding individuals could be realized.

bb) The Combination of Common Law and Civil Law in the Legal System of the International Courts. In the following, we shall examine the sources of the rights of the ICC and the ad hoc tribunals by asking how substantial the Anglo-American and continental European elements are.

(1) The Legal Bases of the Ad Hoc Tribunals (a) Establishment according to the Parameters of the Anglo-American Procedural Model. The Statutes of the ad hoc tribunals for Yugoslavia and Rwanda entered into force by resolution of the Security Council. The work of the Security Council and its adoption of resolutions concerning the organisation of the tribunals were lastingly affected by the United States. Already in the context of the tribunals of Nuremberg and Tokyo, the USA had taken considerable part in the setting up of the courts and the development of the basic foundation for their process. Based on this past procedural practice and its international political weight, the USA could to a large extent use its common law model with the establishment of ad hoc tribunals by the Security Council. On the background of its historical significance for international criminal law and of the political influence of the United States on the decision-making authority of the Security Council, the Anglo- American influence on the statutes is self-explanatory.

"The United States had basically culturally hijacked the institution. (..) It was a common law jurisdiction, and the way of doing business was very North American because the Americans were there from day one"[9].

[9] *L. Arbour*, Crimes against Women under International Law, Berkeley Journal of International Law 21 (2003), p. 196 (209).

As well, the systems of procedure and of proof for the tribunals were first based on the premises of the Anglo-American juridical system.[10] Again, special significance must be given to the USA in the development of the RPE, which reflected the contents of mostly North American legal convictions. The suggestions for the procedural organization submitted by the USA were taken up in the final version of the process systems and adopted without making any fundamental changes.[11] Furthermore, the responsibility for the resolution of the RPE was the legal basis of the ad hoc tribunal established with the judges of these tribunals, who themselves came predominantly from the Anglo-American juridical circle and in principle favoured adversarial tendencies[12]. The development of ad hoc procedural law clarified the close relationship between the normative adjustment of the process systems and the legal background of the organs involved. The competence of the Security Council and the installation of judges from the Anglo-American jurisdiction resulted in common law making a significant impression on the procedural structures.

(b) The Later influence of the Continental-European Juridical System. "Since then there has been much discussion about whether that was a good idea. It may not have been"[13].

During the court's initial work, the weak points of the Anglo-American procedural practice at the level of international criminal procedure became increasingly obvious[14]. Problems arose in particular regarding the position of the defence, whose investigation process was made substantially more difficult by a ruling concerning pre-trial custody and the lack of State co-operation.

In view of the protection of the principles of fairness and equality of arms, the classical model of adversarial procedure could not be used without further restrictions to international criminal law. After adjusting the normative regulations to the challenges of international jurisdiction, practical needs made the inclusion of elements from continental European law necessary. The reality of the judicial procedure proved that implementing Anglo-American elements

---

[10] *S. van Heeck*, Die Weiterentwicklung des formellen Völkerstrafrechts, Düsseldorf, 2006, p. 77.

[11] Suggestions made by the Government of the United States of America for Rules of Procedure and Evidence for the Prosecution of Persons Responsible for Serious Violations of International Humanitarian Law Committed in the Former Yugoslavia, UN Doc.: IT/14, 17 November 1993.

[12] *S. van Heeck*, Die Weiterentwicklung des formellen Völkerstrafrechts, Düsseldorf, 2006, p. 79.

[13] *J. Ackerman/E. O'Sullivan*, Practice and Procedure of the International Tribunal for the Former Yugoslavia, The Hague 2000, p. 110.

[14] *S. Zappala*, Human Rights in International Criminal Proceedings, Oxford 2003, p. 249: "Ad hoc tribunals started to operate on a fundamentally adversarial system. However, it soon appeared that such a model did not fully meet the demands of international criminal proceedings."

without exception in international criminal law was not possible in view of the difficulty in obtaining evidence and the complex juridical system.[15] The role of the judge as mentioned in preliminary proceedings is an example of this. That role was limited to establishing tribunals according to the principles of common law and confirming the arraignment. In changing the RPE, the court's duties were extended to the investigation phase, and a preliminary proceedings judge (Pre Trial Judge) was put in place as a guarantee for improved communication between the parties[16]. In view of the increasing integration of elements of continental European law and their artificial connection with the existing Anglo-American structures, the procedural law had to be understood by the ad hoc tribunals as rules of procedure *sui generis.* [17] Although *Zappalà* characterizes the RPE as, "a sort of hybrid that fits somewhere between adversarial and inquisitorial"[18], its legal justification is still to be seen mainly in common law. Thus the fundamental role of judge and prosecutor corresponds with the Anglo-American model; however, in its embodiment it is modified in accordance with the conditions for inquisitorial procedure. Basically, the prosecutor faces the defence in the context of a contradictory process, but according to regulation 68 i ICTY RPE, he or she is obliged to disclose exonerative material. Such obligation contradicts the strictly adversarial principle of common law and represents an important convergence with the continental European concept of law.

Similarly, the position of the judge was also not changed in the way it was generally conceived, but it was adapted to problems and practical requirements that arose[19]. Whereas the judge's role is basically to be seen as a passive one, he or she can now question the witnesses independently in the context of the hearing (regulation 85 B ICTY RPE). By including both Anglo-American and continental-European elements, the procedural law of the ad hoc tribunals is exposed to a contradictory and systematically inconsistent procedural organization. On the background of this history of the gradual convergence of the elements contained in civil law and in light of the complexity of the regulatory work, critics see the changes of the RPE as problematic.

---

[15] *J. Ackerman/ E. O'Sullivan*, Practice and Procedure of the International Tribunal for the Former Yugoslavia, The Hague 2000, p. 110: "It is one thing to choose a procedural system on paper, and another to see it in operation".

[16] Rule 65-ter B RPE- ICTY.

[17] *P. Robinson*, Ensuring Fair and Expeditious Trials at the ICTY, EJIL 11 (2000), p. 569 (588).

[18] *S. Zappala*, Human Rights in International Criminal Proceedings, Oxford 2003, p. 22.

[19] *E. Hofstetter*, Das Verfahrensrecht internationaler Strafgerichte zwischen Common Law und Civil Law, Bern 2005, p. 192.

"There have been attempts to create a more hybrid system, combining features from both the inquisitorial and the adversarial systems. Largely this has resulted in a creature that is neither one nor the other and in many respects inferior to both"[20].

A further difficulty resulting from the Anglo-American establishment of ad hoc procedural law is its implementation by those participating in the procedure. All the accused and a large majority of the defence come from traditional commitments to juridical systems relating to civil law[21]. If the defence is not sufficiently familiar with the procedural requirements and possibilities, errors can impair the effectiveness of the defence and can be of disadvantage to the accused.

(2) The International Criminal Court's Control System (a) The Development of Procedural Law as a Compromise Solution. The contractual establishment of the International Criminal Court made the participation of all negotiating States in standardising procedural law necessary. By virtue of the parties' identically strong voices in the General Assembly, the Anglo-American model could not again be enforced in its establishment by statute and RPE. Contrary to the development process of the ad hoc tribunals, the USA's conceptual draft of the ICC rules of procedure was not given an exposed position, which would have guaranteed legal validity and priority to common law. The court's contractual formation gave both juridical systems equal possibilities for influence, and fundamentally new conditions were thereby created for the development of criminal procedure standards on an international level. Given the fact that an international agreement required a reconciliation of interests, consent between the States had to be reached. Coming to such a compromise proved to be difficult, as it involved the attempt to meet in a fair way the requirements of fundamentally different legal structures and to agree upon the contrary starting points of Anglo-American and continental European procedural systems.[22] The need for agreement in a community of States based on common procedural law salvaged the chance to develop an autonomous procedural law at an international level that was independent of political convictions.

Due to the absence of a clear majority, a unique possibility arose to discuss the content of procedural matters based on the history of the special needs of

---

[20] *J. Ackerman/ E. O'Sullivan*, Practice and Procedure of the International Tribunal for the Former Yugoslavia, The Hague 2000, p. 110.

[21] *J. Ackerman/ E. O'Sullivan*, Practice and Procedure of the International Tribunal for the Former Yugoslavia, The Hague 2000, p. 110.

[22] *K. Roberts*, Aspects of the ICTY Contribution to the Criminal Procedure of the ICC, p. 572: "The drafters of the Rome Statute were more constrained by the need to compromise, stemming from political concerns emanating from a large number of states representing a broader background of legal systems. This need for compromise inevitably played a major role in shaping the final text."

international criminal jurisdiction. "National Vanities",[23] however, led to the fact that developing procedural law became the lesser goal in making a feasible decision, but it also led to negotiating reciprocal concessions. Observers of the negotiations criticized that the majority of the States involved wanted to obtain the implementation of their national process systems without considering potential divergences in international law.[24] Therefore, the result of the negotiations had more the character of a political compromise than that it represented a real attempt to define the principles of common criminal procedure.

(b) The Combination of Anglo-American and Continental-European Structures. A general survey of the procedural law system shows a fundamental dominance of the Anglo-American model. Nevertheless, the influence of civil law is not necessarily seen only as a corrective, but also as a rare and innovative representation in the International Criminal Court.[25] Already the role of the judge goes against the principles of common law in that it is seen as an active function in the investigation and the consideration of evidence. [26] Although the parties are also responsible for incriminating and exonerating material, the judge can require the proof of additional evidence (art. 69 III ICC- Statute). Also, in the context of the hearing of witnesses, which is on principle done in the Anglo-American way of cross examination, the judge is permitted to do his own independent questioning (regulation 140 ICC RPE). Basically, the adversarial procedure is supplemented by the court's power to interfere with the continental-European requirement of material truth.[27] In comparing the adversarial model of the ad hoc tribunals with that which is to be seen in the restructuring, the most important change lies in the prosecutor's procedural function.

According to 54 ICC-Statute, the prosecutor has the right to cross examine and investigate in view of determining both incriminating and exonerating evidence. The prosecutor is not to contradict the defence, but to serve as an objective authority with a general interest in ascertaining the truth. [28] This corresponds with his power of appeal in favour of the accused after concluding the court proceedings (Art. 81 I b ICC-Statute). However, as the example of *Tho-*

---

[23] *T. Wilhelmini*, Die Verfahrensordnung des Internationalen Strafgerichtshofs – Modell eines universalen Strafverfahrensrechts?, IRP 24 (2004), p. 7 (57).

[24] *S. Zappala*, Human Rights in International Criminal Proceedings, Oxford 2003, p. 248.

[25] *T. Wilhelmini*, Die Verfahrensordnung des Internationalen Strafgerichtshofs – Modell eines universalen Strafverfahrensrechts?, IRP 24 (2004), p. 7 (9).

[26] *T. Wilhelmini*, Die Verfahrensordnung des Internationalen Strafgerichtshofs – Modell eines universalen Strafverfahrensrechts?, IRP 24 (2004), p. 7 (39f).

[27] *T. Wilhelmini*, Die Verfahrensordnung des Internationalen Strafgerichtshofs – Modell eines universalen Strafverfahrensrechts?, IRP 24 (2004), p. 7 (39f).

[28] *T. Wilhelmini*, Die Verfahrensordnung des Internationalen Strafgerichtshofs – Modell eines universalen Strafverfahrensrechts?, IRP 24 (2004), p. 7 (46ff.).

mas Lubanga shows, the problem of obtaining proof for the defence could not be solved, despite the prosecutor's modified obligations.

The ICC's procedural law connects adversarial and inquisitorial components without consistently implementing the procedure's realisation.[29] The result forms a compromise between the juridical systems that follows no logical process. In view of the mosaic-like structure of the statute, the question arises whether or not the normative link between Anglo- American and continental European elements justifies conceptual contradictions. Irrespective of the justified criticism of the politically-influenced negotiations,[30] the extent to which the ICC's procedural law can be proven in practice to be a possible model for future process controls will have to be examined.

cc) In Conclusion. The procedural regulations of international criminal courts have demonstrated various problems regarding the compatibility of national civil law traditions and common law. Alternative ways of processing were developed because of the need for inter-governmental compromises and the practical requirements of the international criminal procedure. As regulations have developed, it has become clear that the court's established forms influence the American emphasis and the continental European process instructions in a relevant way. The connection between diverse juridical systems without a uniform international concept justifies the complexity and partially contradictory rules of procedure. In order to facilitate the practical implementation of procedural systems and strengthen the acceptance of international criminal law via a clear procedural model, international procedural law must be harmonized.

A common procedural law based on the inquisitional trial should be developed, and it should be equally applicable to all tribunals of international law. The development of a universally valid procedural law would give international law a stable foundation and would simplify the work of the parties involved, who then would not have to await new compromise solutions.

Independently of political interests, it must be examined which control system for the rights of the accused can be most effectively transformed. In this process, the question regarding adversarial and inquisitorial elements in defining the role of judge and prosecutor gains special significance. Given the fact that the implementation of the procedure is significantly influenced by the functions exercised, the organs of the court, their rights and obligations must be adapted to the conditions of international criminal procedure.

---

[29] *E. Hofstetter*, Das Verfahrensrecht internationaler Strafgerichte zwischen Common Law und Civil Law, Bern 2005, p. 192.

[30] *S. Zappala*, Human Rights in International Criminal Proceedings, Oxford 2003, p. 248.

b) Plea for the Consistent Use of Civil Law

The best possibility for protecting the rights of the accused at an international level consists in the complete acceptance of civil law procedure. While both common and civil law can guarantee a fair procedure in national law, the characteristics of international criminal law make it necessary to apply continental European structures. The difficulty in obtaining evidence and the different financial and personnel configurations of defence and prosecution complicate the guarantee of equality of arms.

A fair trial is only possible on the basis of adversarial proceedings if both parties have equal opportunity. Since equality of arms does not exist in an international context due to structural and organisational differences, an adversarial system cannot respect the interests of the defence with regard to its rights. In order to ensure an effective defence, judges and the public prosecutor's office must contribute to asserting the rights of the accused. [31] As the following shows, this cannot be achieved in an adversarial trial.

Another aspect which must be considered in choosing the juridical system is the absence of a jury in international criminal procedure. The transfer of decision-making power to a lay jury in the pursuit of democracy is rejected because of its complexity in view of criminal law regarding individuals. Therefore an important prerequisite for American common law procedures, which have in mind the needs and problems of a jury, is missing. In order to deal effectively with the special problems of the accused in international criminal law, the procedure of the international criminal courts must be consistently oriented toward civil law. This applies in particular to the exercise of the functions of the organs involved.

2. The role of the Organs Involved

"A purely adversarial model in international criminal proceedings can lead to some unfairness. It is not possible to leave it only to the defendants to protect their interests in an international context."[32]

On this background it seems necessary that in international criminal procedures the functions of judge and prosecutor be developed in such a way as to ensure optimum protection of the rights of the accused.

[31] *S. Zappala*, Human Rights in International Criminal Proceedings, Oxford 2003, p. 24: "In international criminal trials both the prosecutor and the judges are bound to take all those measures designed to assist the accused in the preparation of his or her defence, which are imposed by the notion of fair trial".

[32] *S. Zappala*, Human Rights in International Criminal Proceedings, Oxford 2003, p. 27.

a) Role of the Prosecutor

The role the prosecutor plays in an inquisitional trial of the civil law system deviates greatly from the principles of the common law system. The prosecutor does not only assume the role of a party, he also acts as a neutral authority and is committed to objectivity and the establishment of the truth. His investigations aim at clarifying facts and circumstances independently and are not carried out solely to the detriment of the defendant. The combination of Anglo-American and continental elements has led to a contradiction in the prosecutor's function: he sees his function as a party of the trial; he is however also obliged to investigate in the name of the defence.

The *Lubanga* case showed that a consistent realisation of the inquisitional approach could prevent problems of the defence. If the prosecutor actually investigated as an objective authority, the non-disclosure of documents would pose fewer problems. In that case the public prosecutor would use the information as a "springboard" to be able to conduct investigations equally in both directions. The defence would thus be at a far lesser disadvantage in the course of its investigations. The principle of equality of arms has to be abided by strictly, if the parties act as opponents, which they mostly do at the ICC. If the prosecutor saw his role as a neutral entity with the goal of collecting evidence, he would also cooperate with the defence more effectively without the need for a court instruction. The defence's practical deficits with respect to the equality of arms have to be compensated for by the prosecutor's objective work in order to guarantee a fair trial as regards the consideration of culpatory and exculpatory information. For this purpose it does not suffice to impose individual responsibilities on him or her – designing the trial according to the principles of civil law alone can fundamentally change the prosecutor's perception of his function. The problems regarding the rules of evidence and the equality of arms can only be solved conclusively if the prosecutor sees him- or herself as a neutral investigation authority instead of an adverse party.

b) Role of the Judge

"The judge is expected not to know anything about the contents of the procedure when it begins. That means he should enter the courtroom with a white piece of paper, first listen to one side and then listen to the other side, the defence plea, the reply to the defence plea, then withdraw and finally pronounce judgement. Thus, the judge has a notably passive role and has to rely on the pleading of the parties in the true sense of the word."[33]

This quotation by Wolfgang Schomburg, judge at the ICTY, shows that the role of the international judge is still generally influenced by the ideas of common

[33] *W. Schomburg*, Vortrag vor der Gesellschaft für Außenpolitik, 18 February 2008, http://www.foreign-affairs.info/volltext.php?id=124 (accessed 22 January 2009).

law. Even though the statutes of international criminal courts contain varying provisions, the judge's role remains essentially passive.

The judge's limited possibilities for engagement according to common law are justified mainly by the participation of a jury in Anglo-American law. When the international criminal procedures are negotiated individually before a judge and not a jury, it is logical that the role of the judge must be clearly defined. The need for a continental European arrangement becomes evident particularly in the context of background information for the judge regarding procedure as well as his or her authority in leading the trial.

aa) The Judge's Information. According to the concept of common law, the judge may not have received any information about the procedure before the trial begins so that he or she will be able to meet both parties impartially. For this reason, a strict separation of judges in the trial and pre-trial will sustain procedures. According to Art. 39 IV 2 ICC-Statute, a judge who participated in preliminary proceedings may under no circumstances take part in the main trial. The main reason for this rule of incompatibility is the idea that the judge is to function as a neutral entity before a jury and therefore is to have no prior information. Although this regulation may be meaningful in national procedures, it loses its persuasive power in international law. Since the accused is sentenced by the judge alone, the latter must receive all information as promptly and comprehensively as possible. A mandatory separation of trial and pre-trial judge is not necessary in view of the structure of the international criminal procedure. Here it can be seen again that the application of continental European law is more compatible with the conditions of international criminal law.

bb) Judge as Head of the Proceedings. "It appears that judges cannot simply be regarded as umpires, but must play a more active role in the conduct of proceedings".[34]

The complexity of international law regarding criminal procedure makes it necessary for the judge to intervene in the process of steering the procedure for the protection of the accused. In order to ensure this and in light of the judge's authority in the procedure, this was extended to the procedural law of tribunals.[35] While the original Anglo-American orientation handed over the organization of the procedure to the parties by means of cross examination, the judge now increasingly received direct access to intervene. Thus, the judge is authorized (for example in Regulation 85 (B) ICTY RPE) to address the witness at any

---

[34] *S. Zappala*, Human Rights in International Criminal Proceedings, Oxford 2003, p. 250f.

[35] *A. Orie*, Accusatorial v. Inquisitorial Approach in International Criminal Proceedings, in: A. Cassese/P. Gaeta/ J. Jones (eds.), The Rome Statute of the International Criminal CourtVol. II, Oxford 2003, p. 1476.

time during the cross examination. At this point the elements of common law and civil law conflict again. The cross examination is planned in detail by the defence and thus has a set operational sequence. Through the possibility of inquiry, the judge can interrupt the argumentation structure of the defence and destroy the intended effect of the cross examination.[36] The extension of the judicial powers was necessary in order to ensure the rights of the accused in the international criminal process. However, the problem of the witness hearing that arises hereby shows clearly that it is not enough to take on individual continental European elements. Common law and civil law have partially contrary starting points, which prevents the combination of a uniform and conclusive juridical system. Thus, if the consistent application of a legal order is sensible, the structure of the international criminal procedure again supports the choice of civil law. One of the first objectives of cross examination is to convince a jury of one's own position. Intermediate questions from the judge are not permitted as these could be seen as possible influence in view of controlling the jury. Since there is no jury in the procedures before international criminal courts, the tool of cross examination essentially loses its meaning. In the end, the judge alone must make a decision so that a restriction of his possibility to question is not at all expedient. Finally, it becomes clear that the absence of a jury as a substantial element of common law in criminal procedure regarding individuals speaks for the application of the continental-European system.

IV. In Conclusion

There are still deficits in the existing procedural systems in international criminal law when it comes to effectively upholding the right of the accused. The specific problems of international law demonstrate that the implementation of equality of arms is possible only by consistently enforcing the civil law procedure. In particular, judges and prosecutors must also represent the defence's interests as neutral investigation authorities in order to achieve the most important objective of international proceedings: a fair trial.

---

[36] *W. Schabas*, The UN International Criminal Tribunals, 3rd ed., Cambridge 2007, p. 511.

Protection of Women against Sexual Violence in Armed Conflicts

Julia Volkmann-Benkert

> *"It is now more dangerous to be a woman than a soldier in modern wars."*
>
> Major General Patrick Cammaert,
> former Deputy Force Commander, MONUC (2008)

This article deals with the legal and factual situation of women in armed conflicts and their rights of protection during and after such conflicts. The question arises as to whether or not women are in need of special protection during and after armed conflicts and, if so, whether the law provides such protection in an adequate way.

First, there will be a brief overview of the *status quo* of women living in armed conflicts, using the example of the Democratic Republic of the Congo. Second, the material and procedural side of the legal position of women will be shown. The main basis of the description will be the Rome Statute, the Statute of the International Criminal Court. Subsequently, the legal position of women in detention will be presented as a benchmark of the protection of women against sexual violence in armed conflicts. Finally, some specific questions regarding the legal protection of women will be pointed out (article 17 and article 124 of the Rome Statute), concluding with a preview for the future.

I. Status Quo of Women in Armed Conflicts Using the Example of the Democratic Republic of the Congo

1. Women in the Democratic Republic of the Congo

During the war in the Democratic Republic of the Congo, thousands of women and girls became victims of sexual violence. The Second Congo War, also known as Africa's World War or the Great War of Africa, began in August 1998 in the Democratic Republic of the Congo (formerly called Zaire), and officially ended in July 2003, when the Transitional Government of the Democratic Republic of the Congo took power (though hostilities continue to this day).[1] The largest war in modern African history, it directly involved eight African nations as well as about 25 armed groups.

The chronic sexual violence is one facet of a broader environment of insecurity that still defines eastern Congo. The International Rescue Committee stated that a decade-long war killed an estimated five million people.[2] The prevalence and intensity of rape and other sexual violence is described as the worst in the world. In 2004, Amnesty International stated that 40,000 cases of rape had been reported over the previous six years, the majority occurring in South Kivu.[3] According to December 2007 UN figures, around 350 rape cases are reported every month in Kivu.[4] This is an incomplete count, as the humanitarian and international organizations compiling the figures do not have access to the complete conflict area. Only women who have reported for treatment are included. The actual number of women raped is assumed to be much higher. Of some 14,200 rape cases registered in the Democratic Republic of the Congo between 2005–2007 just 2% of the perpetrators were ever called to account.[5]

A journalist[6] reported on *Honorata Barinjibanwa*, a woman living in the Democratic Republic of the Congo. He described her as an 18-year-old woman with downcast eyes and high cheekbones. He reported that she was kidnapped from a village that the Rastas raided in April and kept as a sex slave until August. During most of that time she was tied to a tree. The men would untie her for a few hours each day to gang-rape her.

He quoted the woman as follows: "I'm weak, I'm angry, and I don't know how to restart my life." She was taken to the hospital after the captors freed her. She was pregnant at that time.

Henriette Nyota, another woman living in the Democratic Republic of the Congo, told the media that she had been gang-raped while four of her children

---

[1] *M. W. Nest*, The Democratic Republic of Congo: economic dimensions of war and peace, p. 1 ff.; US Government Accounting Office (GAO), U.N. peacekeeping executive branch consultations with Congress in 1999–2000 did not meet expectations fully, p. 52.

[2] International Rescue Committee, IRC Study Shows Congo's Neglected Crisis Leaves 5.4 Million Dead; Peace Deal in N. Kivu, Increased Aid Critical to Reducing Death Toll, http://www.theirc.org/news/irc-study-shows-congos0122.html (accessed 26 January 2009).

[3] Amnesty International United Kingdom, North Kivu: No End to the war against women and children, p. 1 (5 ff.), http://www.amnesty.org.uk/uploads/documents/doc_18687.pdf (accessed 24 January 2008).

[4] Amnesty International United Kingdom, North Kivu: No End to the war against women and children, p. 1 (5 ff.), http://www.amnesty.org.uk/uploads/documents/doc_18687.pdf (accessed 24 January 2008).

[5] 2008 parliamentary hearing at the United Nations New York 2008, background document: Session II, Sexual violence against women and children in armed conflict, p. 1 (1).

[6] *J. Gettlemen*, In Congo, an epidemic of rape, International Herald Tribune – the Global Edition of the New York Times, http://www.iht.com/articles/2007/10/07/news/congo.php (accessed 22 January 2009).

and her husband were forced to watch. She said the men in uniform then disembowelled her husband. Afterwards they continued raping her and her two oldest daughters, 10 and 8 years old. The assault went on for three days.[7]

The media quoted her saying: "I wish they'd killed me right there with my husband. What use am I now? Why did those animals leave me to suffer like this?"[8]

These two experiences of women living in the Democratic Republic of the Congo stand for the fate of thousands of women in zones of armed conflict around the world.

2. *Vulnerability of Women Regarding Sexual Violence in Armed Conflict*

a) *Special Vulnerability of Women Compared to Men and Children*

When we hear about armed conflicts, we know that besides destruction, pillaging and killing, many women are raped by combatant forces – both by enemy and by "friendly forces".[9] Especially in armed conflicts with infantry action, women aren't safe. In these cases, the soldiers on both sides meet women living in the combat area. Many of them become victims of sexual violence. Sexual violence includes rape as well as all other forms of violence with sexual activity against the will of the woman concerned.[10]

The violence is committed against women because of their gender, in addition to their ethnic origin or religion.[11] Additionally, in most cases women and children are the only ones left in the villages, towns or cities while the men fight. Unaccompanied women, girls[12] and lone female households are all frequent targets, because they are even more helpless.[13]

The issue of particular vulnerability is important for the question of special protection of women in armed conflicts, because only a particular vulnerability of women might legitimize the demand for special means of protection. Without a specific vulnerability of women in armed conflicts compared to men and

---

[7] *J. Koinange*, Rape, brutality ignored to aid Congo peace, http://edition.cnn.com/2006/WORLD/africa/05/23/koinange.rape.war/index.html (accessed 22 January 2009).

[8] *J. Koinange*, Rape, brutality ignored to aid Congo peace, http://edition.cnn.com/2006/WORLD/africa/05/23/koinange.rape.war/index.html (accessed 22 January 2009).

[9] *Ch. Chinkin*, Rape and Sexual Abuse of Women in International Law, European Journal of International Law 5 (1994), p. 326 (326).

[10] ICTR, *Prosecutor v Akayesu*, Case No ICTR-96–4, Judgment (1998), para. 688; *O. Triffterer*, Commentary of the Rome Statute of the International Criminal Court, 2nd edition, 2008, paragraph 7, para. 53.

[11] *Ch. Chinkin*, Rape and Sexual Abuse of Women in International Law, European Journal of International Law 5 (1994), p. 326 (326).

[12] *M. Colombini*, Gender based and Sexual Violence against Women in Armed Conflict, Journal of Health Management 4 (2002), p. 167 (168).

[13] *M. Colombini*, Gender based and Sexual Violence against Women in Armed Conflict, Journal of Health Management 4 (2002), p. 167 (170).

children, there would be no reason for special treatment. Special treatment by law requires a special form of vulnerability. In fact, such vulnerability cannot be imputed automatically to women. Vulnerability and the need for protection resulting from it depend on each individual case. The risk of becoming a victim of sexual violence is not only a female phenomenon. Men[14] and children become victims of sexual violence as well. It cannot be argued that all victims are female, because it is generally agreed that the uncertain number of male victims is higher than average.[15] Differentiating would arrive at the conclusion that women would get special protection, but men and children would not. It is as terrible for men and children to become victims of sexual violence as it is for women. The fact that most known cases involve women who have become victims of sexual violence does not allow the conclusion that only women are in need of special treatment by law. Rather, the human being as such has to be protected by law.

b) Focusing on Women's Rights on an International Level

Even though there is no special vulnerability of women compared to men and children, it is questionable whether international law protects women's rights in an adequate way. Is there enough protection against sexual violence in armed conflicts? Therefore the idea is that, even though men and children become victims of sexual violence as well, the number of female victims is still higher. That is why the following will focus on women.

Although sexual violence in armed conflicts is often a tool used to subordinate a group of people, it is in every case a means of subjugating, objectifying and dehumanizing women,[16] even when the intent is aimed at something else. In many cases of armed conflict, the intent is not focused on raping women.[17] Rather, the occasion is the reason for raping women in armed conflicts. Most of the women are helpless, because the men are dominant. But raping and other forms of sexual violence become more and more an intended systematic way of behavior.[18]

But what happens after the armed conflict? Do the perpetrators really get punished for the rape in a criminal procedure? Or is it just a fact that everybody

---

[14] *S. Sivakumaran*, Sexual Violence Against Men in Armed Conflict, The European Journal of International Law 18 (2007), no. 2, pp. 253 ff.

[15] *S. Sivakumaran*, Sexual Violence Against Men in Armed Conflict, The European Journal of International Law 18 (2007), no. 2, pp. 253 ff.; *W. Russel*, Sexual Violence against Men and Boys, Forced Migration Review (FMR) 27 (Sexual Violence), p. 22 (22).

[16] *J. Gardam*, Women and the Law of Armed Conflict: Why the Silence?, International and Comparative Law Quarerly 46 (1997), p. 55 (70).

[17] *M. Colombini*, Gender-based and Sexual Violence against Women during Armed Conflict, Journal of Health Management 4 (2002), p. 167 (170).

[18] *Ch. Lindsey*, Women and war – An overview, International Review of the Red Cross No. 839 (2000), p. 561 (579).

knows about, more a side effect of war than a war crime, rather a "usual" situation for an armed conflict?

Although the international community has made some strides in outlawing and punishing atrocities committed during armed conflict by developing international law, sexual violence against women has been consistently dismissed or marginalized as a natural consequence.

II. International Criminal Law as a Means of Protection

1. Material Criminal Law

a) The Nuremberg and Tokyo Tribunals

For millennia, women and girls have suffered rape, sexual slavery, forced pregnancy and other brutal forms of sexual gender violence during armed conflicts. Like other forms of war-related brutality, such violence is often tolerated or ordered by military, paramilitary or other governmental actors.[19] Neither the Nuremberg nor the Tokyo tribunals from 1945 to 1949 mentioned sexual violence in their Charters. Not a single charge of rape was brought to the Nuremberg Tribunal.[20] Some of the Tokyo charges involved rape charges. But rape was only a side aspect. Not one rape victim was called as a witness. Not one of the defendants has been charged with rape or sexual violence.[21] The reason was that the court focused on other crimes such as crimes against humanity or war crimes committed through mass killings.

b) Geneva Conventions and the Additional Protocols

The law of armed conflict is codified in the Geneva Conventions and the Hague Conventions. The Geneva Conventions impose no restrictions on the means and methods of warfare, but provide for such matters as the treatment of prisoners of war, civilians in occupied territories and persons *hors de combat*. The Hague Conventions deal with the regulation of the conduct of warfare itself.

In 1949, the four Geneva Conventions were revised and expanded. In 1977, two Additional Protocols were added: 1st Protocol: international conflicts, 2nd Protocol: non-international conflicts. The Geneva Conventions and the Addi-

[19] United Nations, Division for the Advancement of Women, Department of Economic and Social Affairs, Women 2000, Sexual Violence and Armed Conflict: United Nations Response, http://www.un.org/womenwatch/daw/public/cover.pdf (accessed 17 January 2009).

[20] *G. Werle*, Principles of International Criminal Law, 2008, p. 248; *J. Gardam*, Women, Human Rights and International Humanitarian Law, International Review of the Red Cross No. 324, p. 421 (421).

[21] *K. Fitzgerald*, Problems of Prosecution and Adjudication of Rape and Other Sexual Assaults under International Law, European Journal of International Law 8 (1997), no. 4, p. 638 (644).

tional Protocols primarily apply to the contracting states. The states are responsible for compliance with regulations written down in the Conventions and the Additional Protocols and their enforcement (article 1 of the Geneva Conventions and of the Additional Protocol I). The states or the International Criminal Court[22] are responsible for prosecuting war crimes committed. The Additional Protocols apply additionally to the Geneva Conventions.

The Conventions chiefly concern the treatment of combatants and non-combatants.[23] The Fourth Geneva Convention protects women (and men) as members of the civilian population not taking part in an armed conflict. A civilian is any person who does not belong to the armed forces.[24]

The Additional Protocol I also affords protection. Women are in general protected against abusive treatment by the parties of the armed conflict, against effects of the fighting, and in addition, women are afforded special protection. Article 27 paragraph 2 of the Fourth Geneva Convention states that

> "women shall be especially protected against any attack on their honor, in particular against rape, enforced prostitution, or any form of indecent assault".

The Conventions and their Protocols arrogate for measures to be taken to prevent or to stop what are known as "grave breaches". However, the ad hoc tribunals have rarely enforced regulations about sexual violence against women in armed conflict.[25] Before the International Criminal Tribunal Yugoslavia and the International Criminal Tribunal Rwanda, rape was not explicitly stated as a grave breach of the Geneva Conventions.[26] Article 147 of the Fourth Geneva Convention states that

> "grave breaches to which the preceding article relates shall be those involving any of the following acts, if committed against persons or property protected by the present Convention: wilful killing, torture or inhuman treatment, including biological experiments, wilfully causing great suffering or serious injury to body or health, unlawful deportation or transfer or unlawful confinement of a protected person, compelling a protected person to serve in the forces of a hostile power, or wilfully depriving a protected person of the rights of fair and regular trial prescribed in the present Convention, taking of hostages and extensive destruction and appropriation of property, not justified by military necessity and carried out unlawfully and wantonly."

---

[22] Cf. under B. I. 4.

[23] Geneva Conventions I – III will be left out at this part, because the Geneva Conventions I-III assume a combatant as protecting subject. Women can be combatants as well in armed conflict. However, this part of the essay focuses on women as civilians in armed conflict. Female combatants in detention Cf. B. IV. 1.

[24] Article 50 of the Additional Protocol I.

[25] *L. Friedman*, The Law of War: A Documentary History, Volume 1, p. 776 (777); *J. Gardam/M. Jarvis*, International Redress, in: Women, Armed Conflict and International Law, 2001, p. 180 (188).

[26] Cf. B. I. 3.

At the time when the Fourth Geneva Convention was adopted, rape was not designated as a war crime for which there is individual responsibility.[27] The ICC Statute states this explicitly and includes sexual slavery, enforced prostitution, forced pregnancy, enforced sterilization or any other form of sexual violence as also being grave breaches of the Conventions (Article 8 (2)(b)(xxii)).[28]

c) International Criminal Tribunal (ICT) Yugoslavia and ICT Rwanda

The International Criminal Tribunal Yugoslavia (established in 1991) as well as the International Criminal Tribunal Rwanda (established in 1994) have been responsible for the most significant developments in the criminalization of sexual violence and rape in international law.[29] Both tribunals were established to prosecute serious crimes committed during the wars in the former Yugoslavia and the Rwandan genocide. Under chapter VII of the UN Charter, they were created as a measure to maintain and restore international peace and security.[30] Both tribunals are ad hoc tribunals.[31] They were established just for a special situation.[32] They do not exist permanently. A constant authority for the future does not exist. In fact the tribunals were established in order to condemn the atrocities in both countries.[33]

In this connection, sexual violence was named as a violation of the laws or customs of war along with genocide, crimes against humanity, grave breaches of the 1949 Geneva Conventions and as a violation of common Art. 3 of the 1949 Geneva Conventions and of the 1977 Additional Protocols.

Key decisions of both tribunals provided blueprints for the new International Criminal Court (ICC) provisions on helping victims of crime.

aa) The Akayesu Judgment. One of the judgments with the most influence was the decision in the *Akayesu* case. It was brought before the Rwanda tribunal and provided further illustrations of the case for gender justice.[34] In 1998, the judges of the International Criminal Court Rwanda found *Jean-Paul Akayesu* guilty of rape as one crime among others.

---

[27] *J. Gardam*, Women and the Law of Armed Conflict: Why the Silence?, International and Comparative Law Quarterly 46 (1997), p. 55 (74).

[28] Cf. under B. I. 3. b).

[29] *J. Gardam*, Women, human rights and international humanitarian law, International Review of the Red Cross No. 324 (1998), p. 421 (432).

[30] *G. Werle*, Principles of International Criminal Law, 2008, p. 18.

[31] *A. Cassese*, International Criminal Law, 2nd edition, 2008, pp. 325 ff.; *W. A. Schabas*, An Introduction to the International Criminal Court, 3rd edition, 2008, p. 290.

[32] *A. Cassese*, International Criminal Law, 2nd edition, 2008, pp. 325 ff.

[33] *G. Werle*, Principles of International Criminal Law, 2008, pp. 48 ff., 54 f.

[34] *M. Glasius*, International Criminal Court, a global civil society achievement, 2006, p. 79.

Akayesu, a former mayor of the Taba commune in Rwanda, was accused of allowing policemen and others under his authority to rape and torture mostly Tutsi women who had sought his protection. With a guilty verdict, this was the first time anyone had been found guilty by an international tribunal for genocide crimes, which include sexual violence. Under pressure from Rwandan and international rights groups, the office of the prosecutor finally amended the charges against *Akayesu* to include sexual violence. Initially, the ICTR had not charged *Akayesu* with crimes of sexual violence in spite of the overwhelming evidence of mass rapes in the Taba commune.

The *Akayesu* case was the first to define rape as an international crime, thereby setting an important legal precedent.[35] The chamber noted that there was at the time no commonly accepted definition of the term rape in international law. The chamber defined rape as "a physical invasion of a sexual nature, committed on a person under circumstances which are coercive".[36] The chamber also defined the term "other forms of sexual violence". Sexual violence is a broader term than rape.[37] The term describes any kind of violence carried out through sexual means or by targeting sexuality.[38] Sexual violence – which includes rape – is not limited to a physical invasion of the human body and may include acts that do not involve penetration or physical contact. Sexual violence covers both physical and psychological attacks directed at a person's sexual characteristics.[39]

The Tribunal underscored in this case that rape and sexual violence

> "constitute genocide in the same way as any other act as long as they were committed with the specific intent to destroy, in whole or in part, a particular group, targeted as such".[40]

In addition, *Akayesu* would be the first non-military leader declared guilty of rape crimes committed in an internal armed conflict.

bb) The Tadic Judgment. Another key judgment was the decision in the *Tadic* case made by the International Criminal Court of the Former Yugoslavia. In this case, *Dusko Tadic*, a member of the Bosnian Serb forces and low-level official at the Omarska camp, was convicted by the ICTY on 7 May 1997 for crimes against

---

[35] *J. A. Williamson*, Overview of the international criminal jurisdiction operating in Africa, International Review of the Red Cross No. 861 (2006), p. 111; ICTR, *Prosecutor v Akayesu*, Case No ICTR-96-4, Judgment (1998).

[36] ICTR, *Prosecutor v Akayesu*, Case No ICTR-96–4, Judgment (1998), paras. 596, 688.

[37] *O. Triffterer*, Commentary of the Rome Statute of the International Criminal Court, 2nd edition, 2008, paragraph 7, para. 53.

[38] ICTR, *Prosecutor v Akayesu*, Case No ICTR-96–4, Judgment (1998).

[39] Final Report of the Special Rapporteur of the Working Group on Contemporary Forms of Slavery, on systematic rape, sexual slavery and slavery-like practices during armed conflict (1998 Slavery Rapporteur Report), UN Doc.E/CN.4/Sub.2/1998/13), para. 23.

[40] ICTR, *Prosecutor v Akayesu*, Case No ICTR-96-4, Judgment (1998).

humanity for criminal acts of persecution that included crimes of rape and other forms of sexual violence. Thirty-one individual counts of persecution, murder, cruel treatment, and inhuman acts were brought against *Tadic*, in relation to events alleged to have occurred in the Prijedor region in northwest Bosnia, more specifically at the Keraterm, Omarska and Trnopolje camps, in Kozarac, and in the area of Sivci and Jaskici. *Tadic* was found guilty on 11 counts, constituting both violations of the laws or customs of war, including violations of Article 3 common to the Geneva Conventions, and crimes against humanity.[41]

He was not convicted for directly committing an act of sexual assault, but for his participation in a general, widespread and systematic campaign of terror. This decision is a key decision, because it states categorically that rape and all other forms of sexual violence can be considered constituent elements of a widespread or systematic campaign of terror against a civilian population. It is not necessary to prove that rape itself was widespread or systematic, but that rape was one of perhaps many types of crimes, the spectrum of which was committed on a widespread or systematic basis and comprised an aggressor's campaign of terror.[42]

d) The International Criminal Court

aa) Facts about the Court. The ICC, established in 2002, is the first permanent international crime court in history. The Rome Statute of the International Criminal Court, approved in 1998 in Rome and entered into force in 2002, remains a significant landmark in the development of international law's response to gender and violence. On 17 July 1998 the Rome Statute was adopted in plenary session with 120 votes. The USA, China, Israel, Iraq, Libya, Yemen and Qatar voted against the Statute. 21 states abstained.[43] The International Criminal Court can prosecute individuals, from common soldiers to heads of state, for genocide, war crimes and crimes against humanity.[44]

bb) The Rome Statute. There was no definition of rape in international humanitarian or human rights law when the Rome Statute was adopted.[45] But an

---

[41] *Rochus J. P. Pronk & Brian D. Tittemore*: ICTY Issues Final Judgment Against Dusan Tadic in First International War Crimes Trial Since World War II, Human Rights Brief 4 (1997), no. 3, http://www.wcl.american.edu/hrbrief/04/3pronk.cfm (accessed 25 January 2009).

[42] *The Shan Human Rights Foundation (SHRF) & The Shan Women's Action Network (SWAN)*, The Burmese military regime's use of sexual violence in the ongoing war in Shan State, http://www.shanland.org/resources/bookspub/humanrights/LtoR/sexual_violence_as_crimes_agains.htm (accessed 18 January 2009).

[43] *G. Werle*, Principles of International Criminal Law, 2008, p. 22.

[44] *M. Glasius*, The International Criminal Court, a global civil society achievement, 2006 p. i (xiii).

[45] Rape and Sexual Assault: A Legal Study, Final Report of the U. N. Commission of Ex-

influential report by the UN Special Rapporteur on the situation of systematic rape, sexual slavery and slavery-like practices during wartime, including internal armed conflicts, published during the Rome Diplomatic Conference, states that rape is

"the insertion under conditions of force, coercion or duress, of any object, including but not limited to a penis, into a victim's vagina or anus; or the insertion, under conditions of force, coercion or duress, of a penis into the mouth of the victim".[46]

Rape does not only include forced sex; it includes also sexual conduct connected with the insertion of the perpetrator's sexual organ into other body cavities (oral or anal penetration). The material element requires an invasion of the victim's body by the perpetrator, which must result in penetration. Furthermore, the literature's convincing hit-off compromises that also the insertion of other parts of the perpetrator's body or objects into the vagina or other parts of the body could be included.[47]

In the Kunarac judgment, the trial chamber of the ICTY was of the view that a comprehensive comparison of the world's national criminal law system shows that the accent has been less on the exercise of coercion or use of force than on whether it occurred against the will of the victim.[48] Since the *Kunarac* judgment, the trial chamber has affirmed the definition. The result is that the focus changed from the perpetrator's objective behaviour to the victim's opposing will.

cc) Article 7 (Crimes Against Humanity) and Article 8 (War Crimes) of the Rome Statute. The Rome Statute includes sexual violence in its definition of both crimes against humanity (article 7 of the Rome Statute) and war crimes (article 8 of the Rome Statute) over which it has jurisdiction in international and non-international armed conflicts. Article 7 (1) (d) of the Rome Statute defines "crimes against humanity" as

"any of the following acts when committed as part of a widespread or systematic attack directed against any civilian population, with knowledge of the attack: Rape, sexual slavery, enforced prostitution, forced pregnancy, enforced sterilization, or any other form of sexual violence of comparable gravity."

---

perts Established Pursuant Security Council Res. 780 (1992), U.N. Doc. S/1994/674/Add.2, Volume 1, annex II, para. 2.

[46] Rape and Sexual Assault: A Legal Study, Final Report of the U.N. Commission of Experts Established Pursuant Security Council Res. 780 (1992), U.N. Doc. S/1994/674/Add.2, Volume 1, annex II, para. 2.

[47] *G. Werle*, Principles of International Criminal Law, 2008, p. 248.

[48] ICTY, *Prosecutor v. Kunarac* et al. Case No IT-96–23-T & IT-96–23/1-T, 2002, para. 128.

Likewise article 8 (2) (b) (xxii) of the Rome Statute defines rape and other forms of sexual violence as a means to war crimes. According to article 8 (2) (b) (xxii) of the Rome Statute,

> "the Court shall have jurisdiction in respect of war crimes in particular when committed as part of a plan or policy or as part of a large-scale commission of such crimes."

Paragraph 2 (b) of article 8 of the Rome Statute regulates that

> "for the purpose of this Statute, 'war crimes' means other serious violations of the laws and customs applicable in international armed conflict, within the established framework of international law, namely, any of the following acts: committing rape, sexual slavery, enforced prostitution, forced pregnancy, as defined in article 7, paragraph 2 (f), enforced sterilization, or any other form of sexual violence also constituting a grave breach of the Geneva Conventions."

To be regarded as an international conflict, military occupation is necessary, that is normally the situation of war. The ICTY proposed a general definition of international armed conflict. In the *Tadic* case, the Tribunal stated that

> "an armed conflict exists whenever there is a resort to armed force between States".[49]

The perception of a non-international conflict is not clear. But at any rate the brink to a civil war in a state is captured.[50] This is important for the situation of women in such conflicts.

The definition advised in article 8 of the Rome Statute is narrower than some of the decisions of the ICTY or ICTR examined above in relation to consent. That means that the element of the crimes is catchier to attest and therefore harder to prosecute. Article 8 of the Rome Statute requires that the aforementioned conduct be part of a plan or policy or part of a large-scale commission of such crimes. Without one of the aforementioned elements, the elements constituting crimes in article 8 of the Rome Statute are not fulfilled, even when rape and other forms of sexual violence are obvious. Then it is part of the national jurisdiction to prove the conduct under national law. In most member states, rape and other forms of sexual violence are a criminal conduct, punishable by national law. International prosecution is not possible. In most cases, a national procedure does not take place, because the perpetrators have already left the country and the identity or the domicile of the perpetrators is unknown or it is even harder for the jurisdiction to find evidence. But even when the national jurisdiction prosecutes the perpetrators before a national court, it is not as effec-

[49] ICTY, *The Prosecutor v. Dusko Tadic*, Decision on the Defence Motion for Interlocutory Appeal on Jurisdiction, IT-94-1-A, 1995, para. 70.

[50] *J. P. Cerone*, Status of Detainees in Non-International Armed Conflict, and their Protection in the Course of Criminal Proceedings: The Case of Hamdan v. Rumsfeld, The American Society of International Law 10 (2006), no. 17, http://www.asil.org/insights060714.cfm (accessed 25 January 2009).

tive as a trial before the international crime court. No international importance is given the interests of the international community. It is known that the international community is more interested in international procedures than in diverse national procedures in the member states. It is not possible to publish all national cases of all member states to all the other member states, so knowledge is limited. The possibility of prosecuting the perpetrators before the International Criminal Court is more difficult because of the aforementioned added elements of crimes, but it is also vitally important.[51]

As mentioned above, rape is also defined as a crime against humanity in article 7 of the Rome Statute. The elements of crime in article 7 of the Rome Statute differ from the elements of crime in article 8 to the effect that rape is committed as part of a widespread or systematic attack directed against a civilian population. Since a policy of committing a widespread or systematic attack must be related to a state or organizational policy and to multiple acts, there is a limitation that is narrower than under customary international law. The application of both provisions (article 7 and article 8 of the Rome Statute) faces the same difficulties. The elements of crime constitute a higher barrier.

dd) Article 6 of the Rome Statute (Genocide). The Statute does not define something comparable in article 6 (genocide), but nevertheless rape and sexual violence could be covered by article 6 (b) of the Rome Statute. As already mentioned, the ICTR stated in the *Akayesu judgment* that rape and other forms of sexual violence can constitute genocide.[52]

The Rome Statute adopted the definition of genocide as accepted in the Genocide Convention. The Genocide Convention is reflected in the Rome Statute.[53] The Convention defines genocide as

"acts committed with the intent to destroy in whole or part a national, ethnical, racial or religious group".

Article 6 of the Rome Statute and the Genocide Convention do not mention sexual violence. Article 6 (b) of the Rome Statute and article 2 of the Genocide Convention define that genocide means interalia "causing serious bodily or mental harm to members of the group". The International Criminal Court acknowledged that rape and other forms of sexual violence could constitute "serious bodily or mental harm" and thereby genocide.[54] This consideration is ap-

---

[51] *B. Bedont/ K. Hall-Martinez*, Ending Impunity for Gender Crimes Under the International Criminal Court, The Brown Journal of World Affairs 6 (1999), p. 65 (70).

[52] Cf. under B. II. 2. b).

[53] Cf. article 6 of the Rome Statute.

[54] *J. Gardam/M. Jarvis*, International Redress, in: Women, Armed Conflict and International Law, 2001, p. 180 (190); see case concerning application of the Convention on the prevention and punishment of the crime of genocide (Bosnia Herzegovina v. Yugoslavia (Serbia Montenegro)), Preliminary Exceptions, 26 February 2007, para. 161.

propriate, because rape and other forms of sexual violence in most cases cause serious bodily or mental harm; the act takes place against the wishes of the victim. The perpetrator ignores the will and also the intimacy of the victim and this causes at least serious mental harm. Furthermore, it is mandatory that genocide includes rape and sexual violence as well, because even though article 7 and article 8 of the Rome Statute contain rules regarding rape and other forms of sexual violence, it is possible that the elements of crime as stated in article 7 or 8 of the Rome Statute are not fulfilled, but the elements of crime in article 6 of the Rome Statute are. If article 6 of the Rome Statute did not contain rape and sexual violence, the criminal conduct would not be covered by international law. As it is seen in article 7 and article 8 of the Rome Statute, the International Community noticed that rape and other forms of sexual violence against women in armed conflicts need to be regulated on an international level. This conclusion must also apply to genocide in article 6 of the Rome Statute. It would be inconsistent to read article 6 of the Rome Statute in a different way. The idea of the Rome Statute concerning rape and other forms of sexual violence has to apply to genocide as well as to war crimes and crimes against humanity.

But even if rape and other forms of sexual violence could constitute genocide, it would be necessary for the perpetrator to act with specific intent, because one important factor in article 6 of the Rome Statute is that the act must be committed with "intent to destroy".[55] Without the specific intent, article 6 of the Rome Statute cannot be fulfilled.

Finally to summarize, rape and sexual violence may also constitute genocide, as these acts may have the effect of destroying the group, particularly if they occur within cultures in which men may reject women who have been the victim of rape or sexual violence.[56]

Thus, regulations to protect women in armed conflicts do generally exist in the Statute of the ICC.

2. *Special Protection of Women in Armed Conflict Using the Example of Women in Detention*

International humanitarian law has, since its inception, accorded women general protection equal to that of men.[57] Women are protected as members of the civilian population if they are interned, and as members of the armed forces when captured and detained by the enemy in international and non-interna-

[55] Cf. article 6 of the Rome Statute.

[56] *R. Layton/V. Bannon*, International law and armed conflict: Implications for emergency and humanitarian organizations, Australian Journal of Emergency Management 15, p. 58 (61).

[57] *F. Krill*, The Protection of Women in International Humanitarian Law, International Review of the Red Cross No. 249 (1985), pp. 337 ff.

tional conflicts.[58] But the law and thereby the international community have also recognized the need to give women special protection according to their specific needs.

a) International Conflict

aa) Women as Civilians. The Fourth Geneva Convention deals with the protection of civilians during times of war "in the hands" of an enemy and under any military occupation by a foreign power. The Fourth Geneva Convention does not protect people who are already protected under one of the other three Geneva Conventions. Whether or not the person took part in hostilities is irrelevant to protection under the Fourth Geneva Convention.[59] But the scope of the Fourth Geneva Convention is limited. It is designed to protect persons in occupied territories from arbitrary acts by the occupying party.[60]

Civilian women deprived of their liberty for reasons related to the conflict are entitled without discrimination to the same general protection as men, but they also benefit from additional specific rules which take into account their specific needs. The special protection regarding women is codified in rules relating to matters such as physiological specificity,[61] pregnancy and childbirth,[62] privacy and modesty, food and clothing,[63] hygiene and medical attention.[64] For example, the two-tiered protection finds expression in articles 76 paragraph 4, and 124 paragraph 3 of the Fourth Geneva Convention, which provide that

> "detained or interned women be held separately from men and that they be under the immediate supervision of women",[65]

and in article 89 paragraph V of the Fourth Geneva Convention, which states

> "expectant and nursing mothers and children under fifteen years of age, shall be given additional food, in proportion to their physiological needs".

By contrast, a similar regulation that men shall be under immediate supervision of men does not exist. The specific right applies only to women.

---

[58] *Ch. Lindsey*, Women and War: the detention of women in wartime, International Review of the Red Cross 2001 No. 842 (2001), p. 505 (507).

[59] *G. Werle*, Principles of International Law, 2008, p. 300: "Unlawful combatants" (persons who take up arms without being permitted to do so under the law of war) are also protected.

[60] *J. Gardam*, Women and the Law of Armed Conflict: Why the Silence?, International and Comparative Law Quarterly 46 (1997), p. 55 (74).

[61] Article 97 paragraph 4 states that "a woman internee shall not be searched except by a woman".

[62] Article 50 paragraph 5, article 89 and article 132 paragraph 2 of the Fourth Geneva Convention.

[63] Articles 89–90 of the Fourth Geneva Convention.

[64] Articles 91–92 of the Fourth Geneva Convention.

[65] So also in article 5 paragraph 2 of the Additional Protocol II.

bb) Women as Combatants. Participation of women in hostilities is not a new development. Many women have taken a more or less active part in armed conflict throughout the centuries.[66]

Like men, women who take part in hostilities are protected by international humanitarian law from the moment they are detained by the enemy. It is essential for them to be members of the armed forces of a party to the conflict if they are to be considered as combatants entitled to the status of prisoners of war, once captured.[67]

In international armed conflict, women, who are actively combats in hostilities as members of the armed forces are protected, if captured by the enemy, by the Third Geneva Convention relative to the Treatment of Prisoners of War. This Convention elaborates the principle that prisoners of war shall be treated humanely in all circumstances. However, the Convention also affords women special protection. Article 14 paragraph 2 of the Third Convention contains a general reference to women by regulating that

> "women shall be treated with all the regard due to their sex and shall in all cases benefit by treatment as favourable as that granted to men".

This principle is followed by a number of provisions, which expressly refer to the conditions of detention for women in prisons. For example, article 25 paragraph 4 of the Third Geneva Convention states that

> "in any camps in which women prisoners of war, as well as men, are accommodated, separate dormitories shall be provided for them".

Also article 29 paragraph 2, 2nd sentence of the Third Geneva Convention contains a special protection of women when it speaks of the obligation to provide separate sanitary conveniences for them. The Third Geneva Convention also contains the obligation to provide separate quarters under the supervision of women in the event of punishment (article 97 and article 107 of the Third Convention). Article 76, paragraph 2 of the Additional Protocol I also includes a direct reference to women; it states that

> "pregnant women and mothers having dependent infants who are arrested, detained or interned for reasons related to the armed conflict, shall have their cases considered with the utmost priority".

Female combatants benefit from special protection, because these women's needs are different from men's needs. The fact that they actively take part in an

---

[66] Along with such historical characters as *Queen Elizabeth I of England* or *Queen Christina of Sweden*, who were both rulers and military commanders, many other women distinguished themselves in combat.

[67] *F. Krill*, The Protection of Women in International Humanitarian Law, International Review of the Red Cross No. 249 (1985), pp. 337 ff.

armed conflict does not change the existence of specific needs of women in detention.

b) Non-International Conflict

aa) Women as Civilians. In the case of internal armed conflict in which women do not take part, the same violations are prohibited. In this context, reference should be made to article 3 common to the four Geneva Conventions and the Additional Protocol II.[68] The regulations of the Additional Protocol II regarding the special protection of women in armed conflict apply to conflicts on a non-international level. While article 3 common to the four Geneva Conventions[69] contains no special treatment of women in an internal armed conflict, it establishes fundamental guarantees for the treatment of all persons not taking part in the hostilities. Furthermore article 4 paragraph 2 of the Additional Protocol rules in general terms that "outrages upon personal dignity, in particular humiliating and degrading treatment, rape, enforced prostitution and any form of indecent assault" are forbidden. Additional Protocol II contains special regulation on the protection of women. Article 5 paragraph 2 (a) of the Additional Protocol II states that

> "those who are responsible for the internment or detention of the persons referred to in paragraph 1 shall also, within the limits of their capabilities, respect the following provisions relating to such persons: except when men and women of a family are accommodated together, women shall be held in quarters separated from those of men and shall be under the immediate supervision of women".

In the event that it is not possible to provide separate quarters, it is essential in any event to provide separate sleeping places and conveniences as well as the supervision of women. Article 6 paragraph 4 of the Additional Protocol II contains a special protection of women regarding penal prosecution.

bb) Women as Combatants. Women[70] who take an active part in the hostilities in a non-international conflict do not have prisoner-of-war status if the enemy detains them. However, in such a case they are entitled to the fundamental guarantees equal to men afforded by article 3 common to the Geneva Conventions and by article 4 of the Additional Protocol II relative to the protection of victims of non-international armed conflict.[71] Additional Protocol II is applicable to persons detained or interned for reasons related to the conflict. Moreover, this Protocol also contains a provision on fundamental guarantees that must be

[68] *A. Cassese*, International Criminal Law, 2nd edition, 2008, p. 90.
[69] It is the only article of the Geneva Conventions that applies in non-international conflicts.
[70] Also men.
[71] *Ch. Lindsay*, Women and War – An Overview, International Review of the Red Cross No. 839 (2000), pp. 561 ff.

ensured to all persons. But women who are arrested or detained in relation to the hostilities are also entitled to specific protection according to their specific needs.[72] Article 5 paragraph 2 (a) of the Additional Protocol II applies to women taking part in the hostilities as well as to civilian women.[73]

So even if women take an active part in hostilities in an internal conflict, international law recognizes and regulates the specific need for protection.

c) Résumé

The special protection of women in detention is justified, because women have different needs for example regarding their body's physical structure. The reproductive role of women, for example, generally makes them particularly vulnerable to shortages in medicine, reliable birth control, and medical treatment. The absence of medical services and basic supplies has vastly different implications for women than for men. It would not be right to treat women exactly the same way as men. Such a distinction between the genders is not regarded as contrary to the general principle of international law forbidding all discrimination.[74] The reason for this is not discrimination against men; rather, they do not have exactly the same needs.

The example of women in detention shows that the international community recognized the special need for protection of women in some areas. As already mentioned, there is no specific legal protection of women against rape and sexual violence. But once more it has been seen that the international community did not ignore the fact that women are in need of special protection under certain specific circumstances. The international community rightly differentiates and does not generally assume the need for special protection of women, or rather, it generally denies the special need for protection.

However, in reality such special protection mostly does not exist in many of the areas mentioned. Women are detained as a result of armed conflict, often in worse conditions than men. The reason for this is that the majority of detainees are men, and there are few prisons or places of detention solely for women. In many cases, female detainees are consequently housed in the men's prison. Since they are fewer in number, their sector is usually the smallest and lacks adequate sanitary and other facilities.[75] Also, women detainees rarely if ever have the possibility to see a gynecologist.

---

[72] *Ch. Lindsay*, Women and War: the detention of woman in wartime, International Review of the Red Cross No. 842 (2001), p. 505 (509).

[73] *Ch. Lindsay*, Women and War: the detention of woman in wartime, International Review of the Red Cross No. 842 (2001), p. 505 (509).

[74] *J. Pejic*, Non-Discrimination and Armed Conflict, International Review of the Red Cross No. 841 (2001), pp. 183 ff.

[75] *Ch. Lindsey*, Women and War – An Overview, International Review of the Red Cross No. 839 (2001), pp. 561 ff.

III. Procedural Aspects

Besides material rules written down in the Rome Statute, procedural rules are of great importance for the protection of women's rights. The protection of both witnesses and victims is a key responsibility of the International Criminal Court.[76]

The Rome Statute contains principles of evidence in cases of sexual violence. These principles do not specifically exist for victims of sexual violence, but they are important in these cases. The reason for this is that the court needs to be guided by some principles to protect the victim.[77] For example the consent of the victim cannot be inferred in some cases (undermining the victim's ability to give her voluntary and informed consent because of threat of force or other comparable conduct). Theses rules provide detailed measures for the protection of victims and witnesses that go far beyond those guaranteed by the previous tribunals. One of these rules is article 68 paragraph (I) (2), which refers directly to women:

"The Court shall take appropriate measures to protect the safety, physical and psychological well-being, dignity and privacy of victims and witnesses. Thereby, the Court shall have regard to all relevant factors, including age, gender as defined in Article 7, paragraph 3, and health, and the nature of the crime, in particular, but not limited to, where the crime involves sexual or gender violence."

This sentence of article 68 (I) substantiates the general provision of article 68 (I) (1) of the Rome Statute on protection as regards the nature of crimes.[78] This helps to identify the particular "group" of vulnerable victims, interalia women, the survivors who are always at risk of re-victimization. Re-victimization can happen in the form of so-called "secondary victimization", which is defined in the UN – Handbook on Victims Rights as the harm that may be caused to a victim by the investigation and prosecution of the case or by publicizing the details of the case in the media.[79]

The International Criminal Tribunal Yugoslavia stated in the *Tadic judgement* mentioned earlier:

"... It has been noted that rape and sexual assault often have particularly devastating consequences, which, in certain instances, may have a permanent detrimental impact on the victim. (...) It has been noted further that testifying about the event is often difficult,

[76] *W. A. Schabas*, An Introduction to the International Criminal Court, 3rd edition, 2008, p. 333.

[77] Rules of Procedure and Evidence, Doc. ICC-ASP/1/3, rule 86; *O. Triffterer*, Commentary of the Rome Statute of the International Criminal Court, 2nd edition, 2008, article 68, para. 2, para. 3.

[78] *O. Triffterer*, Commentary of the Rome Statute of the International Criminal Court, 2nd edition, 2008, article 68, para. 13.

[79] United Nations Office for Drug Control and Crime Prevention, Handbook on Justice for Victims, 1999, p. 9.

particularly in public, and can result in rejection by the victim's family and community. (...) In addition, traditional court practice and procedures have been known to exacerbate the victim's ordeal during trial. Women who have been raped and have sought justice in the legal system commonly compare this experience to being raped a second time."

But article 68 (1) of the Rome Statute concludes with a restriction:

"These measures shall not be prejudicial to or inconsistent with the rights of the accused and a fair and impartial trial."

At the International Criminal Tribunal of the Former Yugoslavia, one of its very first rulings authorized the non-disclosure of the names of witnesses. This decision was discussed according to rule 87 (3) of the Rules of Procedure and Evidence. Rule 87 (3) of the Rules of Procedure and Evidence indicates interalia that

"a chamber may, on a motion or request under sub-rule 1, hold a hearing, which shall be conducted in camera, to determine whether to order measures to prevent the release to the public or press and information agencies, of the identity or the location of a victim, a witness or other person at risk on account of testimony given by a witness by ordering, interalia:

(a) That the name of the victim, witness or other person at risk on account of testimony given by a witness or any information which could lead to his or her identification, be expunged from the public records of the Chamber;

(b) That the Prosecutor, the defence or any other participant in the proceedings be prohibited from disclosing such information to a third party;

(c) That testimony be presented by electronic or other special means, including the use of technical means enabling the alteration of pictures or voice, the use of audio-visual technology, in particular videoconferencing and closed-circuit television, and the exclusive use of the sound media;

(d) That a pseudonym be used for a victim, a witness or other person at risk on account of testimony given by a witness; or

(e) That a Chamber conduct part of its proceedings in camera."

The implication of this provision would seem to be that a truly anonymous witness does not fall within the "special measures" permitted by article 68 (1) of the Rome Statute. Rule 88 gives as an example of such "special measures" those taken

"to facilitate the testimony of a traumatized victim or witness, a child, an elderly person or a victim of sexual violence".

This might involve authorizing testimony in a remote location, behind a screen or by video link, or permitting counsel, a psychologist, a legal representative, or a family member to attend during the testimony of the witness or victim.[80] Judges are instructed to be

[80] Rules of Procedure and Evidence, rule 88 (2).

"vigilant in controlling the manner of questioning a witness or victim so as to avoid any harassment or intimidation, paying particular attention to attacks on victims of crimes of sexual violence".[81,82]

The existence of procedural rules in the Rome Statute is important for the protection of women even after the criminal act. Only if the women can be made to feel safe, will it be possible to call the women as witnesses. That is necessary, because women are witnesses predominantly in cases involving rape and sexual assault, and they are often too scared to stand up as a witness before a court. The identification of the attackers by the victim sometimes needs to be treated with considerable caution. Due to fear of reprisals, many survivors refuse to identify correctly the armed group to which the attackers belong, particularly when the armed groups still control the territory in which they live.[83] That is why it is so important to protect the women even after the criminal act.

4. *Enforcement of Penalization of Sexual Violence against Women*

Having constituted the material and procedural facts regarding the protection of women in armed conflicts, some questions should be highlighted regarding the enforcement of penalization of sexual violence against women by the ICC.

a) *Article 17 (1) (d) of the Rome Statute*

This matter brings us to article 17 of the Rome Statute. It deals with admissibility issues. Article 17 (1) (d) states that a case may be declared inadmissible when

"it is not of sufficient gravity to justify further action by the Court".

The Pre-Trial Chamber I of the ICC held that the following two features must be considered in order to accept the "gravity" in terms of article 17 (1) (d) of the Rome Statute: First, the conduct has to be either systematic or large-scale and second, due consideration must be given to the social alarm such conduct may have caused in the international community. The Chamber stated that if isolated instances of criminal activity were sufficient, there would be no need to establish an additional gravity-driven selection of the crimes.[84] From this point of view, just the need for protection of women in armed conflicts as such does not automatically lead to the affirmation of sufficient gravity in terms of article 17 (1) (d). The law does not make a difference between women and men just because of their gender. Is it necessary to make a difference just because of the

[81] Rules of Procedure and Evidence, rule 88 (5).
[82] *W.A. Schabas*, An Introduction to the International Criminal Court, 3rd edition, 2008, pp. 336 f.
[83] *J. Gardam/ H. Charlesworth*, Protection of Women in Armed Conflict, Human Rights Quarterly 22 (2000), p. 148 (155).
[84] ICC, *Prosecutor v. Lubanga*, para. 41, paras. 65–66.

gender, with the consequence that sexual violence against women would in every case be of sufficient gravity in terms of article 17 of the Rome Statute simply because a woman is the victim? One argument could be to suggest that women are more in the need of protection than men. The special situation of women in armed conflicts could make it necessary to differentiate, because men are fighting and the women stay alone at home. Maybe it could be said that women are still weaker than men and need a special treatment by law. Women could still be the part of the family who need protection by men or by law. Another argument could be that most victims of rape and other forms of sexual violence are women of all ages; male victims are rare.

On the other hand, there are some arguments against the aforementioned differentiation. At present, the role of women has changed. Not all women stay at home while the men fight. The role allocation is not clear anymore. It cannot be right to deny the seriousness in the case of a man, but to confirm the seriousness in that of a woman. As previously mentioned,[85] the vulnerability of a human being is not solely a female trait. From this it follows that gender alone cannot be the determining factor as to whether or not the crime is sufficiently serious. It is the crime, not the gender of the victim, which matters.

The question arises as to whether or not the definition made by the chamber is applicable to the situation of women in armed conflicts. It is questionable whether the first feature "systematic" covers the cases of violence against women in armed conflicts effectually. Systematic conduct in this context means that the behavior is based on a specific attack against the victims affected by such conduct. Systematic attacks do not include typical crimes during armed conflicts, which happen without being methodical. Thus, it is not enough that such conduct occurs mostly in armed conflicts. As was said, the rate of systematic attacks against women increases in armed conflicts.[86] In many armed conflicts, rape and other forms of sexual violence are used as a weapon to destroy an ethnic group. The reason is that in many areas around the world, raped women are ostracized by their ethnic group because they are classified as dishonored. Methodical raping with the corresponding intent is covered by article 17 of the Rome Statute.

But in many cases sexual violence against women in armed conflicts still does not happen systematically.[87] As mentioned previously, in most cases it is a regular side effect of armed conflicts. The definition would lead to the conclusion that many cases of sexual violence in armed conflicts are not of sufficient gravity and are therefore inadmissible in court. This is not convincing, because the

---

85 Cf. under A. II.

86 *Ch. Lindsey*, Women and War – An Overview, International Review of the Red Cross No. 839 (2000), pp. 561 ff.

87 *M. Colombini*, Gender-based and Sexual Violence against Women during Armed Conflict, Journal of Health Management 4 (2002), p. 167 (170).

protection of women as regular victims of severe violations shows the need for another standard to define gravity. Gravity should be regarded as a question of the vulnerability of victims regardless of their gender.

b) Article 124 of the Rome Statute

This rule not only renders the ICC powerless when it comes to crimes of violence against women; it can also be another obstacle to women in enforcing their rights. Especially where sexual crimes are committed against women in armed conflicts, these are the crimes that have to be intensively pursued by the ICC.

Article 124 of the Rome Statute asserts interalia that when a State becomes party to this Statute, it does not accept the jurisdiction of the court with respect to the category of crimes referred to in article 8, when a crime is alleged to have been committed on its territory or by its nationals. It may also be made for a shorter period of time, or according to article 124, second sentence, it may even be unilaterally terminated before the end of the period. According to this article, a declaration may be withdrawn at any time. The seven-year period of time (or where applicable, a shorter period) begins when the Rome Statute enters into force for that respective state.[88] The earliest time is the moment at which the Rome Statute entered into force in accordance with article 126 of the Rome Statute. This article states that

"this Statute shall enter into force on the first day of the month after the 60th day following the date of the deposit of the 60th instrument of ratification, acceptance, approval or accession with the Secretary – General of the United Nations".

That means e.g. 1st July 2002.

Article 124 of the Rome Statute limits the jurisdiction of the ICC. This could be a dangerous breach of the jurisdiction, because this rule authorizes a limited protection of women in armed conflicts. Article 124 of the Rome Statute regulates nothing specifically for sexual violence against women, but the limitation is also a limitation in cases of sexual violence. Therefore article 124 of the Rome Statute is interesting to look at in connection with women as victims of sexual violence in armed conflicts. Of course article 124 of the Rome Statute applies to the other regulations of the Rome Statute as well. For women, it could mean another barrier to prosecuting the perpetrators for their conduct. Because of the fact that rape and sexual violence are less charged on an international level, the regulation in article 124 of the Rome Statute affects women in a special way.

If a state adopts this rule, it is not possible to prove whether or not violence against women in this state constitutes a war crime, a crime against humanity or genocide, and if so, to charge the perpetrators. Impunity may become an addi-

---

[88] *O. Triffterer*, Commentary of the Rome Statute of the International Criminal Court, 2nd edition, 2008, article 68, para. 13.

tional legitimation for the delinquent. Although it is still possible for the state in which the criminal act happened to prosecute such conduct under national law, this is not the same level. As already mentioned, it is different prosecuting on a national or an international level. Furthermore it is problematic for the international community to recognize the criminal conduct and to be unable to react, although the elements of crimes are fulfilled.

III. Establishing Women's Rights in the Future

This article has shown that there are some rules of protection which are especially important for the protection of women during and after an armed conflict. After all, it cannot yet be assumed whether or not international criminal law ensures a broad protection for women in armed conflicts and the enforcement of rights. It is not certain whether the existing rules give all women the most comprehensive protection possible. However, it is certainly important for the future to prove whether or not the protection of women in armed conflicts is sufficient or not. The current situation shows that there is a need for proof and therefore a need to recognize the problematic situation of women in armed conflicts. Sexual violence during armed conflicts needs to be more discussed in public, in order to bring it out of the shadow of other committed war crimes during armed conflicts.

Sexual violence against women is coming more and more into the spotlight of the international community and becoming a less tolerated side effect of armed conflicts. With the establishment of the International Criminal Court, a responsible institution has emerged to prosecute sexual violence against women. The development of the protection of human rights and especially women's rights can be extended.

Sex and Gender[1] Crimes in International Law: Silence, Honor Injury or New International Crime?

Alona Hagay-Frey[2]

"*Where there is war,* there is always sexual assault."[3]

My inquiries into the roots and anchoring of the crime of rape[4] in international law began coincidentally. The vast number of rapes being committed in Sudan, Rwanda, and Yugoslavia were reported frequently in the newspapers. Blurred photos obscured the rape victims' faces, and the interviewees were confused,

---

[1] The term "gender" as opposed to the term "sex" points directly towards the differences between women and men that do not stem from physiological-biological differences, but rather from culture and society. Similarly, the term "gendered crimes" or "gender crimes", in my approach, is preferable to the terms "sex crimes" because it includes crimes directed towards a man or a woman due to gender status. See *J. Halley*, Rape at Rome: Feminist Interventions in the Criminalization of Sex-Related Violence in Positive International Criminal Law, accepted for publication, Michigan Journal of International Law (2009), p. 75.

[2] This article is based upon parts of the final draft of my master's thesis, which was supervised by Professor Daphne Barak-Erez and Professor Aeyal Gross and submitted for acceptance in May 2009. The author expresses her deep gratitude to her mentors Professor Barak-Erez and Professor Gross for their guidance and valuable critique. Thanks also to my dear friend Daphné Richemond-Barak for her patience and helpful comments, to Stefanie Raker and Kristina Kühl for their valuable help and last but not least to my dear husband and my best friend Asaf Hagay-Frey for his infinite support and continuous encouragement.

[3] *K. D. Askin*, War Crimes against Women: Prosecution in International War Crimes Tribunals, The Hague, 1997.

[4] Note that the term "rape" is intended to refer to all violent sex crimes and not only rape in its classic meaning. See *B. S. Moshan*, Women, War, and Words: The Gender Component in the Permanent International Criminal Court's Definition of Crimes Against Humanity, Fordham International Law Journal 22 (1998), p. 154. In her article, *Brook Sari Moshan* discusses a broad array of crimes that have been termed "gendered crimes" and that share a common foundation: women are the victims to a greatly disproportionate degree. I emphasize that I do not intend to exclude male victims. See for example: *S. Sivakumaran*, Sexual Violence against Men in Armed Conflict, European Journal of International Law 18 (2007), p. 253. However, in the majority of sex crimes the victims are women. In addition, rape of men by men is committed mostly against a one-dimensional background, the inter-racial background of the war – the first stratum. In contrast, rape of women is committed mostly against a bi-dimensional background – inter-racial and inter-gender/sexual – *two* distinct strata. Therefore, my argument is that this crime is more complex.

scarred, and shaken; however, the injured, the family members of people killed in the war and other random speakers are filmed in color, interviewed and documented not only as refugees and victims, but also as heroes.

This distorted reality resonated with my experiences working at the Tel Aviv Rape Crisis Center. Over many months, I was taught that those who have been sexually assaulted feel guilty, stigmatized, and rejected. Yet at the same time, I saw instances in Israeli society of attackers holding senior positions, acting as if the bodies of all subordinate women are permitted to them. These same attackers are glorified with ranks and a supportive wife, and they cast an arrogant look that seems intended to clarify that women fall into their hands like ripe and yielding fruit.

In my research, I plunged into the depths of international law, and I waded through various legal eras, until I finally arrived at the most current law, the modern criminal code – the Rome Statute.[5] I conducted my journey armed with feminist critical theories that enable the exposure of gaps and silences and that paint a transparent reality with sharp and prominent colors.

I discovered that the gender subordination that exists in day-to-day reality dictated the slow and differential development of the crime of rape within domestic law, and, in parallel, within international criminal law.

International criminal law began taking its shape and formation, and was finally consolidated in the Rome Statute, the most up-to-date criminal code, which rests on the broad agreement of 108 countries of the world. In this code, sex crimes found their place in *some* of the categories of crime that are anchored in it – despite the fact that in the opinions of the international tribunals in Rwanda and Yugoslavia, sex crimes were anchored in all of the categories of crime in international criminal law.

My argument is that in each and every one of the categories of crime existing in the international law, it is appropriate to include certain aspects of sex crimes, and that there is no legal or other justification for the fact that sex crimes are not included in *all* the categories of crime that exist in international criminal law. However, my argument does not end there. Even if the Rome Statute were to recognize sex crimes as an inseparable part of the traditional crime categories, it would be insufficient. The deeper problem lies in the fact that sex crimes in international law contain two distinct crimes: a racial crime and a gender crime. These crimes have different characteristics and, therefore, at times they require

[5] Rome Statute of the International Criminal Court, July 17, 1998, U.N. Doc. A/CONF. 183/9 (1998), 37 I.L.M. 999 ("Rome Statute"). The Rome Statute unified the entire history of criminal law in an organized manner and thus today constitutes the modern code of international criminal law. To date, 108 countries have ratified the Rome Statute. The vast majority of the Rome Statute can be considered as reflecting international customary criminal law because it rests on such a broad consensus of most of the countries of the world. However, some countries, such as the United States and Israel, have reservations about a limited number of provisions and thus have not signed and/or ratified the treaty.

different legal treatment. Now that the silence has been breached with respect to the racist sex crime, the recognition has been almost completed, but the gender sex crime remains without a solution and it is only recognized indirectly.

In Part One, I begin with the feminist discourse. I discuss the various feminist theories' critiques of international criminal law in general, and the relationship of international law to sex crimes, in particular. In the continuation of the article, this discussion will enrich the critique of the development of international law, beginning with the early absence of any anchoring of sex crimes and concluding with the current normative situation.

In Part Two, I embark on an historical journey, jumping among different eras in international law. This survey begins with what I refer to as the *Era of Silence*, beginning with the creation of international law and concluding in 1949 with the drafting of the Geneva Conventions. The Geneva Conventions mark the start of the second era – the *Era of Honor* – in that, for the first time, they anchor the crime of rape as a crime under international law, enumerated in the list of crimes against honor. I discuss the problems inherent in this link between rape and honor and its roots, as well as the importance of separating the crime of rape from issues of honor and anchoring rape as a "war crime" and "crime against humanity" in all respects. The *Third Era* commences in the 1990s, with the establishment of the international criminal tribunals for Yugoslavia and Rwanda. These ad hoc courts created a temporary revolution in their treatment of sex crimes in international law. Finally, the survey concludes with the permanent International Criminal Court and the new *status quo* it has created.

In Part Three, I complete the puzzle. First, I summarize the achievements of the international law in recent years, predominantly their insertion of sex crimes into the existing categories of crime under international law. Simultaneously, I expose the difficulties that are inherent in these developments, while comparing existing law to desirable law. I also propose a new perspective for the analysis of sex crimes as a separate international crime, and I summarize the complexities of these crimes.

In the Summary, I draw conclusions and summarize a normative proposal – to leave sex crimes as part of the existing crimes, to add sex crimes to the crime of "genocide," and, simultaneously, to recognize sex crimes as separate crimes under certain circumstances.

In the complete thesis that I authored, and on which this article is based, I propose the preliminary draft of a new crime category – "sex and gender crimes" – as a separate international crime. It would be a new category of crime that would compel the international community to undertake action: to harness collective efforts, to apprehend, to bring to trial and to convict the sex criminals who to date have committed their crimes without any hindrance.

I. Feminism and International Law

In order to understand the convoluted development of international criminal law regarding wartime sex crimes, the feminist background has great significance alongside the historical background, which is discussed in Part II. The goal of this section is to gather the tools that will enrich the critique in the rest of this article of the deficient anchoring of sex crimes in international law, from its beginnings to the present day.

At the outset, I wish to emphasize that the aspirations of feminist analysis of international law go beyond the objective of advancing women's issues. It has the ability to contribute to the development and advancement of international law as a legal branch with relevance to modern reality. For example, consider the feminist "search for silences," *i.e.*, inquiries into those subjects that the international law chooses to leave untreated, or treated only partially or secondarily,[6] such as the subject of this article.

The feminist argument is, primarily, that international law was invented and formulated by men in order to protect men, and therefore, historically, it ignored violence against women.[7] This argument is similar to other claims made against other legal branches, yet it is strengthened vigorously in light of the incontestable historical maleness of the battlefield. The lack of women's involvement in decisions to instigate armed conflicts, the minimal number of women in the international legal field, and the nearly exclusive involvement of men as legislators and judges in international law, contributed in the past as well as today to the failure of international law in the area under discussion. These factors perpetuate female inferiority and prevent assistance in subject areas related to women.

The varied tools born from different feminist theories enable a more accurate and sharper exposure of the gender bias in international law. They also create an opening for an intensive and challenging discussion about various aspects of international law from different feminist perspectives.[8] Therefore, as have many others before me, in my research I chose to adopt an eclectic approach drawing on a number of feminist streams of thought.[9]

Despite the developments in humanitarian law with respect to women's rights, the role of women in international law remains peripheral. For example,

---

[6] *N. Gil-Ad*, A Feminist Perspective of International Public Law, in: D. Barak-Erez (ed.), Studies in Law, Gender and Feminism, Sarigim-Leon 2007, p. 195.

[7] *K. D. Askin*, War Crimes against Women: Prosecution in International War Crimes Tribunals, The Hague 1997, pp. 47 ff.

[8] For a discussion of the eclectic feminist approach to international law, see: *N. Gil-Ad*, A Feminist Perspective of International Public Law, in: D. Barak-Erez (ed.), Studies in Law, Gender and Feminism, Sarigim-Leon 2007, p. 191.

[9] *N. Gil-Ad*, A Feminist Perspective of International Public Law, in: D. Barak-Erez (ed.), Studies in Law, Gender and Feminism, Sarigim-Leon 2007, p. 192.

in all the years that the International Court of Justice has existed, only one woman has been appointed to serve as a judge, *Rosalyn Higgins*, who was appointed in 1995. Women have never served as members of the United Nation's International Law Commission, nor has a woman ever served as the general secretary of the United Nations.[10, 11] Moreover, in recent years there has not been any significant increase in the miniscule number of women serving in professional and senior positions within the U. N. system.[12]

Accordingly, an analysis of international law's view of women demonstrates that in each of those rare instances in which international law does relate to women, they are viewed primarily as victims, and especially as mothers or potential mothers, and, on that basis, they are considered worthy of defense. Hence, the absence of women in the international arena highlights the lack of political equality and the inferior power of women, as expressed by radical feminism, which I discuss later.[13]

It is especially noteworthy that Resolution Number 1820, which was adopted unanimously in 2008 by the U. N. Security Council, emphasizes the importance of women's participation in peace conferences and dispute resolution:

> "Reaffirming the important role of women in prevention and resolution of conflicts and in peace-building, and stressing the importance of their equal participation and full involvement in all efforts for the maintenance and promotion of peace and security, and the need to increase their role in decision-making with regard to conflict prevention and resolution."[14]

In other words, the call for appropriate representation of women in the existing system of international law is not just an expression of the doctrine of liberal feminism that accepts the existing "masculine" system as the environment within which women must seek influence and equal opportunities. The demand

---

[10] See *H. Charlesworth/C. Chinkin/S. Wright*, Feminist Approaches to International Law, American Journal of International Law 85 (1991), pp. 624 ff.

[11] I wish to emphasize that the lack of representation of women in the international sphere is but a mirror of the parliamentary lack of representation of women in the domestic legal system. In the complete version of my master's thesis, I discuss at length the gender problems in the domestic legal system.

[12] *Noam Gil-Ad* notes in his article that on 22 December 2003, the General Assembly of the United Nations adopted a resolution (GA Res. 58/144) expressing concern that for two consecutive years there has been a slowing in the narrowing of the gap of representation between women and men in professional roles and senior roles in the U. N. (Report of Secretary General: "Improvement of the Status of Women in the United Nation System", Doc. A/59/357 (20 September 2004), at: http://daccessdds.un.org/doc/UNDOC/GEN/N04/507/76/PDF/N0450776.pdf?OpenElement (accessed 20 August 2008). See: *N. Gil-Ad*, A Feminist Perspective of International Public Law, in: D. Barak-Erez (ed.), Studies in Law, Gender and Feminism, Sarigim-Leon 2007, p. 198.

[13] See *C. MacKinnon*, "Feminism Unmodified: Discourses on Life and Law", Harvard 1987.

[14] Security Council Resolution 1820 (2008), adopted on 19 June 2008 ("Resolution 1820").

for equal representation exposes the silencing and the subjects that international law avoids treating, and points to the boundary line dividing those subjects that are covered under the wing of international law and those that are not. This boundary line overlaps to a great degree with the gender line.

The liberal argument that it is sufficient to provide formal equal opportunities to women and men to serve in these roles turns out to be problematic for two fundamental reasons. The first is the different starting point that men acquire due to their roles as the major-generals and generals in war. This starting point grants to men a fixed advantage over women. The second reason is that, although subjects such as maintaining peace and human rights are not inherently gendered, nonetheless, women's voice in its distinctiveness, uniqueness, and decision-making style, can add variety and stimulate creativity in the international arena with respect to these subjects. The liberal claim about equal opportunities ignores this potential positive contribution of women in law, and therein lies its weakness. Moreover, the impact of these subject areas on men and women is not uniform.[15]

In their books, both *Carol Gilligan*[16] and *Catherine MacKinnon*[17] use the terminology of the "voice" and expose the silence and silencing of the feminine voice in modern society,[18] albeit via different techniques.[19] Giving a "voice" in law in general, and in a legal proceeding in particular, is a political act constituting part of the struggle for change in the hierarchical power structure of society.[20]

Gilligan and "cultural feminism" emphasize the different way that women behave in different contexts and their "different voice."[21] Hence, for example, in the international context, it has been claimed based on empirical research that women tend to support peace initiatives, environmental protection, and the provision of social services to a greater extent than men.[22] Another claim is that

---

[15] On the fact that sometimes human rights affect women and men differently, see *H. Charlesworth/C. Chinkin*, The Gender of Jus Cogens, Human Rights Quarterly 15 (1993), p. 63 (75 f.).

[16] See *C. Gilligan*, In a Different Voice: Psychological Theory and Women's Development, Harvard 1982.

[17] See *C. MacKinnon*, Only Words, Harvard 1993.

[18] *L. Bilsky*, Violence of the mute, Iyunei Mishpat 23 (2000), p. 421.

[19] *Carol Gilligan* calls for listening to the different and silenced female voice. In contrast, *Catherine MacKinnon* believes that this listening is essential, but that it is impossible without a fundamental change in the ways of the world. I discuss this point in the continuation of this section.

[20] *L. Bilsky*, Violence of the mute, Iyunei Mishpat 23 (2000), p. 421; *K. T. Bartlett*, Feminist Legal Methods, Harvard Law Review 103 (1990), p. 829.

[21] For *Gilligan's* theory, which is based on the assumption that the way in which women think is different from that of men's from within an ethic of care and connection, see: *C. Gilligan*, In a Different Voice: Psychological Theory and Women's Development, Harvard 1982.

[22] See *N. Gil-Ad*, A Feminist Perspective of International Public Law, in: D. Barak-Erez (ed.), Studies in Law, Gender and Feminism, Sarigim-Leon 2007, p. 198; *H. Charlesworth/C.*

the decision-making style in those entities with greater representation of women fosters discussions that are rooted in more open and inclusive language, as distinct from "male" discussions characterized by polarized claims and conflict.[23]

In contrast, *Catherine MacKinnon's* view is that it is the long-term silencing of women which is the source of the difference. Male freedom of speech has silenced female freedom of speech. Trampling of women and their subordination has weakened their voice and created an internalized consciousness of subordination. Therefore, maintains *MacKinnon*, we should not sanctify the difference. According to her theory, *Gilligan's* celebration of difference is unwarranted.

In my opinion, the roots of the difference should indeed be condemned and altered, yet if the results of this oppression lend variation and a positive nuance to the discussion and to the international discourse, then they should be embraced. In addition, shattering the existing frameworks and thinking beyond traditional categories is likely to lead to substantive change.

Moreover, in my opinion, the discussion about human rights has a different impact on women than on men. Women have the most to lose and the most to gain from any change, even the slightest, in the human rights arena, particularly with respect to sex crimes during conflict. In other words, any changes regarding human rights are likely to have a greater impact on women than on men, even marginally – not due to differences between the two genders but rather due to the relationships of subordination and control, which to some extent still remain.

The foregoing applies also to the subject of this article. For years, international law was mute about everything related to sex crimes in war, a subject which primarily affects women and, on that basis, presumably, it turned a blind eye and chose to exclude sex crimes from the law.

II. Sex Crimes and International Criminal Law: Past, Present, Future?

"Imagine that for hundreds of years your most formative traumas, your daily suffering and pain, the abuse you live through, the terror you live with, are unspeakable – not the basis of literature. When you try to speak of these things, you are told that it did not happen, you imagined it, you wanted it, you enjoyed it. Books say this. No books say what happened to you. Law says this. No law imagines what happened to you, the way it happened."[24]

Chinkin/S. Wright, Feminist Approaches to International Law, American Journal of International Law 85 (1991), p. 616.

[23] *N. Gil-Ad*, A Feminist Perspective of International Public Law, in: D. Barak-Erez (ed.), Studies in Law, Gender and Feminism, Sarigim-Leon 2007, pp. 191 ff.

[24] *C. MacKinnon*, Only Words, Harvard 1993, p. 3.

In this Part, I embark on an historical journey to the cradle of international criminal law and follow the development of the crime of rape. I present the existing situation and the lessons from history in order to lay a foundation for the discussion about potential reforms of international criminal law, which is undertaken in the third section.

1. *The Era of Silence*

In the midst of the darkness of battle, women have been excluded from and denied protection of the law. Their bodies have been accessible to all claimers with impunity. The existing everyday gender-biased subordination of women has dictated the sluggish and unique development of the rape felony both in domestic law and in international criminal law. This subordination has excluded rape felonies from the law in an era that I refer to as the *Era of Silence*.

Throughout history, women have suffered from mass rape during times of war. In 1204, the Crusaders raped women in Constantinople. In 1937, Japanese soldiers raped women in Nanking. During WWII, German soldiers raped many Jewish and Russian women, and toward the end of the war Russian soldiers raped German women. In 1971, Pakistani soldiers raped Bangladeshi women, and American soldiers raped Vietnamese women.[25]

We cannot identify a specific moment in history when rape during war was declared a criminal act in the international context.[26] The historical development of women's rights in war and their anchoring in international law developed in a non-uniform manner. For example, *Totila the Ostrogoth*, who conquered Rome in 546 A.D., forbade his soldiers from raping the women of the city.[27] One of the oldest legal codes that have survived is the Articles of War published in 1385 A.D. by *Richard II* of England. Among the 124 articles defining the rules of conduct for soldiers, King Richard prescribed the punishment of hanging for any soldier who was brazen enough to force himself upon a woman, and a similar punishment was prescribed for soldiers who dared to plunder a church.[28] Nevertheless, later during the 17th century, the Dutch jurist *Hugo Grotius* was compelled to wonder about the fact that certain states accepted the violation of the dignity of women in wartime as a permissible act, whereas during the same time period other states believed otherwise. In 1785, the United States and Prussia agreed in the Treaty of Amity and Commerce that in the event of a war among them, children and women would not be molested. In order no. 20 of the United States General *Winfield Scott* in 1847, a severe

---

[25] *S. Brownmiller*, Against Our Will: Men, Woman and Rape, New York 1975, pp. 31 ff.
[26] *S. Brownmiller*, Against Our Will: Men, Women and Rape, New York 1975, pp. 31 ff.
[27] *S. Brownmiller*, Against Our Will: Men, Women and Rape, New York 1975, pp. 31 ff.
[28] *S. Brownmiller*, Against Our Will: Men, Women and Rape, New York 1975, pp. 31 ff.

punishment for soldiers was provided for soldiers who committed rape. The Lieber Code of 1863, adopted by the United States and several European countries, provided in article 44 that soldiers committing acts of rape against the population of an invaded country would be punished with death. The Hague Conventions of 1899[29] and 1907[30] ("Hague Conventions") did not explicitly refer to rape and other sexual violence, but they provided in general language that there is an obligation toward "family honors" and "religious convictions and practice." These words were interpreted as granting protection to women against sexual violence.[31]

In light of the horrors of World War I, a commission was established to determine the responsibilities of the war's instigators and to enforce penalties.[32] This commission placed rape and forced prostitution near the top of thirty-two war crimes.[33]

Nearly 20 years later, the greatest horror ever documented in human history began – World War II. Again, sexual attack was an inseparable part of the interracial battle and it concomitantly continued to be a characteristic of gender subordination. During WWII, sex crimes occurred – both as encouragement for the fighting forces and as part of the policies of the conquering forces.[34] Both the Nazi and the Japanese regimes instituted various forms of forced prostitution and ignored the high frequency of acts of rape. For example, the Japanese regime established the institution of "comfort women," women who were kidnapped and imprisoned in order to provide for the sexual desires of the fighting soldiers.[35] Despite the fact that the international community was aware of these sexual horrors, not a single step was taken to prevent them. The *Era of Silence*

---

[29] Hague Convention (II) Laws and Customs of War on Land: 29 July 1899 32 Stat. 1803, 187 Consol. T.S. 429. Located at http://www.yale.edu/lawweb/avalon/lawofwar/hague02.htm (accessed 24 September 2008).

[30] Hague Convention (IV) Respecting the Laws and Customs of War on Land, with Annex of Regulations, 18 October 1907, T.S. No. 539, 1 Bevans 631, 36 Stat. 2277 (entered into force 26 January 1910). Located at http://www.yale.edu/lawweb/avalon/lawofwar/hague04.htm (accessed 24 September 2008).

[31] *Y. Khushalanai*, Dignity and Honor of Women as Basic and Fundamental Human Rights, The Hague 1982.

[32] This commission is referred to by various titles: the "War Crime Commission," the "Peace Conference Commission," "The Commission on Responsibility of Authors of the War," and simply as the "1919 Commission." See *K. D. Askin*, War Crimes against Women: Prosecution in International War Crimes Tribunals, The Hague 1997, p. 42.

[33] The crime of rape is listed fifth and immediately afterwards comes forced prostitution or, in the words of the commission: "kidnapping of children and women for purposes of forced prostitution." History of the United Nations War Crimes Commission and the Development of the Laws of War (HM Stationary), London 1948.

[34] *T. Meron*, Rape as a Crime Under International Humanitarian Law, American Journal of International Law 87 (1993), p. 424 (425 f.).

[35] Note that only in 1993, in a declaration called the "Kono Statement," did the Government of Japan take responsibility for these horrendous crimes and apologize formally to the women who were kidnapped and enslaved as sex slaves to service the Japanese soldiers in war

continued. However, this time, unlike in the past, the Allied forces reacted by establishing two international tribunals to prosecute those accused of war crimes – the International Military Tribunal in Nuremberg and the International Military Tribunal for the Far East in Tokyo. These two tribunals relied on the provisions of the Hague Conventions that had been recognized as part of customary international law. This was a golden opportunity to breach the silence, to recognize sex crimes as international crimes, and to convict for these crimes. Yet despite the numerous testimonies and extensive evidence regarding forced abortion, sexual slavery, forced prostitution, and sexual mutilation, the silence continued, and these crimes were excluded from the trials conducted in Nuremberg against the war criminals. In Tokyo, the heavy silence was breached by whispering. Although the tribunal's Charter was indeed silent, the sex offenders were given sentences for these crimes, in addition to their sentences for other crimes. Although rape and the other sex crimes were not specifically stated in the indictments, rape was deemed to be "inhumane treatment", "ill-treatment", and "a failure to respect family honour and rights."

The foregoing review demonstrates that prohibitions on sexual violence against women during war have existed for over 200 years. However, historically, both treaty and customary international law have ignored sex crimes, have not anchored them explicitly in the law, and have not punished the sex criminals.[36] While there have been legal statements denouncing the practice of sexual violence in war, and an undertaking to end the sexual violence that became widespread during wars and armed conflicts, the measures taken were insufficient to protect women. Moreover, sex crimes in times of conflict always have been perceived as lesser crimes and perhaps even excused, as compared to other crimes against "the rules of war."[37] Or, as summarized by *Theodor Meron*:

> "In many cases, however, rape has been given license, either as an encouragement for soldiers or as an instrument of policy. Nazi and Japanese practices of forced prostitution and rape on a large scale are among the egregious examples of such policies."[38]

Upon the conclusion of the Nuremberg and Tokyo tribunals, the Allied forces began a second series of trials with the objective of bringing to justice lesser war criminals. These trials were conducted in national military courts, which were authorized by Control Council Law No. 10 ("CCL10").[39] The CCL10 included

---

time. See *E. Totsuka*, Commentary on a Victory for 'Comfort Women': Japan's Judicial Recognition of Military Sexual Slavery, Pacific Rim Law & Policy Journal 8 (1999), p. 47.

[36] *J. Campanaro*, Women, War, and International Law: The Historical Treatment of Gender Based War Crimes, Georgetown Law Journal 89 (2001), p. 2565.

[37] *J. Campanaro*, Women, War, and International Law: The Historical Treatment of Gender Based War Crimes, Georgetown Law Journal 89 (2001), p. 2565.

[38] *T. Meron*, Rape as a Crime Under International Humanitarian Law, American Journal of International Law 87 (1993), p. 426.

[39] Allied Control Council Law No. 10, Punishment of Persons Guilty of War Crimes,

"rape" in the crime category of "crime against humanity" (in contrast with gender crimes and even other sex crimes, which were not included in the CCL10). However, the crime of "rape" was not included in the crime category "war crime."[40]

This CCL 10 authorized the prosecution of any war criminal, not solely criminals from the "aggressor" countries, *i.e.*, those that instigated the war. Thus, an opportunity was created to bring many rapists to justice. However, in practice, the crime of rape was not included in even one indictment.[41]

2. *The Era of Honour*

The silence was finally broken upon the signing of the Geneva Conventions in 1949.[42] This was the opening shot of the *Era of Honour*, in which the crime of rape was recognized for the first time as a violation of international law. Article 27 states:

> "Women shall be especially protected against any *attack on their honour*, in particular against rape, enforced prostitution, or any form of indecent assault." (Emphasis added).

As indicated by the provision's express language, the harm recognized by law was the injury to the victim's honour, not to the victim's dignity as a human being.[43] Thus, according to the Geneva Conventions, rape harms women's social

---

Crimes Against Peace and Against Humanity, 20 December 1945, Official Gazette of the Control Council for Germany 3 (1946), p. 49.

[40] There is a substantive difference between the two categories of crime, embedded in the different elements required for each category of crime. See *T. Meron*, Rape as a Crime Under International Humanitarian Law, American Journal of International Law 87 (1993), p. 425.

[41] I note that the name I selected for this historical era (the *Era of Silence*) refers not only to the silence of international law regarding sex crimes, but also to the silence of society and the language regarding sex crimes. As *Fionnuala Ni Aolain* described: "We use the words rape, sexual assault, prostitution, and sexual violation with the sense of a distinct reference model within which the acts are understood and the harms take place. This reference model was not in place either during or immediately following the Second World War. This is not the vocabulary of women describing the violence done to them or to others." *F. N. Aolain*, Rethinking the Concept of Harm and Legal Categorizations of Violence During War, Theoretical Inquiries in Law 1 2000, no. 2, p. 307 (313 ff.).

[42] First Geneva Convention "For the Amelioration of the Condition of the Wounded and Sick in Armed Forces in the Field," 27 July 1949, 118 L. N. T. S. 303; Second Geneva Convention "For the Amelioration of the Condition of Wounded, Sick and Shipwrecked Members of Armed Forces at Sea," 12 August 1949, 75 U. N. T. S. 85; Third Geneva Convention "Relative to the Treatment of Prisoners of War," 12 August 1949, 75 U. N. T. S. 135; Fourth Geneva Convention "Relative to the Protection of Civilian Persons in Time of War," 12 August 1949, 75 U. N. T. S. 287.

[43] *Orit Kamir* analyses the distinction between "*honor*" and "*dignity*" at length. "*Honor societies*" are those in which "honor," on the one hand, and "shame," on the other hand, serve as two sides of the same value by means of which the social structure and hierarchical status are conceptualized. Dishonorable behavior is perceived as casting a stain of disgrace on a person's good name and brings shame and humiliation. This stain of shame adheres to the individual's honor, and also casts its shadow on the honor of everyone who is defined as re-

honour and not their dignity as human beings. This reference to honour not only diminishes the value of the injury itself, but also blurs and hides the cruelty of the physical injury, with respect both to its social aspect and its personal aspect. This focus on honour reduces the motivation to prosecute sex offenders and creates a tendency for the system to punish criminals for crimes that are perceived to be more serious.

Hilary Charlesworth explained:

> "The provision assumes that women should be protected from sexual crimes because they implicate a woman's honour, reinforcing the notion of women as man's property, rather than because they constitute violence."[44]

This reflects the perception that rape in the international legal context is an act committed against another entire race, a crime that is characterized as a struggle of one group against another. This perception ignores the victim and erases the gender aspect. In other words, in the context of the focus on honour, the idea that rape results from women's subordination and men's supremacy is rendered invisible. The focus in the Geneva Conventions on an abstract requirement of an injury to a woman's honour not only transforms the crime of rape into a theoretical crime, but also emphasizes the inferiority of sex crimes under international law.

Also, note that shifting the discussion to the harm to honour both hides the victim's physical and emotional harm, and requires that the measurement of the victim's harm be based on the injury to honour. This shift also distances the criminal from the crime and places the victim at the centre of the investigation.

> "The focus on the victim's protection, dignity and honour serves to distance the crime from the perpetrator. This distance is potentially harmful. It could lead prosecutors and judges considering charges of sexual slavery (or enforced prostitution) to focus on an evaluation of harm to honour or dignity and overlook consideration of sexual autonomy."[45]

This requirement of the abstract injury to "honour" converts the crime of rape into a theoretical offence. In order for the crime of rape to become concrete, the drafters of the Conventions would need to have adapted its elements to those of the crimes "wilful killing, torture, or inhuman treatment" and "wilfully caus-

---

lated to or allied with the person. Thus in many societies the rape of women is considered an injury to the entire community's honor and a "mark of Cain" on the victim that can never be erased. In order to acquire honor, one must act in accordance with a specific social code. On the other hand, "*dignity*" is a universal and uniform feature with which all human beings are born, as an inherent characteristic of their humanity. See *O. Kamir*, Israeli Honor and Dignity: Social Norms, Gender Politics and the Law, Carmel 2004, pp. 19ff.

[44] *H. Charlesworth*, Feminist Methods in International Law, American Journal of International Law (Symposium on Method in International Law) 93 (1999), p. 386.

[45] *H. Charlesworth*, Feminist Methods in International Law, American Journal of International Law (Symposium on Method in International Law) 93 (1999), pp. 650ff.

ing great suffering or serious injury to body or health." However, the drafters of the Conventions did not do this, and they thereby made the chances of submitting an indictment for the crime of rape unlikely.[46, 47]

A discussion of the *Era of Honour* would be incomplete without a reference to *Janet Halley*, who supports the position taken by the Geneva Conventions. In her view, the Geneva Convention protects both women and men as part of its universal protection for human beings. She believes that the addition declaring protection for the honour of women adds to the usual protection for women and men.

> "There is no trace of the patriarchal conception of honour in the pattern or in the words that construct it, I would hazard to say. Rather, we have universal rights of man, and the claim that they require specification because of the special harms that befall women … ."[48]

This position is unconvincing, in my opinion. It appears that this treatment of women distinguishes them from the general rule, which deals with the protection of men. However, the interpretation of the Geneva Convention in retrospect, from today's feminist standpoint, overlooks the historical background of words written in the *Era of Silence*: the choice of the word "honour" and not "dignity" is by no means accidental; it points to the roots of the offence – an injury to the masculine honour.

I will summarize the origin and emphasize the terms that *Halley* ignores: WWII and the immoral treatment of women and even children lead to the conclusion that special treatment of women is required on the basis of respect for the person, honour and family rights.[49] In that respect, *Halley* claims, there is

---

[46] *R. Copelon*, Gendered War Crimes: Reconceptualizing Rape in Time of War, in: J. Peters/A. Wolper (eds.), Women's Rights, Human Rights, New York 1995, p. 197.

[47] I further note that in the 1940s, when the Geneva Conventions were drafted, rape was not considered "torture." Torture was perceived as a means to extract information. However, international law has since expanded the bounds of the definition of the crime of "torture" to all physical and mental harm that is intended: "(to) punish, intimidate, discriminate, obliterate the victim's personality, or diminish her personal capacities." For further discussion regarding the absence of the recognition of "rape as torture", see *H. Charlesworth/C. Chinkin*, The Gender of Jus Cogens, *N. Gil-Ad*, A Feminist Perspective of International Public Law, in: D. Barak-Erez (ed.), Studies in Law, Gender and Feminism, Sarigim-Leon 2007, pp. 191 ff.; see also *A. Kalosieh*, Consent to Genocide? The ICTY's Improper Use of the Consent Paradigm to Prosecute Genocidal Rape in Foca, Women's Rights Law Reporter 24 (2003), p. 121 (123 f.).

[48] See *J. Halley*, Rape at Rome: Feminist Interventions in the Criminalization of Sex-Related Violence in Positive International Criminal Law, accepted for publication, Michigan Journal of International Law (2009), p. 56.

[49] See *J. Halley*, Rape at Rome: Feminist Interventions in the Criminalization of Sex-Related Violence in Positive International Criminal Law, accepted for publication, Michigan Journal of International Law (2009), p. 56.

no defect: "[T]here is no trace of patriarchal conception of honour."[50] However, *Halley* ignores the comparison that is made between women and children, the placing of the situation in the "moral" field, and the use of the language of honour and family.[51] If we attempt to ignore the lenient language of the provisions, we could claim that the prohibition against rape in wartime under the international Conventions demonstrates that many countries consider rape in wartime to be illegal. On this basis, we could claim that the prohibition against rape in wartime, which is embedded in the Geneva Conventions, is a prohibition comprising part of customary international law.[52]

Anchoring the prohibitions of the Geneva Conventions in customary international humanitarian law is significant in several respects. First, today the Geneva Conventions enjoy broad international recognition. Therefore, unlike other treaties that are binding only on those countries that have become parties to them, the claim can be made that the Geneva Conventions have become part of customary international law and that, therefore, they are binding on all states.[53] Second, the principles of international humanitarian law are binding in both international and national conflicts. Third, the interpretations of international treaty law must be compatible with customary international law.[54]

However, it can also be argued that on the contrary, because the anchoring of the crime of rape in international law is handled in such a patchwork manner, whereby it is either given low importance or none whatsoever, the conclusion must be drawn that, as a matter of law, the crime of rape is not part of the existing norms of international humanitarian law. Consequently, it also can be claimed that rape cannot be considered part of the peremptory norms, or *jus cogens*, which no states are permitted to violate. Moreover, it could even be claimed that, according to this perspective as a technical matter, rape is not subject to any legal prohibition in the international arena.

The conclusion arising from this discussion is thus both dual and ambivalent: on the one hand, we can conclude that the prohibitions in various conventions

---

[50] *J. Halley*, Rape at Rome: Feminist Interventions in the Criminalization of Sex-Related Violence in Positive International Criminal Law, accepted for publication, Michigan Journal of International Law (2009), p. 56.

[51] A woman as a victim is perceived by the categories of family law within the framework of the paternalistic protection of the "minor." Moreover, this protection is located entirely within the moral field rather than the legal field.

[52] Customary international law was born out of the general practices that were customary over a long period of time, at a time when acts of states were based on the belief that they were bound to act in accordance with the practices. *B. E. Carte/P. R. Trimble*, International Law, Aspen 1993, 3rd ed.

[53] *B. A. Isenbeg*, Genocide, Rape, and Crimes against Humanity: An Affirmation of Individual Accountability in the Former Yugoslavia in the Kaaradzic Actions, Albany Review 60 (1997), p. 1051.

[54] *J. Kellenberger*, Forward, in: J. Henckaerts/L. Doswald-Beck (eds.), Customary International Humanitarian Law 1, Cambridge 2005.

in general and in the Geneva Conventions in particular against an act injuring a person's honour, and the requirement that women be protected against rape, are part of international customary law. On the other hand, "rape" and "sexual violence" are not enumerated among the crimes that constitute a "grave breach" of the Geneva Conventions, nor are they included in the Article 3 common to all Geneva Conventions, which ensures minimal protection during both international and domestic armed conflicts. And indeed, as I demonstrate further in Part II, 3, when the drafters of the Rome Statute subsequently began to arrange the categories of international crimes, they chose to continue this train of legal thought and to exclude the crime of rape from the list of crimes comprising "grave violations of the Geneva Conventions."

3. A Trend of Transformation, Towards a New Era?

Gradually, a new *status quo* emerged, beginning with the establishment of the International Criminal Tribunals for the former Yugoslavia and for Rwanda. These international tribunals recognized sex crimes within *every* existing category of crime in international law: as a crime against humanity, a war crime, a breach of the Geneva Conventions, and even genocide.

a) The International Criminal Tribunal for the Former Yugoslavia (ICTY)

According to the report of the United Nations Special Rapporteur on Human Rights, over 20,000 women were victims of abuse between 1992 and 1994 in the former Yugoslavia. Most of the incidents of rape were committed by Serbian forces.

In an operation which etched "ethnic cleansing" on its flag, hundreds of thousands of Serbs raped thousands of Muslim and Croatian girls and women for the purpose of "forced impregnation." These horrific acts occurred in approximately twenty rape and death camps.[55] Perhaps even more than the incomprehensible number, the circumstances of these horrific acts are shocking. Women were imprisoned in their homes, in hotels or in one of the tens of detention camps, where they were repeatedly raped by Serbian soldiers over many months, and the acts of rape were accompanied by violence and cruelty.[56] The women were used as a means to humiliate, to abuse, and ultimately, to attempt to annihilate an entire population.

---

[55] Note that some of the UN soldiers sent to protect the local population also compelled refugees to submit sexually in order to receive assistance, see *C. MacKinnon*, Rape, Genocide and the Human Rights of Women, in: A. Stiglmayer (ed.), Mass Rape: the War against Women in Bosnia-Herzegovina Lincoln 1994. In the full thesis, I expand upon the issue of sex crimes committed by peace-keeping forces.

[56] *C. B. Coan*, Rethinking the Spoils of War: Prosecuting Rape as a War Crime in the International Criminal Tribunal for the Former Yugoslavia, North Carolina Journal of International Law & Com. Reg. 26 (2000), p. 183 (185 ff.).

The Statute of the International Criminal Tribunal for the Former Yugoslavia[57] ("ICTY Statute") granted the tribunal broad jurisdiction to bring to trial sex criminals and was an important milestone in the struggle for recognition and protection of women's rights in wartime. For example, article 5(g) of the ICTY Statute provided for the first time in the history of international law that the crime of rape was a "crime against humanity." This explicit point constitutes a considerable advance in light of the charters of the previous tribunals (Nuremberg and Tokyo). The ICTY Statute also applies to all crimes, including rape, committed by any agent of war against citizens in order to advance the war.

The crime of rape is the only sex crime enumerated in the list of crimes over which the court has jurisdiction. Other sex crimes were not listed alongside it. This crime only found refuge in the shade of the crime category "crimes against humanity." The other categories of crime under the ICTY's jurisdiction did not include the crime of rape, a fact which diminished the court's ability to recognize and to treat effectively the considerable harm caused by sex criminals to thousands of women during the war.

Apparently, the reasons for the limitations that restricted the possibilities for filing rape claims were, as usual, the absence of an appropriate political lobby and the international law traditions in this subject area.[58] Inclusion of rape in the crime category of "crime against humanity" indeed constituted a step forward from a procedural perspective. Yet, at the same time, the absence of rape from all of the other crime categories subject to the court's jurisdiction was prominent: "genocide", "war crimes" and "grave breaches of the Geneva Conventions."

The first trial held in the ICTY concerned Dusko Tadic.[59] The decision in the Tadic case forged significant judicially-created precedents that influenced the integration of sex crimes into international law. The first count in the indictment charged Tadic with a "crime against humanity" for his involvement in a "[c]ampaign of terror which included killings, torture, sexual assaults, and other physical and psychological abuse,"[60] and with participation in "[t]orture of

---

[57] Statute of the International Criminal Tribunal for the Former Yugoslavia, annexed to Resolution 827, S.C. Res. 827, U.N. SCORE, 48th Sess., Annex, 3217th mtg. at 6, U.N. Doc. S/RES/827 (1993), 32 I.L.M. 1192.

[58] In other words, the historical non-participation of women in decisions affecting all matters related to international law was perpetuated yet again. This issue reinforces women's secondary status on the map of international decision-making. See *K. D. Askin*, A Decade in Human Rights Law: A Decade of the Development of Gender Crimes in International Courts and Tribunals: 1993–2003, Human Rights Br. 11 (2004), p. 16 (17 f.).

[59] Second Amended Indictment, PP4, 4.3, *Prosecutor v. Tadic*, Indictment, Case No. IT-94-1-T (Int'l Crim. Trib. for Former Yugoslavia Dec. 14, 1995), located at http://www.un.org/icty/indictment/english/tad-2ai951214e.htm (accessed 24 September 2008).

[60] Second Amended Indictment, PP4, 4.3, *Prosecutor v. Tadic*, Indictment, Case No. IT-94-1-T (Int'l Crim. Trib. for Former Yugoslavia Dec. 14, 1995), located at http://www.un.org/icty/indictment/english/tad-2ai951214e.htm (accessed 24 September 2008).

more than 12 female detainees, including several gang rapes."[61] Tadic was convicted of other sex crimes involving violence, sexual assaults and sexual mutilation. Surprisingly (or perhaps not), on the first occasion that an international court recognized sex crimes in such a broad fashion (broad both because the accused was charged with sex crimes under all of the existing traditional crime categories, and because varied sexual content was fit into these categories of crime, and not just rape in the traditional meaning), the convictions concerned incidents involving victims who were men and not women.[62]

In June 1996, for the first time in the history of international criminal law, the ICTY imposed criminal responsibility based only on sexual offences committed against women.[63] In *Gagovic*, Serbian soldiers were charged with more than sixty incidents of sexual assault of non-Serbian women; one of the Serbian officers, Dragoljub Kunarac, was charged with entering a detention camp, selecting Muslim women and girls, and taking them to a military base where they were raped and subjected to grievous sexual abuse. In this decision, based nearly entirely on criminal convictions for sexual offences, Tadic was found guilty of twenty-one incidents of rape and torture as "crimes against humanity" and "war crimes."

b) The International Criminal Tribunal for Rwanda (ICTR)

Also in 1994, women in Rwanda were subjected to sexual abuses and brutality – rape, gang rape, sexual mutilation – as part of the conflict opposing the Hutu tribe to the Tutsi tribe.[64] *Major Brent Beardsley*, an assistant to the general of the peace-keeping forces present in Rwanda prior to the genocide and also for a short period during it, testified before the International Criminal Tribunal for Rwanda ("ICTR"). The following is his response to the question of whether he noticed anything unusual about the women's bodies which he saw while in Rwanda:

---

[61] Second Amended Indictment, PP4, 4.3, *Prosecutor v. Tadic*, Indictment, Case No. IT-94-1-T (Int'l Crim. Trib. for Former Yugoslavia Dec. 14, 1995), located at http://www.un.org/icty/indictment/english/tad-2ai951214e.htm (accessed 24 September 2008).

[62] Acts of sexual abuse were committed primarily against prisoners in the context of ongoing physical and mental abuse of them. These facts lead to the recognition that victims of sex crimes are not just women, and that sex crimes are likely to don the characteristics of torture in the context of a comprehensive inter-racial war to which women and men are exposed, as I claim in Part I above.

[63] *Prosecutor v. Gagovic*, Case No. IT-96-23 (Int'l Crim. Trib. for Former Yugoslavia June 26, 1996, located at http://www.un.org/icty/indictment/english/foc-ii960626e.htm, (accessed 22 September 2008). In 1998, the indictment was amended and *Kunarac* became the only defendant in an indictment based solely on sex crimes, see *Prosecutor v. Kunarac*, Case No. IT-96-23-I (Int'l Crim. Trib. for Former Yugoslavia 13 July 1998, located at http://www.un.org/icty/indictment/english/kun1ai980819e.htm, (accessed 19 September 2008).

[64] Human Rights Watch, Shattered Lives: Sexual Violence During the Rwandan Genocide and its Aftermath, 1–2 (1996).

> "[T]wo things, really. One, when they killed women it appeared that the blows that had killed them were aimed at sexual organs, either breasts or vagina; they had been deliberately swiped or slashed in those areas. And, secondly, there was a great deal of what we came to believe was rape, where the women's bodies or clothes would be ripped off their bodies, they would be lying back in a back position, their legs spread, especially in the case of very young girls. I'm talking girls as young as six, seven years of age, their vaginas would be split and swollen from obviously multiple gang rape, and then they would have been killed in that position. So they were lying in a position they had been raped; that's the position they were in."[65]

Yet again, sexual abuse played a significant role in a militaristic attempt to annihilate a population.[66]

As in the ICTY Statute, the ICTR Statute also declared in article 3(g) that rape is a "crime against humanity."[67] The significant contribution of this new tribunal to international law lies in article 4 of the ICTR Statute, which expanded the tribunal's authority and included the crime of rape in the list of breaches of common article 3 of the Geneva Conventions and Protocol II. By using the term "breaches" and not "grave breaches," the ICTR Statute enabled the tribunal to avoid dealing with the distinction between breaches and grave breaches and thereby to add rape and other crimes that can be prosecuted to the list of crimes. Therefore, the jurisdiction of the ICTR, in contrast to the ICTY, thus explicitly covered the crime of rape via the Geneva Conventions.[68] However, since the crime of rape is covered under the wings of international humanitarian law, the pre-condition that the rape occurs as part of an armed conflict was permitted to cast its shadow here as well.[69]

---

[65] Examination-in-Chief of *Brent Beardsley*, former aide to the force commander, General *Roméo Dallaire*, UN peacekeeping mission in Rwanda, Bagasora, Kabiligi, Ntabakuze, Nsengiyumva (ICTR-98-41-T), trial transcript of 3 February 2004. *K.D. Askin*, Gender Crimes Jurisprudence in the ICTR Positive Developments, Journal of International Criminal Justice 3 (2005), p. 1007 (1008 f.)

[66] Examination-in-Chief of *Brent Beardsley*, former aide to the force commander, General *Roméo Dallaire*, UN peacekeeping mission in Rwanda, Bagasora, Kabiligi, Ntabakuze, Nsengiyumva (ICTR-98-41-T), trial transcript of 3 February 2004. *K.D. Askin*, Gender Crimes Jurisprudence in the ICTR Positive Developments, Journal of International Criminal Justice 3 (2005), p. 1007 (1008 f.)

[67] Statute of the International Criminal Tribunal for Rwanda, annexed to Resolution 955, S.C. Res. 955, U.N. SCORE, 49th Sess., Annex, 3453d mtg. at 3, U.N. Doc. S/RES/955 (1994) (the "ICTR Statute"). However, the ICTR Statute gave a narrow meaning to situations under the definition of "armed conflict": the offense must be committed as part of a widespread or systematic attack against a civilian population, against a national, political, ethnic or religious background. This contrasts with the ICTY Statute, which gave a broader interpretation: the possibility to prosecute the crimes listed when they are committed in an "armed conflict," whether national or international, and directed against a civilian population.

[68] I note that article 2 of the ICTY Statute, which refers to grave breaches, does not include within them the crime of rape.

[69] See *J. Halley*, Rape at Rome: Feminist Interventions in the Criminalization of Sex-Related Violence in Positive International Criminal Law, accepted for publication, Michigan Journal of International Law 30 (2009), p. 62.

As a result, from a procedural perspective, the crime of rape was upgraded by its inclusion among the leading criminal offences. However, from a substantive perspective, the Geneva Conventions were strengthened, despite the problematic language of "honour" embedded therein.

Reports documenting the incidents of mass rape as a weapon of the racist and gendered war in Rwanda began to accumulate. Yet nothing was done to bring the criminals to justice. Judge *Navanethen Pillay*, a female judge, was the only member of the international panel that was established who ordered the prosecutors to re-examine the reports and to investigate the incidents of rape, as well as to employ female investigators.[70] Once again, the different voice noticed that which had been ignored, and initiated a change.[71]

In the end, however, very few of the cases heard by the ICTR concerned sex crimes during the war. Nevertheless, a significant precedent in the matter of *Jean-Paul Akayesu*[72] broke new ground and expanded the ability of the international community to prosecute wartime sex crimes. *Akayesu* was found guilty of sexual abuse committed for the purpose of genocide. The court found that the acts of abuse included the intention to annihilate all or part of the Tutsi tribal community.[73] In its decision, the court explained how the acts of rape constitute the grave international crime of "genocide," because they were committed with an intention to destroy Tutsi tribe members physically and mentally, and many women and girls died from their injuries and were murdered. The court also found *Akayesu* guilty of committing acts of rape and forced nakedness as inhumane acts constituting a "crime against humanity." The court defined the crime of rape as:

(A) "Physical invasion of a sexual nature, committed on a person under circumstances which are coercive."[74]

By recognizing that rape harms the personal dignity of the victim, the court in effect held that rape is a type of torture, and it broadened the recognition that

---

[70] *A. Kalosieh*, Consent to Genocide? The ICTY's Improper Use of the Consent Paradigm to Prosecute Genocidal Rape in Foca, Women's Rights Law Reporter 24 (2003), p. 123.

[71] *C. Gilligan*, In a Different Voice: Psychological Theory and Women's Development, Harvard 1982.

[72] *Prosecutor v. Akayesu*, Case No. ICTR-96-4-T (Int'l Crim. Trib. for Rwanda Trial Chamber I (2/9/1998). http://trim.unictr.org/webdrawer/rec/15154/view/AKAYESU%20-%20%20JUDGEMENT.pdf (accessed 25 September 2008) ("Akayesu Decision").

[73] *Prosecutor v. Akayesu*, Case No. ICTR-96-4-T (Int'l Crim. Trib. for Rwanda Trial Chamber I (2/9/1998). http://trim.unictr.org/webdrawer/rec/15154/view/AKAYESU%20-%20%20JUDGEMENT.pdf (accessed 25 September 2008) ("Akayesu Decision"), section 734.

[74] *Prosecutor v. Akayesu*, Case No. ICTR-96-4-T (Int'l Crim. Trib. for Rwanda Trial Chamber I (2/9/1998). http://trim.unictr.org/webdrawer/rec/15154/view/AKAYESU%20-%20%20JUDGEMENT.pdf (accessed 25 September 2008) ("Akayesu Decision"), section 688.

there is no requirement to prove "physical contact" in order to prove a sexual attack. The court emphasized that, although the crime of rape is traditionally defined under state law as "non-consensual sexual intercourse," this definition is too narrow.

This decision significantly strengthened the possibility of bringing criminals to justice for sex crimes under international law. The strengthening is evident not only in the fact that this is the first time that international law recognized "rape" as a form of "genocide." It was also the first time that an international tribunal recognized the possibility of convicting an international sex criminal for the crime of rape and other sex offences that caused emotional harm to the victims, and not only physical harm.[75] Also, the decision formally recognized for the first time that gender crimes were used systematically as a tool of war and terror, such that these crimes had an impact that was more extensive, having an effect far beyond the immediate victim. In its decision, the court recognized the impact of gender crimes on the victims' families, their community, all of the groups involved in the conflict, and the entire society.[76]

Despite these important achievements, the ICTR was criticized for not conducting appropriate investigations and for refusing to amend indictments related to sex crimes during armed conflict. This occurred despite the many testimonies presented to the court, according to which thousands of Rwandan women were subjected to degradation and an array of gender abuses. In order to contend with the challenges it faced, the ICTR needed to integrate gender issues and treatment aspects into its investigations, but it did not do so.[77]

It is possible that more women with professional training in the treatment of sex crimes victims could have been appointed as investigators and translators for the victims' interviews. Also, the ICTR needed to take steps to ensure protection for victims and trial witnesses. This protection is an essential condition for any legal process dealing with sex crimes. Witness protection is required both pre-trial, during the trial and afterwards. If the women victims are not granted protection, upon returning to their villages or moving elsewhere as well, the proceedings cannot achieve their aims.

Additional criticism focused on the inclusion of the crime of rape only when there is a systematic or widespread attack. *Charlesworth*, for example, denounces the *Akayesu* decision for determining that the crimes of rape that were committed are a breach of international humanitarian law and constitute "genocide"

---

[75] *J. Campanaro*, Women, War, and International Law: The Historical Treatment of Gender Based War Crimes, Georgetown Law Journal 89 (2001), p. 2671.

[76] As discussed, the recognition of sex crimes as tools of war and terror found expression recently in Resolution 1820 of the Security Council, adopted on 19 June 2008 ("Resolution 1820").

[77] Human Rights Watch, Shattered Lives: Sexual Violence During the Rwandan Genocide and its Aftermath, 1–2 (1996), pp. 94–95.

only because of the aspect of "destruction of the community". This determination, she argues, does not give expression to an additional and important stratum, the gender stratum:

"Rape is wrong, not because it is a crime of violence against women and a manifestation of male dominance, but because it is an assault on a community defined only by its racial, religious, national or ethnic composition. In this account, the violation of a woman's body is secondary to the humiliation of the group. In this sense, international criminal law incorporates a problematic public/private distinction: it operates in the public realm of the collectivity, leaving the private sphere of the individual untouched. Because the notion of the community implicated here is one defined by the men within it, the distinction has gendered consequences."[78]

To summarize, the two international tribunals established by the authority of the Security Council during the 1990s undertook very important steps in connection with the recognition of sex crimes in international criminal law, but the path has neither been completed nor is it defect-free. In addition, it must be recalled that the authority of these criminal tribunals is limited both by time and territory.[79]

c) The International Criminal Court (ICC)

Undoubtedly, the attention that the Yugoslavian and Rwandan international criminal tribunals devoted to sex crimes preceded in a meaningful way the treatment of these subjects in the international sphere. However, this progress was accompanied by a fundamental problem, namely, the failure to supply principles that would be absorbed into the international criminal law that is binding on all of the states in the world.[80] Moreover, it must be remembered that these courts were *ad hoc* tribunals established *ex post facto* for the conviction of crimes that occurred during a defined period and in defined events. The establishment of *ex post facto* tribunals reduces the deterrent power of judging, makes the legal proceedings more costly and more complex, and by nature does not lead to orderly legal change. Therefore, the need for establishing a permanent international criminal court was heightened.

Finally, in 1992, the U.N. General Assembly decided to advance the establishment of a permanent international court – the International Criminal Court ("ICC").[81] The International Law Commission ("ILC") was given the authority to draft a constitution to establish the permanent court. In 1994, the ILC sub-

---

[78] *H. Charlesworth*, Feminist Methods in International Law, American Journal of International Law (Symposium on Method in International Law) 93 (1999), p. 387.

[79] *M. R. Mumford*, Building upon a Foundation of Sand: A Commentary on the International Criminal Court Treaty Conference, Journal of International Law & Practice 8 (1999), p. 151 (165 f.).

[80] *S. Kimmel*, Prosecuting Sexual Violence as Crimes of War, PA Law 8 (1999), p. 8.

[81] G.A. Res. 47/33, U.N. GAOR, 47th Sess., Supp. No. 49, at 287, U.N. Doc. A/47/49 (1992).

mitted a draft of the constitution for the court. In addition to the other controversies raised by the proposed constitution, the absence of any treatment of gender issues and sex crimes was prominent.[82]

In order for the process, which had been frozen for decades, not to be halted and as a response to ongoing pressure from several women's organizations and other non-governmental organizations, the General Assembly established a new *ad hoc* committee tasked with preparing "[a] widely acceptable ... convention for an international criminal court."[83] With the cooperation and active interest of many countries and NGOs, the new committee began its complex mission of conducting negotiations on the provisions of the proposed constitution for the ICC.

The Women's Caucus of Gender Justice in the International Criminal Court ("Women's Caucus") was founded in 1997. It currently represents approximately three hundred women's organizations. The Women's Caucus created a strong lobby for the protection of women's rights in the international sphere, and this lobby greatly influenced the development of the ICC's statute. Due to the influence of this group, gender principles and various definitions were expanded and strengthened in the constitution's draft, including gender representation among the prosecutors, judges and the staff in general, establishment of a witness and victims unit, and creation of the position of legal adviser for gender issues, whose role is to advise the prosecutor about gender crimes.

Throughout the entire period during which they worked on the wording of the draft of the statute, stormy discussions were held over gender issues.[84] Indeed, the final form of the draft gives expression to some of the successes achieved regarding recognition of sex crimes as crimes in the international sphere. However, the final document also contained a number of failures in the treatment of these subjects, which require future attention.

In 1998, the signing of the Rome Statute[85] signified a midway point – the treaty did not go the extra mile down the path created by the precedents of the Yugoslavian and Rwanda tribunals. On the one hand, sex crimes had been recognized as a crime against humanity in article 7(1)(g):

"Rape, sexual slavery, enforced prostitution, forced pregnancy, enforced sterilization, or any other form of sexual violence of comparable gravity."

---

[82] Report of the International Law Commission on Its Forty-Sixth Session, Draft Statute for an International Criminal Court, U.N.GAOR, 49th Sess., Supp. No.10, U.N.Doc. A/49/10 (1994).

[83] G.A. Res. 50/46, U.N.GAOR, 50th Sess., Supp. No.49, at 1, U.N.Doc. A/Res/50/46 (1995).

[84] *J. Campanaro*, Women, War, and International Law: The Historical Treatment of Gender Based War Crimes, Georgetown Law Journal 89 (2001), p.2560.

[85] Rome Statute of the International Criminal Court, July 17, 1998, U.N.Doc. A/CONF.183/9 (1998), 37 I.L.M. 999.

Sex crimes were also recognized as a war crime in article 8(2)(b)(12):

"Rape, sexual slavery, enforced prostitution, forced pregnancy, as defined in article 7, paragraph 2 (f), enforced sterilization, or any other form of sexual violence also constituting a grave breach of the Geneva Conventions".

And we also find significant progress in article 7(1)(h), which acknowledges gender persecution as a crime against humanity:

"Persecution against any identifiable group or collectivity on political, racial, national, ethnic, cultural, religious, *gender* as defined in paragraph 3, or other grounds that are universally recognized as impermissible under international law." (Emphasis added)

The inclusion of the term "gender" in the context of groups acknowledges that women are a group that can be persecuted, and thus a group with unique needs and concerns that must be protected under international law.

On the other hand, article 6, which defines the crime of genocide, and article 8 1(a), which lists the grave breaches of the Geneva Convention, do not include any sex crimes whatsoever. This silence is a direct continuation of the eras in which these terms were originally written – the *Era of Silence* and the *Era of Honour.*[86]

In addition, the list of sex crimes is not detailed and cannot be understood without future interpretation. For example, the questions are asked: does forced nakedness constitute sexual assault? What are the elements of the crime of rape from the perspective of the Rome Statute? This gap is prominent in comparison to other terms that the Rome Statute chose to define in an explicit manner. [87]

To summarize: two eras have passed. No more silence. No more harm only to honor. A new era has already begun, an era in which sex crimes are recognized as physical and emotional injuries, an era in which special care for victims of sex crimes is part of international law. The Rome Statute explicitly recognizes gender crimes and embeds sex crimes within some of the existing, traditional categories. However, is this sufficient? Is this the change we hoped for as we embarked on our journey?

Certainly not. The journey has not been completed. Part III focuses on these issues.

---

[86] As I discuss above in section 2.2, the Geneva Convention was signed in 1949, which is the beginning of the Era of Honour, and the Convention on the Prevention and Punishment of the Crime of Genocide, 78 U.N.T.S. 277, entered into force on December 9, 1948, during the Era of Silence.

[87] For example, the term "gender" is defined as "male and female", and the crime of "forced impregnation" has been defined such that its intent is to affect the ethnic composition of the population – article 7(2)(f) of the Rome Statute. Again racist, collective, masculine thinking, if you will. Why indeed should the objective of the forced impregnation be relevant? Is not forced impregnation in and of itself, out of a male desire for control and subordination, sufficient?

III. Existing Law and Preferable Law

The aim of this Part III is to demonstrate the failure of the existing crime categories in today's international law with respect to all aspects of sex and gender crimes. This demonstration will include a gathering of the shards of the criticism that was brought to bear on the historical journey described in Part II of this article, and analysis of their relevance in light of the present situation. The purpose is to clarify that the present arrangement is unsatisfactory and to lay a foundation for proposing a solution that is a more appropriate legal arrangement.

The partial recognition of gender and sex crimes in the modern criminal code – the Rome Statute – is not sufficient. Each and every category of crime in international law could and should cover sex crimes, and there is no justification whatsoever, legal or otherwise, for the fact that sex crimes are not included in *every* category of crime in international criminal law.

For example, rape and forced impregnation are likely to constitute "genocide," as the ICTR tribunal ruled in the *Akayesu* opinion,[88] and sex crimes are likely to constitute "grave breaches of the Geneva Conventions," as was determined explicitly in the ICTR Statute.[89] The final version of the Rome Statute does not incorporate this expended interpretation of international criminal law. The silence as regards the categories of the grave crimes of "genocide" and "grave breaches of the Geneva Conventions" in the Rome Statute indicates that international law still views sex crimes as crimes that are less grave than other international crimes.

The silence as regards these categories of crime draws us back to times we want to believe have passed from our world, those dark times when sexual criminals were allowed, in the absence of law, to do as they pleased with women's bodies. However, my argument amounts to more. Even if we assume that the Rome Statute recognizes sex crimes as inseparable from traditional crime categories, it still will be insufficient. The attempt to formulate the law according to a fundamentally male paradigm makes it impossible to properly address sex and gender crimes due to embedded and hidden differences. The attempt to construct rape during conflict simply as an act of violence ignores racist and gender-biased phenomena, and because it ignores aspects of the crime, it is therefore inefficient. In other words, pursuing crimes of sexual violence using the existing categories views the crime of rape as equal and equivalent to other in-

---

[88] *Prosecutor v. Akayesu*, Case No. ICTR-96-4-T (Int'l Crim. Trib. for Rwanda Trial Chamber I (2/9/1998). http://trim.unictr.org/webdrawer/rec/15154/view/AKAYESU%20-%20%20JUDGEMENT.pdf (last visited 25 September 2008) ("Akayesu Decision").

[89] Article 4(e) of the ICTR Statute, Statute of the International Criminal Tribunal for Rwanda, annexed to Resolution 955, S.C. Res. 955, U.N. SCORE, 49th Sess., Annex, 3453d mtg. at 3, U.N. Doc. S/RES/955 (1994) (the "ICTR Statute").

ternational crimes. This act of recognition, though holding great promise, cannot suffice.

I maintain that the underlying stratum of sex crimes, the gender stratum, must be exposed. In order to do so, a new international crime category that will protect and enforce all violent aspects of the phenomenon must be recognized. For example, in article 7(1) of the Rome Statute, the "crime against humanity" category provides:

> "For the purpose of this Statute, 'crime against humanity' means any of the following acts when committed as part of a widespread or *systematic attack* directed against any *civilian population*, with knowledge of the attack." (emphasis added)

Article 8(1) states the "war crime" category:

> "The Court shall have jurisdiction in respect of war crimes in particular when committed as part of a plan or policy or as part of a large-scale commission of such crimes."

Certain improvements must be included in the new category of crime that I propose:

First, this new international crime category will not refer to systematic attacks as crimes against humanity, because sex and gender crimes are often sporadic crimes. Nor will it require the existence of an armed conflict, since gender crimes and sex crimes can occur even outside of an armed conflict.

Second, this new international crime category must protect all human beings, regardless of their gender, race and whether or not they are civilians. Protection must be provided against all sexual attacks, without any regard to his or her lack of consent. The definition of the prohibited sexual act must be as broad as possible. In this context, I would be pleased to adopt the decision of the ICTY in the matter of *Furundzija*,[90] which strengthened the law according to which rape is likely to be a type of torture and even proposed, for the first time, a broad and clear definition of the crime of rape.[91] The court ruled that, despite the absence of an international consensus on the subject, the objective of humanitarian law is the protection of a person's dignity, without regard to gender. Thus, a forced oral act is a degrading act that harms dignity. Forced oral penetration, the court ruled, is as traumatic to the victim as genital or anal penetration. Any other finding would rest on a shaky foundation, and would undermine the central principle behind the crime of rape – the protection of a person's dignity.

Third, the *means rea* of the accused should be tested objectively. In cases of conflict, the subordination is clear-cut. The coercive nature of the situation indicates that true consent is impossible. I refer to the arguments of *Diana Otto*[92]

---

[90] *Prosecutor v. Furundzija*, Case No. IT-95-17/1-T, PP39-41, 41–46 (Int'l Crim. Trib. for Former Yugoslavia Trial Chamber II, 10 December 1998).

[91] *Prosecutor v. Furundzija*, Case No. IT-95-17/1-T, PP39-41, 41–46 (Int'l Crim. Trib. for Former Yugoslavia Trial Chamber II, 10 December 1998), pp. 174 ff.

[92] *D. Otto*, Making Sense of Zero Tolerance Policies in Peacekeeping Sexual Economies,

and *Janet Halley*[93] in order to explain this last concept. According to *Otto* and *Halley*, sometimes during warfare there could be consent to intercourse when women seek to obtain basic necessities such as food or shelter. I claim that in a coercive environment, there is no place for will. Any sexual relationship in a coercive environment is rape. In the same way that domestic law recognizes statutory rape irrespective of the facts regarding consent, and sexual harassment in the workplace assumes a coercive environment, international law similarly must recognize that survival sex in times of conflict is rape.[94] Furthermore, in the same way that signing a treaty under coercive circumstances is a void act,[95] and signing a contract under coercive conditions is a voidable act,[96] this is true in the matter of consent to sexual relations in times of conflicts.

One could claim that dropping the requirements for the systematic nature of the attack, the armed conflict and the issue of consent leaves an inferior crime unworthy of being litigated in the field of international law. In response to this claim, I would argue that the legal vacuum that has existed for so many years in this arena points to the true meaning of the universal jurisdiction which is the foundation on which the ICC was built. Universal jurisdiction developed where domestic jurisdiction was short-handed, in the areas in which terrible wrongs occurred and where, in the absence of this jurisdiction, there is neither justice nor law.

This new category of crime will introduce sex crimes into international law by granting full protection from sex crimes in international tribunals. Furthermore, it will allow international harmonization of the elements of the crime of rape.

Repeatedly throughout human history, women have been tortured, murdered *and* raped. They have been murdered and tortured as the enemy, and they have been tortured and raped as women. *Therefore, these crimes should bear a double punishment – for murder and torture, and for rape.* Women have been tortured and raped not just because of the colour of their skin or their political view. They have been tortured and raped because of their gender on both sides of the forces in conflict.

---

in: V. Munro/C. F. Stychin (eds.), Sexuality and the Law: Feminist Engagements, Oxon/New York 2007, p. 265.

[93] This issue is central to J. Halley in her article: *J. Halley*, Rape In Berlin: Reconsidering the Criminalisation of Rape in the International Law of Armed Conflict 9(1) Melbourne Journal of International Law 9 (2008), no. 1, p. 78. Are sexual relations between a conquered population and the enemy soldiers rape? Or perhaps it is a woman's decision in the context of war?

[94] In my full thesis, I discuss and expand upon this issue, including analysis of an example from Israeli domestic law.

[95] See Vienna Convention on the Law of Treaties, 23 May 1969, 1155 U. N. T. S. 331, article 52.

[96] See, e.g., Israeli contracts law, Contracts Law (General Law), 1977, section 17.

In this section, I have summarized the changes that must be brought about in international criminal law in order to contend in the most appropriate manner with sex and gender crimes. These changes must be anchored in new, separate crime categories of "sex and gender crimes" that will stand alongside the traditional crime categories. In the complete thesis paper that I anticipate publishing in the future, I will present all of the adaptations required for the new crime category, and I will delineate its boundaries, fill it with content, and propose the appropriate wording in light of my conclusions regarding this crime.

IV. Summary and Clarifications

To summarize, there are two important steps that international law should take. As a first step, the international law should include sex crimes in each existing category of crime and regard them as crimes of violence. But this step can only provide a solution for some of the crimes, since including sex crimes in international law according to male paradigms will create gaps wherever there are differences. Hence, a second step is required: construction of a new category of crime, suitable for sex crimes. This category of crime will present sex crimes as a racial and a gender-biased phenomenon, and will not overlook the social reality in which rape is conducted mostly by men and against women. Only by breaking the male dichotomy will the underlying stratum of sex crimes be revealed – the gender stratum.

To clarify, I am not suggesting that crimes against women are more serious than other crimes. My argument is that each crime has its own unique traits and distinctions. In my opinion, rape should not be elevated to the top of the crime list, but rather a separate category of crime should be created to fit sexual crimes and gender crimes, and this category of crime must stand alongside other grave crimes. The gender-biased subordination of women intensifies in times of conflict, and rape becomes a weapon, a fact recognized 2008 by the U.N. General Assembly in Resolution 1820.[97] Sex crimes must be condemned by international law, similar to actions undertaken in the past by the international community to condemn other insufferable crimes. Just as international law pursued the pirate in the past, and pursues terrorists and plane hijackers in the present, as the "enemy of mankind" – *hostis humani generis*[98] – international law must pursue the sex and gender criminals today.

Will the ICC interpret the categories of crime that exist under its statute as covering sex crimes, even in those provisions where they were not explicitly

[97] Security Council Resolution 1820 (2008), adopted on June 19, 2008 ("Resolution 1820").

[98] *Y. Dinstein*, Samkhuyot ha-medinah kelape penim, Tel Aviv 1972, p. 76.

recognized? Will international law adopt a separate category of crime, specifally designed for sex crimes? The future will tell.

At the time of writing this article, there is an indication that the ICC criminal prosecutor is starting to utilize the new legal provisions related to sex crimes. One of the first matters adjudicated in the ICC concerned *Germain Katanga*, who was charged with "war crimes" and "crimes against humanity" that he allegedly committed in the Congo in 2003. The violent sexual crimes of which he was accused were included in the indictment under the new crime of "sexual slavery" and "rape."[99] In the pre-trial hearing conducted on 29 September 2008, the court unanimously found that the evidence was sufficient to warrant trying him in the ICC on the charge of "sexual slavery" and "rape" as a "crime against humanity," and a majority found sufficient evidence for the charge of "sexual slavery" and "rape" as a "war crime."[100] The trial has not yet commenced.

Will the ICC continue along the course set by its predecessors, the ICTY and the ICTR, and adopt broad interpretations in all matters related to sex crimes? For example, will it utilize its powers of interpretation to rule that forced impregnation, for example, is likely to constitute "genocide"? Will it pave the way for the assimilation of sex crimes into customary law? Will it rule that rape constitutes a "grave breach of the Geneva Conventions"? Will the gender dimension of sex crimes finally be exposed in international law?

My article demonstrates that the ICC has all the tools needed to do so.

[99] Sexual slavery as a "crime against humanity" – Rome Statute, article 7(1)(g); sexual slavery as a "war crime" – Rome Statute, article 8(2)(b)(xxii).

[100] Latest Press Releases, "Decision on the confirmation of charges in the case of The Prosecutor v. Germain Katanga and Mathieu Ngudjolo Chui" (The Hague, 26 September 2008), located at http://www.icc-cpi.int/press/pressreleases/425.html (accessed 3 October 2008). At the time this article was written, the decision in the pre-trial hearing had not been published.

Chapter III

Structures of Implementation of Human Rights in a Globalized World

The Impact of Human Rights Law on Supranational Regimes

Sigrid Boysen

I. Introduction

Initially ignored, human rights are increasingly conceived of as a possible force for European integration, a symbol of shared European identity. With the common market largely achieved, human rights seem to provide a fresh focus and a remedy for the Union's deficit in political legitimacy. Discussing the role of fundamental rights in the European Union, *Eric Posner*[1] went so far as to suggest that the recent *Kadi* judgement[2] gives further evidence of the maturing of the European State: The European Court of Justice (ECJ) held that the EU regulation implementing a United Nations Security Council anti-terrorism resolution to freeze funds of individuals worldwide was in violation of fundamental rights. The Court found that "the obligations imposed by an international agreement cannot have the effect of prejudicing the constitutional principles of the EC Treaty, which include the principle that all Community acts must respect fundamental rights, that respect constituting a condition of their lawfulness which it is for the Court to review in the framework of the complete system of legal remedies established by the Treaty". According to *Posner*, this ruling confirms the Court's insistence on the precedence of the European legal order not only over international law, but over the UN Charter itself. He goes on to establish an analogy with the emergence of modern states: Since, historically, states have been created through war and violence, the birth of states almost always goes hand in hand with violations of international law. This could be explained by political psychology: the new state feels the need to reassure its

[1] *E. Posner*, Panel discussion at NYU on the Kadi judgment, held in the framework of the IILJ's Hauser Colloquium on Globalization and Legal Theory, 17 September 2008, http://globaladminlaw.blogspot.com/2008/10/nyu-kadi-panel-discussion-in-full.html (accessed March 2009).

[2] Joined Cases C-402/05 P and C-415/05 P *Yassin Abdullah Kadi and Al Barakaat International Foundation/Council and Commission*, judgement of 3 September 2008, not yet reported.

own people that they are its first priority, and that their values will be defended in the face of conflicts with any other legal orders, including the international one.[3]

Whether or not this is true, it is an undisputed fact that throughout the last four decades, the European Court of Justice has developed a rich and differentiated fundamental rights case law and, since its judgement in the *Stauder* case,[4] has been ready to revoke Community legislation that violates EC fundamental rights. Having said this, the concept of human rights within the European legal order has always held a somewhat circumstantial, not to say accidental role. The Treaties were written as law concerning economic integration, not human rights. Moreover, European Union law takes place in a complex environment with a plethora of national and international human rights regimes, namely the European Convention on Human Rights and the catalogues of fundamental rights in the national constitutions of the Member States. Regarding the latter, it is well known that the ECJ's human rights jurisprudence was highly influenced if not initiated by the criticism voiced prominently by the German Constitutional Court (*Bundesverfassungsgericht*) in its so called *Solange I* decision[5] of the fact that European Community Law was claiming supremacy over the national legal systems without the safeguard of a human rights catalogue.[6] As for the international level, all EU Member States are parties to the European Convention on Human Rights (ECHR)[7] and to the UN Charter,[8] whereas the EU itself is not. The ECHR, as interpreted by the European Court on Human Rights (ECtHR), can be seen as the world's most advanced and effective regional human rights regime. Since, both the EU and the human rights regime of the European Council rely heavily on the crucial role of the Luxembourg and the Strasbourg Court respectively, for as long as there have been relations between the European Court of Human Rights and the EC/EU, the question has

---

[3] *E. Posner*, Panel discussion ans NYU on the Kadi judgment, held in the framework of the IILJ's Hauser Colloquium on Globalization and Legal Theory, 17 September 2008, http://globaladminlaw.blogspot.com/2008/10/nyu-kadi-panel-discussion-in-full.html (accessed March 2009).

[4] ECJ, Case 29/69 *Stauder/Stadt Ulm* [1969] ECR 419.

[5] BVerfGE 37, 271 – *Solange I (Internationale Handelsgesellschaft)* comprehensive English translation in Common Market Law Reports 1974, p. 540.

[6] *J. Callewaert*, 'Unionisation' and 'Conventionisation' of Fundamental Rights in Europe: The interplay between Union and Convention law and its impact on the domestic legal systems of the Member States, in: J. Wouters/A. Nollkaemper/E. de Wet (eds.), The Europeanisation of International Law, The Hague 2008, p. 109 (110); *D. Thym*, Charter of Fundamental Rights: Competition or Consistency of Human Rights Protection in Europe?, Finnish Yearbook of International Law XI (2000, published 2002), p. 11 (14).

[7] Convention for the Protection of Human Rights and Fundamental Freedoms of 4 November 1950, ETS 5, 213 UNTS 222. The Convention entered into force on 3 September 1953.

[8] Charter of the United Nations, signed on 26 June 1945, 59 Stat. 1031, 993 UNTS 1153. The Charter entered into force on 24 October 1945.

remained as to whether the Convention has been somehow 'unionised' or whether, quite the contrary, it is rather EC law that has been 'conventionalised'.[9]

Against this background, the present article will address the ambiguities and procedural gaps between the human rights acquis in the European Union as laid down in the Charter of Fundamental Rights, the European Convention on Human Rights, the law of the United Nations and national constitutions. It will do so by exploring, in the first part, the interface between the fundamental rights of the European Union and the national constitutions. The second part will focus on the relationship between EU fundamental rights and the European Convention on Human Rights. The article will conclude with an analysis of the impact of international law, which is to say, of the law of the United Nations, on human rights jurisprudence in Europe.

II. The Relationship between National Constitutions and EU Fundamental Rights

The six founding States and their national constitutions had a strong impact on the development of European Community Law and it is well known that the human rights jurisprudence of the European Court of Justice was initiated in the course of the famous 'dialogue' between the Court of Justice on the one hand and the German Constitutional Court (*Bundesverfassungsgericht*)[10] and

[9] *J. Callewaert*, 'Unionisation' and 'Conventionisation' of Fundamental Rights in Europe: The interplay between Union and Convention law and its impact on the domestic legal systems of the Member States, in: J. Wouters/A. Nollkaemper/E. de Wet (eds.), The Europeanisation of International Law, The Hague 2008, p. 109. For further analysis of the interface between the ECJ and the ECtHR, see *G. Harpaz*, The European Court of Justice and its Relations with the European Court of Human Rights: The Quest for Enhanced Reliance, Coherence and Legitimacy, Common Market Law Review 46 (2009), p. 105; *S. Douglas-Scott*, A Tale of Two Courts: Luxembourg, Strasbourg and the Growing European Human Rights Acquis, Common Market Law Review 43 (2006), p. 629; *I. Canor*, Primus Inter Pares – Who is the Ultimate Guardian of Fundamental Rights in Europe?, European Law Review 25 (2000), p. 3; *F. G. Jacobs*, Judicial Dialogue and the Cross-Fertilization of Legal Systems: The European Court of Justice, Texas International Law Journal 38 (2003), p. 547; *M. Bronckers*, The Relationship of the EC Courts with other International Tribunals: Non-Committal, Respectful or Submissive?, Common Market Law Review 44 (2007), p. 601; *J. R. Wetzel*, Improving Fundamental Rights Protection in the European Union: Resolving the Conflict and Confusion between the Luxembourg and the Strasbourg Courts, Fordham Law Review 71 (2003), p. 2823; *A.-M. Slaughter*, A Typology of Transjudicial Communication, University of Richmond Law Review 29 (1994/1995), p. 99.

[10] BVerfGE 37, 271 – *Solange I*, supra n. 5; E 73, 339 – *Solange II*; E 75, 223 – *Kloppenburg*; E 89, 155 – *Maastricht* reported in English in Common Market Law Reports 1994, p. 57; E 102, 147 – *Bananenmarktordnung*. See *K. Hailbronner*, The European Union from the Perspective of the German Constitutional Court, German Yearbook of International Law 37 (1994), p. 93; *M. Herdegen*, Maastricht and the Constitutional Court: Constitutional Re-

the Italian Constitutional Court (*Corte Costituzionale*)[11] on the other. The initial treaties of the European Coal and Steel Community (1951) and the European Economic Community (1957) did not contain a list or bill of human rights. The reasons for these lacunae have been analysed extensively and do not need an elaborate reiteration:[12] Despite the undeniable political motives of the venture, both Communities were formed as economic entities and the Treaties were therefore restricted to the aims of economic integration. It was this "constitutional vacuum"[13] which led to the fundamental criticism of the fact that European Community Law was claiming supremacy over the legal systems of the Member States without ensuring its own compliance with fundamental rights.[14] In this context, it should not be surprising that the four main human rights cases between 1969 and 1979 were preliminary references by lower German courts and one action brought by a German company against the Commission.[15] In all these cases the applicants argued that certain provisions of European Community Law violated their fundamental rights as laid down in the German Constitution (*Grundgesetz*) and should therefore not apply in Germany.

The ECJ tried to resolve these reservations by filling the gap with judicial interpretation. Both in an exercise of "bold judicial activism"[16] and in renunciation of its earlier case law,[17] the Court therefore stated in its preliminary rulings that respect for human rights forms an integral part of the general principles of

straints for an Ever Closer Union, Common Market Law Review 31 (1994), p. 235; *U. Everling*, Will Europe Slip on Bananas? The Banana Judgment's of the Court of Justice and National Courts, Common Market Law Review 33 (1996), p. 401.

[11] Corte costituzionale, Case 183/74 *Frontini* [1974] Foro italiano I-314; Case 170/84 *Granital* [1984] Foro italiano I-2062; see *K. Lenaerts/E. de Smitjer*, A 'Bill of Rights' for the European Union, Common Market Law Review 38 (2001), p. 273 (276, note 17).

[12] See e.g. *J. H. H. Weiler*, Eurocracy and Distrust: Some Questions Concerning the Role of the European Court of Justice in the Protection of Fundamental Human Rights within the Legal Order of the European Communities, Washington Law Review 61 (1986), p. 1103 (1110 f.).

[13] *G. Harpaz*, The European Court of Justice and its Relations with the European Court of Human Rights: The Quest for Enhanced Reliance, Coherence and Legitimacy, Common Market Law Review 46 (2009), p. 105 (107).

[14] BVerfGE 37, 271 (280 f.) – *Solange I (Internationale Handelsgesellschaft)* comprehensive English translation in Common Market Law Reports 1974, p. 540.

[15] ECJ, Case 29/69 *Stauder/Stadt Ulm* [1969] ECR 419; Case 11/70 *Internationale Handelsgesellschaft mbH/Einfuhr- und Vorratsstelle für Getreide und Futtermittel* [1970] ECR 1125; Case 4/73 *Nold/Commission* [1974] ECR 491; Case 44/79 *Hauer/Land Rheinland-Pfalz* [1979] ECR 3727.

[16] *J. H. H. Weiler*, Eurocracy and Distrust: Some Questions Concerning the Role of the European Court of Justice in the Protection of Fundamental Human Rights within the Legal Order of the European Communities, Washington Law Review 61 (1986), p. 1103 (1105).

[17] Earlier attempts by litigants to invoke human rights and other principles recognized by domestic law were rejected by the ECJ, see Case 1/58 *Stork/High Authority* [1959] ECR 17; Joined Cases 36, 37, 38 and 40/59 *Geitling/High Authority* [1960] ECR 423; Case 40/64 *Sgarlata and others/Commission* [1965] ECR 215.

Community law.[18] Since its ruling in *Internationale Handelsgesellschaft*,[19] the ECJ has continually emphasized the autonomy of the Community's general principles of law,[20] thereby rooting the protection of human rights within the Community's legal order, reinforcing the latter's normative supremacy and – last not least – asserting its own institutional autonomy vis-à-vis national courts.[21] On the other hand, the Court has repeatedly stressed that there are two main sources for the general principles of EC law: first, the common constitutional traditions of the Member States, and secondly, international human rights agreements.[22] This approach has very accurately been described by Advocate General *van Gerven* in his Opinion in the case *SPUC/Grogan*:

"A feature of [the ECJ's] (...) case-law is that it does not confer direct effect in the Community legal order on the provisions of (...) international treaties but regards those treaties, together with the constitutional traditions common to the Member States, as helping to determine the content of the general principles of Community law."[23]

Despite the "symbolic prominence"[24] attributed not only by the Court but also by the EU treaties to the 'common constitutional traditions' of the Member States, there are only a few cases in which the Court has drawn on national constitutional traditions. This is hardly surprising, considering the difficulties of asserting a common approach for 27 Member States. As attractive as the concept of 'common constitutional traditions' might sound, it is difficult to put into practice in a constitutional environment with fundamental differences between specific national conceptions of particular human rights.[25]

Moreover and more importantly, the reluctance to draw on national constitutions can be explained by the Court's determination to reinforce the supremacy of EC law. As a matter of fact, in some ways, the same protective impetus which had led the Court to reject the existence of fundamental rights in Community

---

[18] ECJ, Case 29/69 *Stauder/Stadt Ulm* [1969] ECR 419; Case 11/70 *Internationale Handelsgesellschaft mbH/Einfuhr- und Vorratsstelle für Getreide und Futtermittel* [1970] ECR 1125; Case 4/73 *Nold/Commission* [1974] ECR 491; Case 44/79 *Hauer/Land Rheinland-Pfalz* [1979] ECR 3727.

[19] Case 11/70 *Internationale Handelsgesellschaft mbH/Einfuhr- und Vorratsstelle für Getreide und Futtermittel* [1970] ECR 1125.

[20] For details on the concept see *P. Craig/G. de Búrca*, EU Law, 4. ed., Oxford 2008, p. 381 et seq.; *T. Tridimas*, The General Principles of EC Law, 2. ed., Oxford 2007; *J. Usher*, General Principles of EC Law, Edinburgh 1998.

[21] *G. Harpaz*, The European Court of Justice and its Relations with the European Court of Human Rights: The Quest for Enhanced Reliance, Coherence and Legitimacy, Common Market Law Review 46 (2009), p. 105 (107).

[22] See Case 4/73 *Nold/Commission* [1974] ECR 491, para. 13.

[23] Case C-159/90 *Society for the Protection of Unborn Children Ireland Ltd/Stephen Grogan and others* [1991] ECR I-4685, para. 30.

[24] See *P. Craig/G. de Búrca*, EU Law, 4. ed., Oxford 2008, pp. 386 f., who show that fundamental rights claims have been more successful in disputes involving individual administrative acts such as staff cases or competition proceedings.

[25] *P. Craig/G. de Búrca*, EU Law, 4. ed., Oxford 2008, p. 389.

law in its earlier case law, induced it to change this case law in the face of the self-created new supranational order, itself acting as a constitutional court "determined to preserve the *integrity*, *unity*, and *uniformity* of the system it had evolved".[26] Of course, this reading of the Court's case law raises questions as to its credibility, especially when it comes to situations where the integrity of the Community legal order is in conflict with individual rights. In this context, the EU and in particular the ECJ have met with severe criticism of their attitude towards human rights and have been reproached with having a greater commitment to market rights than to human rights.[27] This criticism is supported by the fact that, in spite of an ever increasing number of human rights claims that are brought before the CFI and the ECJ, the number of cases in which the Court has actually revoked EU legislation remains very low.[28]

Despite these problems and the ECJ's overt supremacy and autonomy subtext, the ECJ's case law gained the support of the Member States. The reason is to some extent obvious, in that the human rights jurisprudence was introduced by the Court primarily as a restraint upon the powers of the Community institutions.[29] Nonetheless, the *Bundesverfassungsgericht* was not easily satisfied with the ECJ's human rights jurisprudence. Its grounding in the internal legal order of the EU, initially through the 'general principles' as developed by the Court itself rather than in national or international law, of course implied its development on an *ad hoc* basis and therefore went along with a lack of comprehensiveness, clarity, predictability and sophistication.[30]

In its *Solange I* decision of 29 May 1974, the *Bundesverfassungsgericht* held that it was competent to disapply European law so long as the process of Euro-

[26] *J.H.H. Weiler*, Eurocracy and Distrust: Some Questions Concerning the Role of the European Court of Justice in the Protection of Fundamental Human Rights within the Legal Order of the European Communities, Washington Law Review 61 (1986), p. 1103 (1117), italics in the original.

[27] See, e.g., *J. Coppel/A. O'Neill*, The European Court of Justice: Taking Rights Seriously?, Common Market Law Review 29 (1992), 669; *J.H.H. Weiler/N. Lockhart*, "Taking Rights Seriously" Seriously: The European Court and its Fundamental Rights Jurisprudence, Common Market Law Review 32 (1995), p. 51 and p. 579.

[28] See *P. Craig/G. de Búrca*, EU Law, 4. ed., Oxford 2008, p. 390.

[29] However, in its later case law, the ECJ held that EU fundamental rights are also binding on Member States when they are acting within the scope of application of EC law, see Case C-260/89 *ERT/DEP* [1991] ECR I-2925; Case C-112/00 *Schmidberger/Austria* [2003] ECR I-5659. Article 51 of the EU Charter of Fundamental Rights takes a narrower approach. It states that "the provisions of this Charter are addressed to the institutions and bodies of the Union (...) and to the Member States only when they are implementing Union law". Despite the narrow wording of Article 51, the explanatory memorandum to the Charter purports to read it more broadly.

[30] *G. Harpaz*, The European Court of Justice and its Relations with the European Court of Human Rights: The Quest for Enhanced Reliance, Coherence and Legitimacy, Common Market Law Review 46 (2009), p. 105 (107); *A. v. Bogdandy*, The European Union as a Human Rights Organization? Human Rights and the Core of the European Union, Common Market Law Review 37 (2000), p. 1307 (1330f.).

pean integration did not lead to a legally binding catalogue of fundamental rights enacted by a parliament and that it offered a level of protection that was adequate to the fundamental rights in the *Grundgesetz*.[31] Twelve years later, in its *Solange II* decision of 22 October 1986, it accepted the methodology and the case law of the European Court of Justice as functionally satisfying this requirement even without a formal catalogue of fundamental rights.[32] It was surely no coincidence that the remaining uncertainties as expressed in the *Maastricht* judgement of 12 October 1993[33] were cleared in the year 2000, while the Charter of Fundamental Rights was elaborated under the presidency of the former German chief Justice Roman Herzog. In its *Bananas* decision of 7 June 2000,[34] the *Bundesverfassungsgericht* held that, since the ECJ generally guaranteed an effective protection of fundamental rights against the European public authority, it would no longer apply the fundamental rights of the German Constitution to European law. It explicitly stated that the *Grundgesetz* does not require identical protection of individual rights through European law and that therefore the level of protection guaranteed by the ECJ may vary from German constitutional law in individual cases. In conclusion, the *Bundesverfassungsgericht* held that only if the overall level of protection guaranteed by the general human rights jurisprudence fell beneath a minimum level which ignored the very substance of the fundamental rights guaranteed by the *Grundgesetz*, could it be brought to reassume its subsidiary control function.[35]

Thus, after decades of back and forth, the jurisdictional conflict between the European Court of Justice and the *Bundesverfassungsgericht* was settled by a presumption of conformity which *nota bene* cannot be rebutted on a case-by-case basis, but only by proof of structural or large-scale shortcomings in the protection of fundamental rights under Community law. This is of course a very unlikely scenario and will therefore most probably remain a fairly theoretical eventuality.

---

[31] BVerfGE 37, 271 (285).

[32] BVerfGE 73, 339 (383).

[33] BVerfGE 89, 155 (209).

[34] BVerfGE 102, 147.

[35] BVerfGE 102 147 (161 f.): "Solange die Europäischen Gemeinschaften, insbesondere die Rechtsprechung des Gerichtshofs der Gemeinschaften einen wirksamen Schutz der Grundrechte gegenüber der Hoheitsgewalt der Gemeinschaften generell gewährleisten, der dem vom Grundgesetz als unabdingbar gebotenen Grundrechtsschutz im Wesentlichen gleich zu achten ist, zumal den Wesensgehalt der Grundrechte generell verbürgt, wird das Bundesverfassungsgericht seine Gerichtsbarkeit über die Anwendbarkeit von abgeleitetem Gemeinschaftsrecht, das als Rechtsgrundlage für ein Verhalten deutscher Gerichte und Behörden im Hoheitsbereich der Bundesrepublik Deutschland in Anspruch genommen wird, nicht mehr ausüben und dieses Recht mithin nicht mehr am Maßstab der Grundrechte des Grundgesetzes überprüfen".

As it stands, the EU has an obligation to respect human rights when it acts on its competences,[36] compliance being ensured by the ECJ (at least insofar as the EU acts through the Community). Although EC fundamental rights apply mainly to the EU and its institutions, the ECJ's case law has established that fundamental rights are addressed also to the Member States when they are acting within the scope of application of EC law. The Court elaborated three situations in which EC fundamental rights are binding not only on the EC institutions but also on Member States: first, when applying provisions of EC legislation which are based on the protection of human rights;[37] secondly, when implementing or enforcing EC measures;[38] and finally, when derogating from measures of EC law.[39] However, Article 51 of the EU Charter of Fundamental Rights chooses a narrower approach in stating that the "provisions of this Charter are addressed to the institutions and bodies of the Union (...) and to the Member States only when they are implementing Union law". As long as the Charter has not formally been incorporated into EU law by the Treaty of Lisbon, it is difficult to say whether the general impact of EU fundamental rights on Member State action has been reduced or not. So far, however, the Court has not shown any inclination to reduce the scope of its judicial review in this respect.[40]

---

[36] ECJ, Case 29/69 *Stauder/Stadt Ulm* [1969] ECR 419; Case 11/70 *Internationale Handelsgesellschaft mbH/Einfuhr- und Vorratsstelle für Getreide und Futtermittel* [1970] ECR 1125; Case 4/73 *Nold/Commission* [1974] ECR 491; Case 36/75 *Rutili/Ministre de l'intérieur* [1975] ECR 1219; Case 44/79 *Hauer/Land Rheinland-Pfalz* [1979] ECR 3727; Case 5/88 *Wachauf/Germany* [1989] ECR 2609; Case C-13/94 *P/S and Cornwall* [1996] ECR I-2143; Case C-36/02 *Omega* [2004] ECR I-9609.

[37] See Case 36/75 *Rutili/Ministre de l'intérieur* [1975] ECR 1219; Case 222/84 *Johnston/Chief Constable of the Royal Ulster Constabulary* [1986] ECR 1651; Case 222/86 *UNECTEF/Heylens* [1987] ECR 4097; Case C-185/97 *Coote/Granada Hospitality* [1998] ECR I-5199.

[38] See Case 63/83 *R/Kent Kirk* [1984] ECR 2689, paras. 21 f.; Case 249/86 *Commission/Germany* [1989] ECR 1263; Case C-219/91 *Criminal proceedings against Ter Voort* [1992] ECR I-5485, paras. 33 et seq.; Joined Cases C-74 and 129/95 *Criminal Proceedings against X* [1996] ECR I-6609; Case C-60/02 *Criminal Proceedings against X* [2004] ECR I-651; Case C-387/02 *Berlusconi and others* [2005] ECR I-3565.

[39] See Case C-260/89 *ERT/DEP* [1991] ECR I-2925; Case C-368/95 *Vereinigte Familiapress Zeitungsverlags- und -vertriebs GmbH/Heinrich Bauer Verlag* [1997] ECR I-3689; Case C-413/99 *Baumbast and R/Home Secretary* [2002] ECR I-7091, paras. 72 et seq.; Case C-60/00 *Carpenter/Home Secretary* [2002] ECR I-6279; Case C-109/01 *Home Secretary/Akrich* [2003] ECR I-9607; Case C-441/02 *Commission/Germany* [2006] ECR I-3449, paras. 108 f.

[40] See, e.g., Case C-540/03 *European Parliament/Council* [2006] ECR I-5769, para. 38; *P. Craig/G. de Búrca*, EU Law, 4th. ed., Oxford 2008, p. 402.

III. The European Convention on Human Rights and EU Fundamental Rights: The Relationship between Union and Convention Law from a Judicial and Legislative Perspective

Although technically a part of public international law, the European Convention on Human Rights in itself already represents a form of Europeanisation of international law,[41] expressing – as the preamble states – the will of the governments of European countries "which are like-minded and have a common heritage of political traditions, ideals, freedom and the rule of law, to take the first steps for the collective enforcement of certain of the rights stated in the Universal Declaration" of Human Rights. However, this does not answer the question regarding the specific relationship between EU and Convention law.

If we focus on the interface between the European Convention on Human Rights and the fundamental rights acquis of the European Union, what we see is in fact not so much a unilateral 'unionisation' of the European Convention on Human Rights or a 'conventionalisation' of the ECJ's human rights jurisprudence, but rather a perpetual motion, a constant and reciprocal interaction between EU and Convention law.[42] In some ways, of course, the term "interaction" can be called a euphemism and should not disguise the frictions and paradoxes that characterise the relationship between EU and Convention law. The following analysis will show that these tensions exist both on the judicial and the legislative level, and it will explore the immanent ambiguities of the relationship.

1. The Judiciary

Over the years, a complex relationship has evolved between the ECJ and the ECtHR. The mulit-faceted interaction between the two courts manifests itself, on the one hand, in an ever increasing number of cases in which both the CFI and the ECJ refer to judgements of the ECtHR, and in a growing number of cases in which the ECtHR relies on the jurisprudence of the ECJ.[43] On the other hand, what can also be observed is an ever growing willingness on the part of the Strasbourg Court to indirectly review EC measures. However, considering the progress the ECJ has made with the consent of at least most of the

[41] See *J. Wouters/A. Nollkaemper/E. de Wet* (eds.), The Europeanisation of International Law, The Hague 2008.

[42] *J. Callewaert*, 'Unionisation' and 'Conventionisation' of Fundamental Rights in Europe: The interplay between Union and Convention law and its impact on the domestic legal systems of the Member States, in: J. Wouters/A. Nollkaemper/E. de Wet (eds.), The Europeanisation of International Law, The Hague 2008, p. 109.

[43] This reliance is less extensive than *vice versa*, but its scope is increasing, see *S. Douglas-Scott*, A Tale of Two Courts: Luxembourg, Strasbourg and the Growing European Human Rights Acquis, Common Market Law Review 43 (2006), p. 629 (640f.).

Member States regarding its human rights jurisprudence, and in view of the adoption of the EU Charter on Fundamental Rights, the question arises as to why Article 6 (2) EU as amended by the Lisbon Treaty now finally provides for the EU to accede to the Convention. The answers to that question help to illuminate some of the basic features of the judicial dialogue between the ECJ and the ECtHR and the resulting potential for conflict.

In fact, it is most of all the legacy of the founding Treaties that has continuously subjected the EU and in particular the ECJ to the criticism that its dominant focus is still on economic aims and objectives and precisely not on fundamental rights. With regard to the ECJ, this criticism is translated into the objection that the ECJ was not designed and should not establish itself as a Human Rights Court vis-à-vis the ECtHR, which was specifically entrusted with this task by the Member States.[44] In this context, it has been pointed out that the ECtHR "was not only established with an express human rights jurisdiction, but has acquired expertise and a moral stature which the ECJ does not yet share".[45] However, in spite of all potential for dispute, the case law has shown that serious conflicts of interpretation between both courts have remained the exception.[46]

a) General Principles of Community Law

While the European Convention on Human Rights is not a formal part of EU law, in its function as a 'source of inspiration' for the general principles of EC law, it is the most frequently used source of reference for EU fundamental rights. In this way, over the years, a considerable amount of European Union law has been reviewed by the ECJ in the light of the ECHR, which of course represents a kind of 'conventionalisation' of Union law. Since its general reference in *Nold* to "international treaties for the protection of human rights on which the Member States have collaborated or of which they are signatories" as "guidelines which should be followed within the framework of Community law",[47] and the first specific recourse to the Convention in *Rutili*,[48] the ECJ has not only drawn

[44] See *D. Spielman*, Human Rights Case Law in the Strasbourg and the Luxembourg Courts: Inconsistencies and Complementarities, in: P. Alston/J. Heenan/M. Bustelo (eds.), The EU and Human Rights, 1999, p. 757.

[45] *P. Craig/G. de Búrca*, EU Law, 4. ed., Oxford 2008, p. 419.

[46] For details see *S. Douglas-Scott*, A Tale of Two Courts: Luxembourg, Strasbourg and the Growing European Human Rights Acquis, Common Market Law Review 43 (2006), p. 629 (650); *M. Bronckers*, The Relationship of the EC Courts with other International Tribunals: Non-Committal, Respectful or Submissive?, Common Market Law Review 44 (2007), p. 601.

[47] Case 4/73 *Nold/Commission* [1974] ECR 491 para. 13.

[48] Case 36/75 *Roland Rutili/Ministre de l'intérieur* [1975] ECR 1219, para. 32. Here, the ECJ describes provisions of EC secondary legislation as specific manifestations of more general fundamental principles of Community law that could be found in the ECHR: "Taken as a whole these limitations placed on the powers of Member States in respect of control of aliens

on the Convention ever more frequently[49] but has been confronted with extensive elaborations on the Convention and the ECtHR's case law by both applicants[50] and the Advocates General.[51] The case law shows that the ECJ gradually moved from mere implicit to explicit references, albeit most often not directly to the Convention but rather with the intermediate step of the general principles of Community law, initially developed by the Court itself and later laid down in Article 6 EU. Even though the ECJ now sometimes omits the reference to the general principles, they still form the statutory basis upon which, according to Article 6 (2) EU, compliance with fundamental rights is to be ensured under EU law.

However, the relationship between the two courts still remains ambiguous. This ambiguity is well reflected by the fact that, although the ECJ has over the years demonstrated an ever greater readiness not only to refer to the ECHR but to adopt the Strasbourg case law, there have always been hesitations on the part of the Union's legal experts as to whether accession by the EU to the Convention is compatible with the specific (economic) nature of the EU legal system.[52] Again, the reason was that there were fears that acceding to the Convention would compromise the supremacy, integrity, and autonomy of the EU legal order. In this context, the mediatisation of Convention law through the concept of

---

are a specific manifestation of the more general principle, enshrined in Articles 8, 9, 10 and 11 of the Convention for the Protection of Human Rights and Fundamental Freedoms, signed in Rome on 4 November 1950 and ratified by all the Member States".

[49] See, e.g., Case 222/84 *Johnston/Chief Constable of the Royal Ulster Constabulary* [1986] ECR 1651, para. 18: "That principle is also laid down in Articles 6 and 13 of the European Convention for the Protection of Human Rights and Fundamental Freedoms of 4 November 1950. As the European Parliament, Council and Commission recognized in their joint declaration of April 5 1977 (Official Journal C 103, p. 1) and as the Court has recognized in its decisions, the principles on which that Convention is based must be taken into consideration in Community law"; Joined Cases 46/87 and 227/88 *Hoechst AG/Commission* [1989] ECR 2859, paras. 13 et seq.; Case C-260/89 *ERT/DEP* [1991] ECR I-2925, para. 41; Opinion 2/94 *Accession of the Community to the ECHR* [1996] ECR I-1759, para. 33. For the recent case law, see e.g. Joined Cases C-402/05 P and C-415/05 P *Yassin Abdullah Kadi and Al Barakaat International Foundation/Council and Commission*, judgement of 3 September 2008, not yet reported, paras. 283, 310 et seq., 335, 344, 356, 360, 363 and 368.

[50] See, e.g., Case 4/73 *Nold/Commission* [1974] ECR 491 para. 12; Joined Cases C-402/05 P and C-415/05 P *Yassin Abdullah Kadi and Al Barakaat International Foundation/Council and Commission*, judgement of 3 September 2008, not yet reported, para. 256.

[51] For an extensive analysis see *S. Douglas-Scott*, A Tale of Two Courts: Luxembourg, Strasbourg and the Growing European Human Rights Acquis, Common Market Law Review 43 (2006), p. 629 (645 f.); see also Case C-402/05 P, supra n. 50, Opinion of Advocate General Maduro of 16 January 2008, para. 37.

[52] See *A. Verstichel*, European Union Accession to the European Convention on Human Rights, in: P. Lemmens/W. Vandenhole (eds.), Protocol No. 14 and the Reform of the European Court of Human Rights, Antwerp/Oxford 2005, p. 123; *F. Benoit-Rohmer*, L'adhésion de l'Union à la Convention européenne des droits de l'homme, 12 Revue Universelle des Droits des l'homme (2000), p. 57; *S. Winkler*, Der Beitritt der Europäischen Gemeinschaften zur EMRK, Baden-Baden 2000.

general principles of EC law, again provided the perfect remedy, allowing at one and the same time to draw on the ECHR as a 'source of inspiration' without applying it as such, and thereby neither giving up the integrity of the Community's legal order nor its own institutional autonomy vis-à-vis the ECtHR. The Treaty of Lisbon continues that double strategy by both incorporating the Charter itself and by providing in Article 6 (3) for the EU to accede to the ECHR.

In practice, however, there are only few jurisprudential conflicts between Strasbourg and Luxembourg.[53] A recent one arose in the case *Emesa Sugar* before the ECJ.[54] It concerned the right to reply to the opinion of the Advocate General in proceedings before the ECJ. In a procedure application for leave to submit observations in response to the opinion of the Advocate General, the applicant relied on the *Vermeulen* judgement of the ECtHR before the ECJ.[55] In *Vermeulen*, the ECtHR had found the lack of opportunity to reply to the submissions of the *Procureur Général* before the Belgian *Cour de Cassation* in breach with Article 6 (1) of the Convention. In its order, the ECJ established that there were significant differences between the role of the Advocate General in EC proceedings and that of the *Procureur Général* under Belgian law,[56] and therefore came to the conclusion that the aforesaid case law of the ECtHR was transposable to the Opinions of the Advocates General.[57] However, the subsequent ruling of the ECtHR in the case *Kress/France*[58] seemed to imply that the Strasbourg Court had a different opinion on this matter, i.e. that its case law on Article 6 (1) of the Convention might indeed apply to the EC Advocates General. On this basis, the question was raised again before the ECJ in the *Kaba*

---

[53] For details, see *D. Spielmann*, Human Rights Case Law in the Strasbourg and Luxembourg Courts – Conflicts, Inconsistencies, and Complementarities, in: P. Alston (ed.), The EU and Human Rights, 1999, p. 757 (764 f.); *J. Callewaert*, 'Unionisation' and 'Conventionisation' of Fundamental Rights in Europe: The interplay between Union and Convention law and its impact on the domestic legal systems of the Member States, in: J. Wouters/A. Nollkaemper/E. de Wet (eds.), The Europeanisation of International Law, The Hague 2008, p. 109 (113).

[54] Case C-17/98 *Emesa Sugar/Aruba* Order of the Court of 4 February 2000 concerning a procedure application. The relevant decision of the ECtHR is App. no. 62023/00 *Emesa Sugar/Netherlands*, admissibility decision of 23 May 2002: the ECtHR declared the application inadmissible on substantive grounds since it concerned the payment of import duties which did not fall within the scope of Article 6 (1) of the ECHR.

[55] App. no. 19075/91 *Vermeulen/Belgium*.

[56] Case C-17/98, *Emesa Sugar/Aruba* Order of the Court of 4 February 2000, para. 12: "[...] the Advocates General, none of whom is subordinate to any other, are not public prosecutors nor are they subject to any authority, in contrast to the manner in which the administration of justice is organised in certain Member States. They are not entrusted with the defence of any particular interest in the exercise of their duties".

[57] Case C-17/98 *Emesa Sugar/Aruba* Order of the Court of 4 February 2000, para. 16.

[58] App. no. 39594/98 *Kress/France*.

case.[59] In his Opinion, Advocate General *Colomer* supported the ECJ's reasoning in *Emesa Sugar*,[60] relying *inter alia*, on a judgement of the French Conseil d'État concerning the role of the *Commissaire du Gouvernement*.[61] In fact, the Advocate General criticised the ECtHR's case law quite severely:

"It seems that what was being sought was not so much the protection of a fundamental right as the imposition of a uniform conception of the organisation of the procedure, without explaining the need for it in terms going beyond the 'doctrine of appearances'. It is legitimate to wonder – as did the seven judges who each cast their own independent votes on the matter – whether, for the purposes of the Convention, the limits of 'European control' may not be exceeded in the light of the specific nature of national rules, which remain legitimate in so far as they fulfil the obligations to achieve a certain result which flow from the requirements of the Convention".[62]

Despite the obvious potential for conflict expressed in the Advocate General's statement, both the ECJ and the ECtHR chose to avoid giving contradictory rulings. In *Kaba*, the ECJ simply did not address the controversial issue and decided the case on different grounds. When, with *Emesa Sugar*, the original cause of the controversy, was brought before the ECtHR for violation of the right to a fair hearing by the ECJ, the ECtHR dismissed the application as inadmissible on the grounds that custom duties did not fall within the scope of the right to a fair hearing in Article 6 (1) of the Convention.[63] This reciprocal effort to avoid conflicts on both sides is complemented by many approving references to the ECtHR's case law by the ECJ. In this respect, it can be said that on the whole the ECJ has been referring to and even following the Strasbourg case law ever more frequently. In fact, it thereby prepared the ground for Article 52 (3) of the EU Charter of Fundamental Rights, which drops any reference to the general principles of Community law. The ECtHR too, in the *Stec case*,[64] decided to refer to the "strong persuasive value" of an ECJ ruling on the question of sex discrimination in social security, and, in *Goodwin/United Kingdom*,[65] drew on the provisions of the Charter of Fundamental Rights.

---

[59] Case C-466/00 – *Arben Kaba/ Secretary of State for the Home Department* [2003] ECR I-2219.

[60] Case C-466/00 – *Arben Kaba/ Secretary of State for the Home Department* [2003] ECR I-2219, Opinion of Advocate General Colomer of 11 July 2002, paras. 95f.

[61] Conseil d'État, judgment of 29 July 1998 *Esclatine*, Rec. p. 320.

[62] Case C-466/00 – *Arben Kaba/ Secretary of State for the Home Department* [2003] ECR I-2219, Opinion of Advocate General Colomer of 11 July 2002, para. 105.

[63] App. no. 62023/00 *Emesa Sugar/Netherlands.*

[64] ECtHR, App. nos. 65731/01 and 65900/01 *Stec/United Kingdom*, para. 58: "In reaching a conclusion on this issue which, while not determinative of the issue under Article 14 of the Convention, is nonetheless of central importance, particular regard should be had to the strong persuasive value of the ECJ's finding on this point".

[65] App. no. 28957/95 *Goodwin/United Kingdom*, para. 100.

b) The Bosphorus Saga

As long as the EC/EU has not acceded to the Convention, the EU institutions do not fall under the ECtHR's jurisdiction for review. This is why in its present case law, the ECtHR does not admit complaints brought directly against the EC/EU.[66] However, not only the ECJ is eager to assert its own institutional autonomy vis-à-vis the ECtHR. In this respect, the ECtHR has, over the years, demonstrated an ever growing willingness to accept cases which indirectly challenge EU measures, taking the liberty to decide on issues that were already dealt with by the Luxembourg Court. In *Matthews/UK*, the ECtHR ruled that Member States cannot escape their responsibilities under the ECHR merely because the violation results from EU law.[67] The case was special insofar as the violation in fact resulted from the implementation of a piece of primary EU law which could not be reviewed by the ECJ.[68] There were several other cases in which the ECtHR accepted indirect complaints against EC and EU acts. Although in most of the cases the ECtHR eventually rejected the applications' admissibility or dismissed them for other reasons, it never declared any application inadmissible on the grounds that it had no jurisdiction over acts of the EC/EU.[69] At least in some respects, this case law may resemble a cat-and-mouse game. However, the most important ruling handed down in this judicial dialogue between the ECJ and the ECtHR, the judgement in the *Bosphorus/Ireland* case, can indeed be characterised as a significant form of 'unionisation' of Convention law.[70]

The case concerned the impounding by the Irish authorities of an aircraft which had been leased by the applicant company from a Yugoslavian airline.

---

[66] See, e.g., for decisions of the Commission on Human Rights App. no. 13258/87 *Melcher/Germany*; App. no. 21090/92 *Heinz/Contracting States and Parties to the European Patent Convention*; App. no. 21072/92 *Gestra/Italy*.

[67] App. no. 24833/94 *Matthews/UK*, paras. 34f.

[68] The case arose because of a complaint brought by a British citizen and resident of Gibraltar whose application to be registered as a voter in the elections to the European Parliament had been turned down with reference to the European Community Act on Direct Elections of 1976. Gibraltar was not included in the franchise, exclusion being effected multilaterally by a common decision of the Member States, which modified the text of the founding documents of the Community. Thus, the ECtHR had to review provisions of EC primary law.

[69] See App. no. 51717/99 *Guérin Automobiles/les 15 Etats de l'Union Européenne*; App. no. 56672/00 *DSR-Senator Lines GmbH/The 15 Member States of the European Union*; App. no. 62023/00 *Emesa Sugar/Netherlands*; see further the relevant decision of the ECJ in Case C-17/98 *Emesa Sugar/Aruba* [2000] ECR I-665; App. nos. 6422/02 and 9916/02 *SEGI/The 15 Member States of the EU*.

[70] *J. Callewaert*, 'Unionisation' and 'Conventionisation' of Fundamental Rights in Europe: The interplay between Union and Convention law and its impact on the domestic legal systems of the Member States, in: J. Wouters/A. Nollkaemper/E. de Wet (eds.), The Europeanisation of International Law, The Hague 2008, p. 109 (120f.).

The Irish authorities had acted in pursuance of EC Council Regulation 990/93,[71] which implemented the United Nations sanctions regime against the Federal Republic of Yugoslavia.[72] Bosphorus Airways challenged the seizure of the aircraft before the Irish High Court, which held that Regulation 990/93 was not applicable to the aircraft in question. On appeal from the Irish Government, the Supreme Court referred the matter to the ECJ. In its preliminary ruling of 30 July 1996, the ECJ held that Regulation 990/93 in fact did apply to the impounded aircraft.[73] It went on to state that the consequences of the impounding for the applicant company were not disproportionate and therefore did not constitute a violation of the company's fundamental rights.[74] The ECJ's ruling was applied by the Irish Supreme Court with the effect that Bosphorus Airways lost approximately three years of its four-year lease of the aircraft. Against this background, Bosphorus Airways lodged a complaint with the European Commission of Human Rights on 25 March 1997. The application was transmitted to the ECtHR on 1 November 1998 and declared admissible on 13 September 2001.

Confronted with the applicant's complaint that the seizure of the aircraft constituted a violation of Article 1 of Protocol No. 1 to the ECHR and that – because of the margin of discretion left by the UN resolution – the ECJ lacked jurisdiction to consider whether the treatment of the applicant by the Irish State amounted to a breach of its property rights, the Strasbourg Court found itself in a very difficult situation. Not only was it in direct competition with the Luxembourg Court, but it was also confronted with the need to finally address the

---

[71] Council Regulation (EEC) No. 990/93 of 26 April 1993 concerning trade between the European Economic Community and the Federal Republic of Yugoslavia (Serbia and Montenegro), OJ L 102/14. The Regulation strengthened the already existing embargo against the Federal Republic of Yugoslavia and repealed Council Regulation (EEC) No. 1432/92 of 1 June 1992 prohibiting trade between the European Economic Community and the Republics of Serbia and Montenegro, OJ L 151/4 and Council Regulation (EEC) No. 2656/92 of 18 December 1992 concerning certain technical modalities in connection with the application of Regulation (EEC) No. 1432/92 of 1 June 1992 prohibiting trade between the European Economic Community and the Republics of Serbia and Montenegro, OJ L 266/27.

[72] Security Council Resolution 713 of 25 September 1991, U. N. Doc. S/RES/713; Security Council Resolution 757 of 30 May 1992, U. N. Doc. S/RES/757 and Security Council Resolution 787 of 16 November 1992, U. N. Doc. S/RES/787; Security Council Resolution 820 of 17 April 1993, U. N. Doc. S/RES/820. The Resolutions were adopted pursuant to Chapter VII of the UN Charter to establish a sanctions regime in order to dissuade the Republics of Serbia and Montenegro from violating the integrity and security of the Republic of Bosnia-Herzegovina and to induce the Bosnian Serb party to cooperate in the restoration of peace. Resolution 820 endeavored to strengthen the embargo by providing, *inter alia*, that States should impound all aircraft in their territories "in which a majority or controlling interest is held by a person or undertaking in or operating from" the Federal Republic of Yugoslavia.

[73] Case C-84/95 *Bosphorus Hava Yollari Turizm Ve Ticaret AS/Minister for Transport, Energy and Communications and others* [1996] ECR I-3953, paras. 11–18.

[74] Case C-84/95 *Bosphorus Hava Yollari Turizm Ve Ticaret AS/Minister for Transport, Energy and Communications and others* [1996] ECR I-3953, paras. 19–26.

question of whether a Member State can be held responsible under the Convention for the application of an E(E)C regulation. In this respect, the ECtHR had to weigh two seemingly conflicting principles. It noted that on the one hand, the Convention did not prohibit contracting parties from transferring sovereign power to a supranational organisation but that, on the other hand, Article 1 of the Convention postulated a general responsibility of every contracting party for all acts and omissions of its organs, regardless of whether the act or omission in question was a consequence of domestic law or of the necessity to comply with international legal obligations.

In its judgement, the ECtHR reconciled these conflicting positions by ruling that the complaint was covered by the scope of the Convention, but rejecting the alleged violation of Article 1 of Protocol No. 1. It held that:

> "State action taken in compliance with such legal obligations is justified as long as the relevant organisation is considered to protect fundamental rights in a manner which can be considered to protect fundamental rights, as regards both the substantive guarantees offered and the mechanisms controlling their observance, in a manner which can be considered at least equivalent to that for which the Convention provides".[75]

If such equivalent protection were considered to be provided by the organisation, the presumption would be that a State had not departed from the requirements of the Convention when it did no more than implement legal obligations flowing from its membership of the organisation. The ECtHR went on to state that any such presumption could be rebutted if, "in the circumstances of a particular case, it is considered that the protection of Convention rights was manifestly deficient. In such cases, the interest of international cooperation would be outweighed by the Convention's role as a 'constitutional instrument of European public order' in the field of human rights".[76] According to the parameters set out above, the judgement ends with an in-depth review of the fundamental rights protection under Community law and reaches the conclusion that it indeed is equivalent to that required by the Convention.

Referring to the relationship between EU fundamental rights and national constitutional law as outlined above, one could ask whether the *Bosphorus* approach was a kind of adaptation to the Convention system of the German Constitutional Court's *Solange II* decision.[77]. Although some of the language does indeed resemble the *Bundesverfassungsgericht's* dictum, a major difference lies in the fact that the *Solange* approach requires proof of structural or large-scale shortcomings in the protection of fundamental rights under Community law for the presumption to be rebutted, whereas under the *Bosphorus* judgement,

[75] App. no. 45036/98 *Bosphorus Hava Yollari Turizm Ve Ticaret Anonim Sirketi/Ireland*, para. 155.

[76] App. no. 45036/98 *Bosphorus Hava Yollari Turizm Ve Ticaret Anonim Sirketi/Ireland*, para. 156.

[77] BVerfGE 73, 339 (383).

the presumption can be rebutted on a case-by-case basis.[78] In fact, precisely this difference shows that the ECtHR's answer to the question, whether and in what circumstances it will indirectly review EU action, is not straightforward. However, as we will see below in the context of the ECJ's *Kadi* judgement,[79] the Luxembourg Court itself quite readily referred to the ECtHR's *Bosphorus* judgement to substantiate its findings regarding the appropriate scope of judicial review of UN measures, drawing on the distinction of directly and not directly attributable acts.[80]

2. *The Legislator*

The complex interplay between the European Convention on Human Rights and EU law on the judicial level is taken even one step further on the legislative level. Here, the EU Charter of Fundamental Rights constitutes the most important object of investigation. To date, it is the most comprehensive legislative initiative taken by the EU in the field of fundamental rights, and at the same time it creates the closest link so far between Convention and Union law. About half of the 50 substantial rights contained in the Charter are borrowed from the Convention and/or the Strasbourg case law. On the other hand, Protocol 12 to the ECHR, which imposes a general ban on discrimination, shows that this is no one-way street. In fact, the Protocol is the first example of a visible legislative impact of the EU acquis on Convention standards. Its adoption was obviously inspired by a similar provision drafted in the context of the work on the Charter of Fundamental Rights.

---

[78] See *F. Schorkopf*, The European Court of Human Rights' Judgement in the Case of *Bosphorus Hava Yollari Turizm v. Ireland*, German Law Journal 6 (2005), p. 1255 (1264).

[79] Joined Cases C-402/05 P and C-415/05 P *Yassin Abdullah Kadi and Al Barakaat International Foundation/Council and Commission*, judgement of 3 September 2008, not yet reported.

[80] Joined Cases C-402/05 P and C-415/05 P, supra n. 79, paras. 313 and 314: "By contrast, in paragraph 151 of *Behrami and Behrami v. France and Saramati v. France, Germany and Norway*, the European Court of Human Rights stated that in the case leading to its judgment in *Bosphorus Hava Yollari Turizm ve Ticaret Anonim Sirketi v. Ireland*, concerning a seizure measure carried out by the authorities of the respondent State on its territory following a decision by one of its ministers, it had recognised its competence, notably *ratione personae*, vis-à-vis the respondent State, despite the fact that the source of the contested measure was a Community regulation taken, in its turn, pursuant to a resolution of the Security Council. In the instant case it must be declared that the contested regulation cannot be considered to be an act directly attributable to the United Nations as an action of one of its subsidiary organs created under Chapter VII of the Charter of the United Nations or an action falling within the exercise of powers lawfully delegated by the Security Council pursuant to that chapter.", italics in the original.

a) The EU Charter of Fundamental Rights

Given the difficult interface between the Strasbourg and the Luxembourg Regime described above, one of the major challenges for the drafters of the EU Charter of Fundamental Rights was the balancing act of preserving the autonomy of the EU legal order while avoiding the – hardly maintainable – outcome of completely new and different EU standards. If not harmonised with those of the Convention, these would pose the threat of legal uncertainty, thereby weakening both human rights regimes at the same time. Article 52 (3) of the Charter explicitly addresses this problem and states:

"In so far as this Charter contains rights which correspond to rights guaranteed by the Convention for the Protection of Human Rights and Fundamental Freedoms, the meaning and scope of those rights shall be the same as those laid down by the said Convention. This provision shall not prevent Union law providing more extensive protection."

Thus, the Charter seeks a solution for the dilemma mentioned above by means of a double strategy: First, it guarantees the same (minimum) level of protection as under the Convention, including the Strasbourg case law, thereby ensuring a minimum level of conformity between the Charter and the Convention. At the same time, and secondly, it safeguards the autonomy of the EU legal system by allowing a higher level of protection under the Charter. In fact, the Convention itself accepts that its level of protection may be replaced by a more extensive one. In Article 53 it explicitly states its aim to impose a minimum rather than a uniform standard:

"Nothing in this Convention shall be construed as limiting or derogating from any of the human rights and fundamental freedoms which may be ensured under the laws of any High Contracting Party or under any other agreement to which it is a Party."

The Charter has made use of this leeway in many respects, as, for example, in guaranteeing the right to marry and to found a family (Article 9), the right to an effective remedy (Article 47 (1)) as well as to legal aid (Article 47 (3)). Unlike lower standards, higher standards pose no threat to the coexistence of the Convention and the Charter. The latter, similarly to national legal systems, adopts the Convention standards as its own minimum standards, thereby building upon them when further developing its own level of protection. In this respect, Article 52 (3) of the Charter does indeed constitute a good example of the phenomenon of 'conventionalisation' of EU law: by establishing an identical "meaning and scope" of the rights corresponding to rights guaranteed by the Convention and dispensing with the general principles of Community law as referred to in Article 6 (2) EU, the Charter, when legally binding, will effectively achieve an indirect adoption of these Convention rights by the EU legal order.[81] At the

[81] See *J. Callewaert*, 'Unionisation' and 'Conventionisation' of Fundamental Rights in Europe: The interplay between Union and Convention law and its impact on the domestic

same time, the second sentence of Article 52 (3) ensures the integrity of the EU legal order vis-à-vis the Strasbourg Regime.

b) Protocol No. 12 to the European Convention on Human Rights

A prominent example of legislative 'unionisation' of Convention standards[82] can be found in Protocol No. 12 to the Convention, which imposes a general ban on discrimination. The adoption of the Protocol on 4 November 2000 was clearly influenced by the EC's strong focus on anti-discrimination law and accelerated by the principle of non-discrimination that was being prepared in the context of the work on the Charter. Article 1 of the Protocol states:

"(1) The enjoyment of any right set forth by law shall be secured without discrimination on any ground such as sex, race, colour, language, religion, political or other opinion, national or social origin, association with a national minority, property, birth or other status.

(2) No one shall be discriminated against by any public authority on any ground such as those mentioned in paragraph 1."

It very much resembles Article 21 of the EU Charter of Fundamental Rights which reads as follows:

"(1) Any discrimination based on any ground such as sex, race, colour, ethnic or social origin, genetic features, language, religion or belief, political or any other opinion, membership of a national minority, property, birth, disability, age or sexual orientation shall be prohibited.

(2) Within the scope of application of the Treaties and without prejudice to any of their specific provisions, any discrimination on grounds of nationality shall be prohibited."

This impact of the Charter's provisions on Convention law is all the more worth mentioning since, following the non-ratification of the EU Constitutional Treaty, the legal status of the Charter still remains uncertain. Therefore, it can be expected that there will be more examples of Convention standards being raised under the influence of EU law once the Charter becomes legally binding with the ratification of the Lisbon Treaty.[83]

---

legal systems of the Member States, in: J. Wouters/A. Nollkaemper/E. de Wet (eds.), The Europeanisation of International Law, The Hague 2008, p. 109 (117), who also points out that it is not entirely clear which rights can be considered to "correspond" to rights guaranteed by the Convention, cf. the Declarations Concerning the Provisions of the Consititution, OJ C 310/420 (456 f.).

[82] See *J. Callewaert*, 'Unionisation' and 'Conventionisation' of Fundamental Rights in Europe: The interplay between Union and Convention law and its impact on the domestic legal systems of the Member States, in: J. Wouters/A. Nollkaemper/E. de Wet (eds.), The Europeanisation of International Law, The Hague 2008, p. 125.

[83] *J. Callewaert*, 'Unionisation' and 'Conventionisation' of Fundamental Rights in Europe: The interplay between Union and Convention law and its impact on the domestic legal systems of the Member States, in: J. Wouters/A. Nollkaemper/E. de Wet (eds.), The Europeanisation of International Law, The Hague 2008, p. 125.

Apart from such distinct influences on the Convention itself, there are other areas in which EC secondary law raises the standards set by the Convention. Such raising of standards has been attributed to Directive 2004/58 of 29 April 2004[84] regarding the right of EU citizens and their family members to move and reside freely within the EU territory. Articles 15 and 28–31 of the Directive establish several rights which are not guaranteed by the ECHR, as its Article 6 is not applicable to expulsion procedures. Another area where EU law provides a higher standard of protection than the ECHR is the right to public access to environmental information as laid down in Directive 2003/4/EC of 28 January 2003.[85] It has to be noted, however, that the Directive does not spring from a genuine EU initiative but was passed in order to implement the EC's and Member States' obligations under the Aarhus Convention.[86] As regards other EU legislative initiatives, it is still frequently a point of controversy, whether or not they imply a rise in standards.[87]

IV. Epilogue: The Impact of UN Law on Human Rights Jurisprudence in Europe

Beyond the rather Eurocentric approach that has been outlined above, a final aspect shall be looked at which concerns the relationship between human rights jurisprudence in the European Union and international law. As a matter of fact, for the Member States, participation in the supranational organisation of the European Community has brought about some distinct problems as regards their obligations under international law. Normative conflicts arising from this constellation may and often do include human rights issues. The solution to these conflicts between the EU and the international legal order remains anything but clear, since both normative systems tend to favour their own legal

[84] Directive 2004/58/EC of the European Parliament and of the Council of 29 April 2004 on the right of citizens of the Union and their family members to move and reside freely within the territory of the Member States amending Regulation (EEC) No. 1612/68 and repealing Directives 64/221/EEC, 68/360/EEC, 72/194/EEC, 73/148/EEC, 75/34/EEC, 75/35/EEC, 90/364/EEC, 90/365/EEC and 93/96/EEC, OJ L 229/35.

[85] Directive 2003/4/EC of the European Parliament and of the Council of 28 January 2003 on public access to environmental information and repealing Council Directive 90/313/EEC, OJ L 41/26. Cf. Articles 8 and 10 of the ECHR and ECtHR, App. no. 32555/96 *Roche/United Kingdom*.

[86] Convention on Access to Information, Public Participation in Decision-making and Access to Justice in Environmental Matters of 25 June 1998, UNTS 2161, I 37770 (Aarhus-Convention).

[87] For details see *J. Callewaert*, 'Unionisation' and 'Conventionisation' of Fundamental Rights in Europe: The interplay between Union and Convention law and its impact on the domestic legal systems of the Member States, in: J. Wouters/A. Nollkaemper/E. de Wet (eds.), The Europeanisation of International Law, The Hague 2008, p. 109 (126 f.).

rules. The idea of exclusivity holds especially true for the EU. Although the Treaty of Rome was concluded in the form of an international treaty, it was the ECJ itself which in *van Gend & Loos*[88] announced the character of the European Community as "a new legal order of international law" and in its following case law contrasted it with "ordinary international treaties".[89] As to the UN, the obligations of the Charter are addressed only to the UN Member States, and the EU is not among them. However, implementation of the Member State's duties under the Charter by means of EC/EU legislation has in practice become an important vehicle for EU Member States' compliance. In spite of the obvious practical advantages of such a modus operandi, questions remain with regard to the legal basis of such legislative measures, as well as to the corresponding liability for faulty execution.[90]

It is in this context of normative cross-references and conflicts of supranationality that the case law covering the EU implementation of United Nations Security Council Counter-Terrorism Sanctions has to be examined. In the past few years, a considerable number of private challenges have been brought before both the CFI and the ECJ, prompting the Union's judges to assess the relevant EU legislation that implements United Nations Security Council Counter-Terrorism Sanctions as laid down in the Security Council Resolutions 1267 (1999)[91] and 1333 (2000).[92] Paragraph 4(b) of Resolution 1267 (1999) provides that all the States must, in particular,

"freeze funds and other financial resources, including funds derived or generated from property owned or controlled directly or indirectly by the Taliban, or by any undertaking owned or controlled by the Taliban, as designated by the Committee established by paragraph 6 below, and ensure that neither they nor any other funds or financial resources so designated are made available, by their nationals or by any persons within their territory, to or for the benefit of the Taliban or any undertaking owned or controlled, directly or indirectly, by the Taliban, except as may be authorised by the Committee on a case-by-case basis on the grounds of humanitarian need."

In addition, the Security Council decided to establish a Sanctions Committee that would be responsible for ensuring that the States implemented the measures imposed. Based on information provided by States and regional organisa-

[88] Case 26/62 *van Gend & Loos/Nederlandse Administratie des Belastingen* [1963] ECR 3.

[89] Case 6/64 *Costa/E.N.E.L.* [1964] ECR 1141: "By contrast with ordinary international treaties, the EEC Treaty has created its own legal system which, on the entry into force of the Treaty, became an integral part of the legal systems of the Member States and which their courts are bound to apply".

[90] For a general assessment of the international responsibility of the EC/EU see *P.J. Kuijper/E. Paasivirta*, Does One Size Fit All? The European Community and the Responsibility of International Organizations, Netherlands Yearbook of International Law 36 (2005), p. 169.

[91] SC Resolution 1267 (1999) of 15 October 1999.

[92] SC Resolution 1333 (2000) of 19 December 1999.

tions, the Sanctions Committee published a list of entities and persons to be subjected to the freezing of funds. This list has since been regularly amended and supplemented. In order to implement the Security Council resolution, the Council, on the basis of Articles 60 and 301 EC, adopted Regulations 337/2000[93] and 467/2001.[94] Following the defeat of the Taliban regime, the Security Council adopted a second set of Resolutions, namely Resolutions 1390 (2002)[95] and 1453 (2002).[96] These no longer aim at the former regime, but rather directly at *Usama bin Laden*, the *Al-Qaeda* 'network' and the persons and entities associated with them. The Resolutions were implemented within the EC by Regulations 881/2002[97] and 561/2003.[98] As to the legal basis of the latter, Articles 60 and 301 EC, which deal with sanctions against third *countries*, were this time supplemented by Article 308 EC in order to include sanctions against individuals and non-State bodies. The main part of the sanctions regime is included in Article 2 of Regulation 881/2002:

"(1) All funds and economic resources belonging to, or owned or held by, a natural or legal person, group or entity designated by the Sanctions Committee and listed in Annex I shall be frozen.

(2) No funds shall be made available, directly or indirectly, to, or for the benefit of, a natural or legal person, group or entity designated by the Sanctions Committee and listed in Annex I.

(3) No economic resources shall be made available, directly or indirectly, to, or for the benefit of, a natural or legal person, group or entity designated by the Sanctions Committee and listed in Annex I, so as to enable that person, group or entity to obtain funds, goods or services."

Annex I of the regulation contains the list of persons as set up by the Security Council's Sanctions Committee. That list included, *inter alia*, the names *Ahmed*

---

[93] Council Regulation (EC) No. 337/2000 of 14 February 2000 concerning a flight ban and a freeze of funds and other financial resources in respect of the Taliban of Afghanistan, OJ L 43/1.

[94] Council Regulation (EC) No. 467/2001 of 6 March 2001 prohibiting the export of certain goods and services to Afghanistan, strengthening the flight ban and extending the freeze of funds and other financial resources in respect of the Taliban of Afghanistan, and repealing Regulation (EC) No. 337/2000, OJ L 67/1.

[95] SC Resolution 1390 (2002) of 28 January 2002.

[96] SC Resolution 1453 (2002) of 24 December 2002.

[97] Council Regulation (EC) No. 881/2002 of 27 May 2002 imposing certain specific restrictive measures directed against certain persons and entities associated with Usama bin Laden, the Al-Qaida network and the Taliban, and repealing Council Regulation (EC) No. 467/2001 prohibiting the export of certain goods and services to Afghanistan, strengthening the flight ban and extending the freeze of funds and other financial resources in respect of the Taliban of Afghanistan, OJ L 139/9.

[98] Council Regulation (EC) No. 561/2003 of 27 March 2003 amending, as regards exceptions to the freezing of funds and economic resources, Regulation (EC) No. 881/2002 imposing certain specific restrictive measures directed against certain persons and entities associated with Usama bin Laden, the Al-Qaida network and the Taliban, OJ L 82/1.

Ali Yusuf, Yasin Kadi and the *Al Barakaat International Foundation*, established in Sweden. These challenged the measures taken against them and brought an action for annulment under Article 230 (4) EC before the CFI, claiming that the regulations breached their fundamental rights. Confronted with the difficult task of assessing the legislation that implements (the Member States') UN obligations, both the CFI and the ECJ exhibited a great deal of argumentative effort and originality and offered valuable thoughts on the relationship between the UN and the EU legal order.

In its judgements of 21 September 2005 in the cases *Kadi/Council and Commission*[99] and *Yusuf and Al Barakaat International Foundation/Council and Commission*,[100] the CFI basically dealt with two legal questions, i.e., first, the Community's competence to adopt and implement UN smart sanctions, and, secondly, the scope of judicial review that the court must carry out in this respect. As to the appropriateness of the legal basis of the contested regulation, the CFI held that Article 308 EC, in conjunction with Articles 60 and 301 EC, provided the Community institutions with the necessary competence.[101] As to the second question, the CFI drew on diverse arguments to justify supranational involvement on the UN level and to establish its own competence to review the conformity of the Security Council's resolutions with the norms of *ius cogens*. With regard to the EC's relationship with the UN,[102] the CFI held that even though the EU was not a UN member, it had succeeded in its Member States' obligations and was therefore competent to implement UN measures concerning the maintenance of international peace and security.[103] Concerning the scope of judicial review, the judges went on to state that, as a matter of principle, the Court lacked jurisdiction to review Security Council resolutions,[104] but was nonetheless "empowered to check, indirectly, the lawfulness of the resolutions of the Security Council in question with regard to *jus cogens*, understood as a body of higher rules of public international law binding on all sub-

---

[99] Case T-315/01 *Kadi/Council and Commission* [2005] ECR II-3649, appeal: C -402/05 P.

[100] Case T-306/01 *Yusuf and Al Barakaat International Foundation/Council and Commission* [2005] ECR II-3533, appeal: C-415/05 P.

[101] Case T-306/01 *Yusuf and Al Barakaat International Foundation/Council and Commission* [2005] ECR II-3533, appeal: C-415/05 P, paras. 99f.

[102] Case T-306/01 *Yusuf and Al Barakaat International Foundation/Council and Commission* [2005] ECR II-3533, paras. 231f.

[103] Case T-306/01 *Yusuf and Al Barakaat International Foundation/Council and Commission* [2005] ECR II-3533, para. 248: "It is also to be observed that, in so far as the powers necessary for the performance of the Member States' obligations under the Charter of the United Nations have been transferred to the Community, the Member States have undertaken, pursuant to public international law, to ensure that the Community itself should exercise those powers to that end".

[104] Case T-306/01 *Yusuf and Al Barakaat International Foundation/Council and Commission* [2005] ECR II-3533, para. 276; Case T-315/01 *Kadi/Council and Commission* [2005] ECR II-3649, para. 225.

jects of international law, including the bodies of the United Nations, and from which no derogation is possible".[105] This was in fact the first time that a regional court declared its competence to dismiss a binding Security Council resolution under Chapter VII of the UN Charter.[106]

Three years later, the ECJ decided on the appeals and handed down its long-awaited judgement in the *Kadi and Al Barakaat International Foundation* case.[107] As for the first legal question dealt with by the CFI, regarding the legal basis for the adoption of the contested regulation, the ECJ came to different findings from the CFI, holding that Article 308 EC by no means enabled the Community to pursue an objective under the Common Foreign and Security Policy (CFSP) of the TEU.[108] The Court went so far as to state that such interpretation of Article 308 EC would in fact undermine both the "constitutional architecture of the pillars, as intended by the framers of the Treaties"[109] and the principle of conferred powers.[110] Surprisingly or not, this critique in the end did not change the CFI's conclusion and the ECJ, too, found that Article 308 EC in conjunction with Articles 60 and 301 EC provided an appropriate legal basis for the contested regulation.[111] However, regarding the most important question, "the relationship between the international legal order under the United Nations and the domestic or Community legal order",[112] and the scope of its own jurisdiction, the ECJ not only adopted different positions but also came to different conclusions. The Court overruled the CFI's judgement and – despite the fact that it was intended to give effect to a Security Council Resolution that all

[105] Case T-306/01, supra, para. 277; Case T-315/01 *Kadi/Council and Commission* [2005] ECR II-3649, para. 226, my italics.

[106] For an international law perspective see *M. Licková*, European Exceptionalism in International Law, EJIL 19 (2008), p. 463 (483 f.).

[107] Joined Cases C-402/05 P and C-415/05 P *Yassin Abdullah Kadi and Al Barakaat International Foundation/Council and Commission*, judgement of 3 September 2008, not yet reported.

[108] Joined Cases C-402/05 P and C-415/05 P *Yassin Abdullah Kadi and Al Barakaat International Foundation/Council and Commission*, judgement of 3 September 2008, not yet reported, para. 201.

[109] Joined Cases C-402/05 P and C-415/05 P *Yassin Abdullah Kadi and Al Barakaat International Foundation/Council and Commission*, judgement of 3 September 2008, not yet reported, para. 202.

[110] Joined Cases C-402/05 P and C-415/05 P *Yassin Abdullah Kadi and Al Barakaat International Foundation/Council and Commission*, judgement of 3 September 2008, not yet reported, para. 203.

[111] Joined Cases C-402/05 P and C-415/05 P *Yassin Abdullah Kadi and Al Barakaat International Foundation/Council and Commission*, judgement of 3 September 2008, not yet reported, paras. 166 et seq. For a detailed analysis see *M. Tzanou*, Case-note on Joined Cases C-402/05 P & C-415/05 P *Yassin Abdullah Kadi & Al Barakaat International Foundation* v. *Council of the European Union & Commission of the European Communities*, German Law Journal 10 (2009), p. 123 (126 f.).

[112] Case T-315/01 *Kadi/Council and Commission* [2005] ECR II-3649, para. 178.

EU Member States were obliged to implement – annulled[113] the contested regulation (881/2002)[114] on the basis of its failure to respect fundamental rights. In this respect, the Court held that the regulation in question did amount to an unjustified restriction of the exercise of the appellant's fundamental rights, namely of his right to be heard,[115] his right to an effective legal remedy,[116] and his right to property.[117]

The argumentative path that led the ECJ to this conclusion was completely different from the course of the CFI's analysis. On the one hand, the ECJ held that its jurisdiction was entirely limited to the review of Community acts and thereby rejected the approach taken by the CFI that Security Council action could – in terms of compliance with norms of *ius cogens* – itself be reviewed by European courts.[118] However, on the other hand, the Court left no doubt that Community actions, regardless of whether taken in execution of an international obligation, must respect fundamental rights. In fact, the Court put out a strong statement and held that the constitutional principles of the European legal order will take precedence not only over international law, but over the UN Charter itself:

"It follows from all those considerations that the obligations imposed by an international agreement cannot have the effect of prejudicing the constitutional principles of the EC Treaty, which include the principle that all Community acts must respect fundamental rights, that respect constituting a condition of their lawfulness which it is for the Court to review in the framework of the complete system of legal remedies established by the Treaty."[119]

---

[113] In fact the Court orderd the effects of Regulation No. 881/2002 to be maintained for a maximum period of three months after the judgment.

[114] Council Regulation (EC) No. 881/2002 of 27 May 2002 imposing certain specific restrictive measures directed against certain persons and entities associated with Usama bin Laden, the Al-Qaida network and the Taliban, and repealing Council Regulation (EC) No. 467/2001 prohibiting the export of certain goods and services to Afghanistan, strengthening the flight ban and extending the freeze of funds and other financial resources in respect of the Taliban of Afghanistan, OJ L 139/9.

[115] Joined Cases C-402/05 P and C-415/05 P *Yassin Abdullah Kadi and Al Barakaat International Foundation/Council and Commission*, judgement of 3 September 2008, not yet reported, para. 348.

[116] Joined Cases C-402/05 P and C-415/05 P *Yassin Abdullah Kadi and Al Barakaat International Foundation/Council and Commission*, judgement of 3 September 2008, not yet reported, para. 349.

[117] Joined Cases C-402/05 P and C-415/05 P *Yassin Abdullah Kadi and Al Barakaat International Foundation/Council and Commission*, judgement of 3 September 2008, not yet reported, paras. 355 f., 370.

[118] Joined Cases C-402/05 P and C-415/05 P *Yassin Abdullah Kadi and Al Barakaat International Foundation/Council and Commission*, judgement of 3 September 2008, not yet reported, para. 287.

[119] Joined Cases C-402/05 P and C-415/05 P *Yassin Abdullah Kadi and Al Barakaat International Foundation/Council and Commission*, judgement of 3 September 2008, not yet reported, para. 285.

Pointing out that the European Community was based on the rule of law, the Court stated that neither the Member States nor the Community institutions could avoid judicial review of their actions for compliance with the "basic constitutional charter, the EC Treaty",[120] and with fundamental rights as "an integral part of the general principles of law whose observance the Court ensures".[121] The Court added that any decision at the European level to annul a European measure of implementation would not, under international law, affect the validity of the international measure; however, this claim is fairly weak.

True, the Court seems to adopt here a purely internal, constitutional law perspective in line with the distinctly dualistic approach of its Advocate General. In his view, the ECJ was bound to apply Community law to Community measures.[122] Yet, different from the Advocate General's approach, who had eventually adopted the same stance towards the Security Council as the *Bundesverfassungsgericht* had previously towards the ECJ in *Solange I*,[123] the ECJ – chose to follow a more inclusive path of argument and, thus, avoided what *Julio Baquero Cruz* - speaking of the *Bundesverfassungsgericht* - recently called "constitutional idolatry".[124] Unlike the *Bundesverfassungsgericht* in *Solange I*, the ECJ valued the role of the Security Council in maintaining international peace and security.[125] Moreover, it explicitly acknowledged the possibility of serious and irreversible effects resulting from an immediate annulment on the restrictive measures imposed by it.[126] The Court therefore left itself some room for ma-

---

[120] Joined Cases C-402/05 P and C-415/05 P *Yassin Abdullah Kadi and Al Barakaat International Foundation/Council and Commission*, judgement of 3 September 2008, not yet reported, para. 281.

[121] Joined Cases C-402/05 P and C-415/05 P *Yassin Abdullah Kadi and Al Barakaat International Foundation/Council and Commission*, judgement of 3 September 2008, not yet reported, paras. 283 et seq.

[122] Joined Cases C-402/05 P and C-415/05 P *Yassin Abdullah Kadi and Al Barakaat International Foundation/Council and Commission*, judgement of 3 September 2008, not yet reported, para. 23: "Yet, in the final analysis, the Community Courts determine the effect of international obligations within the Community legal order by reference to conditions set by Community law", also see para. 22: "This does not mean, however, that the Community's municipal legal order and the international legal order pass by each other like ships in the night. On the contrary, the Community has traditionally played an active and constructive part on the international stage. The application and interpretation of Community law is accordingly guided by the presumption that the Community wants to honour its international commitments".

[123] BVerfGE 37, 271 – *Solange I (Internationale Handelsgesellschaft)* comprehensive English translation in Common Market Law Reports 1974, p. 540.

[124] *J. Baquero Cruz*, The Legacy of the Maastricht-Urteil and the Pluralist Movement, European Law Journal 14 (2008), p. 389 (407).

[125] Joined Cases C-402/05 P and C-415/05 P *Yassin Abdullah Kadi and Al Barakaat International Foundation/Council and Commission*, judgement of 3 September 2008, not yet reported, para. 294.

[126] Joined Cases C-402/05 P and C-415/05 P *Yassin Abdullah Kadi and Al Barakaat International Foundation/Council and Commission*, judgement of 3 September 2008, not yet reported, para. 373.

noeuvre by ordering the effects of the regulation to be maintained for three months, thereby both allowing the Council to remedy the infringements found[127] and mooting the possibility that new procedures at the Security Council could lead to a more deferential approach.

Nonetheless, what is important is not that the ECJ decided to scrap the contested regulation on the basis of "constitutional guarantees"[128] enshrined in the European legal order, but that it did so on the basis of an analysis of EU, ECHR and general international law. Very similar to the ECtHR's approach in *Bosphorus*,[129] the ECJ entered its argumentative path by stating that the autonomy of the EU legal order, as established by the Treaties, could not be altered by any international agreement.[130] Of course, from a strictly dualist perspective, such clarification is rather redundant. Moreover, the ECJ seems to draw this respectful *laissez-faire* from the sphere of international law itself:

> "[It is] not a consequence of the principles governing the international legal order under the United Nations that any judicial review of the internal lawfulness of the contested regulation in the light of fundamental freedoms is excluded by virtue of the fact that that measure is intended to give effect to a resolution of the Security Council adopted under Chapter VII of the Charter of the United Nations."[131]

As for a dogmatic solution to the problem, the Court drew explicitly on the recent ECtHR jurisprudence in *Behrami and Saramati*[132] and *Bosphorus*.[133] In

---

[127] As for the reaction of the Commission, see Commission Regulation (EC) No. 1109/2008 of 6 November 2008 amending for the 100th time Council Regulation (EC) No. 881/2002 imposing certain specific restrictive measures directed against certain persons and entities associated with Usama bin Laden, the Al-Qaida network and the Taliban, OJ L 299/23, and Commission Regulation (EC) No. 1190/2008 of 28 November 2008 amending for the 101st time Council Regulation (EC) No. 881/2002 imposing certain specific restrictive measures directed against certain persons and entities associated with Usama bin Laden, the Al-Qaida network and the Taliban, OJ L 322/25.

[128] Joined Cases C-402/05 P and C-415/05 P *Yassin Abdullah Kadi and Al Barakaat International Foundation/Council and Commission*, judgement of 3 September 2008, not yet reported, paras. 290 and 316.

[129] See App. no. 45036/98 *Bosphorus Hava Yollari Turizm Ve Ticaret Anonim Sirketi* and III. 1. b).

[130] Joined Cases C-402/05 P and C-415/05 P *Yassin Abdullah Kadi and Al Barakaat International Foundation/Council and Commission*, judgement of 3 September 2008, not yet reported, para. 282.

[131] Joined Cases C-402/05 P and C-415/05 P *Yassin Abdullah Kadi and Al Barakaat International Foundation/Council and Commission*, judgement of 3 September 2008, not yet reported, para. 299.

[132] Joined Cases App. no. 71412/01 *Agim Behrami and Bekir Behrami/France* and App. no. 78166/01 *Ruzhdi Saramati/France, Germany and Norway*, admissibility decision of 2 May 2007 (GC). The cases concerned complaints brought by *Agim Behrami* and *Bekir Behrami* for the death and serious injury of their two children in Kosovo by the explosion of undetonated cluster bombs which had been dropped by the NATO, and the complaint brought by *Ruzhdi Saramati* for his extra-judicial detention by KFOR.

[133] App. no. 45036/98 *Bosphorus Hava Yollari Turizm Ve Ticaret Anonim Sirketi/Ireland*.

Behrami and Saramati the ECtHR held that it lacked jurisdiction *ratione personae* to review the contested acts and omissions since they were not attributable to the respondent states, but directly to the UN. Referring to this dictum, the ECJ, in *Kadi*, held that "[I]n the instant case it must be declared that the contested regulation cannot be considered to be an act *directly attributable* to the United Nations as an action of one of its subsidiary organs created under Chapter VII of the Charter of the United Nations or an action falling within the exercise of powers lawfully delegated by the Security Council pursuant to that chapter".[134] By adopting the ECtHR's approach, the ECJ established a crucial distinction, i.e. the Security Council resolutions on the one hand, and EC implementing regulations on the other. While the Community judicature can by no means review the former, it is obliged by the Treaty to examine the legality of the latter. At first glance, the distinction between directly and not directly attributable acts might seem artificial. However, the *Bosphorus* case law, which has been analysed at length above, might suggest otherwise. Very similar to the situation in *Kadi*, the case concerned the seizure of goods and assets (here: of an airplane) carried out in conformity with an EC regulation that for its part implemented a UN Security Council resolution. Here, the ECtHR did not question its own jurisdiction and, regarding a possible violation of human rights, established the 'presumption of equivalence'. Against this background, the ECJ's ruling in *Kadi* seems without alternative. Declining competence to review a piece of EC secondary legislation implementing UN law when the ECtHR has assumed its jurisdiction over national measures, implementing community legislation could very well prove that the presumption of the EU's ECHR compliance has been rebutted.[135]

While conceding that greater deference might be shown regarding the judicial review of implementing regulations if the Security Council improved the judicial remedies available under UN law, the ECJ firmly rejected the suggestion that the recently improved 're-examination procedure' was sufficient to support such considerations.[136] However, this conditionality approach vis-à-vis the Security Council puts the Court distinctly apart from the *Bundesverfassungsgericht's* approach in *Solange I*. It does not argue for legal isolation, exclusivity or even open confrontation, but for an inclusive approach that would accommodate expectations and claims at all of the various levels, i.e. the national con-

---

[134] Joined Cases C-402/05 P and C-415/05 P *Yassin Abdullah Kadi and Al Barakaat International Foundation/Council and Commission*, judgement of 3 September 2008, not yet reported, para. 314, my italics.

[135] See *M. Tzanou*, Case-note on Joined Cases C-402/05 P & C-415/05 P *Yassin Abdullah Kadi & Al Barakaat International Foundation* v. *Council of the European Union & Commission of the European Communities*, German Law Journal 10 (2009), p. 123 (145).

[136] Joined Cases C-402/05 P and C-415/05 P *Yassin Abdullah Kadi and Al Barakaat International Foundation/Council and Commission*, judgement of 3 September 2008, not yet reported, paras. 318 et seq.

stitutions, the Strasbourg Regime and UN law. It does so by simultaneously safeguarding the autonomy of the EC/EU legal order, reflecting the case law of the ECtHR and demonstrating its respect towards international law and the challenges of the fight against terrorism. In this respect, and once more with a prominent reference to the ECtHR's jurisprudence, the Court acknowledges the need for balancing security concerns with the rights of the individuals involved:

"(...) according to the case-law of the European Court of Human Rights, there must also exist a reasonable relationship of proportionality between the means employed and the aim sought to be realised. The Court must determine whether a fair balance has been struck between the demands of the public interest and the interest of the individuals concerned. In so doing, the Court recognises that the legislature enjoys a wide margin of appreciation, with regard both to choosing the means of enforcement and to ascertaining whether the consequences of enforcement are justified in the public interest for the purpose of achieving the object of the law in question [see, to that effect, in particular, European Court of Human Rights, judgment in *J. A. Pye (Oxford) Ltd. and J. A. Pye (Oxford) Land Ltd.* v. *United Kingdom* of 30 August 2007, (...) §§ 55 and 75]."[137]

In conclusion, the ECJ has thus insisted on a human rights-centred approach in the most unlikely of settings: the UN Security Council's fight against global terrorism. From a perspective of global administrative law, the crucial point is that it did so by drawing on an amalgam of EU, ECHR and general international law.[138] From an institutional perspective, by imposing its own human rights standards on the measures of implementation, the ECJ once more ensured its own institutional autonomy on the national, Community and international plane. By acting as it did, the ECJ made it clear that Member States cannot use Community institutions to circumvent national human rights standards. Otherwise the national constitutional courts might well have felt obliged to strike down legislation for implementation and to challenge the ECJ's authority. This, of course, would have posed a major threat to both the unity and the supremacy of Community law.

V. Conclusion

The purpose of this article was to analyse the complex interaction between national, supranational, and international law when it comes to human rights law. The results paradigmatically exemplify the interdependence of the two domi-

[137] Joined Cases C-402/05 P and C-415/05 P *Yassin Abdullah Kadi and Al Barakaat International Foundation/Council and Commission*, judgement of 3 September 2008, not yet reported, para. 360, italics in the original.

[138] See *E. MacDonald*, Kadi, the ECJ and the UN Security Council: A watershed moment for GAL?, http://globaladminlaw.blogspot.com/2008/09/un-security-council-watershed-moment.html (accessed March 2009).

nant debates in current international law: constitutionalism and fragmentation. European human rights protection, although regulated by two distinct and independent human rights regimes, has evolved into the world's most advanced and effective regional human rights regime. Yet precisely because of this success, it raises difficult questions as to its relationship with general international law. The antipodal judgements of the CFI and the ECJ in the Security Council smart-sanctions cases clearly demonstrate that there are no easy answers to these questions. While the ECJ decided to uphold the integrity and supremacy of the EC legal order, the CFI refused to apply the EC human rights acquis and reviewed the Security Council's resolutions' conformity with the norms of *ius cogens*. However, although this approach has been characterised as "limit[ing] the dangers of eroding the U.N. system",[139] it is evident from the ECJ's early judicature in *Foto-Frost*[140] that regionally varying interpretations of *ius cogens* could weaken the position of international law rather than strengthen it. By contrast, the ECJ's judgement, though at first glance adopting an internal, strictly dualistic constitutional law perspective, embraces international law by drawing on an amalgam of EU, ECHR and general international law and – alongside the Strasbourg Court – dismissing judicial parochialism.

[139] See *A. von Arnauld*, UN-Sanktionen und gemeinschaftrsrechtlicher Grundrechtsschutz, Archiv des Völkerrechts 44 (2006), p. 201 (215): "To choose an international ordre public standard instead of a domestic European one, is a wise decision, as it limits the dangers of eroding the U.N. system by encouraging desertion on grounds of national dissent".

[140] Case 314/85 *Foto-Frost/Hauptzollamt Lübeck-Ost* [1987] ECR 4199.

The Correlation between Human Rights and the Loan Policies of the World Bank and the EBRD

Felicitas Chen

In a globalized world, economic activities cannot be considered exempt from political considerations anymore. Economics has a serious impact on politics and vice-versa. Thus, multilateral development banks are commonly expected to consider political issues when giving development assistance. However, the legal prerequisites usually do not allow for politically motivated development strategies. On the contrary, as most international development organizations unite countries with differing historical and political backgrounds, political issues are often not on the agenda. This is especially problematic with regard to human rights aspects as political considerations. The depiction of the loan policies of the World Bank and the EBRD will illustrate how these organizations deal with human rights in theory and practice.

The first part of this article will give an understanding of the World Bank's loan policy with respect to human rights issues. The second part will move on to explaining the legal framework and development practice of the EBRD. The third part will deal with a comparison of the two development institutions before reaching a conclusion in the fourth part.

I. The International Bank for Reconstruction and Development / the World Bank

1. Introduction

The International Bank for Reconstruction and Development (IBRD) is a specialized agency of the United Nations working in the field of international development policy. In July 1944, the United and Associated Nations held the International Monetary and Finance Conference in Bretton Woods (New Hampshire, USA) where they established the IBRD along with the International Monetary Fund (IMF). When talking about the World Bank, the IBRD and the International Development Association (IDA) are usually referred to as the core organizations of the World Bank Group. However, this essay will focus on the IBRD, and thus the World Bank will refer solely to the IBRD. The World Bank has currently 185 member states organized as a cooperative society. According to Article VII Section 2 of its constituent treaty, the Articles of Agreement,[1] the World Bank possesses full juridical personality. Voting power within the World Bank is proportionate to the number of shares. The three largest shareholders are the United States (holding 16.84% of subscriptions that correspond to 16.38% of voting power), Japan (8.07% subscriptions corresponding to 7.86% voting power) and Germany (4.6% subscriptions corresponding to 4.49% voting power).[2] Article I (i) of the World Bank's Articles of Agreement illustrates that at the time of its foundation the main purpose was the reconstruction and economic development of member countries devastated by World War II.[3] Since then, its purposes have developed towards the promotion of sustained development and the reduction of global poverty.[4]

2. *The World Bank's Non-Political Mandate*

How do human rights affect the World Bank's work? Looking at it from a legal perspective, Article III, Section 5 (b) of its Articles of Agreement must be taken into account:

> "The Bank shall make arrangements to ensure that the proceeds of any loan are used only for the purposes for which the loan was granted, with due attention to considerations of economy and efficiency and without regard to political or other non-economic influences or considerations."

This provision makes it clear that political ambitions of any kind, including the promotion of human rights, are prohibited. Furthermore, Article IV, Section 10 outlines even more explicitly that the World Bank is not to interfere in the politics of a member country:

> "The Bank and its officers shall not interfere in the political affairs of any member; nor shall they be influenced in their decisions by the political character of the member or members concerned. Only economic considerations shall be relevant to their decisions, and these considerations shall be weighed impartially in order to achieve the purposes stated in Article I."

---

[1] *IBRD*, Articles of Agreement, as amended effective 16 February 1989, http://go.worldbank.org/0FICOZQLQ0 (permanent URL); see also Forschungsstelle für Völkerrecht und ausländisches öffentliches Recht der Universität Hamburg (ed.), Dokumente. Satzungen der Sonder-Organisationen der Vereinten Nationen, Vol. IV, Frankfurt am Main 1951, pp. 13 ff.

[2] *The World Bank*, http://go.worldbank.org/X96KDQODL0 –> IBRD (accessed 22 May 2009).

[3] Cf. also *R. Peet*, Unholy trinity: the IMF, World Bank and WTO, Kuala Lumpur et al. 2003, p. 114.

[4] http://go.worldbank.org/DM4A38OWJ0 (permanent URL); *S. George*, Kredit und Dogma. Ideologie und Macht der Weltbank, Hamburg 1995, p. 16.

Article 5, Section 5 (c) clarifies that the non-political mandate applies to every decision or action of every World Bank member:

"The President, officers and staff of the Bank, in the discharge of their offices, owe their duty entirely to the Bank and to no other authority. Each member of the Bank shall respect the international character of this duty and shall refrain from all attempts to influence any of them in the discharge of their duties."

Hence, according to the World Bank's own Articles of Agreement, political considerations such as the fostering of human rights as conditions for granting loans to recipient member states must not be of importance. Project proposals solely qualify for promotion on economic grounds.

3. *The World Bank's Loan Policy*

During the first years or even decades of its existence, the World Bank hardly considered political aspects like human rights when lending money. Of course, this was consistent with the non-political mandate as stated in its Articles of Agreement. However, as a consequence, there were Bank projects that had long-term or even irreversible effects on the political, social or ecological framework of a country.[5]

A very prominent example is the so-called *Polonoroeste Program*, a development program for the Brazilian Amazon region. Implementation of the program began in 1982. Its objective was to develop new areas by building a highway through the Amazon rainforest from Cuiaba to Porto Velho.[6] The program had serious effects on the environment[7] as well as on indigenous tribal life in the region.[8] Even after the conclusion of the program, it is being debated whether positive effects prevailed over the negative.[9]

Within the World Bank, criticism of its own development policy came up first under the presidency of *Robert McNamara*.[10] In the 1970's and 80's, interna-

[5] *B. Copur/A. Schneider*, IWF & Weltbank: Dirigenten der Globalisierung, Hamburg 2004, p. 34; *P. Nunnenkamp*, IWF und Weltbank: trotz aller Mängel weiterhin gebraucht?, Kiel 2002, p. 26; M. Hauff (ed.), Strukturanpassungspolitik der Weltbank: Will die Weltbank mehr als Wirtschaftswachstum in Entwicklungsländern?, Berlin 1992, pp. 19 f.; *R. Tetzlaff*, Weltbank und Währungsfonds – Gestalter der Bretton-Woods-Ära: Kooperations- und Integrations-Regime in einer sich dynamisch entwickelnden Weltgesellschaft, Opladen 1996, p. 25.

[6] *C. Junqueira/B. Mindlin*, The Aripuana Park and the Polonoroeste Programme, IWGIA Document No. 59, Copenhagen 1987, p. 3.

[7] *A. L. O. de Almeida/J. S. Campari*, Sustainable Settlement in the Brazilian Amazon, New York 1995, p. 85, No. 23; *C. Junqueira/B. Mindlin*, The Aripuana Park and the Polonoroeste Programme, IWGIA Document No. 59, Copenhagen 1987, p. 7.

[8] *C. Junqueira/B. Mindlin*, The Aripuana Park and the Polonoroeste Programme, IWGIA Document No. 59, Copenhagen 1987, pp. 5 ff.

[9] *A. L. O. de Almeida/J. S. Campari*, Sustainable Settlement in the Brazilian Amazon, New York 1995, p. 85, No. 23.

[10] *Robert Strange McNamara*, President of the World Bank, April 1968 – June 1981.

tional criticism of World Bank projects increased noticeably.[11] Especially the World Bank's financial support of the Indian Sardar Sarovar Dam project has caused enormous protests and opposition internationally[12] as well as from the Indian population since the beginning of its implementation in 1987[13]: It is the core part of the Narmada Valley Project that intends to establish an extensive irrigation system in the northwest of India by building more than 3000 dams regulating the flow of the Narmada River and its affluents.[14] The Sardar Sarovar Dam is designed to produce a reservoir lake with a storage capacity of about 700 000 000 cubic meters.[15] Apart from disastrous ecological effects, e.g. the flooding of huge areas of cultivated land,[16] this project affects hundreds of thousands of people – many of them indigenous tribal peoples[17] – from rural areas subject to involuntary resettlement and displacement.[18] Thus, it has become another well-known example for the negative effects of the World Bank's ignorance as regards political, social and environmental considerations.

As a consequence of all this criticism, the World Bank ran an internal investigation in 1992, the so-called Wapenhans Report,[19] named after the chairman of the responsible task force. In this report, it became clear that there were shortcomings in the quality of the World Bank's loan policy. One of the main factors identified as crucial for deficiencies in the World Bank's project performances was that World Bank staff felt under pressure to conclude a certain

---

[11] *R. Tetzlaff*, Weltbank und Währungsfonds – Gestalter der Bretton-Woods-Ära: Kooperations- und Integrations-Regime in einer sich dynamisch entwickelnden Weltgesellschaft, Opladen 1996, p. 73; *S. Killinger*, The World Bank's non-political mandate, Berlin et al. 2003, p. 63; *B. Copur/A. Schneider*, IWF & Weltbank: Dirigenten der Globalisierung, Hamburg 2004, p. 35.

[12] *W.F. Fisher*, Development and Resistance in the Narmada Valley, in: W.F. Fisher (ed.), Toward Sustainable Development? Struggling Over India's Narmada River, New York 1995, p. 5; *A. Roy*, Die Politik der Macht, 4th edition, Munich 2002, pp. 58ff.

[13] *A. Roy*, Die Politik der Macht, 4th edition, Munich 2002, pp. 25, 57ff.; *W.F. Fisher*, Development and Resistance in the Narmada Valley, in: W.F. Fisher (ed.), Toward Sustainable Development? Struggling Over India's Narmada River, New York 1995, pp. 4f.

[14] *V. Böge*, Das Sardar-Sarovar-Projekt an der Narmada in Indien – Gegenstand ökologischen Konflikts, Environment and Conflicts Projekt (ENCOP), Occasional Paper No. 8, Zurich 1993, p. 1.

[15] *V. Böge*, Das Sardar-Sarovar-Projekt an der Narmada in Indien – Gegenstand ökologischen Konflikts, Environment and Conflicts Projekt (ENCOP), Occasional Paper No. 8, Zurich 1993, p. 1.

[16] *V. Böge*, Das Sardar-Sarovar-Projekt an der Narmada in Indien – Gegenstand ökologischen Konflikts, Environment and Conflicts Projekt (ENCOP), Occasional Paper No. 8, Zurich 1993, p. 3.

[17] *A. Patel*, What Do the Narmada Valley Tribals Want?, in: *W.F. Fisher* (ed.), Toward Sustainable Development? Struggling Over India's Narmada River, New York 1995, pp. 179ff.

[18] *A. Roy*, Die Politik der Macht, 4th edition, Munich 2002, p. 54.

[19] *The World Bank Portfolio Management Task Force*, Effective Implementation: Key to Development Impact, Washington, DC 1992.

amount of loan agreements so that quality was neglected.[20] Another aspect was inadequate resources in time.[21]

Because it was exposed to vehement criticism on an international as well as internal level, the World Bank's loan policy has changed insofar as it has constantly been developing new and different mechanisms to support socially and environmentally sustainable development by means of World Bank projects. Since the 1980's, for example, so-called safeguard policies have existed, been revised and developed. These safeguard policies are compulsory guidelines for every decision or measure taken by World Bank staff. Their objective is to maintain certain social and environmental standards in projects supported by the World Bank.[22] Social and environmental soundness is now an imperative requirement in the project's assessment of progress; only if this requirement is fulfilled is the project eligible for a loan agreement.[23]

4. *Compatibility with Articles of Agreement*

How are these Safeguard Policies and other measures with social and environmental impact compatible with the World Bank's Articles of Agreement? Since according to Article IV, Section 10, "[o]nly economic considerations shall be relevant to their [the World Bank's and its officers'] decisions", any action that can be justified economically is in conformity with its charter.

At this point, it becomes clear that political considerations in the form of human rights obligations are to be distinguished in the World Bank context. A differentiation ought to be made between human rights in the form of civil and political rights and in the form of economic, social and environmental rights. Although there is interaction between politics and economy,[24] the World Bank's Articles of Agreement demand that a measure be economically efficient, and at the same time they exclude political considerations. Thus, the Articles of Agreement evidently distinguish between the two terms. According to *Shihata*[25], everything related to the governing and party system of a country therefore falls under the prohibition of political activity as stated in the Articles of Agreement.[26] With regard to human rights as a political issue, it becomes apparent

---

[20] *The World Bank Portfolio Management Task Force*, Effective Implementation: Key to Development Impact, Washington, DC, 1992, p. 17.

[21] *The World Bank Portfolio Management Task Force*, Effective Implementation: Key to Development Impact, Washington, DC, 1992, pp. 18 f.

[22] There are currently 10 safeguard policies dealing with Environmental Assessment, Forests, Involuntary Resettlement, Indigenous Peoples, Safety of Dams, Pest Management, Physical Cultural Resources, Natural habitats, Projects in Disputed Areas, Projects on International Waterways.

[23] See http://go.worldbank.org/1YXPMBNDO0 (permanent URL).

[24] *I. F. I. Shihata*, The World Bank in a Changing World, Dordrecht 1991, pp. 69 f.

[25] Dr. Ibrahim F. I. Shihata, General Counsel of the World Bank, 1983–1998.

[26] *I. F. I. Shihata*, The World Bank in a Changing World, Dordrecht 1991, p. 70.

that civil and political rights usually do not seem to be of relevance to the World Bank's loan decisions.[27] Since there is a much stronger link between social and environmental considerations and economic development, as e.g. in the field of labor law and labor rights, an economic justification for social and environmental rights appears to be more compatible with the World Bank's Articles of Agreement.

5. *The World Bank's Attitude towards Human Rights*

Despite the distinction mentioned above between political aspects regarding government issues of a borrowing member country and social factors, World Bank practice seems to be partly incoherent. In 1966, the World Bank refused to continue lending to South Africa and Portugal, which was in conformity with UN General Assembly Resolutions 2202 (XXI)[28] and 2184 (XXI).[29] However, it emphasized that this was no intervention in the political affairs of the member states concerned but a result of the economic implications of the respective political situation.[30] Another example is the World Bank's reaction to the Chinese Tiananmen massacre of 4 May, 1989: the World Bank stopped lending to China and considering new loans.[31] In that case, only in part World Bank staff did not deny the political motivations for these measures.[32]

Hence, even if there is evidence of the World Bank's interest in civil and political rights in its practice, in official announcements these rights have usually been regarded as beyond the World Bank's legitimate scope of activities.[33] Thus, the World Bank's attitude towards the promotion of "purely political" human rights is in line with its Articles of Agreement.

With respect to economic, social and environmental rights, the World Bank takes a different view: It openly promotes the fostering of social, economic and ecological development as being coherent with the strict economic mandate as stated in its Articles of Agreement.[34] But even in this area, official announce-

---

[27] *I.F.I. Shihata*, The World Bank in a Changing World, Dordrecht 1991, p. 79.

[28] UN GA Res. No. 2202 (XXI), The Policies of Apartheid of the Government of the Republic of South Africa, 16 December 1966.

[29] UN GA Res. No. 2184 (XXI), Question of Territories under Portuguese Administration, 12 December 1966.

[30] *I.F.I. Shihata*, The World Bank in a Changing World, Dordrecht 1991, pp. 103 f.

[31] *D. Gillies*, Human Rights, Democracy and Good Governance: Stretching the World Bank's Policy Frontiers, in: *J.M. Griesgraber/B.G. Gunter*, The World Bank. Lending on a Global Scale (Vol. III), London et al. 1996, pp. 101 ff. (126).

[32] *David Gillies*, Human Rights, Democracy and Good Governance: Stretching the World Bank's Policy Frontiers, in: *J.M. Griesgraber/B.G. Gunter*, The World Bank. Lending on a Global Scale (Vol. III), London et al. 1996, pp. 101 ff. (127).

[33] See also *S. Killinger*, The World Bank's non-political mandate, Berlin et al. 2003, pp. 99, 116, 122.

[34] *S. Killinger*, The World Bank's non-political mandate, Berlin et al. 2003, pp. 74, 98, 121 ff.

ments of the World Bank say clearly that sensitive topics such as women's rights do not have an impact on the World Bank's loan policy.

The distinction between different kinds of human rights standards made by the World Bank may be problematic as regards their "*indivisibility and interdependence*"[35] as well as their equal importance,[36] which, however, will not be further elaborated in this context.

II. The European Bank for Reconstruction and Development

1. Introduction

The European Bank for Reconstruction and Development (EBRD) is a regional development organization with its headquarter in London, United Kingdom. Its charter, the Agreement Establishing the EBRD,[37] was signed in Paris on 29 May, 1990 and came into force on 28 March, 1991. The EBRD is currently owned by 61 member countries and 2 inter-governmental institutions, the European Community (EC) and the European Investment Bank (EIB). Like the World Bank, it is organized as a cooperative society; therefore as in the World Bank, voting power is proportionate to the number of shares. The largest shareholders are the United States (with a capital subscription of 2 billion euros), Japan, the United Kingdom, Italy, France and Germany (with a capital subscription of 1,703.50 billion euros each). The EC and the EIB have a share of 600 million euros each. Under Article 45 of the Agreement Establishing the EBRD, the Bank possesses full legal personality. The organizational structure of the EBRD is similar to that of the World Bank,[38] yet these are totally independent institutions. Nonetheless, Article 2, paragraph 2 of the Agreement Establishing the EBRD demands that it work closely with the IBRD.

The EBRD's objective is to help countries from Central Europe to Central Asia in their transition towards market-oriented economies.[39] Originally, its main purpose was the support of the transition of Central and Eastern European countries as well as the CIS countries towards a free market economy and multiparty democracy after the collapse of the Soviet Union.[40] Economic devel-

---

[35] See also *S. Killinger*, The World Bank's non-political mandate, Berlin et al. 2003, p. 127.

[36] *K. Ipsen*, Völkerrecht, 5th edition, Munich 2004, p. 788.

[37] *EBRD*, Agreement Establishing the EBRD, http://www.ebrd.com/pubs/insti/basics.htm → Basic Documents of the EBRD, pp. 4 ff. (accessed 22 May 2009).

[38] *I. F. I. Shihata*, The European Bank for Reconstruction and Development. A Comparative Analysis of the Constituent Agreement, London et al. 1990, p. 82.

[39] http://www.ebrd.com/about/index.htm (accessed 22 May 2009).

[40] *U. Suchsland-Maser*, Menschenrechte und die Politik multilateraler Finanzinstitute, Frankfurt am Main 1999, p. 266; *EBRD*, Chairman's Report on the Agreement Establishing the European Bank for Reconstruction and Development, http://www.ebrd.com/pubs/insti/basics.htm → Basic Documents of the EBRD, p. 48 (accessed 22 May 2009).

opment and reconstruction were to be seen more as secondary aims in the early years of the EBRD's existence.[41]

2. *Agreement Establishing the EBRD*

The legal mandate of the EBRD is special in the way that it was the first to explicitly include political aspects for an institution of this kind.[42] Its political orientation is reflected in various provisions of the Agreement Establishing the EBRD, which even refer explicitly to human rights. They start with the Preamble to the Agreement that explicitly upholds respect for human rights in its first and third paragraphs:

"The Contracting Parties,
Committed to the fundamental principles of multiparty democracy, the rule of law, respect for human rights and market economics;
Recalling the Final Act of the Helsinki Conference on Security and Co-operation in Europe, and in particular its Declaration on Principles;
Welcoming the intent of Central and Eastern European countries to further the practical implementation of multiparty democracy, strengthening democratic institutions, the rule of law and respect for human rights and their willingness to implement reforms in order to evolve towards market-oriented economies;
[...]"

The reference to the Final Act of the Helsinki Conference of the OSCE[43] is also a reference to respect for human rights as it is promoted in the 7th Principle Guiding Relations between Participating States in the Final Act.[44]

Furthermore, Article 1 explaining the purpose of the EBRD especially refers to market-oriented economies, private entrepreneurship, multiparty democracy, pluralism and market economics:

"In contributing to economic progress and reconstruction, the purpose of the Bank shall be to foster the transition towards open market-oriented economies and to promote private and entrepreneurial initiative in the Central and Eastern European countries committed to and applying the principles of multiparty democracy, pluralism and market economics. [...]"

Article 8, paragraphs 1 and 2 of the Agreement make reference to the purposes outlined in Article 1, whereas Article 8, paragraph 3 provides for sanctions in a case where a member state does not comply with these purposes:

---

41 *I. F. I. Shihata*, The World Bank in a Changing World, Dordrecht 1991, p. 57.

42 *I. F. I. Shihata*, The European Bank for Reconstruction and Development. A Comparative Analysis of the Constituent Agreement, London et al. 1990, p. 103.

43 *OSCE*, Conference on Security and Co-Operation in Europe. Final Act, in: Archiv des Völkerrechts 17 (1977/78), pp. 84 ff.

44 *OSCE*, Conference on Security and Co-Operation in Europe. Final Act, in: Archiv des Völkerrechts 17 (1977/78), p. 88.

"In cases where a member might be implementing policies which are inconsistent with Article 1 of this Agreement, or in exceptional circumstances, the Board of Directors shall consider whether access by a member to Bank resources should be suspended or otherwise modified and may make recommendations accordingly to the Board of Governors. [...]"

Thus, non-compliance with the purposes of the EBRD may be sanctioned by the suspension of access by a member state to EBRD resources. This appears to be quite a severe but reasonable penalty if the EBRD seriously pursues its objectives.

Furthermore, the Agreement explicitly includes the EBRD's commitment to environmental protection:

Article 2, paragraph 1 (vii):

"the Bank shall assist the recipient member countries [...] to promote in the full range of its activities environmentally sound and sustainable development".

Article 11, paragraph 1 (v):

"The Bank shall carry out its operations in furtherance of its purpose and functions as set out in Articles 1 and 2 of this Agreement in any or all of the following ways: [...] including environmental programmes, necessary for private sector development and the transition to a market-oriented economy".

These explicit references to environmental sustainability are remarkable as again the EBRD is the first institution of its kind to include such provisions.[45] They are further supported by a report mechanism provided for in Article 35, paragraph 2 of the Agreement.

3. *The EBRD's Political Mandate*

The historical circumstances that caused the establishment of the EBRD were exceptional. After four decades of political and ideological confrontation between East and West, the EBRD was designed by the Western community to help countries in Central and Eastern Europe and in the CIS to develop a political and economic system according to their ideals. Hence, the EBRD's explicit political mandate might not be surprising.[46] Yet, the drafters of the Agreement Establishing the EBRD deliberately refrained from mentioning human rights in the agreement itself, and included them explicitly only in the Preamble.[47] This should be interpreted as meaning to include only human rights

---

[45] *I. F. I. Shihata*, The European Bank for Reconstruction and Development. A Comparative Analysis of the Constituent Agreement, London et al. 1990, p. 103.

[46] *I. F. I. Shihata*, The World Bank in a Changing World, Dordrecht 1991, p. 58.

[47] *EBRD*, Political Aspects of the Mandate of the European Bank for Reconstruction and Development, London 1993, p. 4, http://www.ebrd.com/pubs/insti/aspects.htm (accessed 22 May 2009).

standards with significant importance to multiparty democracy, pluralism and market economics – hence, mostly civil and political rights.[48] According to the EBRD itself, these are for example equal protection under the law, a fair criminal procedure, freedom of speech and media, freedom of assembly, freedom of conscience and religion, of movement and the right to private property.[49]

Although the Agreement does not refer to ecological *rights*, the EBRD has been the first multilateral financial institution that has made the furthering of environmental soundness a mandatory requirement for development measures.[50]

4. *The EBRD's Loan Policy*

The EBRD's initial focus of operation were the Central European countries that tended to be more open-minded towards the EBRD objectives.[51] Over the years, it moved towards a more diverse operation policy in geographical terms, including more and more countries in Eastern Europe and the CIS.[52] The EBRD now supports member countries in central-eastern Europe, the Baltic, southeastern Europe and the CIS as well as Mongolia. It operates in 29 member countries. As of 2007 the EBRD reported that overall development in the structural and institutional framework of recipient member states is advancing, although not as much as in former years.[53]

With regard to its political mandate, the EBRD discovered in 2007 that in the Central and Eastern European as well as Baltic states, 40% of the people are of the opinion that political circumstances have worsened since 1989.[54] In the southeastern European member countries, the majority think the political situation has aggravated compared to 1989, whereas in the CIS and Mongolia, some countries have a more positive public view of the political situation and in some, public opinion is definitely negative.[55] This is quite a diverse pattern of how people in recipient countries view the political development since the establishment of the EBRD. It shows that despite the political mandate of the EBRD, its

[48] *EBRD*, Political Aspects of the Mandate of the European Bank for Reconstruction and Development, London 1993, p. 4, http://www.ebrd.com/pubs/insti/aspects.htm (accessed 22 May 2009).

[49] *EBRD*, Political Aspects of the Mandate of the European Bank for Reconstruction and Development, London 1993, p. 5 (showing a more detailed exemplary list), http://www.ebrd.com/pubs/insti/aspects.htm → Political Aspects of the Mandate of the EBRD (accessed 22 May 2009).

[50] See http://www.ebrd.com/enviro/index.htm (accessed 22 May 2009).

[51] *Canadian Department of Finance*, Report on Operations Under the European Bank for Reconstruction and Development Agreement Act 1997, Ottawa 1997, p. 11.

[52] *Canadian Department of Finance*, Report on Operations Under the European Bank for Reconstruction and Development Agreement Act 1997, Ottawa 1997, pp. 10 f.

[53] *EBRD*, Transition Report 2007, London 2007, p. 3.

[54] *EBRD*, Transition Report 2007, London 2007, p. 49.

[55] *EBRD*, Transition Report 2007, London 2007, pp. 49 f.

loan policy has not made a definitely positive impression on the citizens where political development is concerned.

The EBRD has interpreted its environmental mandate comprehensively, as comprising not only ecological issues but also labour, health, safety, gender and community aspects, as well as indigenous peoples, involuntary resettlement, cultural heritage and basic services issues.[56] Environmental standards have to be complied with in every internal or external EBRD decision and development measure[57] with due diligence; for example, ecological aspects should function as conditions in loan agreements.[58] While sustainable development is seen as an essential element in efficient management and "among the highest priorities" in EBRD operations,[59] a sound political and institutional organization of a country is regarded as the necessary prerequisite for ecologically and socially sustainable development.[60] Therefore the transition towards market-oriented economies in EBRD-supported member states appears hardly achievable, to say the least, without environmental and social sustainability.

III. The World Bank and the EBRD – A Comparison

1. The Legal Prerequisites

(a) The (Non-)Political Mandate

The initial purpose of the World Bank was the reconstruction and development of Western European countries devastated during World War II.[61] The founders of the World Bank consisted of 44 states, the United and Associated Nations, joined together by the experiences of World War I, its economic aftermath and the ongoing occurrences of World War II. Their history and traditions, political evolution and ideological beliefs, economic orientation and social constitution

---

[56] *EBRD*, Environmental and Social Policy of 12 May 2008, p. 3, http://www.ebrd.com/about/policies/enviro/policy/index.htm (accessed 22 May 2009); cf. also http://www.ebrd.com/enviro/index.htm (accessed 22 May 2009).

[57] See http://www.ebrd.com/enviro/policy/standard.htm (accessed 22 May 2009).

[58] *Canadian Department of Finance*, Report on Operations Under the European Bank for Reconstruction and Development Agreement Act 1997, Ottawa 1997, pp. 20f.; see also http://www.ebrd.com/enviro/policy/standard.htm (accessed 22 May 2009).

[59] *EBRD*, Environmental and Social Policy of 12 May 2008, p. 3, http://www.ebrd.com/about/policies/enviro/policy/index.htm → Environmental and Social Policy 2008 (accessed 22 May 2009).

[60] *D. Fisher*, Introduction, in: European Bank for Reconstruction and Development (ed.), Environmental impact assessment legislation, London et al. 1994, p. xi.

[61] See *R. Peet*, Unholy trinity: the IMF, World Bank and WTO, Kuala Lumpur et al. 2003, p. 114.

varied greatly. In this situation, the common denominator and necessary focus was the creation of a stable postwar economic order on an international level.[62]

The EBRD initially aimed at helping Central and Eastern European as well as CIS countries in the transition towards free market economics and multiparty democracy after 1989.[63] Emerging in the aftermath of the Cold War, it might seem like a logical consequence that the EBRD was quite a political institution right from the start.[64] The Western founder states had come to share the same ideals and aims over the years,[65] which was partly due to the support towards development granted to Western European countries by the United States under the Marshall Plan.[66] These ideals included the conviction that there is a strong correlation between the formation of market-oriented economies and the development of democracy and the rule of law.[67] At the same time, more than 40 years after the establishment of the World Bank, a tendency could be observed in the international, albeit bilateral donor practice, to tie economic assistance with human rights and democracy requirements.[68]

In any case, the historical, political and also economic circumstances in the formation of the two international financial institutions were quite different. Hence, the significant difference in their constituent treaties – one with the explicit prohibition of political activity, the other expressly linking political development with economic support – is due to their respective genesis.

(b) Human Rights Aspects

When it comes to human rights aspects, a differentiation between civil/political rights and economic/social/ecological rights has to be made.

Regarding civil and political rights, the World Bank's Articles of Agreement are quite clear in that they qualify political considerations as overstretching the Bank's legitimate scope. The EBRD, on the contrary, is bound to the promotion of multiparty democracy, pluralism and market economics, hence clearly po-

---

62 Cf. *I. F. I. Shihata*, The European Bank for Reconstruction and Development. A Comparative Analysis of the Constituent Agreement, London et al. 1990, p. 44.

63 See *U. Suchsland-Maser*, Menschenrechte und die Politik multilateraler Finanzinstitute, Frankfurt a. M. 1999, p. 266.

64 Cf. *I. F. I. Shihata*, The World Bank in a Changing World, Dordrecht 1991, pp. 57 f.

65 *A. Bronstone*, The European Bank for Reconstruction and Development. The building of a bank for East Central Europe, Manchester et al. 1999, pp. 3 f.

66 *A. Bronstone*, The European Bank for Reconstruction and Development. The building of a bank for East Central Europe, Manchester et al. 1999, p. 7.

67 *EBRD*, Political Aspects of the Mandate of the European Bank for Reconstruction and Development, London 1993, p. 3, http://www.ebrd.com/pubs/insti/aspects.htm → Political Aspects of the Mandate of the EBRD (accessed 22 May 2009).

68 *D. Gillies*, Human Rights, Democracy and Good Governance: Stretching the World Bank's Policy Frontiers, in: *J. M. Griesgraber/B. G. Gunter*, The World Bank. Lending on a Global Scale (Vol. III), London et al. 1996, pp. 101 ff. (110 f.).

litical concepts that are inevitably linked to certain standards of civil and political rights.[69]

With respect to economic, social and ecological rights, it has to be emphasized that the dominating concept in the World Bank's Articles of Agreement is the concept of economic efficiency. Since economic development mostly has strong social and ecological implications, the relevant human rights standards may be considered even under the World Bank charter.

On the contrary, the EBRD seems to promote economic and social rights only insofar as they are essential to multiparty democracy, pluralism and market economics. However, the Agreement Establishing the EBRD also expressly provides for environmental protection. This is interpreted by the EBRD itself as encompassing not only ecological issues but also economic and social implications.[70]

Thus, both constituent treaties allow for the protection of economic, social and ecological human rights standards.

(c) Focus on Public/Private Sector Development

As regards operation policy, the World Bank's development assistance is primarily focused on the public sector. This is illustrated especially by Article I (i), (iii)-(v) of its Articles of Agreement, explaining the purposes of the World Bank, as well as by Articles III (especially Section 1, 2, 4) and IV, dealing with General Provisions Relating to Loans and Guarantees and a detailed elaboration of the three basic types of operations. Although the Articles of Agreement do also envisage the promotion of the private sector in Article I (ii), the World Bank's operation policy under the constituent treaty is to be interpreted as being more state-oriented.

The Agreement Establishing the EBRD, however, puts a special focus on private sector development: Article 1 explicitly encompasses the promotion of "*private and entrepreneurial initiative*" with the purposes of the EBRD.

According to Article 2, paragraph 1 (i),

> "to promote, through private and other interested investors, the establishment, improvement and expansion of productive, competitive and private sector activity, in particular small and medium-sized enterprises",

qualifies as a crucial means for economic development. Furthermore, the EBRD charter contains in Article 11, paragraph 3 (i) a clear limitation of rates for public sector activities and thus a definite preference for private sector activities:

---

[69] See EBRD, Political Aspects of the Mandate of the European Bank of Reconstruction and Development, London 1993, p. 4, http://www.ebrd.con/pubs/insti/aspects.htm Caccessed 22 May 2009).

[70] See EBRD, Environmental and Social Policy of 12 May 2008, p. 3, http://www.ebrd.com/about/polities/enviro/policy/index.htm (accessed 22 May 2009); cf. also http://www.ebrd.com/lenviro/index.htm (accessed 22 May 2009).

"Not more than forty (40) per cent of the amount of the Bank's total committed loans, guarantees and equity investments, without prejudice to its other operations referred to in this Article, shall be provided to the state sector. [...]"

This provision constitutes a clear preference for private sector development that shall amount to not less than 60% of the EBRD's development activities.

2. *Lending Practice*

As outlined above, World Bank lending practice has sometimes shown evidence or at least strong indications of the consideration of civil and political rights. Nevertheless, in official statements World Bank staff has persistently denied the intentional furthering of these rights. This discrepancy should be seen in the light of the prohibition of political activity in its Articles of Agreement; it leaves little discretion for World Bank staff when making announcements.

Since the EBRD charter even provides for a sanction mechanism if the political requirements of the treaty are disregarded, chances for controlled political development seemed to be high; however, over the years, expectations were rather disappointed.[71]

With regard to economic, social and cultural rights, it is remarkable that they are practically and officially promoted by the World Bank, e.g. by applying the Safeguard Policies mentioned above to loan projects.

Although the environmental mandate of the EBRD includes social and other political aspects as well,[72] ecological issues play a dominant role in the EBRD loan practice.[73] This even contributes to the promotion of democracy and human rights in that political awareness and participation in issues of ecological concern are fostered.[74]

It can therefore be noted that despite their totally contrary legal mandates regarding political considerations, the loan policies of the World Bank and the EBRD are not as different as one might have expected.[75]

---

[71] *U. Suchsland-Maser*, Menschenrechte und die Politik multilateraler Finanzinstitute, Frankfurt am Main 1999, p. 285.

[72] See EBRD, Environmental and Social Policy of 12 May 2008, p. 3, http://www.ebrd.com/about/policies/envirolpolicy/index.htm (accessed 22 May 2009); cf. also http://www.ebrd.com/enviro/index.htm (accessed 22 May 2009).

[73] *U. Suchsland-Maser*, Menschenrechte und die Politik multilateraler Finanzinstitute, Frankfurt am Main 1999, p. 285.

[74] *U. Suchsland-Maser*, Menschenrechte und die Politik multilateraler Finanzinstitute, Frankfurt am Main 1999, pp. 285 f.

[75] Cf. also *I. F. I. Shihata*, The European Bank for Reconstruction and Development. A Comparative Analysis of the Constituent Agreement, London et al. 1990, pp. 103 f.

IV. Conclusion

The World Bank and the EBRD are international development organizations that differ remarkably in their statutory premises regarding their political objectives. Whereas political activities are expressly prohibited to the World Bank, the EBRD has an explicit political mandate. In practice, however, the differences between the World Bank and the EBRD are not as evident. The two development banks even tend to approach the same level of consideration for aspects of human rights.

There is no hierarchy in the quality of different types of human rights, but there is a strong correlation between all of their types. However, both constituent treaties of the two international financial institutions examined here seem to divide civil/political rights and economic/social/ecological rights. Both banks seem to have difficulties in the direct promotion of civil and political rights, which seems quite astonishing in the case of the EBRD. Between economic, social and ecological rights, the latter seem to get the most attention in both organizations. This might be due to ecological issues not being quite as sensitive a matter ideologically as other aspects of human rights.

Besides human rights obligations in customary international law, most of the member countries of the World Bank and the EBRD have ratified international human rights agreements or are obliged to respect human rights through their membership in international organizations. Furthermore, keeping in mind the tendency in a globalized world to be mindful of aspects of human rights in economics, it is not surprising that even the World Bank is influenced by human rights issues. Moreover, considering the World Bank's and the EBRD's economic power, it seems likely that their activities in view of development, which are influenced by human rights standards, also strengthen human rights by helping to implement them. Hence, there is indeed a correlation between human rights and the loan policies of the World Bank and the EBRD, just as a correlation between economics and politics can generally be observed in this globalized world.

Theoretical Thoughts on the Relationship of Non-State Actors and Human Rights

Ferry Bühring

I. Introduction

Traditionally, public international law aims at regulating inter-state relations. In a globalized world, however, with its "widening, deepening and speeding up of worldwide interconnectedness in all types of contemporary social life, from the cultural to the criminal, the financial to the spiritual",[1] the role of the sovereign nation state is changing.[2] Having lost the capacity to autonomously regulate collective affairs on the national level, states are increasingly confronted with supra- and transnational processes producing internal effects beyond a single state's control.[3] A major pathology of the globalization process is the factual decay of governmental structures.[4] Common to both phenomena – globalization and failing statehood[5] – is the rising influence of "non-state actors".[6]

---

[1] *D. Held/A. McCrew/D. Goldblatt/J. Perraton*, Global Transformation: Politics, Economics and Culture, Cambridge 2005, p. 2.

[2] See *J. Habermas*, Die postnationale Konstellation, Frankfurt 1998; *M. Zürn/S. Leibfried*, Transformation des Staates, Frankfurt 2006; *M. Zürn*, Regieren jenseits des Nationalstaates, Frankfurt 2005.

[3] See Report of the UN Secretary General, Impact of international commitments, policies and processes on the scope and implementation of national development strategies, 25 August 2007, UN-Doc. A/62/303; from a constitutional law perspective see: *C. Tietje*, Die Staatsrechtslehre und die Veränderung ihres Gegenstandes: Konsequenzen von Europäisierung und Internationalisierung, Deutsches Verwaltungsblatt 118 (2003), pp. 1081 ff.

[4] *G. Nolte*, Das Verfassungsrecht vor den Herausforderungen der Globalisierung, VVDStRL 67 (2008), p. 129 (130, 157).

[5] *G. B. Helman/ S. Ratner*, Saving Failed States, Foreign Policy 89 (1992/93), p. 3 ff. and the contributions in: *I. W. Zartman* (ed.), Collapsed States – The Disintegration and Restoration of Legitimate Authority, London 1995; for an international law perspective see *R. Geiß*, "Failed States". Die normative Erfassung gescheiterter Staaten, Berlin 2005; *D. Thürer*, Der Wegfall effektiver Staatsgewalt im Völkerrecht: "The Failed State", Berichte der Deutschen Gesellschaft für Völkerrecht 34 (1995), pp. 9 ff.; *M. Herdegen*, Der Wegfall effektiver Staatsgewalt im Völkerrecht: "The Failed State", Berichte der Deutschen Gesellschaft für Völkerrecht 34 (1995), pp. 49 ff.

[6] *G. F. Schuppert*, The Changing Role of the State Reflected in the Growing Importance of Non-State Actors, in: G.F. Schuppert (ed.), Global Governance and the Role of Non-State

It correlates with a demise of public power exercised by the state and consequently leads to a growing divergence between the normative expectations of a state-centred conception of international law and social reality.

With regard to international human rights law, this divergence manifests itself in constant and severe infringements by non-state actors, which states, as the prime addressees of international law, seem unable to master. Faced with transnationally operating corporations (TNCs) whose economic power frequently transcends their own,[7] states increasingly lose the capacity to effectively guarantee the human rights compliance of the latter, whose activities shape the social reality of millions of lives around the globe. Pharmaceutical corporations are causing the premature and avoidable death of thousands of people living with HIV/AIDS by way of excessive pricing.[8] Multinational oil companies meet the local population with excessive force, while destroying their livelihoods and causing substantial damage to the natural environment.[9] The global garment industry shocks potential consumers through appalling working conditions in many low-wage countries around the world.[10] This list is not exhaustive. At the same time, these companies do not fear sanctions imposed by the state on whose territory they act, but rather dread the medial power wielded by transnational non-governmental organizations (TNGOs). Every now and then, the latter – mostly perceived as "the good guys" – press ahead without verifying their facts, thus causing substantial damage to those they accuse on the basis of wrong information.[11] Having been identified not only as

---

Actors, Baden-Baden 2004, pp. 203 ff.; from an international law perspective see: *S. Hobe*, Die Zukunft des Völkerrechts im Zeitalter der Globalisierung, Archiv des Völkerrechts 37 (1999), p. 253 (261); *A. Reinisch*, The Changing International Legal Framework for Dealing with Non-State Actors, in: Ph. Alston (ed.), Non-State Actors and Human Rights, Oxford 2005, p. 37 (74 f.); *Ph. Kunig*, Das Völkerrecht und die Interessen der Weltbevölkerung, in. P.-M. Dupuy et al. (eds.), Völkerrecht als Wertordnung – Common Values in International Law, Kehl 2006, p. 377 (380); *Ph. Kunig*, Macht und Recht in den internationalen Beziehungen, Verfassung und Recht in Übersee 38 (2005), p. 105 (107).

[7] See *C. Wells/ J. Elias*, Catching the Conscience of the King: Corporate Players on the International Stage, in: Ph. Alston (ed.), Non-State Actors and Human Rights, Oxford 2005, p. 141 (148); for comprehensive information on Transnational Corporations see: United Nations Conference on Trade and Development (UNCTAD), World Investment Report 2007: Transnational Corporations, Extractive Industries and development, UN Symbol: UNCTAD/WIR/2007, available under www.unctad.org (accessed 3 March 2009).

[8] South Africa Competition Commission, Hazel Tau et al. vs. GlaxoSmithKline, Boehringer Ingelheim et al, decision of 16 December 2003, available under: www.compcom.co.za (accessed 3 March 2009); see: *G. Teubner*, The Anonymous Matrix: Human Rights Violations by 'Private' Transnational Actors, Modern Law Review 69 (2006), pp. 327 ff.

[9] *K. Sarow-Wiwa*, Genocide in Nigeria: the Ogoni tragedy, London 1992.

[10] *A. Fung et al.*, Can We Put an End to Sweatshops?, Ann Arbor 2004.

[11] *J. Delbrück*, contribution to the discussion, in: R. Hofmann (ed.), Non-State Actors as New Subjects of International Law, Berlin 1999, p. 67; *A. Reinisch*, The Changing International Legal Framework for Dealing with Non-State Actors, in: Ph. Alston (ed.), Non-State Actors and Human Rights, Oxford 2005, p. 48.

advocates but also as violators of human rights,[12] NGOs increasingly make use of self-regulatory mechanisms.[13] These and similar observations have brought the human rights dimension of non-state actor behaviour to the attention of the international community and have fuelled interdisciplinary discourse on the globalization process and its deficiencies.

In what follows, I intend to show that the international legal order is not entirely blind to these developments and that the current state of human rights law offers promising starting points that might contribute towards clarifying the relationship between human rights law and non-state actors. After some preliminary observations and terminological clarification (II.), the traditional approach of international law as regards human rights relations on the horizontal level will be presented (III.). Against this background, I shall outline some theoretical thoughts on new ways of dealing with non-state actors and human rights under international law (IV.), before offering my conclusion (V.).

II. Terminology and Preliminary Observations

As an analytical tool, the term "non-state actor" seems to be of limited value, since it offers but one criterion of differentiation. By using the word "non-state actor" one is compelled to define the relevant entities by what they are not.[14] Apart from the negatively determined characteristic of not being a state, most of the actors identified have rarely anything in common: Shell, the World Bank, the Lord's Resistance Army in Uganda, Greenpeace, as well as every human being not acting on behalf of the state; all of them qualify as "non-state actors". With its descriptive power and seemingly shoreless scope of applicability, the term represents a cornerstone in the debate about the changing power structure of the international system.[15] A prominent part of this phenomenon is the transfer of competencies from the national to the international and supranational

[12] *A. Reinisch*, The Changing International Legal Framework for Dealing with Non-State Actors, in: Ph. Alston (ed.), Non-State Actors and Human Rights, Oxford 2005, p. 64 with further references.

[13] See, for instance, in the area of humanitarian assistance International Committee of the Red Cross/ International Federation of the Red Cross and Red Crescent Societies, Code of Conduct for the International Red Cross and Red Crescent Movement and Non-Governmental Organizations (NGOs) in Disaster Relief, Geneva 1994.

[14] See *Ph. Alston*, The 'Not-a-Cat' Syndrome: Can the International Human Rights Regime Accommodate Non-State Actors?, in: Ph. Alston (ed.), Non-State Actors and Human Rights, Oxford 2005, pp. 3ff.

[15] See generally the contributions in: G.F. Schuppert (ed.), Global Governance and the Role of Non-State Actors, Baden-Baden 2004; for an international law perspective: R. Hofmann (ed.), Non-State Actors as New Subjects of International Law, Berlin 1999, see also the early contribution by: *H. Mosler*, Die Erweiterung des Kreises der Völkerrechtssubjekte, Berichte der Deutschen Gesellschaft für Völkerrecht 4 (1961), pp. 39ff.

levels. In the following, though, I intend to fade out actors created by the will of states and to concentrate on collective entities of a private nature. Hence, I shall not deal with international or supranational organizations and their human rights relations,[16] but concentrate on two major groups of private collective actors, i.e. multi- or transnational corporations (TNCs) and transnational non-governmental organizations (TNGOs).

Likewise, these terms for their part comprise a plethora of diverse entities. To a certain extent, however, some consensus seems to have been reached in the international debate. Since the early 1970s, various UN bodies have been addressing the issue of defining TNCs, among them the Commission on Transnational Corporations[17] and the Sub-Commission on the Promotion and Protection of Human Rights,[18] the latter being a subsidiary body of the former Human Rights Commission. Since the beginning, finding a generally accepted definition has proved to be difficult.[19] Certainly, the OECD Guidelines for Multinational Enterprises[20] serve as a strong point of reference, not with a precise definition but with a series of typical characteristics that are mirrored in the draft of the UN Code of Conduct on Transnational Corporations.[21] According to these guidelines, multinational enterprises "usually comprise companies or other entities established in more than one country and so linked that they may co-ordinate their operations in various ways. While one or more of these entities may be able to exercise a significant influence over the activities of others, their degree of autonomy within the enterprise may vary widely from one mul-

---

[16] See *S. Boysen*, The Impact of Human Rights an Supranational Regimes, in this volume, pp. 209ff.

[17] See UN Economic and Social Council, Resolutions 1908 LVII, 2 August 1974 and 1913 LVII, 5 December 1974; *S.J. Rubin*, Developments in the Law and Institutions of International Economic Relations. Reflections Concerning the United Nations Commission of Transnational Corporations, American Journal of International Law 70 (1976), p. 70 (73ff.).

[18] See UN-Doc. E/CN.4/Sub.2/RES/1998/8, 20 August 1998 and UN-Doc. E/CN.4/Sub.2/RES/2001/3, 15 August 2001; *K. Nowrot*, Die UN-Norms on the Responsibility of Transnational Corporations and Other Business Enterprises with Regard to Human Rights. Gelungener Beitrag zur transnationalen Rechtsverwirklichung oder das Ende des Global Compact?, in: C. Tietje et al. (eds.), Beiträge zum Transnationalen Wirtschaftsrecht 21 (2006), pp. 6ff.; *N. Rosemann*, The UN Norms on Corporate Human Rights Responsibilities – An Innovative Instrument to Strengthen Business' Human Rights Performance, Dialogue on Globalization – Occasional Paper No. 20, Friedrich Ebert Stiftung, Geneva 2005, pp. 29f.

[19] See *P. Fischer*, Transnational Enterprises, in: R. Bernhardt (ed.), Encyclopedia of Public International Law, Vol. IV, Amsterdam 2000, pp. 921ff.; *S.J. Rubin*, The Transnational Corporations, Proceedings of the Academy of Political Science 32 (1977), pp. 120ff.

[20] OECD Guidelines for Multinational Enterprises, 27 June 2000, in: International Legal Materials 40 (2001), pp. 237ff.

[21] See www.globalcompact.org (accessed 3 March 2009); *S. von Schorlemer*, Der "Global Compact" der Vereinten Nationen. Ein Faust'scher Pakt mit der Wirtschaftswelt?, in: S. von Schorlemer (ed.), Praxishandbuch UNO. Die Vereinten Nationen im Lichte globaler Herausforderungen, Berlin 2003, pp. 507ff.

tinational enterprise to another. Ownership may be private, state or mixed."[22] As with multinational corporations, whose origins date back to the times of the British East India Trading Company and its Dutch counterparts in the 16th century, NGOs operating on an international level are by no means a new phenomenon. On 17 April 1839, the British and Foreign Anti-Slavery Society was founded under British Law, declaring its commitment to abolishing slavery throughout the world.[23] Today known as Anti-Slavery International, this human rights organization belongs to one of the most politically influential types of non-state actors. Although prominently recognized by legal scholarship in the 1960s[24] as an "overwhelming phenomenon in international law", hardly any substantial progress has been made in reaching a consensus in view of a definition until today. The *Encyclopaedia of Public International Law*, for instance, suggests also thinking of multinational companies as NGOs,[25] which certainly confuses NGOs with the wider concept of non-state actors.[26] In 2004, a UN report conceded that "(t)here is considerable confusion surrounding this term in United Nations circles."[27] It seems that instead of a precise definition one has to be satisfied with a terminological approximation. For the purpose of this article, it suffices to delineate two basic types of TNGOs, i.e. *service NGOs* and *political NGOs*.[28] *Political NGOs* predominantly address states, international organizations as well as TNCs in order to exert political influence on their conduct and norm-setting activities. Organizations such as Human Rights Watch, Transparency International or Greenpeace are among the most prominent representatives of this category. *Service NGOs* on the other hand, such as the International Red Cross or Médecins Sans Frontières, are typically concerned

[22] *S. von Schorlemer*, Der "Global Compact" der Vereinten Nationen. Ein Faust'scher Pakt mit der Wirtschaftswelt?, in: S. von Schorlemer (ed.), Praxishandbuch UNO. Die Vereinten Nationen im Lichte globaler Herausforderungen, Berlin 2003, p. 237 (239).

[23] *British and Foreign Anti-slavery Society*, British and Foreign Anti-slavery Society for the abolition of slavery and the slave-trade throughout the world: address, 1839.

[24] *H. Mosler*, Die Erweiterung des Kreises der Völkerrechtssubjekte, Berichte der Deutschen Gesellschaft für Völkerrecht 4 (1961), p. 39 (40f.): "Die Wahl des Themas meines Berichts rechtfertigt sich durch die Notwendigkeit, diesem überwältigenden Phänomen in der Völkerrechtsordnung einen Platz zuzuweisen."

[25] *H. Rechenberg*, Non-Governmental Organizations, in: R. Bernhardt (ed.), Encyclopedia of Public International Law, Volume III (1997), p. 612.

[26] *M. T. Kamminga*, The Evolving Status of NGOs under International Law: A Threat to the Inter-State System?, in: Ph. Alston (ed.), Non-State Actors and Human Rights, Oxford 2005, p. 93 (95).

[27] Report of the Panel of Eminent Persons on United Nations-Civil Society Relations: We the peoples: civil society, the United Nations and global governance, UN-Doc. A/58/817, 11 June 2004, p. 13.

[28] *G. F. Schuppert*, The Changing Role of the State Reflected in the Growing Importance of Non-State Actors, in: G. F. Schuppert (ed.), Global Governance and the Role of Non-State Actors, Baden-Baden 2004, p. 203 (212) drawing on: *J. Curbach*, Global Governance und NGOs. Transnationale Zivilgesellschaft in internationalen Politiknetzwerken, Opladen 2003.

with the provision of public goods such as health, food, or other aspects of basic infrastructure in regions affected by conflicts, poverty, or other disasters. It is crucial to note that *political NGOs* and *service NGOs* assume distinct positions, i.e. they act in different capacities. Whereas the former truly act as representatives of a "world civil society" when promoting norms and values in order to translate them into political programs,[29] the latter take over public functions that typically fall within the state's sphere. This capacity to act in the public interest and in *co-operation with* and/or *instead of* the state – which I shall call "functional statehood"[30] – is not limited to NGOs. TNCs can also be said to assume a "functional statehood" capacity in areas such as security,[31] health care,[32] and environmental protection.[33]

As regards the "relationship" between non-state actors and human rights, I shall distinguish two phenomena: "horizontal effects" and "transnational effects". Whereas the former concept is part of a well-established debate based on the current state of the law, the latter forms part of an ideological orientation process and remains largely uncertain. At this point, it shall suffice to submit that the "horizontal effects" of international human rights law are always mediated through national law, while the "transnational effects" are not. They rather presuppose new ways of looking at the international/global legal order as a whole and at human rights and non-state actors in particular.

---

[29] *G.F. Schuppert*, The Changing Role of the State Reflected in the Growing Importance of Non-State Actors, in: G.F. Schuppert (ed.), Global Governance and the Role of Non-State Actors, Baden-Baden 2004, p. 212.

[30] See for a functional perception of non-state actor activities *R. Wedgwood*, Legal Personality and the Role of Non-Governmental Organizations and Non-State Political Entities in the United Nations System, in: R. Hofmann (ed.), Non-State Actors as New Subjects of International Law, Berlin 1999, p. 21 (36); *F. Bühring/N. Hüfken*, Menschenrechtsstandards für Governance in schwachen und zerfallen(d)en Staaten, in: S. de la Rosa et al. (eds.), Transdisziplinäre Governanceforschung, Baden-Baden 2008, p. 187 (198ff.).

[31] *C. Schaller*, Private Sicherheits- und Militärfirmen in bewaffneten Konflikten, SWP Studie, Stiftung für Wissenschaft und Politik, Berlin September 2005.

[32] See, for instance, the Global Health Initiative (GHI) launched at the 2002 World Economic Forum and designed to engage businesses in public private partnerships in order to tackle HIV/AIDS, Tuberculosis, and health systems in general (http://www.weforum.org/en/initiatives/globalhealth/index.htm (accessed 20 February 2009).

[33] See for the influence of TNCs on the promotion of environmental state-, self- and/or public private partnership regulation *J. Hönke et al.*, Fostering Environmental Regulation? – Corporate Social Responsibility in Countries with Weak Regulatory Capacities: The Case of South Africa, SFB Governance Working Paper Series, No. 11, DFG-Sonderforschungsbereich 700, Berlin 2008.

III. Non-State Actors and the State-Centred Conception of International Human Rights Law

During the 1961 session of the German Society of International Law, *Hermann Mosler* in his widely recognized account "Die Erweiterung des Kreises der Völkerrechtssubjekte"[34] – which he conceded could also be called "non-state participants of international legal relations"[35] – submitted that "today" no one truly conceives of international law as being confined to the legal relations between states.[36] *Mosler* maintained that the international personality of intergovernmental organisations – forming an important group within the circle of non-state entities – had to be accepted as a *fait accompli*.[37] Remarkably, he already devoted a considerable amount of attention to those entities ("Wirkungseinheiten")[38] not created by the will of states, i.e. the ones which should form an integral aspect of the academic debate starting about three decades later. Of course, *Mosler* based his considerations on the undisputed supremacy of states as being the principal subjects of international law. Nearly half a century later, few things have changed in that respect.[39] Despite the structural difference of human rights law as opposed to the classical fields of international law – i.e. rules addressing intra-state situations as opposed to inter-state relations – the axiomatic fact remains that states continue to represent the cornerstone of the international system.

---

[34] *H. Mosler*, Die Erweiterung des Kreises der Völkerrechtssubjekte, in: Berichte der Deutschen Gesellschaft für Völkerrecht 4 (1961).

[35] *H. Mosler*, Die Erweiterung des Kreises der Völkerrechtssubjekte, Berichte der Deutschen Gesellschaft für Völkerrecht 4 (1961), p. 39 (41): "Man könnte auch, statt von der 'Erweiterung des Kreises der Völkerrechtssubjekte' zu sprechen, ebensogut 'nichtstaatliche Teilnehmer des Völkerrechtsverkehrs' sagen."

[36] *H. Mosler*, Die Erweiterung des Kreises der Völkerrechtssubjekte, in: Berichte der Deutschen Gesellschaft für Völkerrecht 4 (1961), p. 39 (40): "Die Beschränkung der völkerrechtlichen Beziehungen auf den Verkehr zwischen Staaten wird heute von niemandem mehr vertreten (...)."

[37] *H. Mosler*, Die Erweiterung des Kreises der Völkerrechtssubjekte, Berichte der Deutschen Gesellschaft für Völkerrecht 4 (1961), p. 39 (76).

[38] *H. Mosler*, Die Erweiterung des Kreises der Völkerrechtssubjekte, Berichte der Deutschen Gesellschaft für Völkerrecht 4 (1961), p. 39 (44 f.).

[39] *J. Ruggie*, Protect, Respect and Remedy: a Framework for Business and Human Rights – Report of the Special Representative of the Secretary-General on the issue of human rights and transnational corporations and other business enterprises, UN-Doc. A/HRC/8/5, 7 April 2008, para 50: "the bedrock role of States"; see also: *Ph. Kunig*, Das Völkerrecht und die Interessen der Bevölkerung, in: P.-M. Dupuy et al. (eds.), Völkerrecht als Wertordnung – Common Values in International Law, Kehl 2006, p. 377 (377): "im Kern ein Recht der Völker in Staaten, welche seine ursprünglich einzigen und heute noch immer strukturbildenden Rechtssubjekte sind".

1. *Horizontal Effects of International Human Rights Law*

a) Indirect Horizontal Effects

The philosophical conception of human rights as spheres of *freedom from* the state,[40] translated into the negative function of human rights law, is reflected in international human rights instruments. Whereas the "negative function" is well established, the "protective function",[41] forming part of the positive obligation of states to ensure these rights and their implications for the horizontal level, seem to have been given a somewhat lesser kind of attention.[42] However, most human rights treaties provide an explicit grammatical basis for this positive dimension of human rights law. Its strongest expression can be found in the UN specialized conventions. Art. 2 lit. (e) of the Convention on the Elimination of All Forms of Discrimination against Women (CEDAW), for instance, requires state parties "to take all appropriate measures to eliminate discrimination against women by any person, organization or enterprise." Commenting on that provision, the CEDAW-Committee maintained that the protective function of the state is not to be perceived as limited to specific treaty law:

> "Under general international law and specific human rights covenants, States may also be responsible for private acts if they fail to act with due diligence to prevent violations of rights or to investigate and punish acts of violence, and for providing compensation".[43]

Less elaborate as compared to art. 2 lit. (e) CEDAW but still explicit, art. 2 para. 1 of the International Covenant on Civil and Political Rights (ICCPR) requires state parties "to ensure to all individuals within its territory and subject to its jurisdiction the rights recognized in the present Covenant". The UN Human Rights Committee held the view that:

> "the positive obligations of State parties to ensure Covenant rights will only be fully discharged if individuals are protected by the State, not just against the violations of

---

[40] *I. Berlin*, The two concepts of liberty: an inaugural lecture delivered before the University of Oxford on 31 October 1958, Oxford 1959.

[41] See for the German Schutzpflicht conception *D. Grimm*, The protective function of the state, in: G. Nolte (ed.), European and US Constitutionalism, Cambridge 2005, p. 137 (143 ff.).

[42] But see *J. Ruggie*, Business and human rights: mapping international standards of responsibility and accountability for corporate acts – Report of the Special Representative of the Secretary-General on the issue of human rights and transnational corporations and other business enterprises, UN-Doc. A/HRC/4/35, 19 February 2007, paras 10 ff.; *J. Ruggie*, Protect, Respect and Remedy: a Framework for Business and Human Rights – Report of the Special Representative of the Secretary-General on the issue of human rights and transnational corporations and other business enterprises, UN-Doc. A/HRC/8/5, 7 April 2008, paras 27 ff.

[43] Committee on the Elimination of Discrimination against Women, General Recommendation No. 19: Violence Against Women, 1992, para 9.

Covenant rights by its agents, but also by acts committed by private persons or entities."[44]

Even more conclusive is the protective dimension of the so-called "second generation rights" as laid down in the International Covenant on Economic Social and Cultural Rights (ICESCR), since they are not primarily designed as *freedoms from* the state but as a positive obligation of the latter. According to the ICESCR-Committee:

"States parties' obligation to protect under Article 3 of the ICESCR includes [...] the adoption of legislation to eliminate discrimination and to prevent third parties from interfering directly or indirectly with the enjoyment of this right [...]. State parties have an obligation to monitor and regulate the conduct of non-state actors to ensure that they do not violate the equal right of men and women to enjoy economic, social, and cultural rights."[45]

Keeping in mind the gradual caveat of the states' discretion with regard to the implementation of these obligations,[46] it appears noteworthy that the treaty bodies of the UN Human Rights System generally seem to agree upon the protective function of human rights law requiring states to ensure a horizontal human rights compliance. Furthermore, there are strong indications that the same is true for the regional human rights systems. With regard to the right to life under the European Convention on Human Rights (ECHR), for instance, the Strasbourg Court in *Keenan vs. the United Kingdom* held that art. 2 para. 1 ECHR does not only contain the negative obligation of the state to refrain from the taking of lives, but also the positive duty of state authorities to take preventive measures in order to protect an individual whose life is at risk from the criminal acts of another individual.[47] In fact, the duty to protect has been established with regard to most of the human rights guarantees under the ECHR.[48]

---

[44] Human Rights Committee, General Comment No. 31: The Nature of the General Legal Obligations Imposed on State Parties to the Covenant, 29 March 2004, para 8.

[45] Committee on Economic Social and Cultural Rights, General Comment No. 16, Article 3: the equal right of men and women to the enjoyment of all economic, social and cultural rights, 2005, paras 19f.

[46] *J. Ruggie*, Business and human rights: mapping international standards of responsibility and accountability for corporate acts – Report of the Special Representative of the Secretary-General on the issue of human rights and transnational corporations and other business enterprises, UN-Doc. A/HRC/4/35, 19 February 2007, para 12.

[47] European Court of Human Rights, *Keenan vs. The United Kingdom*, judgement of 3 April 2001, Reports 2001-III, § 89; see also: *Osman vs. The United Kingdom*, judgement of 28 October 1998, Reports 1998-VIII, § 115; and recently: *Pereira Henriques c. Luxembourg*, arrêt du 9 mai 2006, Requête n° 60255/00, § 54 (only available in French).

[48] *H. Krieger*, Comment, in: G. Nolte (ed.), European and US Constitutionalism, Cambridge 2005, p. 181 (184 ff.); see also *A. Bleckmann*, Die Entwicklung staatlicher Schutzpflichten aus den Freiheiten der Europäischen Menschenrechtskonvention, in: U. Beyerlin et al. (eds.), Recht zwischen Umbruch und Bewahrung, Berlin 1995, pp. 309 ff.

Similar developments can be observed in the African and the American human rights systems.[49]

This brief and incomplete survey of the legal practice of major treaty bodies on the universal and regional levels indicates that the protective function of international human rights law as part of the positive obligations of states to ensure human rights constitutes a widely accepted concept under international law. It requires states to take positive steps in the form of domestic legislation and is therefore adequately described as an *indirect horizontal effect*.

b) Direct Horizontal Effects

Along with these indirect impacts of international human rights law, the debate revolves around a "direct horizontal effect", asking whether certain treaty provisions have the capacity to directly produce a legal relationship between private entities on the national level.[50] A *direct horizontal effect* requires that the respective treaty form part of the domestic legal order – either by way of incorporation or transformation –[51] and that the relevant provision is "self-executing"[52] while at the same time producing a "third party effect".

Firstly, the self-executing character of a norm or its direct applicability requires that the norm's content be adequately structured and possess a sufficient degree of determinacy in order for national administrative authorities and courts to deduce legal consequences with regard to the individual case.[53] This prerequisite is, in principle, given in the case of classical civil and political rights.[54] The self-executing character of "second generation rights", however, which are of particular relevance with regard to the behaviour of TNCs, is subject to a controversial debate. Whereas some authors maintain that due to art. 2 para. 1 ICESCR and the principle of progressive realization, economic, social and cultural rights lack direct applicability,[55] others submit that the dogmatic

---

[49] *G. Nolte*, Das Verfassungsrecht vor den Herausforderungen der Globalisierung, 67 VVDStRL (2008), p. 129 (147) with references in note 90.

[50] *A. Emmerich-Fritsche*, Zur Verbindlichkeit der Menschenrechte für transnationale Unternehmen, Archiv des Völkerrechts 45 (2007), p. 541 (554 ff.).

[51] See *Ph. Kunig*, Völkerrecht und staatliches Recht, in: W. G. Vitzthum (ed.), Völkerrecht, 4th ed., Berlin 2007, p. 86 (98 ff.).

[52] See for the concept of self-executing treaty provisions *A. Bleckmann*, Self-Executing Treaty Provisions, in: R. Bernhardt (ed.), Encyclopedia of Public International Law Volume IV (2000), pp. 374 ff.

[53] *R. Geiger*, Grundgesetz und Völkerrecht, 4th ed., München 2009, p. 142, drawing on: *M. Zuleeg*, Abschluß und Rechtswirkung völkerrechtlicher Verträge in der Bundesrepublik Deutschland, Juristische Arbeitsblätter 1983, p. 1 (6): "wenn die innerstaatlichen Verwaltungsbehörden und Gerichte aus dem Vertrag Rechtsfolgen für den Einzelfall ableiten dürfen".

[54] *Ph. Kunig*, Völkerrecht und staatliches Recht, in: W. G. Vitzthum (ed.), Völkerrecht, 4th ed., Berlin 2007, p. 103 (for an applicability of the rights under section I. of the ECHR).

[55] *P. Kirchhof*, Verfassungsrechtlicher Schutz und internationaler Schutz der Menschenrechte – Konkurrenz oder Ergänzung?, Europäische Grundrechte-Zeitschrift 1994, p. 16

difference between first and second generation rights – i.e. the negative as opposed to the positive function – cannot be perceived as excluding all rights of the latter category from being justiciable.[56] In its General Comment on the nature of the states parties' obligations, the ICESCR-Committee differentiated between rights requiring a "progressive realization", rights with an "immediate effect",[57] and certain "core obligations".[58] A couple of years later, the Committee went on to maintain that "there is no Covenant right which could not, in the great majority of systems, be considered to possess at least some significant justiciable dimensions".[59] However, the Committee distinguishes "between justiciability (which refers to those matters which are appropriately resolved by the courts) and norms which are self-executing (capable of being applied by courts without further elaboration)".[60] Given the progressive interpretation of the ICESCR by its committee and the necessity of renouncing dichotomic dogmatic considerations,[61] combined with the need for a differentiating analysis of the justiciable character of second generation rights,[62] there seems to be enough room for a direct applicability of several ICESCR guarantees.[63] However, it is vital to note that it is up to the respective state to decide whether the legal quality of a norm as "self-executing" can take effect in the domestic legal order or not.[64]

Secondly, in order to establish a horizontal human rights relationship, the self-executing treaty provision in addition requires a "third party effect". Under

---

(28); *K Hailbronner*, Der Staat und der Einzelne als Völkerrechtssubjekte, in: W. G. Vitzthum (ed.), Völkerrecht, 4th ed., Berlin 2007, p. 157 (232).

56 *B. Simma*, "Die vergessenen Rechte": Bemühungen zur Stärkung des VN-Sozialpakts, in: F. Ruland et al. (eds.), Verfassung, Theorie und Praxis des Sozialstaats, Heidelberg 1998, p. 867 (871 ff.); see also the contributions in: F. Coomans/G. J. H. van Hoof (eds.), The Right to complain about Economic, Social and Cultural Rights, Utrecht 1995.

57 Committee on Economic Social and Cultural Rights, General Comment No. 3, The nature of States parties obligations, 1990, para 1.

58 Committee on Economic Social and Cultural Rights, General Comment No. 3, The nature of States parties obligations, 1990, para 10.

59 Committee on Economic, Social and Cultural Rights, General Comment No. 9, The domestic application of the Covenant, 1998, para 10.

60 Committee on Economic, Social and Cultural Rights, General Comment No. 9, The domestic application of the Covenant, 1998, para 10.

61 *B. Simma*, "Die vergessenen Rechte": Bemühungen zur Stärkung des VN-Sozialpakts, in: F. Ruland et al. (eds.), Verfassung, Theorie und Praxis des Sozialstaats, Heidelberg 1998, p. 867 (871 f.).

62 *B. Simma*, "Die vergessenen Rechte": Bemühungen zur Stärkung des VN-Sozialpakts, in: F. Ruland et al. (eds.), Verfassung, Theorie und Praxis des Sozialstaats, Heidelberg 1998, p. 867 (872 f.); F. Coomans/ G. J. H. van Hoof (eds.), The Right to complain about Economic, Social and Cultural Rights, Utrecht 1995.

63 For a more detailed analysis see *A. Emmerich-Fritsche*, Zur Verbindlichkeit der Menschenrechte für transnationale Unternehmen, Archiv des Völkerrechts 45 (2007), p. 541 (555 ff.).

64 *A. Bleckmann*, Self-Executing Treaty Provisions, in: R. Bernhardt (ed.), Encyclopedia of Public International Law, Volume IV (2000), p. 374 (375).

German constitutional law – home of the *Drittwirkung* –[65] a direct effect on the horizontal level (*unmittelbare Drittwirkung*) does not exist. A third party effect of fundamental rights as guaranteed under the Basic Law is always mediated through statutory law in the sense that the constitutional rights are to be considered by the courts when deciding civil law cases. Certainly, this German conception of a *mittelbare Drittwirkung* ("indirect third party effect") does not preclude the dogmatic possibility of a direct third party effect under international human rights law. However, even the usually progressive practice of the competent treaty organs hints in the opposite direction. According to the Human Rights Committee:

"[...] obligations are binding on States [Parties] and do not, as such, have direct horizontal effect as a matter of international law. The Covenant cannot be viewed as a substitute for domestic criminal or civil law."[66]

c) *Intermediate Summary*

To sum up, the protective function of the state is the answer given by the state-centred conception of international law regarding the relationship between non-state actors and human rights. Mediated through national law, this function produces an "indirect horizontal effect" with a wide margin of discretion as regards the implementation of the respective human rights treaty. A *direct effect* of human rights norms on the horizontal level, however, cannot be asserted under the current state of the law. Although a considerable number of human rights guarantees possess the legal quality of a self-executing character, a "direct third party effect" (*unmittelbare Drittwirkung*) cannot be established within the domestic legal systems.

2. *Some Deficiencies*

Can the protective function of international human rights law master the downsides of the globalization process? The answer to that question depends on the scope of that dogmatic category's definition. Understood as the obligation to guarantee horizontal human rights compliance exclusively *under national law*, it reveals predominantly deficiencies. The most evident shortcomings arise in the context of failed or failing statehood.[67] The partial or complete breakdown

[65] German Federal Constitutional Court, Judgement of 15 January 1958 (Lüth), in: Entscheidungen des Bundesverfassungsgerichts 7 (1958), pp. 198 ff.; for a concise explanation of the concept and its resonance in international legal scholarship see: *A. Clapham*, Human Rights Obligations of Non-State Actors, Oxford 2006, pp. 521 ff.

[66] Human Rights Committee, General Comment No. 31: The Nature of the General Legal Obligations Imposed on State Parties to the Covenant, 29 March 2004, para 8.

[67] See *G. B. Helman/ S: Ratner*, Saving Failed States, 89 Foreign Policy (1992/93), pp. 3 ff. and the contributions in: *I. W. Zartman* (ed.), Collapsed States – The Disintegration and Restoration of Legitimate Authority, London 1995; for an international law perspective see: *R.*

of effective governmental structures results in the gradual incapacity of the respective state to fulfil its obligations under general international law and human rights law in particular. Depending on the degree of institutional failure, some authors are inclined to see the Hobbesian anthropological premise as empirically verified.[68] With regard to the human rights infringements by the types of non-state actors in question, it is noteworthy that the overwhelming majority of the alleged human rights infringements occur on the territory of weak or failing states.[69] Certainly, there are legal concepts and mechanisms that are capable of seizing the described phenomena on a theoretical basis. Under the laws of state responsibility, for instance, the conduct of non-state actors can either be attributed to the respective state in accordance with the rules as reflected in articles 4–11 of the ILC-Draft on State Responsibility,[70] or it constitutes an internationally wrongful omission.[71] However, I submit that the international personality of a *failed state* that – for good reasons – continues despite the factual decay of the state, amounts to a legal fiction. The same is true of the fictional state's international responsibilities. Bearing in mind that weak and failing states account for two-thirds of all states in the world,[72] this mechanism can hardly be perceived as offering adequate solutions.

Geiß, "Failed States". Die normative Erfassung gescheiterter Staaten, Berlin 2005; *D. Thürer*, Der Wegfall effektiver Staatsgewalt im Völkerrecht: "The Failed State", Berichte der Deutschen Gesellschaft für Völkerrecht 34 (1995), pp. 9ff.; *M. Herdegen*, Der Wegfall effektiver Staatsgewalt im Völkerrecht: "The Failed State", Berichte der Deutschen Gesellschaft für Völkerrecht 34 (1995), pp. 49ff.

[68] *R. Geiß*, "Failed States". Die normative Erfassung gescheiterter Staaten, Berlin 2005, p. 18.

[69] *N. Rosemann*, The UN Norms on Corporate Human Rights Responsibilities – An Innovative Instrument to Strengthen Business' Human Rights Performance, Dialogue on Globalization – Occasional Paper No. 20, Friedrich Ebert Stiftung, Geneva 2005, p. 10; Organisation for Economic Co-operation and Development (OECD), Multinational Enterprises in Situations of Violent Conflict and Widespread Human Rights Abuses, Working Papers on International Investment, No. 2002/1, available under: www.oecd.org (accessed 3 March 2009); see also: OECD Council, 8 June 2006, OECD Risk Awareness Tool for Multinational Enterprises in Weak Governance Zones, available under: www.oecd.org (accessed 3 March 2009).

[70] UN General Assembly, Responsibility of States for internationally wrongful acts, 12. December 2001, UN-Doc.: A/RES/56/83.

[71] Special Rapporteur *R. Ago*, Yearbook of the International Law Commission 2 (1970), p. 188 para 35 remarked: "With regard to the conduct which must be susceptible of being considered as conduct of the State, what can be said in general is that it can be either positive (action) or negative (omission). [...] There have been innumerable cases in which States have been held responsible for damages caused by individuals [...]"; see generally for the international responsibility of failed and failing states: *H. Schröder*, Die völkerrechtliche Verantwortlichkeit im Zusammenhang mit failed und failing states, Baden-Baden 2007; and specifically for failed states: *R. Geiß*, "Failed States". Die normative Erfassung gescheiterter Staaten, Berlin 2005, pp. 251ff.

[72] *T. Risse*/ *U. Lehmkuhl*, Regieren ohne Staat? – Governance in Räumen begrenzter

A second aspect that highlights the deficiencies of the state-centred conception is the transnational "playing field" of non-state actors. An obligation that solely aims at horizontal human rights compliance mediated through national law can hardly cope with transnational phenomena. It could be argued that this assessment is too simplistic since the extended use of extraterritorial jurisdiction might offer an effective tool to tame transnational power excesses.[73] Considering that the majority of the non-state actors under scrutiny here are headquartered in industrialised (OECD) states and/or have been founded under the national law of the latter, private international law suits might indeed represent a viable path for (Western) states to exert pressure on their nationals. However, the protective function of present international human rights law does not require them to do so.[74] Moreover, the frequent use of concepts leading to the inadmissibility of the respective lawsuit, such as the *forum non conveniens* doctrine in common law countries, indicates the reluctance of Western states to adjudicate extraterritorial human rights infringements that might lead to a comparative disadvantage of their nationals.[75] Along with the parochial motivation of national courts to decline jurisdiction in the economic interest of their home country, there are also significant obstacles of a legal nature deriving from conflicting claims of state sovereignty. In the context of transnational corporate accountability, the (corporate) structure of the respective entity may lead to difficulties with regard to the attribution of certain acts, e.g. the subsidiary whose activities are challenged does not share the nationality of the parent company.[76] Hence, the jurisdiction of the forum state may be barred by the sover-

---

Staatlichkeit, in: T. Risse/U. Lehmkuhl (eds.), Regieren ohne Staat? – Governance in Räumen begrenzter Staatlichkeit, Baden-Baden 2007, p. 13 (13).

[73] See generally the contributions in C. Scott (ed.), Torture as Tort, Oxford 2001.

[74] *J. Ruggie*, Business and human rights: mapping international standards of responsibility and accountability for corporate acts – Report of the Special Representative of the Secretary-General on the issue of human rights and transnational corporations and other business enterprises, UN-Doc. A/HRC/4/35, 19 February 2007, para 15; *S. Joseph*, Taming the Leviathans: Multinational Enterprises and Human Rights, Netherlands International Law Review 1999, p. 171 (181); *M. Weschka*, Human Rights and Multinational Enterprises: How Can Multinational Enterprises Be Held Responsible for Human Rights Violations Committed Abroad?, Zeitschrift für ausländisches öffentliches Recht und Völkerrecht 66 (2006), p. 625 (631).

[75] *C. Scott*, Introduction to Torture as Tort: From Sudan to Canada to Somalia, in: C. Scott (ed.), Torture as Tort, Oxford 2001, pp. 10f.; see also *S. Joseph*, Taming the Leviathans: Multinational Enterprises and Human Rights, Netherlands International Law Review 1999, p. 171 (184) suggesting uniform international standards in order to overcome comparative disadvantages.

[76] This phenomenon – also referred to as the problem of the "corporate veil" – is a consequence of the ICJ's rejection of the "control theory": International Court of Justice, Case concerning the Barcelona Traction, Light and Power Company, Limited, Judgement of 5 February 1970, ICJ-Reports 1970, p. 4 (39ff.). See also *M. Weschka*, Human Rights and Multinational Enterprises: How Can Multinational Enterprises Be Held Responsible for Human

eignty of the subsidiary's home state.[77] An interesting route taken by U.S. courts, which avoids the prerequisite of nationality as a legitimate link for exercising extraterritorial jurisdiction, is the application of the principle of universal jurisdiction in civil law proceedings.[78] Based on the 1789 Alien Tort Claims Act (ATCA), which establishes that "[...] district courts shall have original jurisdiction of any civil action by an alien for a tort only, committed in violation of the law of nations [...]",[79] a number of cases concerning transnational non-state actor involvement in severe human rights violations have been entertained.[80] In contrast to typical international civil law suits, the substantive legal norms referred to in these cases derive from international law and not from the domestic legal systems of the forum state or of the state on whose territory the alleged violation occurred. In theory, applying the principle of universal jurisdiction in civil law proceedings might increase the probability of lawsuits against transnational non-state actors. However, only few domestic systems provide for such a possibility[81] and even the ones that do, apply it with a considerable amount of restraint with a view to not interfering in the domestic affairs of other states.[82]

Failing institutional structures in the overwhelming number of states, the reluctance of Western courts to expose their nationals to comparative disadvantages, conflicting claims of state sovereignty, as well as the hesitant use of universal jurisdiction in civil law proceedings indicate some deficiencies of a highly state-centred conception of international law. In the face of paramount human

Rights Violations Committed Abroad?, Zeitschrift für ausländisches öffentliches Recht und Völkerrecht 66 (2006), p. 625 (629 ff.).

[77] See *C. Scott*, Translating Torture into Transnational Tort: Conceptual Divides in the Debate on Corporate Accountability for Human Rights Harms, in: C. Scott (ed.), Torture as Tort, Oxford 2001, p. 45 (54).

[78] See *G. Nolte*, Universal Jurisdiction in the Area of Private Law – The Alien Tort Claims Act, in: C. Tomuschat/ J.-M. Thouvenin (eds.), The Fundamental Rules of the International Legal Order – Jus Codens and Obligations Erga Omnes, Leiden 2006, pp. 373 ff.

[79] United States Code, Title 28, Part IV, Chapter 85, § 1350.

[80] See, for instance *Doe I vs. Unocal Corporation*, 248 F.3d 915 (9th Cir. 2002); *A. Siebert-Fohr*, Die Deliktshaftung von Unternehmen für die Beteiligung an im Ausland begangenen Völkerrechtsverletzungen – Anmerkungen zum Urteil Doe I v. Unocal Corp. des US Court of Appeal (9th Circuit), Zeitschrift für ausländisches öffentliches Recht und Völkerrecht 63 (2003), pp. 195 ff.; *Wiwa et al. v. Royal Dutch Petroleum et al.*, 226 F.3d 440 (2d Cir. 2000); *M. Rau*, Domestic Adjudication of International Human Rights Abuses and the doctrine of forum non conveniens – The Decision of the U.S. Court of Appeals for the Second Circuit in Ken Wiwa v. Royal Dutch Petroleum Company, Zeitschrift für ausländisches öffentliches Recht und Völkerrecht, 61 (2001), p. 177.

[81] For similar developments in other common law countries see *A. Clapham*, Human Rights Obligations of Non-State Actors, Oxford 2006, pp. 450 ff.; *A. Siebert Fohr/ R. Wolfrum*, Die einzelstaatliche Durchsetzung völkerrechtlicher Mindeststandards gegenüber transnationalen Unternehmen, Archiv des Völkerrechts 43 (2005), p. 153 (178 ff.).

[82] See for the international legal limits of the principle of universal jurisdiction in civil law proceedings *G. Nolte*, Universal Jurisdiction in the Area of Private Law – The Alien Tort Claims Act, in: C. Tomuschat/ J.-M. Thouvenin (eds.), The Fundamental Rules of the International Legal Order, Leiden 2006, p. 373 (376 ff.).

rights infringements by non-state actors, it seems worthwhile to ponder on new ways of looking at the relationship between non-state actors and human rights.

IV. Transnational Effects of International Human Rights Law?

The theoretical conceptions suggested by legal scholars of how to overcome the deficiencies of the state-centred conception of international law are manifold. There are those who argue that with the demise of the state and the rise of non-state actors, a fragmented "global law" is emerging.[83] Characterized by a legal pluralism based on communicative processes, its rules are not constrained by the territorial sovereignty of nation states but rather confined "by 'invisible colleges', 'invisible markets and branches', 'invisible professional communities', 'invisible social networks' that transcend territorial boundaries but nevertheless press for the emergence of genuinely legal forms."[84] In this privatized global order, non-state actors "create our understanding of human rights [...] independently of the existence of binding obligations under international law".[85] Other authors predict a "neomedieval system (in which) the notion that *states* create international law through their consent (...) would have to be expanded".[86] Within this conception, non-state actors enter the realm of true rule-makers, actively forming diverse layers of customary law.[87] The complexity of the images drawn by these and similar kinds of theories[88] is fascinating. However, the pivotal question of how the emerging rules of a neomedieval order or a

[83] See *G. Teubner*, 'Global Bukowina': Legal Pluralism in the World Society, in: G. Teubner (ed.), Global law without a state, Aldershot 1997, pp. 3ff.; and recently: *A. Fischer-Lescano/ G. Teubner*, Regime-Kollisionen: Zur Fragmentierung des globalen Rechts, Frankfurt 2006; see also *G. Teubner*, Globale Zivilverfassungen: Alternativen zur staatszentrierten Verfassungstheorie, Zeitschrift für ausländisches öffentliches Recht und Völkerrecht 63 (2003), pp. 1ff., introducing the idea of "global civil constitutions" to his global law conception, which is largely inspired by Niklas Luhmans' "system theory": *N. Luhmann*, Die Gesellschaft der Gesellschaft, Frankfurt 1997, pp. 595ff.; for the relationship between the works of Luhmann and Teubner see: *A. Fischer Lescano*, Die Emergenz der Globalverfassung, Zeitschrift für ausländisches öffentliches Recht und Völkerrecht 63 (2003), pp. 717ff.

[84] *G. Teubner*, Global Bukowina': Legal Pluralism in the World Society, in: G. Teubner (ed.), Global law without a state, Aldershot 1997, p. 3 (8).

[85] *A. Bianchi*, Globalization of Human Rights: The Role of Non-State Actors, in: G. Teubner (ed.), Global law without a state, Aldershot 1997, p. 179 (201); for a critique see: *A. Clapham*, Human Rights Obligations of Non-State Actors, Oxford 2006, pp. 26f.

[86] *A. C. Arend*, Legal Rules and International Society, New York 1999, p. 176; see also the conception of the international society by: *Hedley Bull*, The Anarchical Society, New York 1995.

[87] *A. C. Arend*, Legal Rules and International Society, New York 1999, pp. 176f.

[88] See also *A. M. Slaughter*, A New World Order, Princeton 2004, who is observing the disintegration of the nation-state and the simultaneous formation of functional networks between the competent governmental authorities.

global law of fragmented communicative processes are legitimatized remains obscure.[89]

Against this background, I suggest a different approach when considering new ways of how to adjust international law. I submit that instead of a radical rethink, an adjustment in the perception of existing norms is required. With regard to the relationship between human rights and non-state actors, the crucial question should be whether or not international human rights law also produces *transnational effects*, i.e. a direct relationship between the individual and the respective non-state actor under international law that is complementary to the *indirect horizontal effects* mediated through national law.[90] In that perspective, the protective function of international human rights law could be translated into a collective responsibility of all states[91] and international organizations obliged to ensure a specific human right norm. Instead of a single state's obligation to ensure human rights compliance on the (national) horizontal level, a clearly defined group of states and international organizations – depending on the norm in question – would collectively have to ensure transnational human rights compliance. That idea can be understood as a dogmatic proposal for a future legal order, in which human rights are perceived as common values of the international community[92] that are collectively enforced with a potent institutional structure. That structure may take the form of an International Court of Human Rights.[93]

---

[89] *Ph. Kunig*, Das Völkerrecht und die Interessen der Bevölkerung, in: P.-M. Dupuy et al. (eds.), Völkerrecht als Wertordnung – Common Values in International Law, Kehl 2006, p. 377 (386) on the conceptions of Günther Teubner and Anne Marie Slaughter. See also for the open question of legitimacy of the law-making process in networks *S. Boysen et al.*, Networks in Public Law, German Law Journal 8 (2007), p. 1079 (1085); *L. Viellechner*, Können Netzwerke Demokratie ersetzen? Zur Legitimation der Regelbildung im Globalisierungsprozess, in: S. Boysen et al. (eds.), German Law Journal 8 (2007), pp. 36 ff. For the concept of legitimacy in international law see *T. M. Franck*, The Power of Legitimacy and the Legitimacy of Power: International Law in an Age of Power Disequilibrium, in: American Journal of International Law 100 (2006), pp. 88 ff.; and generally the contributions in: R. Wolfrum/ V. Röben (eds.), Legitimacy in International Law, Heidelberg 2008.

[90] Sub III. 1.

[91] For a similar approach, cf.: *G. Abi-Saab*, as quoted in: A. Clapham, Human Rights Obligations of Non-State Actors, Oxford 2006, p. 238: "[...] a duty on all States to co-operate in rendering this control effective. Indeed as the activities of transnational corporations straddle several States, their effective control necessitates the co-operation of those states [...]".

[92] *W. Friedmann*, The Changing Structure of International Law, London 1964; *H. Mosler*, The International Society As a Legal Community, The Hague Academy of International Law, Collected courses 40 (1974-IV); *C. Tomuschat*, Die internationale Gemeinschaft, Archiv des Völkerrechts 33 (1995), pp. 1 ff.; *B. Simma*, From Bilateralism to Community Interest in International Law, in: The Hague Academy of International Law, Collected courses 250 (1994-IV), pp. 221 ff.; *A. L. Paulus*, Die internationale Gemeinschaft im Völkerrecht, München 2000.

[93] For the idea of a World Court of Human Rights see *M. Nowak*, Ein Weltgerichtshof für Menschenrechte – Eine utopische Forderung?, Vereinte Nationen 2008, p. 205 (208 ff.).

I argue that current international law offers promising starting points that hint at *transnational effects* of human rights law. Assuming that "legal capacity" constitutes an indispensable element of all forms of legal relationships,[94] the capacity of TNCs and TNGOs as bearers of international rights and duties will be examined first in order to clarify whether these non-state actors qualify, in principle, as (partial) subjects of international law (1.).[95] In a second step it will be asked whether and under what circumstances international human rights law can be perceived as imposing direct duties on these entities (2.).

1. *The International Legal Capacity of Non-State Actors*

Are non-state actors in principle capable of being the bearer of international rights and duties? Do they qualify as (partial) subjects of international law?[96] In 1949, the International Court of Justice in its *Reparations for injuries* opinion remarked that "(t)he subjects of law in any legal system are not necessarily identical in their nature or in the extent of their rights, and their nature depends on the needs of the community".[97] As there are no dogmatic reasons for a *numerus clausus* of international legal persons, this status depends entirely on whether or not an entity is the addressee of international legal norms.[98] Certainly, such a partial subjectivity might only encompass a highly limited status under international law. However, it would prove that the respective entity has been recognized as such by the international legal order and would indicate its capacity to bear further rights and duties.

Whereas intergovernmental organizations derive their existence from an international treaty, TNGOs are founded as legal persons under national law. International agreements addressing the legal personality of these actors are, therefore, concerned with the mutual recognition of their national subjectivi-

---

[94] *H. Mosler*, Die Erweiterung des Kreises der Völkerrechtssubjekte, Berichte der Deutschen Gesellschaft für Völkerrecht 4 (1961), p. 39 (53).

[95] For a detailed discussion on the relevance of "international subjectivity" and non-state actors, see *A. Clapham*, Human Rights Obligations of Non-State Actors, Oxford 2006, pp. 59 ff.

[96] *R. Wedgwood*, Legal Personality and the Role of Non-Governmental Organizations and Non-State Political Entities in the United Nations System, in: R. Hofmann (ed.), Non-State Actors as New Subjects of International Law, Berlin 1999, pp. 21 ff.; *D. Thürer*, The Emergence of Non-Governmental Organizations and Transnational Enterprises in International Law and the Changing Role of the State, in: R. Hofmann (ed.), Non-State Actors as New Subjects of International Law, Berlin 1999, pp. 37 ff.

[97] International Court of Justice, Reparations for Injuries suffered in the service of the United Nations, Advisory Opinion of 11 April 1949, ICJ Reports 1949, p. 174 (179).

[98] *S. Hobe*, Die Zukunft des Völkerrechts im Zeitalter der Globalisierung, Archiv des Völkerrechts 37 (1999), p. 253 (263); *J. Delbrück*, Perspektiven für ein "Weltinnenrecht"? – Rechtsentwicklungen in einem sich wandelnden Internationalen System, J. Jickeli et al. (eds.), Gedächtnisschrift für Jürgen Sonnenschein, Berlin 2003, p. 793 (798).

ty.[99] However, there is no reason why a certain entity cannot be endowed with legal personality under several legal orders.[100] The International Committee of the Red Cross, for instance, founded and organized as a private society under Swiss law, is awarded with the function of a potential "Protecting Power" under international humanitarian law.[101] With regard to international human rights law, NGOs are addressed as rights bearers. Their *jus standi* before international human rights courts and treaty monitoring bodies is widely recognized.[102] Another crucial aspect of NGO involvement in international legal relations is their procedural inclusion in the work of international organizations such as the UN, the ILO or UNESCO.[103] The most prominent example of its kind is the consultative relationship between NGOs and the UN Economic and Social Council (ECOSOC). On the basis of article 71 of the UN Charter, which provides for "suitable arrangements for consultation with non-governmental organizations", the ECOSOC passed resolutions 1286 (XLIV) of 24 May 1968 and 1996/31 of 25 July 1996 establishing a gradual system of procedural rights granted to NGOs. These rights encompass limited rights of attendance and permanent observer positions, as well as the entitlement to actively participate in the deliberation process by delivering statements or submitting proposals.[104]

Likewise, TNCs are founded as legal persons under national law and predominantly assume their personality under international law as bearers of internationally recognized human rights.[105] Certainly, in that capacity TNCs are

---

[99] European Convention on the Recognition of the Legal Personality of International Non-Governmental Organizations, 24 April 1986, European Treaty Series No. 124; see *S. Hobe*, Der Rechtsstatus der Nichtregierungsorganisationen nach gegenwärtigem Völkerrecht, Archiv des Völkerrechts 37 (1999), p. 152 (160).

[100] *H. Mosler*, Die Erweiterung des Kreises der Völkerrechtssubjekte, Berichte der Deutschen Gesellschaft für Völkerrecht 4 (1961), p. 39 (53).

[101] See article 5 para. 4 of the Protocol Additional to the Geneva Conventions of 12 August 1949, and Relating to the Protection of Victims of International Armed Conflict (Protocol I), of 8 June 1997, United Nations Treaty Series, Vol. 1125, p. 3.

[102] *S. Hobe*, Der Rechtsstatus der Nichtregierungsorganisationen nach gegenwärtigem Völkerrecht, Archiv des Völkerrechts 37 (1999), p. 152 (162 ff.); *J. Delbrück*, Perspektiven für ein "Weltinnenrecht"? – Rechtsentwicklungen in einem sich wandelnden Internationalen System, in: J. Jickeli et al. (eds.), Gedächtnisschrift für Jürgen Sonnenschein, Berlin 2003, p. 793 (798).

[103] *E. Riedel*, The Development of International Law. Alternatives to Treaty Making? International Organizations and Non-State Actors, in: R. Wolfum/ V. Röben (eds.), Developments in International Law in Treaty Making, Berlin 2005, pp. 301 ff.

[104] *P. MacAllister-Smith*, Non-Governmental Organizations, Humanitarian Action and Human Rights, in: U. Beyerlin et al. (eds.), Recht zwischen Umbruch und Bewahrung. Festschrift für Rudolf Bernhardt, Berlin 1995, p. 477 (491); *S. Hobe*, Der Rechtsstatus der Nichtregierungsorganisationen nach gegenwärtigem Völkerrecht, Archiv des Völkerrechts 37 (1999), p. 152 (161 f.); *F. Bühring/N. Hüfken*, Menschenrechtsstandards für Governance in schwachen und zerfallen(d)en Staaten, in: S. de la Rosa et al. (eds.), Transdisziplinäre Governanceforschung, Baden-Baden 2008, p. 187 (190).

[105] *M. K. Addo*, The Corporation as a Victim of Human Rights Violations, in: idem (ed.), Human Rights Standards and the Responsibility of Transnational Corporations, The Hague

addressed as private entities subordinated under the domestic legal order of the respective state. Their status is even more limited as compared to private individuals, since not all entitlements under human rights law are applicable to TNCs. The role of these non-state actors in the international system of investment arbitration, on the other hand, shows distinctive features. It represents a strong indication that their capacity to act as an international person has grown into a status virtually transcending their role as private entities. Based on the "Washington Convention",[106] TNCs can act as a party in investment arbitrations, encountering their host states before the International Centre for the Settlement of Investment Disputes (ICSID), which leads to legally binding decisions under international law.[107] According to article 27 of the Convention, the home state refrains from exercising diplomatic protection. At the same time, a dense net of bilateral investment treaties ensures the prior consent of the adversary, i.e. the host state. This framework can be perceived as leading to a quasi-unmediated status of TNCs under international law.[108] A similar mechanism is established under article 26 of the Energy Charter Treaty (ECT),[109] providing for a prior consent of the host state, with the investor not being required to exhaust the local remedies in the host state's domestic system.[110] The legal positions conferred upon TNCs in the system of international investment arbitration represent a strong case in favour of their legal capacity under international law.[111] The same can be said for international conventions on the liability of TNCs for environmental pollution.[112]

1999, p. 187 ff.; *K. Schmalenbach*, Multinationale Unternehmen und Menschenrechte, Archiv des Völkerrechts 39 (2001), p. 57 (63 ff.); *K. Nowrot*, Nun sag, wie hast du's mit den Global Players? Fragen an die Völkerrechtsgemeinschaft zur internationalen Rechtsstellung transnationaler Unternehmen, Die Friedenswarte 79 (2004), p. 119 (125).

[106] Convention on the Settlement of Investment Disputes between States and the Nationals of Other States, 18 March 1965, International Legal Materials 4 (1965), pp. 524 ff.

[107] *M. Herdegen*, Internationales Wirtschaftsrecht, 3rd ed., München 2005, pp. 225 f.

[108] *K. Schmalenbach*, Multinationale Unternehmen und Menschenrechte, Archiv des Völkerrechts 39 (2001), p. 57 (64); *P.-M. Dupuy*, L'Unité de l'Ordre Juridique Internationale, Receuil de Cours, Vol. 297 (2002), p. (105,117); *G. Dahm et al.*, Völkerrecht, Vol. I/2, 2nd ed., Berlin 2002, p. 253.

[109] Energy Charter Treaty, Final Act of the European Energy Charter Treaty Conference, Lisbon, 12 December 1994, International Legal Materials 34 (1995), pp. 360 ff.

[110] *K. Nowrot*, Nun sag, wie hast du's mit den Global Players? Fragen an die Völkerrechtsgemeinschaft zur internationalen Rechtsstellung transnationaler Unternehmen, Die Friedenswarte 79 (2004), p. 119 (127); *M. Herdegen*, Internationales Wirtschaftsrecht, 3rd ed., München 2005, p. 224

[111] *C. Tietje*, Grundstrukturen und aktuelle Entwicklungen des Rechts der Beilegung internationaler Investitionsstreitigkeiten, in: C. Tietje et al. (eds.), Arbeitspapiere aus dem Institut für Wirtschaftsrecht, Halle-Wittenberg 2003, Heft 10, p. 16; *D. Kinley/J. Tadaki*, From Walk to Talk. The Emergence of Human Rights Responsibilities at International Law, Virginia Journal of International Law 44 (2004), p. 931 (946 f.).

[112] International Convention on Civil Liability for Oil Pollution Damage, 29 November 1969, United Nations Treaty Series 14097; International Convention on Civil Liability for

This brief survey indicates that international law has recognized the capacity of non-state actors to bear rights and duties, thus identifying them as potential candidates for further obligations and establishing the possibility of *transnational effects* of international human rights law.

2. *Non-State Actors as Duty Bearers under International Human Rights Law*[113]

Due to the increased ratification of international treaties, it seems that the customary law of human rights has taken "the back seat". For methodological reasons, international lawyers concentrate on the more specific treaty provisions, disposing of a higher degree of determinativeness than the unwritten rules of customary law with their mystic way of detection. Although I shall not rule out the dogmatic possibility of interpreting treaty law in a way that could give rise to an unmediated transnational effect of human rights law, there are as yet no indications of such a perception. Next to several good reasons why renewed attention should be given to its dynamics,[114] customary international law seems to provide the most promising ground for human rights obligations of non-state actors. Serving as an undisputed point of reference with regard to the evolution of customary rules, the Universal Declaration of Human Rights shall serve as my starting point. In the last paragraph of its preamble[115] it is proclaimed:

> "[...] that every individual and every organ of society, keeping this Declaration constantly in mind, shall strive by teaching and education to promote respect for these rights and freedoms and by progressive measures, national and international, to secure their universal and effective recognition and observance".

Commenting on that passage on the occasion of the 50th anniversary of the Declaration, *Louis Henkin* held that "(e)very individual includes juridical persons. Every individual and every organ of society excludes no one, no company, no market, no cyberspace. The Universal Declaration applies to them all."[116] Although it is certainly correct that until today this convincing interpretation has not evolved into a binding rule of customary law,[117] I submit that next to

---

Damage Resulting from Activities Dangerous to the Environment, 21 June 1993, European Treaty Series No. 150.

[113] For an overview of the extensive body of literature on the topic, see *C. Tomuschat*, Human Rights: Between Idealism and Realism, Oxford 2003, p. 90.

[114] *A. Clapham*, Human Rights Obligations of Non-State Actors, Oxford 2006, pp. 85 f.

[115] With regard to articles 29 and 30 see: *J. Paust*, Human Rights Responsibilities of Private Corporations, Vanderbuilt Journal of Transnational Law 35 (2002), p. 801 (819 ff.).

[116] *L. Henkin*, Keynote Address: The Global Market as Friend or Foe of Human Rights: The Universal Declaration at 50 and the Challenges of Global Markets, Brooklyn Journal of International Law 25 (1999), p. 17 (25).

[117] *J. Ruggie*, Business and human rights: mapping international standards of responsibility and accountability for corporate acts – Report of the Special Representative of the Secretary-General on the issue of human rights and transnational corporations and other business

several *soft-law* documents[118] as well as a plethora of self-regulating *codes of conduct*,[119] developments in the fields of international criminal and civil liability represent a strong indication in favour of transnational human rights effects.

First of all, the criminal responsibility of the individual shows that direct obligations of private entities under international law are possible and cannot be ruled out as a matter of principle. International law not only confers rights upon private entities, but has proven capable of imposing certain duties as well. Furthermore, as *John Ruggie* pointed out in his second report to the former Commission on Human Rights on the issue of human rights and TNCs, there is a tendency towards a criminal liability of private collective actors.[120] Although no criminal norm can be found in that respect in the Rome Statute itself, it was debated within the ICC preparatory committee and at the Rome conference.[121] Moreover, it could be argued that where national legal systems already provide for criminal punishment of companies, the international standards for individuals may thereby be extended to corporate entities.[122] In that case, the interplay of national criminal doctrine and the incorporated norms of international criminal law may, in conjunction with the principle of universal jurisdiction,[123] cata-

enterprises, UN-Doc. A/HRC/4/35, 19 February 2007, para 37; *K. Schmalenbach*, Multinationale Unternehmen und Menschenrechte, Archiv des Völkerrechts 39 (2001), p. 57 (65 f.); *D. Kinley/ J. Tadaki*, From Walk to Talk. The Emergence of Human Rights Responsibilities at International Law, Virginia Journal of International Law 44 (2004), p. 931 (949): "ethical duties at its best"; on the history of its establishment, cf. *C. Tomuschat* 1983, 302 ff.

[118] OECD Guidelines for Multinational Enterprises, 27 June 2000, International Legal Materials 40 (2001); ILO Tripartite Declaration, 16 November 1977, as amended on 17 November 2000, International Legal Materials 41 (2002), pp. 186 ff.; UN Global Compact, www.unglobalcompact.org (accessed 3 March 2009).

[119] See *A. Reinisch*, The Changing International Legal Framework for Dealing with Non-State Actors, in: Ph. Alston (ed.), Non-State Actors and Human Rights, Oxford 2005, p. 37 (42 ff.).

[120] *J. Ruggie*, Business and human rights: mapping international standards of responsibility and accountability for corporate acts – Report of the Special Representative of the Secretary-General on the issue of human rights and transnational corporations and other business enterprises, UN-Doc. A/HRC/4/35, 19 February 2007, paras 19 ff.

[121] *A. Clapham*, The Question of Jurisdiction Under International Criminal Law Over Legal Persons: Lessons from the Rome Conference on an International Criminal Court, in: M. Kamminga/ S. Zia-Zarifi (eds.), Liability of Multinational Corporations Under International Law, The Hague 2000, pp. 139 ff.; *A. Clapham*, Human Rights Obligations of Non-State Actors, Oxford 2006, p. 244 f.; *J. Ruggie*, Business and human rights: mapping international standards of responsibility and accountability for corporate acts – Report of the Special Representative of the Secretary-General on the issue of human rights and transnational corporations and other business enterprises, UN-Doc. A/HRC/4/35, 19 February 2007, para 21.

[122] *J. Ruggie*, Business and human rights: mapping international standards of responsibility and accountability for corporate acts – Report of the Special Representative of the Secretary-General on the issue of human rights and transnational corporations and other business enterprises, UN-Doc. A/HRC/4/35, 19 February 2007, para 24.

[123] *A. Zimmermann*, Violations of Fundamental Norms of International Law and the Ex-

lyze a customary evolution, thus leading to a corporate criminal liability for serious human rights violations. In reverse, this permits the conclusion that non-state actors are bound to respect human rights guarantees whose violation translates into an international crime[124] such as slavery, genocide, other crimes against humanity, certain war crimes, and torture.

A similar development can be found in civil law. As already outlined above,[125] national courts in the United States as well as in other common law countries entertain law suits against non-state actors on the basis of a tort in violation of international law. Present U.S. case law shows that even in the absence of a *state nexus*, international crimes such as genocide, slave-trading, slavery, forced labour, and war crimes are actionable under the ATCA.[126] Moreover, the potential liability of non-state actors is not limited to the violation of international rules constituting *jus cogens*.[127] U.S. courts, for instance, also recognize the arbitrary exercise of force against a peaceful demonstration as a violation of international customary law.[128] According to the legal practice recently confirmed by the U.S. Supreme Court,[129] the crucial requirement for applying an international norm is not its fundamental character but its specificity.[130] However, it must be stressed that all lawsuits founded on human rights violations of a lesser

---

ercise of Universal Jurisdiction in Criminal Matters, in: C. Tomuschat/ J.-M. Thouvenin (eds.). The Fundamental Rules of the International Legal Order, Leiden 2006, pp. 335 ff.

[124] For a knowledgeable account on the relationship of human rights and international criminal law see: *S. Nimaga*, The International Criminal Law Regime and International Human Rights Law in this volume, pp. 101 ff.

[125] Sub III 2.

[126] *A. Clapham*, Human Rights Obligations of Non-State Actors, Oxford 2006, p. 253 with reference to Wiwa v Royal Dutch Shell Petroleum, US District Court for the Southern District of New York, 28 February 2002, Doe I v Unocal Corp (18 September 2002); see also the analysis by: *A. Siebert-Fohr/ R. Wolfrum*, Die einzelstaatliche Durchsetzung völkerrechtlicher Mindeststandards gegenüber transnationalen Unternehmen, Archiv des Völkerrechts 43 (2005), p. 153 (166).

[127] Commenting on article 26 of the ILC-Draft on the responsibility of states for internationally wrongful acts, (UN General Assembly, Responsibility of States for internationally wrongful acts, 12 December 2001, UN-Doc.: A/RES/56/83) and thereby indicating the non-exhaustive body of rules constituting *jus cogens*, the International Law Commission maintained that "peremptory norms that are clearly accepted and recognized include the prohibition of aggression, genocide, slavery, racial discrimination, crimes against humanity, and torture, and the right to self-determination", Yearbook of the International Law Commission, Volume II, Part II, Geneva 2001, p. 85.

[128] Wiwa et al. V. Royal Dutch petroleum Co et al., United States District Court, S. D. New York, 2002, WL 319887, para 11; for an analysis see: *A. Siebehrt-Fohr/ R. Wolfrum*, Die einzelstaatliche Durchsetzung völkerrechtlicher Mindeststandards gegenüber transnationalen Unternehmen, Archiv des Völkerrechts 43 (2005), p. 153 (158 f.).

[129] Supreme Court of the United States, 29 June 2004, *Sosa v. Alvarez-Machain*, 542 U.S. 692 (2004), 331 F.3d 604.

[130] See *G. Nolte*, Universal Jurisdiction in the Area of Private Law – The Alien Tort Claims Act, in: C. Tomuschat/ J.-M. Thouvenin (eds.), The Fundamental Rules of the International Legal Order, Leiden 2006, p. 373 (375 f.).

magnitude than international crimes are only actionable in the presence of a *state nexus*, i.e. in cases of complicity between governmental authorities and non-state actors.[131] Taken together, civil and criminal liability based on the principle of universal jurisdiction[132] and enforced on the national level may eventually affect the development of customary law with respect to the human rights obligations of non-state actors.

This brief survey of the legal practice under the ATCA also indicates the relevance of the *state nexus*. Whereas an independent non-state actor's responsibility under international criminal law appears to be in reach, the requirement of state complicity regarding all other forms of human rights violations still signifies the intellectual prison built by the state-centred conception of human rights law. There seems to be a reluctance on the part of international legal practice to abandon the *state nexus*, even in cases where that bond takes the form of criminal complicity. In contrast, I suggest a functional approach when determining the human rights obligations of non-state actors beyond the field of international criminal law. It has been established that non-state actors fulfil public functions.[133] It could be argued that by exercising these functions, non-state actors are bound to respect the human rights obligation of the state on whose territory they act. From that perspective, the public function of a non-state actor would replace the requirement of a state-nexus. The idea that non-state actors may act on behalf of the state is a well founded concept under international law. Under the customary rules of state responsibility, for instance, "(t)he conduct of a person or group of persons shall be considered an act of a State under international law if the person or group of persons is in fact exercising elements of the governmental authority in the absence or default of the official authorities and in circumstances such as to call for the exercise of those elements of authority".[134] Moreover, a functional approach would be compatible with the current architecture of international law since it respects the primacy of states. It does not confer primary obligations and thereby international legitimacy on non-state actors *per se*, but rather determines their international duties derivatively,

---

[131] For a detailed analysis see *A. Clapham*, Human Rights Obligations of Non-State Actors, Oxford 2006, pp. 254 ff.; *A. Siebert-Fohr/ R. Wolfrum*, Die einzelstaatliche Durchsetzung völkerrechtlicher Mindeststandards gegenüber transnationalen Unternehmen, Archiv des Völkerrechts 43 (2005), pp. 166 ff.

[132] *A. Zimmermann*, Violations of Fundamental Norms of International Law and the Exercise of Universal Jurisdiction in Criminal Matters, in: C. Tomuschat/ J.-M. Thouvenin (eds.). The Fundamental Rules of the International Legal Order, Leiden 2006; *G. Nolte*, Universal Jurisdiction in the Area of Private Law – The Alien Tort Claims Act, in: C. Tomuschat/ J.-M. Thouvenin (eds.), The Fundamental Rules of the International Legal Order, Leiden 2006.

[133] Sub II.

[134] Article 9 of the ILC-Draft on the responsibility of States for internationally wrongful acts, UN General Assembly, Responsibility of States for internationally wrongful acts, 12. December 2001, UN-Doc.: A/RES/56/83.

i.e. in accordance with the host state's international obligations. The envisaged results can be compared to the approach taken in the General Policies of the OECD Guidelines on Multinational Enterprises requiring TNCs to respect the human rights "of those affected by their activities consistent with the host government's international obligations and commitments".[135]

V. Conclusion

In a globalized world, the rising influence of non-state actors correlates with a demise of the state and leads to a growing divergence between the normative expectations of a state-centred conception of international law and the social reality of transnational relationships. Especially in states with weak or failing institutional structures, non-state actors increasingly exercise public functions and threaten the most basic enjoyment of human rights. Present international law proves to be incapable of adequately addressing these downsides of the globalization process, since the protective function of human rights law is limited to horizontal effects mediated through national law. With the decay of governmental structures worldwide and the restraint of Western courts in exercising extraterritorial jurisdiction, and hampered by conflicting claims of sovereignty, a new approach with regard to the relationship between human rights and non-state actors is crucial. Whereas thought-provoking suggestions on how to reconceptualise the global legal order as a whole lack a clear basis of legitimacy, a reinterpretation of existing norms seems preferable. With regard to the relationship between non-state actors and human rights, the efforts should focus on *transnational effects* of human rights law, i.e. the unmediated relationship between non-state actors and the individual as a matter of international law. Whereas the international legal capacity of non-state actors can in principle be established, their human rights obligations remain rudimental. Along with customary developments in the field of civil and criminal responsibility based on the principle of universal jurisdiction, a functional approach is suggested that would replace the requirement of a *state nexus* and lead to a derivated set of human rights obligations in accordance with the host state's international commitments. Certainly, many of these thoughts do not reflect the current state of the law and may even seem incompatible with some of its major assumptions. However, the globalization process has induced developments beyond the imagination of traditional legal doctrine.

---

[135] OECD Guidelines for Multinational Enterprises, 27 June 2000, International Legal Materials 40 (2001), p. 237 (239).

Chapter IV

Selected Human Rights Aspects

Women Negotiating for Peace

Political Rights of Women in Post-Conflict Situations

Sarah Wittkopp

I. Introduction

In modern conflict, the overwhelming majority of victims are civilians.[1] When wars are fought between warring factions within one state – e.g. governments and rebel armies, clans or religious factions – civilians, mostly women, the children and the elderly, are often the main target of armed violence, of gross violations of human rights and of ethnic cleansing; they are the ones who suffer most. When former enemies are members of the same community, reconciliation after these 'new wars'[2] is a cumbersome and lengthy process. To this end, peace negotiations and agreements are increasingly seen to be a vital means to pacify the community and to re-establish security for the civilian population.[3] The peace agreement must therefore not only end the war but bring peace. It must include a solution for the legal and political restructuring of society.[4] Women and their rights and concerns are one aspect that has often been absent from the formal negotiations, but that has gained increasing international rec-

---

[1] Civilians make up 2/3 of direct conflict deaths; *Centre for Security Studies*, The Growing Importance of Civilians in Armed Conflict, CSS Analyses in Security Policy, vol. 3, nr. 45, 2008, p. 2, available at: http://se2.isn.ch/serviceengine/FileContent?serviceID=ISFPub&fileid=A65C770A-0CF0-5C97-71EC-1DA3456E2221&lng=en (accessed 02 January 2009); *Geneva Declaration Secretariat*, The Global Burden of Armed Violence, Geneva 2008, p. 3, available at: http://www.genevadeclaration.org/pdfs/Global-Burden-of-Armed-Violence.pdf (accessed 02 January 2009).

[2] For the concept of new wars, see *M. Kaldor*, New & Old Wars, Organized Violence in a Globalized Area, 2nd ed., Cambridge 2006.

[3] *Ch. Chinkin*, Gender, Human Rights and Peace Agreements, Ohio State Journal on Dispute Resolution 2003, p. 867.

[4] *Ch. Chinkin*, Peace Agreements as a Means for Promoting Gender Equality and Ensuring Participation of Women, Background Paper to the Expert Group Meeting on "Peace Agreements as a Means for Promoting Gender Equality and Ensuring Participation of Women – A Framework of Model Provisions?", 10–13 November 2003, UN Doc. EGM/PEACE/2003/BP.1, p. 7.

ognition as being of great importance to the resolution and prevention of conflict. *Gender balancing* in the negotiations and *gender mainstreaming* in the agreement reached are the two concepts employed to ensure that women's concerns are taken into account in the peace process.[5]

This article is concerned with the former as it deals with women's rights to political participation in peace negotiations. On October 31, 2000, the Security Council adopted Resolution 1325[6] on women, peace and security, which provides a comprehensive political framework on all gender-related aspects of peace processes.[7] Without negating the importance of this resolution, which has been thoroughly discussed by scholars,[8] this article will concentrate on the right of women to be included in peace processes that arise from human rights treaty law, and more specifically from the Convention on the Elimination of All Forms of Discrimination against Women (CEDAW).[9] The question this article is concerned with is whether human rights treaty law compels actors in a peace process to include and empower women.

II. Practical Examples of Participation of Women

Two examples of peace processes shall serve to illuminate the position of women in these processes. In 1997–1998 in Northern Ireland, multi-party peace negotiations took place between representatives of political parties of Northern Ireland and the British and Irish governments to end the civil unrest between British Unionists (mostly Protestant) and Irish Nationalists (mostly Catholic).[10] Already in the pre-negotiation phase, the Northern Ireland Women's

---

[5] *Ch. Chinkin*, Peace Agreements as a Means for Promoting Gender Equality and Ensuring Participation of Women, Background Paper to the Expert Group Meeting on "Peace Agreements as a Means for Promoting Gender Equality and Ensuring Participation of Women – A Framework of Model Provisions?", 10–13 November 2003, UN Doc. EGM/PEACE/2003/BP.1, p. 8; *Ch. Chinkin*, Gender, Human Rights and Peace Agreements, Ohio State Journal on Dispute Resolution 2003, p. 867 (870).

[6] Security Council Resolution 1325 (2000), UN Doc. S/RES/1325 (2000), 31 October 2000.

[7] *Ch. Chinkin*, Gender, Human Rights and Peace Agreements, Ohio State Journal on Dispute Resolution 2003, p. 867 (877).

[8] *C. Cohn/H. Kinsella/S. Gibbings*, Women, Peace and Security, International Feminist Journal of Politics, 6 (2004)1, pp. 130–140; *M. Datan*, Women, Peace and Security: A Feminist Analysis of Security Council Resolution 1325, LLM Research Paper, Laws 582, Law Faculty, Victoria University of Wellington, 2004; *J. Neuwirth*, Women and Peace and Security: The Implementation of U. N. Security Council Resolution 1325, Duke Journal of Gender Law and Policy 9 (2002), pp. 253–260; *J. F. Klot*, Women and Peace Processes – an Impossible Match?, in: L. Olsson (ed.), Gender and Peace Processes – an Impossible Match?, Uppsala 2003 p. 17–25.

[9] United Nations Convention on the Elimination of All Forms of Discrimination against Women, New York, 18 December 1979.

[10] *Ch. Bell*, Human Rights and Peace Agreements, Oxford 2000, p. 61.

Coalition was created, the first political party whose primary focus was on issues of concern to women.[11] They defined themselves as a cross-community political party working for inclusion, human rights and equality in Northern Ireland. When the delegates to the multi-party talks were elected, the Women's Coalition earned 1,03% of the votes, coming ninth among the parties, and two of their delegates entered the formal peace negotiations on the future of Northern Ireland.[12] While they were numerically only a few and politically untested, their impact on the negotiation process and its outcome was substantive.[13] The Irish Peace Process led to the so-called Good Friday or Belfast Agreement, upon which the parties agreed on April 10, 1998.[14] In the chapter on Rights, Safeguards and Equality of Opportunity the agreement included a provision that affirmed the political rights of women as well as an equality-clause:

> 1. The parties affirm their commitment to the mutual respect, the civil rights and the religious liberties of everyone in the community. Against the background of the recent history of communal conflict, the parties affirm in particular: (...)
>
> – the right of women to full and equal political participation.
>
> 3. Subject to the outcome of public consultation underway, the British Government intends, as a particular priority, to create a statutory obligation on public authorities in Northern Ireland to carry out all their functions with due regard to the need to promote equality of opportunity in relation to religion and political opinion; gender; race; disability; age; marital status; dependants; and sexual orientation. (...)

It also created a national Northern Ireland human rights commission whose task was to oversee the fulfilment of human rights.[15] The peace agreement for Northern Ireland provides us with one of the rare examples of women becoming part of the formal peace process.

The peace agreement for Northern Uganda shall serve as a more recent example; it is unfortunately not signed and, in the light of the most recent developments,[16] will presumably not be signed in the near future. After years of unsuccessful peace negotiations, a new round of negotiations between the Ugandan

---

[11] *F. Ni Aoláin*, Case Study on Northern Ireland, Expert Meeting of the DAW "Peace Agreements as a Means of Promoting Gender Equality and Ensuring Participation of Women – A Framework of Model Provisions", 10–13 November 2003, EGM/PEACE/2003/EP.4, p. 4.

[12] *Ch. Bell*, Human Rights and Peace Agreements, Oxford 2000, p. 60.

[13] *K. Fearon*, Women's Work: The Story of the Northern Ireland Women's Coalition, Belfast 1999, p. 89 (106, 121); *K. Fearon*, Northern Ireland Women's Coalition: Institutionalizing a political voice and ensuring representation, in: C. Barnes (ed.), Owning the Process. Public Participation in Peacemaking, Conciliation Resources 2002, p. 1 (3), available at: www.c-r.org/our-work/accord/public-participation/ni-womens-coalition.php (accessed 02 January 2009).

[14] The Northern Ireland Peace Agreement: The Agreement reached in the Multi-Party Negotiations, 04 October 1998.

[15] The Northern Ireland Peace Agreement, Chapter on Rights, Safeguards and Equality of Opportunity, para. 5.

[16] *R. Crilly*, Regional Neighbours turn Guns Against Bush Rebels in Uganda, TimesOn-

government and the LRA began in Juba in July 2006.[17] Shortly afterwards, the sides signed a landmark agreement on the cessation of hostilities. Over the next two years, further agreements were reached on comprehensive solutions, reconciliation and accountability, and disarmament. But despite this substantial progress, the LRA's elusive leader Joseph Kony failed to appear at the signing of a final peace agreement in April 2008.[18] Women were very active in the peace process. As early as August 2006, the Uganda Women's Coalition for Peace was formed, an experienced group of Ugandan NGOs working on gender and conflict issues and women leaders at national and district levels.[19] Early in the process, they demanded that women have a voice in the negotiations taking place between the government of Uganda and the Lord's Resistance Army.[20] With the financial and technical support of UNIFEM and the Gender Advisor to the Special Envoy for the LRA Affected Areas, the group held consultations with women from conflict areas on the proposed final peace agreement.[21] From these consultations, the Women's Coalition developed a detailed proposal on the gender aspects of the peace negotiation. Despite the presence of women in the negotiating teams for both the Ugandan government and the LRA, with further assistance from UNIFEM, some members of the Uganda Women's Coalition for Peace travelled to the Peace Talks in Juba in a bid to acquire observer status and to give input into the process. While they were not able to obtain an official role in the talks, they did attempt to contribute to the negotiation positions based on their developed proposals.[22] It is difficult to determine whether the positions put forward by the Women's Peace Coalition have had a direct impact on the parties' negotiating positions. Yet it is important to note that women were empowered to be a part of the peace process; however, they remained on its periphery. In any case, the peace agreement is remarkably progressive regarding the inclusion of women, as it provides for affirmative action on the basis of gender. In Point 2 of the strand of the agreement headed Comprehensive So-

line 16 December 2008, available at: www.timesonline.co.uk/tol/news/world/africa/article5348823.ece (accessed 05 January 2009).

[17] *Oxfam Briefing Paper*, From Emergency to Recovery, September 2008, p. 5.

[18] For a timeline of the conflict, see http://northernuganda.usvpp.gov/peacerec2.html (accessed 02 January 2009).

[19] *A. Sheriff/K. Barnes*, Enhancing the EU Response to Women and Armed Conflict. With particular reference to development policy, Discussion Paper No. 84, European Centre for Development Policy Management, Maastricht 2008, p. 59.

[20] *A. Sheriff/K. Barnes*, Enhancing the EU Response to Women and Armed Conflict. With particular reference to development policy, Discussion Paper No. 84, European Centre for Development Policy Management, Maastricht 2008, p. 59.

[21] *UNIFEM*, Northern Uganda Women Speak Out on Juba Talks, Press Statement, 19 October 2006.

[22] *Uganda Women's Coalition for Peace*, Annual Report 2006, Uganda 2007, pp. 7f., 10f., available at: www.uwonet.or.ug/index.php?page=publications (accessed 02 January 2009).

lutions to the War,[23] Principles of Governance, the Final Peace Agreement for Northern Uganda includes the following:

2.1 The Parties shall adhere to the following objectives and directive principles enshrined in the Constitution as the guiding principles in the implementation of this Agreement:
a) The State shall be based on democratic principles, which empower and encourage the active participation of all citizens at all levels in their own governance.
b) The composition of Government shall be broadly representative of the national character, gender and social diversity of the country. (…)
f) The government shall take affirmative action in favour of groups marginalised on the basis of gender, age, disability or any other reason created by history, tradition or custom, for the purpose of redressing imbalances, which may exist against them.

Since about 1995, there have been many examples of peace agreements that take women and their rights and concerns into account.[24] It is, however, too early to say that this has become the rule rather than an exception. Progress is indeed slow and women are still only seldom part of the formal peace process, as was the case in Northern Ireland; they often remain trapped in informal processes.[25] It can, however, be stated that there is a growing number of women taking part in peace talks and a growing number of peace accords that take women's rights into account. Women are not only a "vulnerable group in society" that has suffered disproportionately during the conflict and whose needs (not rights) need to be respected, as was the view of Boutros Boutros-Ghali in his Agenda for Peace back in 1996.[26] They are increasingly viewed as actors on the international plane, as stakeholders who have to have their say in the public affairs of their State.

III. Reasons for the Inclusion of Women

There are quite a few answers to the question why women have to be included in peace negotiations. In his address to the Security Council in October 2002,

---

[23] Agreement on Comprehensive Solutions between the Government of the Republic of Uganda and Lord's Resistance Army/Movement, Juba, Sudan, 2 May 2007.

[24] E.g. the peace agreement for Liberia, Sierra Leone, Burundi, East Timor, Afghanistan, etc.

[25] *Ch. Chinkin*, Peace Agreements as a Means for Promoting Gender Equality and Ensuring Participation of Women, Background Paper to the Expert Group Meeting on "Peace Agreements as a Means for Promoting Gender Equality and Ensuring Participation of Women – A Framework of Model Provisions?", 10–13 November 2003, UN Doc. EGM/PEACE/2003/BP.1, p. 4.

[26] An Agenda for Peace, Preventive Diplomacy, Peacemaking and Peace-Keeping, Report of the Secretary-General pursuant to the Statement adopted by the Summit Meeting of the Security Council on 31 January 1992, UN Doc. A/47/277, at para. 81; see also *H. Charlesworth/Ch. Chinkin*, The Boundaries of International Law. A Feminist Analysis, Manchester 2000, p. 286.

Secretary General Kofi Annan stated: "If women suffer the impact of conflict disproportionately, they are also the key to the solution of conflict".[27] This hints at a view according to which the inclusion of women has instrumental value. This might indeed be true, since women can provide a different view on the root causes and consequences of the conflict and therefore can provide invaluable information to the parties to the agreement.[28] Not confined to women only, but applicable to minority groups as well, is the argument that inclusion of women enhances the inclusiveness and sustainability of the process: The more sectors of the population are included in the formulation of the peace accord, the better will be its implementation. Local ownership of the process will facilitate lasting and sustainable peace.[29] Also, women's inclusion in the transitional phase is viewed as a 'compensation', so women can ensure at this time that their voices are heard and their needs catered to. For women the post-conflict transitional phase can mean a "window of opportunity" for their advancement. For them, peace is not meant to include a return to the status quo before the conflict, but can be a possibility for change in society and in gender relations.[30]

Some writers also say that women are better peacemakers, for they speak in a "different voice", as Gilligan put it in 1982[31]; they are perceived as having a disposition that makes them ideal negotiators because they are consensus-oriented instead of seeking confrontation, which is believed to be a male attribute.[32] That predisposition is explained by the female need to care for her family and her

[27] *K. Annan*, Secretary General's Statement to the Security Council on Women, Peace and Security, 29. October 2002, UN Doc. SG/SM/8461.

[28] *UNIFEM*, Women, Peace & Security. CEDAW and Security Council Resolution 1325: A Quick Guide, New York 2006, p. 15; *E. Onubogu/ L. Etchart*, Achieving Gender Equality and Equity in Peace Processes, in: R. Baksh/ L. Etchart/ E. Onubogu/ T. Johnson (eds.), Building Sustainable Peace, London 2005, pp. 34, 40f.; *Ch. Chinkin*, Peace Agreements as a Means for Promoting Gender Equality and Ensuring Participation of Women, Background Paper to the Expert Group Meeting on "Peace Agreements as a Means for Promoting Gender Equality and Ensuring Participation of Women – A Framework of Model Provisions?", 10–13 November 2003, UN Doc. EGM/PEACE/2003/BP.1, p. 10.

[29] *S. N. Anderlini*, Women Building Peace: What They Do, Why It Matters, London 2007, p. 79.

[30] *Ch. Chinkin*, Peace Agreements as a Means for Promoting Gender Equality and Ensuring Participation of Women, Background Paper to the Expert Group Meeting on "Peace Agreements as a Means for Promoting Gender Equality and Ensuring Participation of Women – A Framework of Model Provisions?", 10–13 November 2003, UN Doc. EGM/PEACE/2003/BP.1, p. 11; *S. Meintjes*, War and Post-war Shifts in Gender Relations, in: M. Turshen/ S. Meintjes/A. Pillay (eds.), The Aftermath. Women in Post-Conflict Transition, London 2002, p. 64.

[31] *C. Gilligan*, In a Different Voice: Psychological Theory and Women's Development, Cambridge Mass (et al.) 1982.

[32] *T. Greenblatt*, speech to the UN Security Council, September 2002 "Even when we are women whose very existence and narrative contradicts each other, we will talk – we will not shoot."; *S. Anderson*, "My only clan is womanhood": Building Women's Peace Identities, International Fellowship on Reconciliation, 2005, available at: www.ifor.org/WPP/article_May_05.pdf (accessed 02 January 2009).

community and to keep them together. Such arguments are grounded in the assumption that women may reason and think in an essentially different way from men, which is associated with cultural feminism.[33] This concept is certainly doubtful and, in any case, it runs the risk of reinforcing stereotypical perceptions of male and female behaviour, which the CEDAW sets out to eliminate.[34] Nonetheless, it has to be noted that due to their common experiences, women have repeatedly manifested an ability to unite beyond the boundaries of race, class and age to find common ground in their quest for peace. In Somalia, women united across boundaries of ethnicity to form what was to become known as the "sixth clan", obtaining a role in the Somali Peace and Reconciliation Conference in Djibouti and later securing a quota for women in the Transitional National Assembly.[35] Similarly, in the Democratic Republic of Congo in 2001, 60 women from all parties to the "Inter-Congolese Dialogue" came together in a cross-party workshop which resulted in the Nairobi Declaration and Action Plan calling for a mainstreaming of gender sensitivity throughout the process.[36]

But apart from these instrumental considerations, the inclusion of women has intrinsic value. It takes distributive justice or participative democracy into consideration,[37] since women make up 50% of the population – in post-conflict situations often even more.[38] This leads to the assumption that they should supply 50% of the decision-making bodies.[39] If asymmetries of representation continue in peace times, they enact and reinforce the asymmetries of power existing

---

[33] *N. Lacey*, Feminist Legal Theory and the Rights of Women, in: K. Knop (ed.), Gender and Human Rights, Oxford, New York 2004, pp. 13, 23.

[34] Art. 5 a) of the CEDAW; critical to the concept are also: *R. Manchanda*, Interrogating Stereotypes: Women Making Peace, in: R. Samaddar/ H. Reifeld (eds.), Peace as Process. Reconciliation and Conflict Resolution in South Asia, Manohar 2001, pp. 80, 84 ff.; *E. Onubogu/ L. Etchart*, Achieving Gender Equality and Equity in Peace Processes, in: R. Baksh/ L. Etchart/ E. Onubogu/ T. Johnson (eds.), Building Sustainable Peace, London 2005, p. 40.

[35] *E. Rehn/E.J. Sirleaf*, Women, War, Peace. The Independent Expert Assessment on the Impact of Armed Conflict on Women and Women's Role in Peacebuilding, New York 2002, p. 78; *S. Anderson*, "My only clan is womanhood": Building Women's Peace Identities, International Fellowship on Reconciliation 2005, available at: www.ifor.org/WPP/article_May_05.pdf. (accessed 02 January 2009), p. 2.

[36] *UNIFEM*, Securing the Peace. Guiding the International Community Towards Women's Effective Participation Throughout Peace Processes, New York 2005, p. 6. The Nairobi Declaration and Action Plan is available under http://www.peacewomen.org/resources/DRC/NairobiDec2002en.pdf. (accessed 02 January 2009).

[37] *S. Fredman*, Discrimination Law, London 2002, pp. 20 f.

[38] After the conflict in Rwanda, 70% of the population were female and 50% of the households were headed by women; Human Rights Watch, Shattered Lives: Sexual Violence during the Rwandan Genocide and its Aftermath, 1996, available at: http://www.unhcr.org/refworld/docid/3ae6a8510.html (accessed 12 December 2008).

[39] For a theoretical defence of parity and mirror representation, see *F. Gaspard*, The French Parity Movement, in: J. Clausen/Ch. S. Maier, Has Liberalism Failed Women? Assuring Equal Representation in Europe and the United States, New York 2001, pp. 62 ff.

in a society before and during the conflict. Moreover, it is important to note that the inclusion of women is a matter of the rule of law: States and maybe even other actors are legally obliged under public international law to include women in all political processes of the transitional phase from conflict to peace. The obligations arising from the CEDAW will be discussed in detail in the next section.

However, the inclusion of women also has its critics. For one thing, it is not enough to "add women and stir", as this approach is sometimes termed. Research has shown that a threshold of 30% has to be met (the so called critical mass) in order to effect a more women-centered, gender-sensitive outcome. It has to be admitted that the inclusion of women alone cannot guarantee the emergence of a 'gender perspective' in the political process. Nonetheless, this is more likely to develop when a critical mass of women are in decision-making positions.[40] There is also a more general critique. Some writers believe that human rights issues (and women's rights are human rights[41]) should not play a major role in peace negotiations, and this not because of sexism or a belief that women lack the ability to take part in politics, but out of a general concern: Respecting human rights in peace negotiations can present an obstacle to a quick solution of the conflict.[42] When actors are compelled to meet or to commit to certain human rights standards in their behaviour and actions, this might hinder them from taking part in negotiations or agreeing on other issues, thus threatening the fragile peace[43]. In the long run, however, the observance of human rights and its institutions in the peace process – bills of rights, human rights commissions etc. – play an important role in the solution, management and transformation of the conflict and thus contribute to a more sustainable peace.[44] If human rights are neglected in a peace process, human rights violations might recur in the form of civil unrest and even renewed conflict.[45]

---

[40] *E. Rehn/ E.J. Sirleaf*, Women, War, Peace. The Independent Expert Assessment on the Impact of Armed Conflict on Women and Women's Role in Peacebuilding, New York 2002, p. 80.

[41] Beijing Platform for Action, adopted at the Fourth World Conference for Women, Beijing, September 1995, endorsed by GA Resolution 50/203, 22 December 1995, para. 213.

[42] *Anonymous*, Human Rights in Peace Negotiations, Human Rights Quarterly 18(1996), p. 249 (250).

[43] *J. Boehme*, Human Rights and Gender Components of UN and EU Peace Operations. Putting Human Rights and Gender Mandates into Practice, German Institute for Human Rights, Berlin 2008, p. 44.

[44] *Ch. Bell*, Human Rights and Peace Agreements, Oxford 2000, p. 6.

[45] *J. Boehme*, Human Rights and Gender Components of UN and EU Peace Operations. Putting Human Rights and Gender Mandates into Practice, German Institute for Human Rights, Berlin 2008, p. 44.

IV. Obligations Arising from CEDAW

The Convention on the Elimination of all Forms of Discrimination against Women (CEDAW) was adopted by the General Assembly on December 18, 1979, and after it was signed by 20 States, it entered into force on September 3, 1981. It is the most important human rights treaty especially for women, and covers such diverse areas as public life, education, health, employment, nationality, marriage and family relations, the rights of rural women, etc. The Convention aims at equality for women in all areas and aspects of their lives through the prohibition of discrimination. Nowadays, it enjoys almost universal ratification, since 185 States are party to the Convention.[46] As a mechanism for implementation, it provides for a reporting duty of States parties to the treaty organ – the Committee for the Elimination of All Discrimination against Women – every four years,[47] and since 2000, when the Optional Protocol (OP) entered into force (which has 94 parties as of November 2008), it also provides for an individual complaint mechanism (referred to in the OP as "communications") as well as an investigation procedure (referred to as "inquiry").[48] The Committee has also formulated 26 General Recommendations on specific topics of the treaty, which interpret and refine the obligations of States under the treaty.

CEDAW is also significant as regards the conflict and post-conflict environment. Art. 7 and 8 of the CEDAW are central to the human rights obligations concerning women's participation in peace processes arising under CEDAW, because they codify women's right to political participation. Article 7 reads:

> States Parties shall take all appropriate measures to eliminate discrimination against women in the political and public life of the country and, in particular, shall ensure to women, on equal terms with men, the right:
>
> (a) To vote in all elections and public referenda and to be eligible for election to all publicly elected bodies;
>
> (b) To participate in the formulation of government policy and the implementation thereof and to hold public office and perform all public functions at all levels of government;
>
> (c) To participate in non-governmental organizations and associations concerned with the public and political life of the country.

---

[46] For the list of ratifications, declarations and reservations, see http://www2.ohchr.org/english/bodies/ratification/8.htm.

[47] For an overview of the Committee's work, see *B. Schöpp-Schilling*, The Nature and Mandate of the Committee, in: B. Schöpp-Schilling/ C. Flinterman (eds.), The Circle of Empowerment, New York 2007, pp. 248–261.

[48] *A. Byrnes/J. Connors*, Enforcing the Human Rights of Women: A Complaints Procedure for the Women's Convention? Draft Optional Protocol to the Convention on the Elimination of all Forms of Discrimination against Women, Brooklyn Journal of International Law 21 (1996) p. 679; *C. Flinterman*, Strengthening Women's Human Rights Through Individual Complaints, in: B. Schöpp-Schilling/C. Flinterman (eds.), The Circle of Empowerment, New York 2007, pp. 286–297.

Art. 7 a) codifies the formal right to vote and to be elected and is relevant when there is a formal election process for the negotiating teams, as was the case in Ireland in 1995. Otherwise, Article 7 b) is of interest: It names the right to take part in the formulation and implementation of government policy at all levels. This encompasses a very broad concept that does not stop at the formal right to vote and to be elected, but includes the de facto participation of women in all public affairs, which must be ensured by the State.[49] The post- Cold War peace agreements often set out to rearrange the whole political and societal setting in a country;[50] the formulation and negotiation of a peace agreement between the government and another actor after an internal armed conflict thus implies the formulation of government policy.

In addition, in the case of an interstate conflict or of negotiations taking place between States and other actors on the international level, Article 8 becomes important. It reads as follows:

> States Parties shall take all appropriate measures to ensure to women, on equal terms with men and without any discrimination, the opportunity to represent their Governments at the international level and to participate in the work of international organizations.

Besides the opportunity to represent their governments as diplomats, this guarantees to women the possibility of attending international conferences and meetings as delegates of their country.[51] The representation of government at the international level includes such peace negotiations as they are carried out by government delegations.

We can conclude that women have the right to political participation, not only in elections but also in every other aspect of political and public life. The subject matter of these provisions covers peace talks. By CEDAW, women are not given the right to participate politically; this is granted by other human rights conventions like the ICCPR.[52] But CEDAW gives them the right not to be discriminated against in these matters. This leads us to the concept of discrimination in the CEDAW. Article 1 defines discrimination as follows:

> For the purposes of the present Convention, the term "discrimination against women" shall mean any distinction, exclusion or restriction made on the basis of sex which has the effect or purpose of impairing or nullifying the recognition, enjoyment or exercise

---

[49] *Japanese Association of International Women's Rights*, Convention on the Elimination of All Forms of Discrimination against Women. A Commentary, Tokyo 1992, p. 143.

[50] See *Ch. Chinkin*, Peace Agreements as a Means for Promoting Gender Equality and Ensuring Participation of Women, Background Paper to the Expert Group Meeting on "Peace Agreements as a Means for Promoting Gender Equality and Ensuring Participation of Women – A Framework of Model Provisions?", 10–13 November 2003, UN Doc. EGM/PEACE/2003/BP.1, p. 7.

[51] *Japanese Association of International Women's Rights*, Convention on the Elimination of All Forms of Discrimination against Women. A Commentary, Tokyo 1992, p. 153.

[52] Art. 25 International Covenant on Civil, Political and Cultural Rights.

by women, irrespective of their marital status, on a basis of equality of men and women, of human rights and fundamental freedoms in the political, economic, social, cultural, civil or any other field.

The CEDAW gives a very broad definition of discrimination; it does not require a discriminatory intent and covers direct, indirect,[53] and structural discrimination[54] of women in the enjoyment of their human rights.

When applying this definition to the case of peace talks, differing patterns of discrimination become apparent. That women actually be prohibited from taking part in peace talks is quite seldom. Women might, however, be indirectly discriminated against, for example when the negotiating delegations are made up of former combatants or representatives of clans – which traditionally are mostly men[55] – or when they are selected on the basis of posts held: the defence minister, the chief of staff of the army, etc.[56] Women do not often hold such posts.[57] Indirect discrimination occurs where the effect of certain requirements, conditions or practices imposed by the State that appear to be gender-neutral have an adverse impact disproportionately on women.[58] When only persons that represent the clan or hold certain posts are allowed to be part of the solution of the conflict, women are thus indirectly discriminated against, although seen from the outside, the selection criterion is gender-neutral.

Most often, however, the general and widespread invisibility of women in public life poses the greatest difficulty in discerning suitable female candidates for the negotiations.[59] Women are often excluded from public life by culture and tradition.[60] Structural discrimination is discrimination that is embedded in rules, norms and patterns of attitudes and behaviour in institutions and other societal structures; these constitute obstacles to women in achieving the same rights and opportunities that are available to men.[61] When women are absent

---

[53] *CEDAW Committee*, General Recommendation No. 19 on violence against women, 1992, UN Doc. HRI/GEN/1/Rev. 6, 245, para. 10; CEDAW Committee, General Recommendation No. 25 on Article 4, paragraph 1 of the Convention on the Elimination of All Forms of Discrimination against Women, on temporary special measures, 2004, UN Doc. CEDAW/C/2004/I/WP.1/Rev.1., para. 7.

[54] *R. Holtmaat*, Towards Different Law and Public Policy. The significance of Article 5a CEDAW for the elimination of structural gender discrimination, The Hague 2004, p. 11.

[55] This was the case in Somalia during the first Peace and Reconciliation Conference in 2002.

[56] This happened in the case of Uganda's peace process.

[57] *S. N. Anderlini*, Women Building Peace: What They Do, Why It Matters, London 2007, p. 58.

[58] *S. Fredman*, Discrimination Law, London 2002, pp. 106ff.

[59] *S. N. Anderlini*, Women Building Peace: What They Do, Why It Matters, London 2007, p. 58.

[60] *C. Chinkin*, Gender, Human Rights and Peace Agreements, Ohio State Journal on Dispute Resolution 2003, p. 867 (871).

[61] *R. Holtmaat*, Towards Different Law and Public Policy. The significance of Article 5a CEDAW for the elimination of structural gender discrimination, The Hague 2004, p. 90.

from political life due to the predominant role assumptions that confine women to the private sphere, it is thus also structural discrimination that keeps women from taking part in negotiations. Changing dominant stereotypical gender ideology is a cumbersome process, but CEDAW can nonetheless be of help in redressing this problem.[62] As one of the suggested tools, UNIFEM calls for a strict 30% quota of women in peace negotiations;[63] it also calls for training of women to develop their negotiating skills and to enable them to participate.[64] This claim finds legal support in the CEDAW norms, as they call for affirmative action to accelerate women's equality. Human rights create not only an obligation to respect on the side of the State, which is to say that it is not only bound to refrain from violations of human rights, in this case of discrimination. As *Asbjorn Eide* has developed in the context of social, economic and cultural rights, all human rights also entail an obligation to protect and to fulfill.[65] States must protect the rights of women against violations by third parties (the non-State actors)[66] and they must ensure that women are brought into a situation that enables them to make full use of their human rights. This last dimension of human rights obligations goes well with Article 4 (1) of the Convention, which reads:

> 1. Adoption by States Parties of temporary special measures aimed at accelerating de facto equality between men and women shall not be considered discrimination as defined in the present Convention, but shall in no way entail as a consequence the maintenance of unequal or separate standards; these measures shall be discontinued when the objectives of equality of opportunity and treatment have been achieved.

Art. 4 (1) of CEDAW on affirmative action – in the language of the Convention: temporary special measures[67] – at first sight only states that under the Convention, temporary special measures do not constitute discrimination, and there-

---

[62] Art. 5 (a) CEDAW explicitly calls for "the elimination of prejudices and customary and all other practices which are based on the idea of the inferiority or the superiority of either of the sexes or on stereotyped roles for men and women."

[63] *UNIFEM*, Securing the Peace. Guiding the International Community Towards Women's Effective Participation Throughout Peace Processes, New York 2005, p. 7; *E. Rehn/E.J. Sirleaf*, Women, War, Peace. The Independent Expert Assessment on the Impact of Armed Conflict on Women and Women's Role in Peacebuilding, New York 2002, pp. 80 ff.

[64] *E. Rehn/ E.J. Sirleaf*, Women, War, Peace. The Independent Expert Assessment on the Impact of Armed Conflict on Women and Women's Role in Peacebuilding, New York 2002, pp. 79 f.

[65] *A. Eide*, Right to Adequate Food as a Human Right, UN Doc. E/CN.4/Sub.2/1987/23, UN Publications New York 1989, para. 66–69, pp. 14 f.; *A. Eide*, Realization of Social and Economic Rights and the Minimum Threshold Approach, HRLJ 10 (1989), p. 35, 37 ff.; *A. Eide*, Economic, Social and Cultural Rights as Human Rights, in: *A. Eide./C. Krause/A. Rosas*, Economic, Social and Cultural Rights. A Textbook, Dordrecht 1995, p. 12 (37 ff.).

[66] Cf. Art. 2 (e) CEDAW.

[67] On temporary special measures, see I. Boerefijn et al. (eds.), Temporary Special Measures, Antwerpen et al. 2003.

fore the article merely allows for them. But taken together with Art. 3 I, Art. 4 (1) means more than that. Article 3 obliges States to take all appropriate measures to ensure the advancement of women in all fields. It reads:

States Parties shall take in all fields, in particular in the political, social, economic and cultural fields, all appropriate measures, including legislation, to ensure the full development and advancement of women, for the purpose of guaranteeing them the exercise and enjoyment of human rights and fundamental freedoms on a basis of equality with men.

As all appropriate measures have to be taken, States are under an obligation to use temporary special measures to advance women's equality in a given field, if such a measure is the most suitable to reach equality in that field.[68] Given the above-mentioned exclusion of women from the political sphere in virtually every society as well as their exclusion from the peace table, this is a field where temporary special measures, for example in the form of quotas, are especially needed.[69] As women's participation is not yet systematic or assured, there is a need for affirmative action in this area.[70] That is also the view of the CEDAW Committee, the treaty body of the CEDAW, as expressed in the General Recommendation 25 on temporary special measures, the relevant passages of which read as follows:

24. Article 4, paragraph 1, read in conjunction with articles 1, 2, 3, 5 and 24, needs to be applied in relation to articles 6 to 16 which stipulate that States parties "shall take all appropriate measures". Consequently, the Committee considers that States parties are obliged to adopt and implement temporary special measures in relation to any of these articles if such measures can be shown to be necessary and appropriate in order to accelerate the achievement of the overall, or a specific goal of, women's de facto or substantive equality."[71]

---

[68] *A. F. Bayefsky*, The Principle of Equality and Non-Discrimination in International Law, HRLJ 11 (1990), p. 27 f.; *R. Holtmaat*, Building Blocks for a General Recommendation on Article 4 (1) of the CEDAW Convention. Report of the Expert Meeting in Maastricht (Valkenburg), 10–12 October 2002, in: I. Boerefijn et al. (eds.), Temporary Special Measures, Antwerpen et al. 2003, p. 213 (227).

[69] *R. Cook*, Obligations to Adopt Temporary Special Measures Under the Convention on the Elimination of All Forms of Discrimination against Women, in: I. Boerefijn et al. (eds.), Temporary Special Measures, Antwerpen et al. 2003, p. 119 (135 f.); CEDAW Committee, General Recommendation No. 23, on Political and Public Life, 2000, UN Doc. HRI/Gen/1/Rev.4, para. 15.

[70] *C. Hannan*, Affirmative Action and Security Council resolution 1325 (2000), CEDAW General Recommendation 25 and women's participation in conflict prevention and conflict resolution, Statement, Genf 2004.

[71] *CEDAW Committee*, General Recommendation 25 on Article 4, paragraph 1, of the Convention on the Elimination of All Forms of Discrimination against Women, on temporary special measures, 2004, UN Doc. CEDAW/C/2004/I/WP.1/Rev.1., para. 24.

V. Post-conflict Derogation from Human Rights Obligations?

One objection exists as regards the last conclusion. Armed violence and threats to security of the population do not cease to occur as soon as a ceasefire has been signed and the negotiations are under way. On the contrary. The transitional phase is still one of severe insecurities and weak or limited statehood. The situation of States thus resembles in some ways a state of emergency, which is the underlying rationale for the derogation clauses in a number of human rights treaties.[72] In a state of emergency, the state is allowed under certain circumstances to derogate temporarily from a part of its treaty obligations. The CEDAW does not contain a derogation clause. This does not necessarily mean that there is no possibility of derogation for States in an emergency situation. If a human rights treaty does not contain the *legal regime* applicable in such situations, a right to derogation can be based on general international law.[73] If such right is applicable in post-conflict situations, it could serve as a justification for the temporary weakening of the States' obligations arising from CEDAW. The Special Rapporteur on Human Rights and States of Emergency, *Leandro Despouy*, has written several reports on the subject and has listed the requirements that must be met so that a State can lawfully invoke a state of emergency.[74] Some of them will be applied to the present matter.

First, there must be an emergency situation. Such a situation is characterised by exceptional circumstances that involve an actual and imminent threat to the community as a whole.[75] Terms like exceptional circumstances and imminent threat are difficult to define in abstract terms, and in any case they require an evaluation of the situation on a case to case basis. It is clear that the emergency situation in a post-conflict state must still reach a certain degree of gravity. Given the often widespread continuing violence in a conflict-ridden country during the peace process, it is in fact likely that an emergency situation might still exist.

Secondly, the measures taken to address the emergency, which constitute the derogation from the human rights obligations, must be proportionate, which is to say that they are acceptable only if events make them necessary and if they are proportionate to the danger that those events present.[76] In other words, the

---

[72] See Art. 4 ICCPR, Art. 15 ECHR, Art. 30 European Social Charta, Art. 27 American Convention on Human Rights and Art. 4 Arab Charter on Human Rights.

[73] *J. Oraá*, Human Rights in States of Emergency in International Law, Oxford 1992, p. 209. This would either be an application of the principle of necessity (Art. 25 ILC Articles on State Responsibility) or a general principle of law recognized by civilized nations.

[74] *UN Special Rapporteur on Human Rights and States of Emergencies*, 23 June 1997, E/CN.4/Sub.2/1997/19, p. 13 ff.

[75] *UN Special Rapporteur on Human Rights and States of Emergencies*, 23 June 1997, E/CN.4/Sub.2/1997/19, para. 34 p. 10, para. 76 ff., p. 19 ff.

[76] *UN Special Rapporteur on Human Rights and States of Emergencies*, 23 June 1997, E/

measures taken must be suitable to end or at least mitigate the emergency situation.[77] As regards our topic, this is doubtful. The omission of States to include women in the peace process, which constitutes a violation of their human right to political participation and the state's obligation under CEDAW, can not be viewed to have a positive impact on the security situation, as its aim is not to end the emergency.

A third principle regulating states of emergency in international law is the principle of non-discrimination.[78] The prohibition of discrimination is arguably either one of the non-derogable rights[79], or it might be a precondition for the derogation,[80] as it is in the derogation clauses in the ICCPR and in the ACHR. That is to say that measures taken by States in the case of an emergency have to be non-discriminatory. Accordingly, if they establish differences in the treatment of several ethnic, religious or gender groups, the State has to prove that this differentiation is necessary.[81] Since in our case the exclusion of women is discriminatory, as it establishes different treatment of men and women, a possible justification would have to coincide with the above-mentioned proportionality test. It would therefore meet with the same objections.

In conclusion, the application of the state of emergency in post-conflict situations might be feasible, but the case in question, the exclusion of women from the peace process, cannot be justified under that heading.

VI. The Right to Derogation in the Practice of the CEDAW Committee

Let us verify this conclusion by examining the practice of the Committee on the Elimination of Discrimination as regards this matter. When the reporting dialogue between States and the committee is analyzed, it becomes clear that the committee does not turn a blind eye on the situation of States. The members

CN.4/Sub.2/1997/19, para. 83ff., pp. 21 ff.; *R. Higgins*, Derogations under Human Rights Treaties, BYBIL 48 (1976–7), 282 (283).

[77] *UN Special Rapporteur on Human Rights and States of Emergencies*, 23 June 1997, E/CN.4/Sub.2/1997/19, para. 88, p. 22.

[78] *UN Special Rapporteur on Human Rights and States of Emergencies*, 23 June 1997, E/CN.4/Sub.2/1997/19, para. 92ff., p. 23; *A. Svensson-McCarthy*, The International Law of Human Rights and States of Exception, The Hague, Boston, London 1998, pp. 640ff.

[79] *UN Special Rapporteur on Human Rights and States of Emergencies*, 23 June 1997, E/CN.4/Sub.2/1997/19, para. 93, p. 23; Human Rights Committee, General Recommendation No. 29 on States of Emergency (Art. 4), 31 August 2001, para. 8.

[80] *Human Rights Committee*, General recommendation No. 5 on Derogation of Rights (Art. 4), 31 July 1981, para. 1; *J. Oráa*, Human Rights in States of Emergency in International Law, Oxford 1992, p. 263.

[81] *J. Oráa*, Human Rights in States of Emergency in International Law, Oxford 1992, p. 180.

recognize the State's difficulties during the transitional period as well as the severe hardships the people have to endure. The committee's consideration of Burundi's initial report might serve as an example.[82] In its principle areas of concern and recommendations, the committee says:

49. The Committee considers the absence of peace to be the most serious obstacle to the full implementation of the Convention. It also expresses its concern about the number of women who have been affected by violence during conflict.

50. The Committee recommends that, in the implementation of the Arusha Accords and in accordance with those Accords, emphasis be placed on the role of women in reconstruction and that the acceleration of women's equality be integrated in all its aspects. It urges that special efforts be made to include women in national reconciliation and peace-building initiatives.

The Committee recognizes the obstacles, but goes on to emphasize that in the implementation of the Peace Accord, the acceleration of women's equality must be emphasized. The Committee does not seem to alter the standards of human rights performance. This also becomes clear in the Committee's consideration the combined first, second and third report of Bosnia-Herzegovina.[83] It reads

11. While aware of the difficulties confronting the State party owing to the impact of the armed conflict and the political, economic and social transformation processes in the reconstruction period, the Committee is concerned that in the postwar period women's enjoyment of their human rights has been negatively affected by several factors: the lack of a gender analysis of the consequences of the armed conflict and the lack of women's participation in and gender analyses of the peace, reconstruction and transformation processes. The Committee is also concerned that the creation of a constitutional framework as well as of political and administrative structures based on ethnicity as the determining factor has contributed to a limited recognition and implementation of gender equality principles.

12. The Committee urges the State party to comply with its obligations under the Convention to eliminate discrimination against women without delay, to include women in all political, economic and social transformation processes at the State, entity, cantonal and municipal levels on a basis of equality with men and to make gender analyses an integral part of these processes.

In conclusion, in the reporting process no evidence of a right to derogation can be found in the Committee's dialogue with the States in transition. Similarly, States in post-conflict situations have not invoked a state of emergency in order to justify their non-compliance with obligations under the CEDAW. At times the Committee has even put additional obligations on a State in transition. Bosnia-Herzegovina was requested by the Committee to provide financial resourc-

[82] *CEDAW Committee*, Report of the Committee on the Elimination of Discrimination against Women, UN Doc. A/56/38, para. 32, p. 7.

[83] *CEDAW Committee*, Concluding comments of the Committee on the Elimination of Discrimination against Women: Bosnia and Herzegovina, Thirty-Fifth Session, CEDAW/C/BIH/CO/3.

es for health care and trauma counselling for female victims of the armed conflict.[84] Similarly, in Burundi the Committee suggested that Burundi supply greater assistance and carry out rehabilitative efforts directed at women in refugee camps and provide post-trauma counselling for women who were victims of gender-based violence during the conflict.[85] These requests could be evidence of the "Window of Opportunity" or a repetition of the obligations arising from the Convention at any time. In any case, they confirm the conclusion that States in the transitional phase do not have a right to derogate from their obligations under the Convention.

VII. Conclusion

This conclusion is reflected in the *soft law* that exists regarding this matter. In its area of concern "Women and Armed Conflict", the Beijing Platform for Action calls for increased participation of women in conflict resolution.[86] In Resolution 1325, women's participation in peace processes is a key component, as it urges all actors in a peace process to include women at all levels of decision-making in post-conflict negotiations and to adopt a gender perspective in the resolution of the conflict.[87]

Human rights violations including those of women are often the root cause of armed conflict and in any case, they accompany it. If they continue during peace-time, and if the unequal power relationships between men and women are not addressed, no sustainable and lasting peace can be brought to a region. Women's participation in negotiating for peace is an essential component of gender equality and of an effective and responsive peace agreement. However, progress has been slow and significant political pressure is necessary to ensure that women really do participate in peace processes. The CEDAW can be an important tool in exerting pressure on actors and in providing leverage to stakeholders in post-conflict situations.

---

[84] *CEDAW Committee*, Concluding comments of the Committee on the Elimination of Discrimination against Women: Bosnia and Herzegovina, Thirty-Fifth Session, CEDAW/C/BIH/CO/3, para. 38.

[85] *CEDAW Committee*, Report of the Committee on the Elimination of Discrimination against Women, UN Doc. A/56/38, paras. 53 and 54.

[86] Beijing Declaration and Action Plan, adopted at the Fourth World Conference for Women, Beijing, September 1995, para. 142.

[87] Security Council Resolution 1325 (2000), UN Doc. S/RES/1325 (2000), 31 October 2000, paras. 1 and 8.

Economic, Social and Cultural Rights and the Question of Justiciability: International Legal Protection of the Right to Food

Kristina Roepstorff

I. Introduction

At the international level, the main treaty acknowledging economic, social and cultural (esc) rights is the ICESCR (1976), which forms, together with the ICCPR (1976), the two Optional Protocols to the ICCPR and the Universal Declaration of Human Rights (1948), the International Bill of Human Rights.

Yet, already when the United Nations Charter was drafted, disagreement arose concerning the extent to which esc rights should be included. It was eventually agreed to include a provision regarding international economic and social cooperation into the United Nations Charter.[1] The human rights movement gained momentum after the world witnessed two gruesome World Wars, and in 1948 the Universal Declaration of Human Rights (UDHR) was adopted. The UDHR, that encompasses civil and political as well as esc rights, elaborated on the human rights already acknowledged in the United Nations Charter. Subsequently, the UDHR had to be translated into binding treaty obligations. Although it was widely recognised that the two sets of human rights were interdependent and interrelated, disagreement on the status of esc rights and their inclusion in a legally binding treaty arose again.[2] Those who were in favour of drafting a single covenant including both sets of rights argued that human rights could not be clearly divided into different sets of rights and emphasised the interdependence of all human rights. Those in favour of drafting two separate covenants based their arguments on the assumed differing nature of the two sets of rights. As no agreement could be reached, two separate treaties, the ICCPR[3]

---

[1] UN Charter, 1945, Article 55.

[2] P. Alston/H. Steiner (eds.), International Human Rights in Context: Law, Politics, Morals, Oxford 2000, p. 244.

[3] International Covenant on Civil and Political Rights, 1976.

and the ICESCR[4] were finally adopted in 1966, coming into force in 1976.[5] At the same time, an Optional Protocol to the ICCPR providing for an individual complaints procedure was adopted.[6] No similar procedure was established in relation to the ICESCR. Indeed, the ICESCR differs from the ICCPR in various ways. The most significant difference lies in the nature of state obligations and in the monitoring mechanisms set out in the covenants. The main reason for this is the alleged weak legal quality of esc rights enshrined in the ICESCR. It is widely claimed that these rights, in contrast to the rights recognised under the ICCPR, do not ground individual legal entitlements and that their implementation depends on the availability of resources. According to this view, civil and political rights have an absolute character making them justiciable, while esc rights, due to their alleged programmatic character, were considered as non-justiciable rights.[7]

Thus, while the UDHR recognised both civil and political rights and esc rights, emphasising the indivisibility and interdependence of all human rights,[8] esc rights have ever since been differentiated from civil and political rights and treated as a distinct category of human rights.[9] The positions range from the view that esc rights are superior to civil and political rights to the view that esc rights are not legal rights at all.[10] This has led to a hierarchical perception of the

---

[4] International Covenant on Economic, Social and Cultural Rights, 1976.

[5] *M. Craven*, The International Covenant on Economic, Social and Cultural Rights, Oxford 1995, p. 9.

[6] Second Optional Protocol to the International Covenant on Civil and Political Rights, 1976; the ICCPR is not the only treaty establishing an individual complaint procedure. For a discussion of various individual complaint procedures see Human Rights Fact Sheet No. 7: Complaint Procedures, Geneva 2002 http://www.unhchr.ch/html/menu6/2/sheets.htm (accessed 19 January 2009).

[7] Annotations on the Text of the Draft International Covenants on Human Rights, UN Doc. A/2929, 1995, Par. 7; see also *M. J. Dennis/D. P. Stewart*, Justiciability of Economic, Social and Cultural Rights: Should There Be an International Complaints Mechanism to Adjudicate the Rights to Food, Water, Housing, and Health?, American Journal of International Law 3 (2004).

[8] The idea of the indivisibility, interdependence and universality of all human rights was reemphasised during the 1993 World Conference on Human Rights: Vienna Declaration and Programme of Action, UN doc. A/CONF:157/23, Part I, para. 5; see also *R. Künnemann*, A Coherent Approach to Human Rights, Human Rights Quarterly 17 (1995), pp. 323–342; *C. Scott*, The Interdependence and Permeability of Human Rights Norms: Towards a Partial Fusion of the International Covenants on Human Rights, Osgoode Hall Law Journal 27 (1989), p. 769.

[9] *M. Craven*, The International Covenant on Economic, Social and Cultural Rights, Oxford 1995, p. 9.

[10] This last position is represented by *Vierdag*, see *E. Vierdag*, The Nature of the Rights Granted by the International Covenant on Economic, Social and Cultural Rights, Netherlands Yearbook of International Law 9 (1978), p. 82. Vierdag's position has, however, been challenged, among others by *Van Hoof*, see *G. J. H Van Hoof*, The Legal Nature of Economic, Social and Cultural Rights: A Rebuttal of Some Traditional Views, in: P. Alston/K. Tomasevski (eds.), The Right to Food, Dordrecht 1984, p. 103.

rights where civil and political rights are given priority over economic and social rights or *vice versa*.[11]

II. Nature of Economic, Social and Cultural Rights

The historical evolution and development of the concept of human rights is often explained in terms of 'first generation rights', 'second generation rights' and 'third generation rights'.[12] According to this categorisation, esc rights are defined as welfare or 'second generation rights' that evolved from the socialist ideology in the late nineteenth and early twentieth century, and the rise of the labour movement in Europe.[13] They are distinguished from the so-called 'first generation rights', the civil and political rights, that have their origin in the liberal tradition, and from the 'third generation rights' that represent group or so-called solidarity rights.[14] This distinction of different sets of rights results to some extent from the ideological conflict during the Cold War.[15] Whereas Communist states emphasised economic and social rights that they associated with the socialist ideology, Western states gave priority to civil and political rights that they, on the other hand, associated with liberty rights of non-interference.[16]

Though the motivation for the categorisation of human rights into two sets of rights springs to a large extent from the particular political setting at the time of drafting, the separation has since then been interpreted as evidence of the distinct nature of the two sets of rights, leading to monolithic views of their nature and philosophical conceptualisation.[17] There are at least two different but intertwined lines of argument in the debate concerning the status and nature of esc rights: first, arguments that are based on a theoretical distinction between civil

---

[11] *A. Eide/A. Rosas*, Economic, Social and Cultural Rights: A Universal Challenge, in: A. Eide/A. Rosas et al. (eds.) Economic, Social and Cultural Rights, Dordrecht 1995, p. 17.

[12] *M. Craven*, The International Covenant on Economic, Social and Cultural Rights, Oxford 1995, p. 8.

[13] *M. Craven*, The International Covenant on Economic, Social and Cultural Rights, Oxford 1995, p. 8; see also *I. Szabo*, Historical Foundations of Human Rights and Subsequent Developments, in: K. Vasak/P. Alson (eds.), The International Dimensions of Human Rights, Westport 1982.

[14] This classification was proposed by the French jurist, Karel Vasak. While not universally accepted, this classification of three generations of human rights has received general recognition.

[15] *M. Craven*, The International Covenant on Economic, Social and Cultural Rights, Oxford 1995, p. 8.

[16] *M. Craven*, The International Covenant on Economic, Social and Cultural Rights, Oxford 1995, p. 8.

[17] *M. Craven*, The International Covenant on Economic, Social and Cultural Rights, Oxford 1995, p. 9; see also *M. Cranston*, What are Human Rights, London 1973.

and political rights and esc rights; second, arguments that derive from practical and political reasons for distinguishing between these two sets of rights.

Theoretically, the idea of human rights is grounded in moral thought about how people ought to be treated.[18] However, human rights as legal rights, and in contrast to mere moral rights, give rise to enforceable claims that citizens make against their governments.[19] The basic structure of any legal right requires that there is a right-holder, an addressee, and a determinable content or subject of the right.[20] A complete concept of human rights as legal rights therefore has to specify the correlative duties and responsibilities, as well as determining the content of the right.[21] Human rights as legal rights are then enforceable and give rise to corresponding duties, which are the conditions for their successful implementation.[22] The basic characteristics of human rights thereby are their universality and absoluteness.[23]

Esc rights have been criticised on the basis of two main conceptual assertions: first, the universal and absolute character of esc rights has been challenged. Human rights are universal in the sense that they are ascribed to every human being just by being human. But it has been argued that esc rights only refer to particular (vulnerable) groups and therefore are not universal rights. This argument, however, is based on a logical misconception: esc rights are universal because they are rights that every individual has. That only specific groups are to exercise these rights in particular situations does not diminish their universal scope. In fact, the same applies to civil and political rights – as for example, not all persons are detained, but the rights of detained people are of universal scope and everybody is entitled to those rights.[24] The second claim, that esc rights are not absolute rights, is linked to pragmatic considerations and is derived from the assumption that their enforcement depends on the availability of resources. Since not all governments have the same amount of resources available to guarantee economic and social well-being of their citizens, implementation is only progressively possible. But only those rights that can be implemented immedi-

---

[18] *R. Mckeon*, The Philosophical Bases and Material Circumstances of the Rights of Man, UNESCO Symposium, Human Rights Comments and Interpretations, 1949, p. 37; *J. Morsink*, The Philosophy of the Universal Declaration, Human Rights Quarterly 6, 309 (1984).

[19] *R. Plant*, Modern Political Thought, Oxford 1991, p. 253; for a differentiation between moral and legal rights see for instance *M. Cranston*, What are Human Rights, London, 1973.

[20] *P. Koller*, Die Kontroverse um die Menschenrechte; in: S. Gosepath/G. Lohmann (eds.), Philosophie der Menschenrechte, Frankfurt (am Main) 1998, p. 99.

[21] *H. Shue*, The Interdependence of Duties, in: P. Alston/K. Tomasevski (eds.), The Right to Food, Dordrecht 1984, p. 83.

[22] *M. Cranston*, What are Human Rights, London 1973.

[23] *M. Craven*, The International Covenant on Economic, Social and Cultural Rights, Oxford 1995, p. 10.

[24] *M. Craven*, The International Covenant on Economic, Social and Cultural Rights, Oxford 1995, p. 14.

ately and enforced are regarded as real human rights.[25] Thus, esc rights are considered to constitute long term aspirational goals[26] and it is therefore not possible to realise them immediately and fully like civil and political rights. Consequently, esc rights are perceived as being not precise, not justiciable, and therefore not enforceable. By contrast, civil and political rights are considered to allow precise definition, hence to be justiciable and enforceable.[27]

According to the second assertion, esc rights are understood as positive egalitarian or welfare rights, whereas civil and political rights are associated with negative and traditional liberal rights.[28] Accordingly, latter rights are associated with negative obligations of non-interference while the former are perceived as welfare rights that require states to take measures in order to meet their obligations – even if this means interfering with the liberty of the individual.[29] This is why esc rights are widely considered to be ideological claims that are incompatible with a free market economy and to lead to a high degree of intervention in domestic policies and individual liberties.[30] However, as all rights have to be understood as interrelated and indivisible, the assumption that one category of rights may 'trump' and override the other category of rights is not reasonable.

Related to this conceptual distinction between the two sets of rights is the more pragmatic distinction that is made between resource-intensive and cost-free rights. The claim is that the implementation of esc rights as positive rights imposes positive obligations on states and thus requires costly resources, while the negative civil and political rights are cost-free rights, merely demanding non-interference.[31] This distinction between negative civil and political rights versus positive esc rights does not seem viable.[32] For instance, while the esc right

---

[25] *M. Craven*, The International Covenant on Economic, Social and Cultural Rights, Oxford 1995, p. 15.

[26] *J.K. Mapulanga-Hulston*, Examining the Justiciability of Economic, Social and Cultural Rights, International Journal of Human Rights 4 (2002), p. 30; see also *T. Pogge*, World Poverty and Human Rights, Cambridge 2005, p. 67.

[27] *J.K. Mapulanga-Hulston*, Examining the Justiciability of Economic, Social and Cultural Rights, International Journal of Human Rights 4 (2002), p. 40.

[28] See for instance *M. Bossuyt*, La distinction juridique ebtre los droits civil et politiques et les droits économiques, sociaux et culturels, Revue des Droits de l'Homme 8 (1975), pp. 791–792.

[29] See *R. Plant*, Modern Political Thought, Oxford 1991, p. 272.

[30] *P. Alston/G. Quinn*, The Nature and Scope of States Parties' Obligations under the International Covenant on Economic, Social and Cultural Rights, Human Rights Quarterly 9 (1987), p. 159.

[31] *J.K. Mapulanga-Hulston*, Examining the Justiciability of Economic, Social and Cultural Rights, International Journal of Human Rights 4 (2002), p. 40.

[32] The argument here is that many civil and political rights require positive action as well, see for instance *J. Donnelly*, The Social Construction of International Human Rights, in: T. Dunne/N.J. Wheeler (eds.), Human Rights in Global Politics, Cambridge 1999, p. 87; *S. Holmes/C. Sunstein*, The Cost of Rights, New York 1999, pp. 37–48; *R. Plant*, A Defence of Welfare Rights, in: R. Beddard/D.M. Hill (eds.), Economic, Social and Cultural Rights. Progress and Achievement, Houndmills 1992.

to form trade unions does not require positive action by the state, the civil and political right to take part in genuine periodic elections or the right to a fair trial requires a vast amount of resources.[33] Indeed, all rights do impose negative obligations of non-interference as well as positive obligations to take measures. Thus, the twofold classification of negative and positive rights and obligations has been subject to criticism as being simplistic and artificial. It was considered to be more fruitful to:

> "[...] examine the relatively negative (duties to avoid depriving), the relatively positive (duties to aid the deprived), and the intermediate (duties to protect from deprivation) elements that are mixed together in various proportions in the implementation of just about every right."[34]

Thus, a tripartite understanding of the different dimensions of obligations has been proposed, according to which each right poses three different dimensions of obligations: the obligation to respect, the obligation to protect, and the obligation to fulfil.[35] Understood in this way, the outlined theoretical and pragmatic reasons for distinguishing between the two sets of rights must not be maintained. While the implementation of positive measures may depend on the availability of resources, this is true not only in the case of esc but also in relation to civil and political rights. Yet, negative obligations of non-interference (or of respect) are independent of the availability of resources and are to be implemented immediately.

The objections raised against esc rights are not feasible – neither theoretically nor practically. If human rights are to respect and protect the inherent value of every human being, they have to be understood as a complex concept of human rights, guaranteeing the autonomy and the well-being of the individual.[36] The application of a tripartite model of human rights obligations allows for a holistic approach towards the implementation of all human rights. Only the combina-

---

[33] On this point see *H. Shue*, Rights in the Light of Duties, in: P. Brown/D. MacLean (eds.), Human Rights and US Foreign Policy, Lexington 1979, p. 69; *G.J.H Van Hoof*, The Legal Nature of Economic, Social and Cultural Rights: A Rebuttal of Some Traditional Views, in: P. Alston/K. Tomasevski (eds.), The Right to Food, Dordrecht 1984, p. 103.

[34] *H. Shue*, The Interdependence of Duties, in: P. Alston/K. Tomasevski (eds.): The Right to Food, Dordrecht 1984, p. 84.

[35] *H. Shue*, The Interdependence of Duties, in: P. Alston/K. Tomasevski (eds.): The Right to Food, Dordrecht 1984, p. 84.

[36] *R. Plant*, Modern Political Thought, Oxford 1991, p. 267. Indeed, the relevance of esc rights can be justified in at least two ways: first, to understand them as essential conditions for the full enjoyment of civil and political rights. But this presents a weak argument as this view only ascribes an instrumental value to esc rights. Secondly, to understand esc rights as inherently valuable in themselves, regardless of what instrumental value they have for the realisation of civil and political rights. This view is, for instance, expressed by human needs theories of human rights and presents a stronger argument.

tion of civil and political rights and esc rights gives due regard to all aspects of the concept of human rights.[37]

III. Obligations under the International Covenant on Economic, Social and Cultural Rights

Looking at the respective covenants, the above discussed conceptual differentiation between esc rights and civil and political rights is reflected and supported in the different terminology and wording used in the ICCPR and the ICESCR.[38] This is particularly noticeable in relation to the nature of state obligations. Article 2 (1) of the ICESCR, which deals with the nature of state obligations, reads:

"Each State Party to the present Covenant undertakes to take steps, individually and through international assistance and co-operation, especially economic and technical, to the maximum of its available resources, with a view to achieving progressively the full realisation of the rights recognised in the present Covenant by all appropriate means, including particularly the adoption of legislative measures."[39]

Article 2 further requests states to guarantee that the rights set out in the ICESCR are to be exercised without discrimination of any kind.[40] The respective article in the ICCPR differs in the strength of state obligations. Article 2 (1) of the ICCPR reads:

"Each State Party undertakes to respect and to ensure to all individuals within its territory and subject to its jurisdiction the rights recognised in the Covenant, without distinction of any kind, such as race, colour, sex, language, religion, political or opinion, national or social origin, property or other status."

And in Article 2 (2):

"Where not already provided for by existing legislative or other measures, each State Party to the present Covenant undertakes to take the necessary steps, in accordance with its constitutional processes and with the provisions of the present Covenant, to adopt such legislative or other measures as may be necessary to give effect to the rights recognised in the present Covenant."

The Article continues by demanding states to provide for effective remedy in case of violations of the rights; to have the remedy determined by competent

[37] *G. Peces-Barba*, Reflections on Economic, Social and Cultural Rights, Human Rights Law Journal 2 (1981), p. 287.

[38] *M.J. Dennis/D.P. Stewart*, Justiciability of Economic, Social, and Cultural Rights: Should There Be an International Complaints Mechanism to Adjudicate the Rights to Food, Water, Housing, and Health?, American Journal of International Law 3 (2004).

[39] ICESCR, 1976, Article 2 (1).

[40] ICESCR, 1976, Article 2 (1).

judicial, administrative or legislative authorities; and it asks states to develop possibilities of judicial remedy and to ensure the enforcement of such remedy. The assumption of the different nature of esc and civil and political rights and therefore of state obligations is obvious. However, the nature of obligations as set out in the ICESCR has been subject to various critiques.[41]

The primary obligation in the ICESCR is to 'take steps' towards the realisation of esc rights. The obligations of state parties under the ICESCR are, however, subject to the availability of resources and of progressive achievement and realisation. This wording has led to the claim that because the ICESCR only imposes programmatic obligations, it is difficult to determine whether a government is complying with its obligations under it or not.[42] The problem here is one of threshold. However, one proposal put forward to conceptualise the main components of human rights obligations is to translate human rights into quantitative indicators. These indicators allow capturing two key factors – the willingness and the capacity of a government to protect and promote esc rights.[43] It has further been claimed that the concept of progressive realisation in relation to the availability of resources takes away the meaningful content and strength of the obligations and that governments will not be able to comply with their obligations since they are too onerous.[44] Thus, Article 2 (1) of the ICESCR has been interpreted as imposing 'obligations of result' rather than 'obligations of conduct'.[45] But, as the Committee on Economic, Social and Cultural Rights (CESCR) – the body in charge of monitoring the implementation of the esc rights in those states which are party to the ICESCR – has stated in General Comment No. 3 Article 2 (1) is best explained as incorporating a mixture of both types of obligations.[46]

---

[41] *P. Alston/H. Steiner* (eds.), International Human Rights in Context: Law, Politics, Morals, Oxford 2000, p. 246.

[42] *P. Alston/H. Steiner* (eds.), International Human Rights in Context: Law, Politics, Morals, Oxford 2000, p. 246; see also *R. E. Robertson*, Measuring State compliance with the obligation to devote the "maximum available resources" to realising economic, social and cultural rights, Human Rights Quarterly 4 (1994).

[43] *K. Tomasevski*, Indicators, in: A. Eide/A. Rosas (eds.), Economic, Social and Cultural Rights, Dordrecht 1995, pp. 389–401; with special reference to the right to food K. Tomasevski, Human Rights Indicators, The Right to Food as a Test Case, in: P. Alston/K. Tomasevski (eds.), The Right to Food, Dordrecht 1984, pp. 135–167.

[44] P. Alston/H. Steiner (eds.), International Human Rights in Context: Law, Politics, Morals, Oxford 2000, p. 244.

[45] *G. S. Goodwin-Gill*, Obligations of Conduct and Result, in: P. Alston/K. Tomasevski (eds.), The Right to Food, Dordrecht 1984, pp. 111–118; *R. Künnemann*, A Coherent Approach to Human Rights, Human Rights Quarterly 17 (1995), pp. 323–342.

[46] CESCR General Comment No. 3: The nature of States parties' obligations (art. 2, para. 1, of the Covenant), 1990; see also *P. Alston/G. Quinn*, The Nature and Scope of States Parties' Obligations under the International Covenant on Economic, Social and Cultural Rights, Human Rights Quarterly 9 (1987), p. 165.

As discussed earlier, the distinction between the two sets of human rights is based on the assumption that civil and political rights are negative rights that generate negative obligations, whereas esc rights impose positive obligations.[47] However, as discussed in the previous section, this distinction is not feasible. While civil and political rights impose obligations at all levels, even positive ones, esc rights can often be best safeguarded through states' non-interference with the use of resources possessed by the individual.[48] Thus, the tripartite model of the different state obligations better reflects the unity between the two sets of rights, as it recognises that each form of obligation exists in each and every right.[49] The model therefore allows for an integral approach to human rights and offers guidance for enforcement and implementation of esc rights.[50] The tripartite model of human rights obligations, distinguishing between the obligation to respect, the obligation to protect and the obligation to fulfil (the obligation to fulfil includes an obligation to facilitate and an obligation to provide),[51] was taken on by the CESCR in General Comment No 3.[52] In the same Comment, the CESCR determined the nature of obligations and further stated that each right generates minimum core obligations.[53] The CESCR holds that:

"[...] a minimum core obligation to ensure the satisfaction of, at the very least, minimum essential levels of each right is incumbent upon every State party. Thus, for example, a State party in which any significant number of individuals is deprived of essential foodstuffs, of essential primary health care, of basic shelter and housing, or of the most basic forms of education is, prima facie, failing to discharge its obligations under the Covenant. If the Covenant were to be read in such a way as not to establish such a minimum core obligation, it would be largely deprived of its *raison d'être*."[54]

According to the former Special Rapporteur on the realisation of esc rights, *Danilo Türk*, and in line with the principle of minimum core obligations, states are obliged to respect and ensure minimum subsistence rights for all – regard-

---

[47] *A. Eide*, Economic, Social and Cultural Rights: A Textbook, Dordrecht 2001, p. 25.

[48] *A. Eide*, Economic, Social and Cultural Rights: A Textbook, Dordrecht 2001, p. 25.

[49] *G. J. H Van Hoof*, The Legal Nature of Economic, Social and Cultural Rights: A Rebuttal of Some Traditional Views, in: P. Alston/K. Tomasevski (eds.), The Right to Food, Dordrecht 1984, p. 107.

[50] *G. J. H Van Hoof*, The Legal Nature of Economic, Social and Cultural Rights: A Rebuttal of Some Traditional Views, in: P. Alston/K. Tomasevski (eds.), The Right to Food, Dordrecht 1984, p. 108.

[51] *A. Eide*, Economic, Social and Cultural Rights: A Textbook, Dordrecht 2001, p. 23.

[52] CESCR General Comment No. 3: The nature of States parties' obligations (art. 2, para. 1, of the Covenant), 1990, Par. 10.

[53] For a detailed analysis of the mandate of the CESCR see *M. Craven*, The International Covenant on Economic, Social and Cultural Rights, Oxford 1995, pp. 35–105; see also *P. Alston*, Out of the abyss: the challenges confronting the new U. N. Committee on Economic, Social and Cultural Rights, Human Rights Quarterly 3 (1987), p. 353.

[54] CESCR General Comment No. 3: The nature of States parties' obligations (art. 2, para. 1, of the Covenant), 1990.

less of the level of economic development.[55] This ensures a basic level of enjoyment of each right.[56] Against this background, the Commission on Human Rights (CHR) urged states to consider identifying specific national benchmarks designed to give effect to the minimum core obligations in order to ensure the satisfaction of minimum essential levels of esc rights.[57] This principle of minimum core obligations was reaffirmed in the 1997 Maastricht Guidelines on Violations of Economic, Social and Cultural Rights that were elaborated by a group of distinguished experts convened by the International Commission of Jurists.[58] It is important to note, however, that minimum core obligations must not be considered to be more than a first step in realising esc rights. In particular, they do not imply that only the minimum core of esc rights is justiciable. Rather, the basic components, obligations and entitlements of each esc right need to be established.[59]

The potential qualification for esc rights to be justiciable depends greatly on what obligations arise from these rights.[60] Though the language used in the ICESCR suggests that esc rights generate different obligations from those of civil and political rights, this distinction between esc rights and civil and political rights is feasible neither on conceptual nor on pragmatic grounds. Despite the various efforts to show possible ways of implementing esc rights by way of establishing minimum core obligations and the widely acknowledged tripartite model of human rights obligations, esc rights are to this day considered as non-justiciable rights that differ significantly from civil and political rights. The main argument against considering esc rights as human rights proper has been their alleged non-justiciable nature.[61]

---

[55] CESCR General Comment No. 3: The nature of States parties' obligations (art. 2, para. 1, of the Covenant), 1990, para. 10.

[56] *United Nations/High Commissioner for Human Rights*, Economic, social and cultural rights: handbook for national human rights institutions, New York 2005, p. 22.

[57] Commission on Human Rights Resolution 1993/14.

[58] *V. Dankwa et al.*, Commentary to the Maastricht Guidelines on Violations of Economic, Social and Cultural Rights, Human Rights Quarterly 3 (1998), p. 717.

[59] *United Nations/High Commissioner for Human Rights*, Economic, social and cultural rights: handbook for national human rights institutions, New York 2005, p. 23; see also *S. Leckie*, Another step towards indivisibility; identifying the key features of violations of economic, social and cultural rights, Human Rights Quarterly 1 (1998).

[60] *J. Schneider*, Die Justiziabilität wirtschaftlicher, sozialer und kultureller Menschenrechte, Deutsches Institut für Menschenrechte, Berlin 2004.

[61] *K. Arambulo*, Strengthening the Supervision of the International Covenant on Economic, Social and Cultural Rights, Antwerp 1999, p. 55.

IV. Justiciability of Economic, Social and Cultural Rights

The ICCPR and the ICESCR differ in their terminology, in the nature of their obligations imposed upon state parties, and in their provisions for implementation and enforcement mechanisms. Despite their inclusion in international human rights law, the legal status of esc rights as human rights has all too often been denied.[62] The question of justiciability of esc rights arises in light of the nature of obligations as set out in the ICESCR. In order to be a legal right, the right must be legally definable, which in turn makes the right legally enforceable and justiciable.[63] The language used in the ICESCR is considered to be too vague for establishing clear legal entitlements and obligations. Whereas the ICCPR requires immediate compliance with its provisions, the ICESCR relativises the obligations of state parties by using a vague and indeterminate language. All these particularities have supported the perception that esc rights are not justiciable.[64] But what makes a right justiciable? Justiciability, which must be distinguished from enforceability[65], refers to the possibility of presenting a case of human rights violations before a court or to invoke the right through quasi-judicial procedures. To be justiciable, human rights must be formulated in such a way that their violation can be established by a court or through court-like mechanisms. In this sense, justiciability refers to the possibility of applying a right in a specific case by judicial or quasi-judicial bodies.[66] This requires the right to be precise enough. Thus, the fact that esc rights are often perceived as not being justiciable is linked to the assertion that these rights are dependent on a variety of factors and that due to the vagueness of their formulation, no precise

---

[62] See *E. Vierdag*, The Nature of the Rights Granted by the International Covenant on Economic, Social and Cultural Rights, Netherlands Yearbook of International Law 9 (1978), p. 82.

[63] *G.J. H Van Hoof*, The Legal Nature of Economic, Social and Cultural Rights: A Rebuttal of Some Traditional Views, in: P. Alston/K. Tomasevski (eds.), The Right to Food, Dordrecht 1984, p. 99.

[64] *P. Alston/H. Steiner* (eds.), International Human Rights in Context: Law, Politics, Morals, Oxford 2000, p. 276.

[65] While the enforcement of human rights refers to the identification of entitlements and duties created by the legal regime that need to be maintained and executed, justiciability presupposes the existence of a review mechanism to determine violations of human rights. Yet, the two concepts are closely connected. In addition, justiciability, which refers to those matters which are appropriately resolved by the courts, has to be distinguished from norms which are self-executing and therefore capable of being applied by courts without further elaboration. See for instance *J.K. Mapulanga-Hulston*, Examining the Justiciability of Economic, Social and Cultural Rights, International Journal of Human Rights 4 (2002), p. 37; and *K. Arambulo*, Strengthening the Supervision of the International Covenant on Economic, Social and Cultural Rights, Antwerp 1999, p. 56.

[66] *K. Arambulo*, Strengthening the Supervision of the International Covenant on Economic, Social and Cultural Rights, Antwerp 1999, p. 55.

legal formulation can be achieved.[67] In relation to civil and political rights, it is generally taken for granted that judicial remedies for violations are essential. However, the contrary assumption is often made in relation to economic, social and cultural rights.[68] This discrepancy is, however, justified neither by the nature of the rights nor by the relevant covenant provisions. In line with the discussion in this paper's previous sections, the claim that esc rights differ from civil and political rights and therefore are not justiciable cannot be justified.[69] In fact, the CESCR has made clear that it considers many of the provisions in the covenant to be capable of immediate implementation.[70] There is no covenant right which could not be considered to possess at least some significant justiciable dimensions – as for instance the minimum core obligation and the obligation to respect, which is in accordance with the requirement of non-discrimination.[71] Thus, the fact that esc rights are considered to be non-justiciable seems to be a consequence of their not having been transformed into positive legislation and of a lack of practice, rather than of their unique nature: there seems to be confusion between what is actually done (treated as being not justiciable) with what can be done (being justiciable). In so far as the Committee is given the authority to assume a quasi-judicial role over the rights in the covenant, those rights will be justiciable.[72]

Objections to the justiciability of esc rights stem to a large extent from the incapacity of courts to make decisions about the implementation of these rights, as they relate to policy issues and the implementation of political programmes, allocating resources and rearranging budgets. This seems to be in tension with the idea of the separation of powers.[73] It has been criticised that a court's deci-

---

[67] *K. Arambulo*, Strengthening the Supervision of the International Covenant on Economic, Social and Cultural Rights, Antwerp 1999, p. 55; see also *A. Berenstein*, Economic and Social Rights: Their Inclusion in the European Convention on Human Rights: Problems of Formulation and Interpretation, Human Rights Law Journal 2 (1981), p. 271.

[68] CESCR General Comment 9: The domestic application of the Covenant, 1998.

[69] *M. Addo*, The justiciability of economic, social and cultural rights, Commonwealth Law Bulletin 4 (1988).

[70] In its General Comment No. 3 on the nature of States parties' obligations, the CESCR cited, by way of example, articles 3; 7, para. (a) (i); 8; 10, para. 3; 13, para. 2 (a); 13, para. 3; 13, para. 4; and 15, para. 3.

[71] *J. Schneider*, Die Justiziabilität wirtschaftlicher, sozialer und kultureller Menschenrechte, Deutsches Institut für Menschenrechte, Berlin 2004, p. 24. Moreoevr, the CESCR clearly stressed in its General Comment No. 14 the justiciability of esc rights, see CESCR, General Comment No. 14: The right to the highest attainable standard of health (article 12 of the Covenant), 2000, Par. 60.

[72] *M. Craven*, The International Covenant on Economic, Social and Cultural Rights, Oxford 1995, p. 102.

[73] *F. Coomans* (ed.), Justiciability of Economic and Social Rights. Experiences from Domestic Courts, Antwerp 2006, p. 5; see also *J. Cottrell/Y. Ghai*, The Role of the Courts in the Protection of Economic, Social & Cultural Rights, in: J. Cottrell/Y. Ghai (eds.), Economic, Social and Cultural Rights in Practice, London 2004, p 86.

sion on economic and social policies threatens the separation of powers, and it has been suggested that matters involving the allocation of resources should be left to the political authorities rather than to the courts.[74] However, this argument can be raised in the context of civil and political rights as well and is not a particularity of esc rights. While the competences of the various branches of government must be respected,

> "[...] it is appropriate to acknowledge that courts are generally already involved in a considerable range of matters which have important resource implications. The adoption of a rigid classification of economic, social and cultural rights which puts them, by definition, beyond the reach of the courts would thus be arbitrary and incompatible with the principle that the two sets of human rights are indivisible and interdependent. It would also drastically curtail the capacity of the courts to protect the rights of the most vulnerable and disadvantaged groups in society."[75]

A right is justiciable if it is not only recognised as such but if there are also procedural mechanisms allowing victims of violations access to judicial or quasi-judicial review and providing adequate remedy or redress.[76] This condition for justiciability is also stressed in Article 9 of the 1984 Limburg Principles on the Implementation of the International Covenant on Economic, Social and Cultural Rights, which emphasise that states should provide for effective remedies, including judicial remedies.[77] It is further supported by CESCR General Comment No. 9, which calls upon states to provide for appropriate measures and effective administrative or judicial remedies at the domestic level.[78] In the further development of the Limburg Principles, the Maastricht Guidelines call upon states to allow for effective national and international remedies for all victims of violations of esc rights, reaffirming the justiciability of esc rights.[79] In recent years, an increasing number of states have developed judicial remedies for violations of esc rights at the national level.[80] In addition, at present, complaints are received under a number of international and regional procedures,

---

[74] *P. Alston/G. Quinn*, The Nature and Scope of States Parties' Obligations under the International Covenant on Economic, Social and Cultural Rights, Human Rights Quarterly 9 (1987), p. 170.

[75] Report of the Special Rapporteur on the right to food, *Jean Ziegler*, to the United Nations Human Rights Council, A/HRC/7/5,10 January 2008.

[76] CESCR General Comment No. 3: The nature of States parties' obligations (art. 2, para. 1, of the Covenant), 1990, Par. 5; see also F. Coomans (ed.), Justiciability of Economic and Social Rights. Experiences from Domestic Courts, Antwerp 2006, p. 4.

[77] The Limburg Principles on the Implementation of the ICESCR of 1984, principle 9.

[78] CESCR General Comment 9: The domestic application of the Covenant, 1998, Par. 10.

[79] The Maastricht Guidelines on Violations of Economic, Social and Cultural Rights (1997), Guideline 22.

[80] *United Nations/High Commissioner for Human Rights*, Economic, social and cultural rights: handbook for national human rights institutions, New York 2005, p. 23; see also F. Coomans (ed.), Justiciability of Economic and Social Rights. Experiences from Domestic Courts, Antwerp 2006.

giving guidance on how esc rights may be reviewed or may be invoked through quasi-judicial procedures.[81] Creating precedents benefits not only the victims in a particular case but can be used positively in other cases as well.

For many years the inferior status of esc rights has had a negative impact on the possibilities to claim effective implementation of these rights, both at the international and the domestic level. However, over the last ten years, developments at the international level supported the justiciability of esc rights, culminating in the recent adoption of the Optional Protocol to the ICESCR.[82] The ICESCR so far has only allowed for monitoring through state reports, but the coming into force of the Optional Protocol to the ICESCR, allowing for an individual complaint procedure, marks a significant progress at the international level in developing the justiciability of esc rights. The Optional Protocol is the result of in-depth discussions during five sessions of the open-ended working group on the nature of esc rights and on the best ways to ensure respect, protection and fulfilment of these rights. With the adoption of the Optional Protocol, the Human Rights Council brings to completion a process that started in 1993 at the Vienna World Conference on Human Rights. The CESCR was asked to prepare a first draft Optional Protocol in 1996; inter-governmental negotiations commenced in 2004.[83] Adopted by the Human Rights Council on 18 June 2008, the Protocol was given final approval by the UN General Assembly in December of the same year. The adoption of the Optional Protocol on the 60th anniversary of the UDHR reaffirmed the Council's commitment to the interdependence and indivisibility of human rights:

"Since the adoption of the two core international human rights covenants in 1966, the lack of a complaint procedure for economic, social and cultural rights has been a missing piece in the international human rights protection system [...] As we are celebrating the 60 years anniversary of the Universal Declaration of Human Rights, the Optional Protocol reaffirms our commitment to a unified and comprehensive vision of human rights, sending a strong, unequivocal message about the equal value and importance of all human rights."[84]

---

[81] For instance the International Labour Organisation, UNESCO, San Salvador Protocol to the American Convention on Human Rights, the African Charter on Human and Peoples' Rights and the European Social Charter, and the Optional Protocol to the International Convention on the Elimination of All Forms of Discrimination against Women and the Convention on the Rights of the Child among others.

[82] *P. Alston*, No Right to Complain About Being Poor: The Need for an Optional Protocol to the Economic Rights Covenant, in: A. Eide/J. Helgesen (eds.), The Future of Human Rights Protection in a Changing World: Fifty Years Since the Four Freedoms Address – Essays in Honour of Torkel Opsahl, Oslo 1991; see also F. Coomans (ed.), Justiciability of Economic and Social Rights. Experiences from Domestic Courts, Antwerp 2006.

[83] Vienna Declaration and Programme of Action, 1993; see also UN.Doc. Gen A/HRC/8/7, 2008.

[84] See http://www.unog.ch/unog/website/news_media.nsf/(httpNewsByYear_en)/91C1 D8EE6730CD72C 125746C0054 8987?Open Document (accessed 19 January 2009).

The Optional Protocol builds on the experience of the existing mechanisms established in similar instruments related to other UN human rights treaties, as well as on the developments in case law at the national, regional and international level. It allows persons to petition an international human rights body concerning violations of rights guaranteed under the ICESCR. As the High Commissioner stressed in her address to the Working Group on 31 March 2008, the establishment of a communication procedure under the ICESCR presents a milestone in the history of universal human rights, "putting to rest the notion that legal and quasi-judicial remedies are not relevant for the protection of esc rights".[85]

The Optional Protocol, which reaffirms the universality, indivisibility, interdependence and interrelatedness of all human rights, covers Part II and III of the ICESCR.[86] This new instrument allows communications from or on behalf of individuals or groups of individuals concerning alleged violations of states' obligations under the covenant[87], provides the CESCR with the possibility to decide upon interim measures[88] and to carry out inquiries in situations of grave and systematic violations of esc rights.[89] The CESCR must thereby not consider communications unless it has ascertained that all *available* domestic remedies have been exhausted.[90] The wording of this article suggests that if such domestic remedies are not available, communications may be made to the CESCR directly. This is an important provision, as in some countries, the justiciable nature of esc rights remains contested and no domestic remedies exist. Furthermore, the Optional Protocol takes into account the importance of international assistance and cooperation in the progressive realisation of esc rights.[91]

---

[85] See: http://www.unog.ch/unog/website/news_media.nsf/(httpNewsByYear_en)/91C1 D8EE6730CD72C 125746C0054 8987?Open Document (accessed 19 January 2009).

[86] Report of the Open-ended Working Group on an optional protocol to the International Covenant on Economic, Social and Cultural Rights, Gen. A/HRC/8/7, Geneva 2008, Annex I, Preamble.

[87] Report of the Open-ended Working Group on an optional protocol to the International Covenant on Economic, Social and Cultural Rights, Gen. A/HRC/8/7, Geneva 2008, Annex I, Article 2.

[88] Report of the Open-ended Working Group on an optional protocol to the International Covenant on Economic, Social and Cultural Rights, Gen. A/HRC/8/7, Geneva 2008, Annex I, Article 5.

[89] Report of the Open-ended Working Group on an optional protocol to the International Covenant on Economic, Social and Cultural Rights, Gen. A/HRC/8/7, Geneva 2008, Annex I, Article 11.

[90] Report of the Open-ended Working Group on an optional protocol to the International Covenant on Economic, Social and Cultural Rights, Gen. A/HRC/8/7, Geneva 2008, Annex I, Article 13.

[91] Report of the Open-ended Working Group on an optional protocol to the International Covenant on Economic, Social and Cultural Rights, Gen. A/HRC/8/7, Geneva 2008, Annex I, Article 14.

While compromises have been made, the Optional Protocol is a significant achievement.[92] The Optional Protocol, that will enter into force once it has been ratified by ten states[93], finally places esc rights on an equal footing with civil and political rights in terms of international legal protection. It provides victims of violations of esc rights with an international complaint mechanism, and encourages states to ensure greater protection of these rights at the national level.

V. The Right to Food and its Justiciability

The right to food is both enshrined in the UDHR, Article 25, and in the ICESCR, Article 11. Article 25 of the 1948 UDHR states:

"Everyone has the right to a standard of living adequate for the health and well-being of himself and of his family, including food, clothing, housing and medical care and necessary social services, and the right to security in the event of unemployment, sickness, disability, widowhood, old age or other lack of livelihood in circumstances beyond his control."[94]

The ICESCR recognises in Article 11 the right to an adequate standard of living, including adequate food, as well as the fundamental right to be free from hunger.[95] It further recognises that the right to freedom from hunger requires international cooperation, and relates to matters of production, the agriculture and global supply.[96] In line with the tripartite model of human rights obligations, the CESCR in General Comment No. 12 of 1999 defined the obligations that states parties have to meet in order to implement the right to adequate food at the national level. These are as follows:

1. The obligation to *respect* existing access to adequate food requires state parties not to take any measures that result in preventing such access;
2. the obligation to *protect* requires measures by the state to ensure that enterprises or individuals do not deprive individuals of their access to adequate food;
3. the obligation to *fulfil (facilitate)* means the state must pro-actively engage in activities intended to strengthen people's access to and utilization of resources and means to ensure their livelihood, including food security. Whenever for reasons beyond their control, and individual or group is unable to enjoy the right to adequate food by the means

[92] Though previous negotiations supported an ‚à la carte' approach, where state parties pick and choose the rights which will be justiciable under the Optional Protocol to the ICESCR, a comprehensive approach was eventually agreed on. See UN Doc. E/1997/22, Annex IV, Par. 25.

[93] Report of the Open-ended Working Group on an optional protocol to the International Covenant on Economic, Social and Cultural Rights, Gen. A/HRC/8/7, Geneva 2008, Annex I, Article 18.

[94] UDHR, 1948, Article 25.

[95] ICESCR, 1976, Article 11; see also *M. Craven*, The International Covenant on Economic, Social and Cultural Rights, Oxford 1995, pp. 306–329.

[96] ICESCR, 1976, Article 2.

at their disposal, states have the obligation to *fulfil (provide)* that right directly. This obligation also applies to persons who are victims of natural or other disasters.[97]

Using the tripartite model of human rights obligations, the CESCR was in a position to render more precisely the nature of state obligations entailed in Article 2 of the ICESCR. In 2000, the Special Rapporteur on the Right to Food, *Mr. Jean Ziegler*[98], was appointed with the task of advancing the topic at the international level, of observing the worldwide situation of food security, and of writing a yearly report on this.[99] The Special Rapporteur implements the mandate through different means and activities. He presents annual reports to the UN Human Rights Council and to the UN General Assembly on the activities and studies undertaken in the view of implementing the mandate and monitors the situation of the right to food throughout the world, he identifies general trends related to the right to food, he visits countries which provide him with a firsthand account of the situation concerning the right to food in a specific country, and he communicates with states and other concerned parties with regard to alleged cases of violations of the right to food and other issues related to the mandate; and he promotes the full realisation of the right to food through dialogue with relevant protagonists by participating in seminars, conferences, meetings of experts.[100]

In 2002, *Jean Ziegler* defined the right to food as the human right to have regular, permanent and unrestricted access, either directly or by means of financial purchases, to quantitatively and qualitatively adequate and sufficient food corresponding to the cultural traditions of the people to whom the consumer belongs, and which ensures physical and mental, individual and collective fulfilment and dignified life free of fear.[101] This definition compromises all normative elements included in General Comment 12 of the CESCR, which states that:

"[...] the right to adequate food is realized when every man, woman and child, alone or in community with others, have the physical and economic access at all times to adequate food or means for its procurement. The right to adequate food shall therefore not be in-

[97] CESCR General Comment No. 12: The right to adequate food (Art. 11), 1999; see also *H. Shue*, The Interdependence of Duties, in: P. Alston/K. Tomasevski (eds.), The Right to Food, Dordrecht 1984.

[98] Since 2008 *Oliver De Schutter* is Special Rapporteur on the Right to Food.

[99] The mandate of the Special Rapporteur on the right to food was originally established by the Commission on Human Rights in April 2000 by resolution 2000/10. Subsequent to the replacement of the Commission by the Human Rights Council in June 2006, the mandate was endorsed and extended by the Human Rights Council by its resolution 6/2 of 27 September 2007.

[100] See http://www2.ohchr.org/english/issues/food/overview.htm (accessed 19 January 2009).

[101] Report to the Commission on Human Rights, UN. Doc. E/CN.4/2002/58; see *M. Craven*, The International Covenant on Economic, Social and Cultural Rights, Oxford 1995, pp. 306–329.

terpreted in a narrow or restrictive sense which equates it with a minimum package of calories, proteins and other specific nutrients. The right to adequate food will have to be realized progressively. However, States have a core obligation to take the necessary action to mitigate and alleviate hunger even in times of natural or other disasters."[102]

Freedom from hunger, which General Comment 12 designates as more pressing and immediate, could be measured by the number of people suffering from malnutrition and in the extreme, dying of starvation. The right to *adequate* food is thereby a much higher standard, including not only the absence of malnutrition, but the full range of qualities associated with food, including safety, variety and dignity, in short, all those elements needed to enable an active and healthy life.[103]

As outlined in the previous sections, while all the rights under the ICESCR are meant to be achieved through progressive realisation, states do have some minimum core obligations which are of immediate effect. As regards the right to food, states have the obligation to refrain from any discrimination in access to food as well as to means and entitlements for its procurement, on the grounds of race, colour, sex, language, age, religion, political or other opinion, national or social origin, property, birth or other status.[104] According to the CESCR, food is available when a person has the possibility to feed him- or herself through the products of the land and natural resources or if the availability of food is guaranteed by way of functioning systems of distribution, processing, and commercialisation.[105] States are further prohibited from taking retrogressive or deliberate measures which result in the deterioration of the current level of fulfilment of the right to food. In its General Comment No. 12, the CESCR made it clear that in most regions of the world the problem is not one of scarcity of resources, but of lacking access to food or the resources necessary for the procurement of food.[106] Indeed, it is well established that there is enough food produced in the world to feed the present world population. Thus, rather than being a matter of availability of resources, it is a question of their just distribution and the structure of the global economic system.[107] Yet, while the ICESCR requires that states take whatever steps are necessary to ensure that everyone is free from hunger and can enjoy the right to adequate food as soon as possible, they do have a margin of discretion in choosing the ways and means of imple-

---

[102] CESCR General Comment No. 12: The right to adequate food (Art. 11), 1999.

[103] CESCR General Comment No. 12: The right to adequate food (Art. 11), 1999; see also *M. Craven*, The International Covenant on Economic, Social and Cultural Rights, Oxford 1995, pp. 306–329.

[104] CESCR General Comment No. 12: The right to adequate food (Art. 11), 1999, para. 18.

[105] CESCR General Comment No. 12: The right to adequate food (Art. 11), 1999, para. 25.

[106] CESCR General Comment No. 12: The right to adequate food (Art. 11), 1999, para. 25.

[107] See *F. Moore et al.*, World Hunger: 12 Myths, Institute for Food and Development Policy, 2006, http://www.foodfirst.org/files/pdf/BG%20SU06%2012%20Myths%20About%20Hunger.pdf (accessed 19 January 2009).

menting the right to adequate food – as long as they ensure the satisfaction of the minimum essential level required to be free from hunger.[108]

Regarding the acknowledgement of the right to food, positive trends can be observed.[109] The right to food was included in the plan of action at the 1996 World Food Summit with the goal to halving the number of starving people by 2015. As a response to the 1996 World Food Summit, the Food and Agriculture Organization of the United Nations (FAO) set up an inter-governmental working group five years later, in 2001, to draft voluntary guidelines to assist states in achieving the progressive realisation of the right to food. In 2004, The Voluntary Guidelines to Support the Progressive Realization of the Right to Adequate Food in the Context of National Food Security were adopted.[110] Among other things, the Voluntary Guidelines show how the right to food can be incorporated into government strategies and institutions.[111] They provide a detailed interpretation of the right to food, emphasising its international dimension and stressing the importance of food security.

Despite these positive trends, the number of starving people has actually increased since then. While states are obliged to progressively realise the right to food, the number of people suffering from hunger has increased significantly in the last decade – from about 848 million to 923 million in 2007/2008.[112] In 2008, the CESCR expressed its concern at the rapid worldwide rise in food prices and the high energy prices that have caused a global food crisis and are adversely affecting the right to adequate food and freedom from hunger as well as other human rights of more than 100 million people.[113] As a result of domestic and global challenges, there is an urgent need to re-examine and strengthen the sta-

---

[108] CESCR General Comment No. 12: The right to adequate food (Art. 11), 1999, para. 21.

[109] For a summary of success stories and demonstration of how the right of food may be realised see W. Strothenke (ed.), Success for Human Dignity, FIAN International Publication, Heidelberg 2007.

[110] Voluntary Guidelines fort the Realization of the Right to Adequate Food in the Context of National Food Security, FAO, Rom 2005; *A. Kundu/ J. Stish*, Right to Food Case Study: India. Study conducted for FAO in support of the Intergovernmental Working Group in the Elaboration of a set of Voluntary Guidelines fort the Realization of the Right to Adequate Food in de context of national Food Security, FAO, Rom 2004. On the relation between the right to food and food security see *A. Eide, et al.*, Food Security and the Right to Food in International Law and Development, Transnational Law & Contemporary Problems 1 (1991); *K. Mechlem*, Food Security and the Right to Food in the Discourse of the United Nations, European Law Journal 5 (2004), pp. 631–648.

[111] *FAO*, Right to Food in Action. Examples of How FAO Member Countries Make it Happen, Rome 2007.

[112] *International Food Policy Research Institute (IFPRI)*, The Global Hunger Index. The Challenge of Hunger 2008, http://www.ifpri.org/pubs/cp/ghi08.pdf (accessed 19 January 2009).

[113] See CESCR Statement: The World Food Crisis, UN Doc. E/C.12/2008/1, 2008.

tus of esc rights.[114] The recognition of the individual esc rights at the national and international level is thereby of utmost importance for their implementation.[115] Justiciability is essential for the realisation of the right to food:

> "[...] the real test of the effectiveness of a system of international protection for human rights is whether it provides an international remedy for the individual whose rights are violated. From that perspective, possibilities for complaints by individuals are a necessary component of a future supervisory system related to the human right to food."[116]

As determined earlier, the right to food is justiciable when victims may not only claim their right politically, but have the possibility of bringing their case to court and getting a positive verdict.[117] The alleged differing natures of the two sets of rights are reflected in the various wordings used in the ICESCR and the ICCPR. These resulted not only from a different perception of these rights at the time of drafting, but also had consequences on the later perception and implementation of esc rights, which received a weaker formulation. As a result, there are questions to this day around the justiciability of esc rights.[118] However, international recognition of the justiciability of esc rights is increasing rapidly, particularly due to the frequent consideration of esc rights by domestic courts in many states and because of recent developments at the international level.[119] In several countries, these developments have led to the recognition of the right to food at the national level.[120] For instance, India provides one of the best examples in showing ways to adjudicate the right to food.[121] The right to

[114] See *J.K. Mapulanga-Hulston*, Examining the Justiciability of Economic, Social and Cultural Rights, International Journal of Human Rights 4 (2002), p. 30; *J. Mowbray*, The Right to Food and the International Economic System: An Assessment of the Rights-Based Approach to the Problem of World Hunger, Leiden Journal of International Law 20 (2007), pp. 545–569.

[115] Report of the Special Rapporteur on the right to food, *Jean Ziegler* to the Human Rights Council, A/HRC/7/5,10 January 2008. For an extensive discussion of several case studies at the national level see: F. Coomans (ed.), Justiciability of Economic and Social Rights. Experiences from Domestic Courts, Antwerp 2006.

[116] *G. Westerveen*, Towards a System for Supervising States. Compliance with the Right to Food, in: P. Alston/K. Tomasevski (eds.), The Right to Food, Dordrecht 1984.

[117] This includes compensation for the damage suffered, a guarantee for non repetition, and the expeditious enforcement of the court's orders.

[118] *J.K. Mapulanga-Hulston*, Examining the Justiciability of Economic, Social and Cultural Rights, International Journal of Human Rights 4 (2002), p. 36; for a discussion of the different dimensions of state obligations see *A. Eide*, The Right to an Adequate Standard of Living including the Right to Food, in: A. Eide (ed.), Economic, Social and Cultural Rights, Dordrecht 1995, pp. 99–105.

[119] *United Nations/High Commissioner for Human Rights*, Economic, social and cultural rights: handbook for national human rights institutions, New York 2005, p. 23; see also F. Coomans (ed.), Justiciability of Economic and Social Rights. Experiences from Domestic Courts, Antwerp 2006.

[120] See GTZ (2005): http://www.gtz.de/de/themen/laendliche-entwicklung/armut-hunger/2298.htm (accessed 19. January 2009).

[121] See E/CN.4/2006/44/Add.2.

life is recognised as a directly justiciable fundamental right by the Indian Constitution,[122] while the right to food is defined as a directive principle of state policy.[123] As it has interpreted these provisions, the Supreme Court of India has found that the government has a constitutional obligation to take steps to fight hunger and extreme poverty and to ensure a life with dignity for all individuals.[124] In South Africa, all economic and social rights have been declared justiciable under South African law. The South African Bill of Rights, incorporated into the 1996 Constitution, explicitly provides that every person has the right to access to sufficient food and water.[125] Dealing with concrete cases contributes to further clarification and better understanding of the content and scope of esc rights in general and the right to food in particular – thereby supporting the justiciability of esc right.[126] Indeed:

> "[...] to achieve realisation of the right to food – and one might add: of human rights in general – the limited monitoring system of the ICESCR as it exists today is insufficient and needs to be supplemented by a mechanism of communications for individuals and groups, which makes identification and potential redress of violations or non-compliance in the framework of the ICESCR possible."[127]

The adoption of the Optional Protocol to the ICESCR adds an individual complaints procedure to the existing monitoring system of the ICESCR, thus allowing persons to petition an international human rights body about violations of rights guaranteed in the ICESCR, among others the right to food. The Optional Protocol represents a particular success in the acknowledgment of the justiciability and in advanced protection of esc rights. By determining the content of particular esc rights, the Optional Protocol allows the CESCR to continue its interpretative work that began with the General Comments and Concluding Observations.[128] This said, like all other individual complaint procedures, the Optional Protocol to the ICESCR only provides a limited monitoring

---

[122] Article 21 of the Indian Constitution.

[123] Article 47 of the Indian Constitution.

[124] For an examination of the right to food in India see for instance *FIAN-Gruppe Berlin*, Der Kampf umd das Menschenrecht auf Nahrung in Indien, in: K. Roepstorff/E. Töpfer/Subin Nijhawan (eds.), Menschenrechte in Indien, Südasien-Informationen Nr. 8, September 2005.

[125] Section 27, para. 1 (b) of the South African Constitution; see also *FIAN*, Decision by South African High Court ends long lasting fight of fishermen, retrieved from http://www.fian.org (accessed 19. 01. 2009).

[126] *K. Arambulo*, Strengthening the Supervision of the International Covenant on Economic, Social and Cultural Rights, Antwerp 1999, p. 176.

[127] *K. Arambulo*, Strengthening the Supervision of the International Covenant on Economic, Social and Cultural Rights, Antwerp 1999, p. 125.

[128] *M. Engels*, Verbesserter Menschenrechtsschutz durch Individualbeschwerdeverfahren?, Zur Frage der Einführung eines Fakultativprotokolls für den Internationalen Pakt über wirtschaftliche, soziale und kulturelle Rechte, München 2000, p. 326.

mechanism. Final enforcement of esc rights largely depends on the willingness and commitment of states.

VI. Conclusion

Esc rights have been challenged as not being legal rights and as being categorically different from civil and political rights. However, a categorical distinction is not tenable. While there might be differences in terms of historical evolution, philosophical justification or ways of implementation between the various human rights, these differences cannot be made by ascribing negative rights and duties only to civil and political rights and positive rights and duties to esc rights. A distinction based on this categorisation is arbitrary and does not derive from the nature of the rights themselves.

The perception of esc as non-justiciable rights is more a consequence of their not having been transformed into positive legislation and of lack of practice than a result of their unique nature. Indeed, there is confusion between what is actually done (treated as not justiciable) and what can be done (being justiciable). This argument finds support in the recent adoption of an Optional Protocol to the ICESCR that will allow persons to petition an international human rights body concerning violations of rights guaranteed in the ICESCR, among others the right to food. Moreover, the work of a number of international and national human rights organisations has led to the thematic prioritisation of esc rights in development work and the increasing acceptance of esc rights both in the wider public and among experts. However, final enforcement of esc rights largely depends on the willingness and commitment of states.

Children's Rights in Practice: The Participation of Children in Care and Protection Decisions

Tali Gal[*]

I. Introduction

The goal of this chapter is to explore the percolation of international children's rights (mainly the participation right) into child protection decision making processes, where professionals, representatives of the State, make decisions regarding children and families. A decision to place a child in a foster care, kinship care or adoption, changes the child's life fundamentally, and has long and short term psychological, physical and social effects. Therefore, it is important to examine the status given to children in such decisions and the implementation of international standards regarding the participation of children in decision making processes that concern their lives.

After a short discussion of international children's rights, I suggest that the standard way to understand and implement these international norms can be considered a liberal approach to children's human rights, and I discuss the central characteristics of such an approach. To demonstrate its main characteristics, the Israeli child protection administration will be considered as a case study. Then, an alternative way to perceive human rights, called a restorative approach, is presented and discussed. The introduction of the restorative approach uncovers the limitations of the liberal approach to human rights and offers a broader discourse regarding children's human rights. Family Group Conferencing is then reviewed as a central instrument for implementing a restorative approach to children's human rights. Empirical findings regarding both its potential and its challenges are considered. The concluding part highlights the central differences emerging between liberal and restorative implementations of children's rights, based on the two case studies presented in this paper.

* I am in debt to David Levi-Faur for many helpful conversations and especially for coning the phrase "restorative bureaucracy". Part of the research conducted for this paper was supported by the Adler Research Center for Child Welfare and Protection at the Tel Aviv University, and I am grateful for their help.

II. Children's Human Rights

In 1989 the adoption of the United Nations Convention on the Rights of the Child (CRC) by the UN General Assembly marked a watershed in discourse around children's rights.[1] The CRC has been the single most widely ratified treaty ever.[2] The Convention sets up a comprehensive bill of children's rights, which include both self-determination and protective rights. For the first time, the Convention acknowledged children as individuals fully entitled to human rights, without neglecting their special needs for protection.[3] The Convention is also unique because of its coherent nature and indivisible articles, with children's dignity as its central theme that should be read into each one of its articles.[4] The CRC includes the widest variety of rights for children – social, legal, cultural, civil and human rights – and therefore represents a new, broader approach to children's rights. Children are no more regarded as merely objects of protection (although the right to be protected is a central principle); they are human beings, part of the world's community, and thus deserve to be treated with respect for their human rights and freedoms. Most importantly, the CRC provides a broad framework of citizenship for children through the introduction for the first time of the *participation principle.*[5]

The participation principle includes two aspects: First, it provides children who are capable of doing so with the right to *express* their opinions freely in all matters affecting them. Second, and for the first time in an international document, it provides that their opinions will be considered and given *due weight* according to their age and maturity.[6] Article 12(2) specifies the application of the participation principle with respect to judicial and administrative proceedings, where the child's views should be heard particularly, expressed either by the child personally or by a representative.

---

[1] *S. Bessel/T. Gal*, Forming Partnerships: The Human Rights of Children in Need of Care and Protection, International Journal of Children's Rights 17 (2009), p. 283.

[2] *C.P. Cohen*, The Relevance of Theories of Natural Law and Legal Positivism, in: M. Freeman/P. Veerman (eds.), The Ideologies of Children's Rights, Dordrecht 1992, pp. 53 ff.

[3] *S. Detrick/J. Doek/N. Cantwell*, The United Nations Convention on the Rights of the Child: A Guide to the "Travaux Preparatories", Boston 1992.

[4] *G.B. Melton*, Socialization in the Global Community: Respect for the Dignity of Children, American Psychologist 46 (1991), no. 1, pp. 66 ff.; *G. Van Bueren*, Combating Child Poverty: Human Rights Approaches, Human Rights Quarterly 21, (1999), no. 3, pp. 680 ff.

[5] *J. Roche*, Children: Rights, Participation and Citizenship, Childhood 6 (1999), pp. 475 ff.

[6] *R. Hodgkin/P. Newell*, Implementation Handbook for the Convention on the Rights of the Child, New York 2002, p. 145.

III. "Standard" Implementation of Children's Human Rights: A Liberal Approach

The CRC has been extremely successful in triggering rhetoric around children's rights, and in particular the right to participation. But what participation means and how it can be achieved in a manner that is practically useful and meaningful for children is often unclear. In many cases, children's participation has been translated into practice as the presence of children. Rarely is the format of these processes changed sufficiently to ensure that children are able to genuinely participate and affect the outcome.[7] When comprehensive children's rights reforms have been introduced to child protection policies, they have led to a significant increase in child abuse reports and investigations on the one hand (based on the child's right to protection), and an emphasis on procedural rights for children and parents during decision making processes on the other (based on the participation right).[8] Therefore, the standard and most common way of understanding children's human rights can be called liberal: formal, adversarial, and individualistic.

The centrality of due process rights is typical in liberal reforms. The uniqueness of liberalism is the constant contest between competing rights and interests of individuals.[9] The traditional liberal theory of rights assumes independent, rational individuals who are capable of making choices and expect freedoms from governmental interference. Children, then, present a challenge to the liberal theory of rights, because they do not fit into this theoretical framework.[10] Consequently, it has been argued that children cannot be rights-holders, as they are incapable of making choices and exercising or waiving their rights.[11] Therefore, in modern rights-based reforms of bureaucracies dealing with children (such as child protection), tests and assumptions regarding children's maturity and capability act as central gatekeepers for the inclusion of children in decision making processes.

A further characteristic of the liberal human rights perspective is the centrality of the individual and his/her privacy. A liberal reform in child protection

---

[7] *S. Bessel*, Adult Attitudes towards Children's Participation in the Philippines, under review, Childhood (2007).

[8] See Australian Law Reform Commission/Human Rights and Equal Opportunity Commission 1997, regarding care and protection legislation; *A. Cooper/R. Hetherington/I. Katz*, The Risk Factor: Making the Child Protection System Work for Children, London 2003, on the British reform.

[9] *D. Williams/T. Young*, Governance, the World Bank and Liberal Theory, Political Studies 42 (1949), no. 1, pp. 84 ff.

[10] *M. Minow*, Children's Rights: Where we've Been, and Where we're Going, Temple Law Review 68 (1995), p. 1573 (1579).

[11] *H. L. A. Hart*, Essays on Bentham: Studies in Jurisprudence and Political Theory, Oxford 1982.

centers on the child's and the parents' interests as represented by them (or their authorized representative) only. Other people having meaningful relationships with the direct stakeholders are typically excluded from the process in order to uphold their privacy. Although the exclusion of supporters from the discussion has its justifications, it also limits the scope of ideas for a treatment plan for the child and local resources for supporting the family in safeguarding the child's best interests.

IV. The Case of Israeli Child Protection Decision Making Processes

One recent example of such a liberal approach based on rights is the Israeli child protection administration and its 2006 reform. Until recently, children's right to participate was not regulated, and in practice children's inclusion in the process was lacking to non-existent. The 2006 reform is significant, then, in the promotion of children's rights in the context of child protection. At the same time, the liberal-restorative delineation discussed later in this chapter illuminates the limitations of this reform and others resembling it in other parts of the world, and proposes a step forward in the implementation of children's human rights. The following section provides a brief review of the work of child protection decision committees in Israel, the critiques against their work and the consequent reform. It then highlights its liberal characteristics.

'Decision Committees' are a central instrument in Israeli child protection administration. Decision Committees provide a forum in which all relevant professionals meet together to exchange information, evaluate current and future risks, explore various treatment options, and develop a detailed treatment plan – all regarding children who are at risk of abuse or neglect.

Prior to the 2006 reform, the Israeli Social Work Regulations[12] was the single normative guidance for child protection workers treating at-risk children and their families. In addressing the work of decision committees, the regulations stated that it is "… *recommended* to invite the child's parent *or* the child him/herself to the discussion *or parts of it*, according to the needs and the *discretion* of the committee's coordinator or the committee as a whole." (Emphasis added by the author.)

It is easy to see that the Regulations viewed children not as partners to the process, but as potential "guests" in it, whenever this seemed appropriate to the committee's coordinator and members. Not surprisingly, a 2001 comprehensive

[12] *State of Israel, Ministry of Social Affairs and Social Services*, Social Work Regulations, Section 8.9, updated 30 November 30 1995. http://www.molsa.gov.il/MisradHarevacha/HomePageMenu/Regulations/SocialRegulations/Tas_Perek_8.htm (accessed 7 December 2008).

study on the work of Israeli decision committees by the Brookdale institute[13] found very limited participation of children and their families, and other problems in the work of decision committees. The following is a summary of these findings.

- There was little or no physical inclusion of children in meetings (only 15–25% of children were present and only 5% of coordinators reported that children in the appropriate age group were routinely invited to the committees).[14]
- Even when children were invited, it was to get their input, and they were typically excluded from the critical stages of the discussion.[15]
- The preparation of children and their parents for the committees was minimal to non-existent.[16]
- There was no reference to child representation or any other means to support their active participation in an adult-oriented forum.
- Information exchanged within the decision committee was typically not presented to children or their parents.[17]
- The decision was eventually reached by professionals, without the family's knowledge of the process (no transparency).[18]
- Cultural and professional gaps were obstacles to involving family members in the discussions.[19]

It seems that concerns about exposing children to potentially harmful situations, combined with insufficient knowledge regarding ways of involving children of various ages in decision making processes were at the heart of this lacking-to-non-existent inclusion of children and youth in the work of Israeli Decision Committees. Indeed, the inclusion of children in an adult-based process where painful matters are discussed presents considerable challenges that require special attention.[20] There are indications, however, that children and

[13] *T. Dolev/R. Benbenishty/A. Timer*, Decision Committees in Israel: Their Structure, Work Procedures and Outcomes – Final Report (Hebrew), Jerusalem 2001.

[14] *T. Dolev/R. Benbenishty/A. Timer*, Decision Committees in Israel: Their Structure, Work Procedures and Outcomes – Final Report (Hebrew), Jerusalem 2001, p. 59.

[15] *T. Dolev/R. Benbenishty/A. Timer*, Decision Committees in Israel: Their Structure, Work Procedures and Outcomes – Final Report (Hebrew), Jerusalem 2001, p. 57.

[16] *T. Dolev/R. Benbenishty/A. Timer*, Decision Committees in Israel: Their Structure, Work Procedures and Outcomes – Final Report (Hebrew), Jerusalem 2001, p. 90.

[17] *T. Dolev/R. Benbenishty/A. Timer*, Decision Committees in Israel: Their Structure, Work Procedures and Outcomes – Final Report (Hebrew), Jerusalem 2001, pp. 59 ff.

[18] *T. Dolev/R. Benbenishty/A. Timer*, Decision Committees in Israel: Their Structure, Work Procedures and Outcomes – Final Report (Hebrew), Jerusalem 2001, p. 65.

[19] *T. Dolev/R. Benbenishty/A. Timer*, Decision Committees in Israel: Their Structure, Work Procedures and Outcomes – Final Report (Hebrew), Jerusalem 2001, p. 61.

[20] *P. Nixon*, Seen but Not Heard? Children and Young People's Participation in Family Group Decision Making: Concepts and Practice Issues, American Humane 22 (1) (2006), pp. 20 ff.

young people usually want to participate in such proceedings and are willing to take the risk of being exposed to more harmful information than most professionals are willing to give.[21]

In response to public criticism against the work of child protection workers in Israel, the General Director of the Ministry of Welfare in 2004 presented a proposal for reform.[22] In 2006 the reform was launched, and today it is in the process of assimilation. The 2004 governmental proposal stated that the reform should be based on values such as partnership with parents, stakeholders' empowerment, and the focusing on strengths. In practice, the reform emphasizes the procedural rights of parents and children and strengthens their status in the decision making process. The reform explicitly refers to the UN Convention on the Rights of the Child while discussing the right of children to participate in the process, but leaves it to the discretion of the committees to balance it with protection considerations (which of course are also part of the Convention). Importantly, the reform creates age-based assumptions for the inclusion (or exclusion) of children in the discussions: children under 12 shall not take part in discussions unless decided otherwise. Children over 12 shall participate if they want to, but protective considerations might prevent their inclusion. All children, however, shall be given the opportunity to give their opinion, be it before the whole committee or in person with their social worker or the head of the committee. In addition, participating children will be prepared and informed beforehand, and will be supported by someone of their choice. All children will be informed about the committee's decision.

The 2006 reform significantly strengthened the status of children in the decision making process regarding their placement. However, a deeper look at the reform's provisions reveals that the liberal assumptions of capacity and rationality are still at the heart of the decision whether a child can actively participate or not. Indeed, although the reform includes provisions regarding the preparation of the child for the meeting and their right to have their views considered, their actual participation in the process depends on estimations regarding the child's maturity and level of understanding of the matter discussed, as well as the child's best interests. Clearly, there is tension between the right to participate

---

[21] *G. B. Melton/S. P. Limber*, What Children's Rights Mean to Children: Children's Own Views, in: M. Freeman/P. Veerman (eds.), The Ideologies of Children's Rights, Dordrecht 1992, pp. 167 ff.; *A. J. Hicks/J. A. Lawrence*, Children's Criteria for Procedural Justice: Developing a Young People's Procedural Justice Scale, Social Justice Research 6 (1993), no. 2, pp. 163 ff.; *K. Marshall*, Children's Rights in the Ballance: The Participation-Protection Debate, Edinburgh 1997; *J. A. Lawrence*, Safeguarding Fairness for Children in Interactions with Adults in Authority: Computer-Based Investigations of the Judgments of Secondary School Students, Report to Criminology Research Council 2003.

[22] *State of Israel*, Committees for Planning, Treatment and Evaluation: Decisions of the Implementation Team, Ministry of Social Affairs and Social Services, unpublished policy statement, 29 April 2004.

and (in some cases) the child's best interests, and this reform chose to leave much discretion to the committee in balancing the two. In practice this means that only if a participating child is evaluated (by the decision making professionals themselves) as mature enough to form a reasonable view (and could that be a view that contradicts the professionals' view?), can his or her opinion be considered seriously.

In addition, the suggested reform emphasized procedural rights of parents and children, including the right to be present, be provided with information, adequate preparation for the discussion, a right to appeal to a higher institution, and a right to be represented. The reform resembles other reforms based on the liberal notion that no intervention in the private sphere is justified unless due process rules have been fully implemented. Similar to incarceration, coerced physical examination, telephone monitoring and so on, state intervention in the family unit based on the Decision Committee's assessment can only be executed, according to the reform, if all procedural safeguards have been maintained.[23] The emphasis on procedural rights and representation at every stage of the decision making process leads to an adversarial relationship between the child, the family and the child-protection social worker. In such an adversarial atmosphere resembling that of the criminal court, it is difficult to imagine an open, trustful and effective deliberation regarding the various options available to the child and the parents.

V. From Liberal to Restorative Understandings of Children's Rights

Perhaps there could be another direction: a restorative reform based on a broader understanding of the CRC, in which children are perceived as respected members of their communities and of society in general; a reform in which power is shifted to families and children in a way that enables them, with the support of significant others, to reach decisions in true partnership with professionals; one that is less adversarial, less focused on procedural rights and more on respect for children and other individuals; a reform that welcomes a pluralistic, informal, participatory process.

Restorative justice, most commonly used in youth justice as a diversion from the criminal justice process, can be seen as an example of such a broad understanding of children's human rights.[24] Born out of disappointment with both the retributive and rehabilitative justice paradigms, restorative justice has

[23] See *C. Lupton/P. Nixon*, Empowering Practice? A Critical Appraisal of the Family Group Conference Approach, Bristol 1999, p. 14, for a similar description of the New Right ideology in the UK during the 1980's and 1990's.

[24] *T. Gal*, Victims to Partners: Child Victims and Restorative Justice, Australian National

emerged as a 'third lense',[25] according to which "... crime is a violation of people and relationships. It creates obligations to make things right. Justice involves the victim, the offender, and the community in a search for solutions which promote repair, reconciliation, and reassurance".[26]

Tony Marshall[27] provided the most widely accepted definition of restorative justice, according to which it is

> "... a process whereby parties with a stake in a specific offence collectively resolve how to deal with the aftermath of the offence and its implications for the future".

According to *Braithwaite*,[28] the parties with a stake in the offence are typically victims, offenders and the affected community; the damage to be restored is whatever the stakeholders see as needing to be restored.

The United Nations' *Basic Principles on the Use of Restorative Justice Programmes in Criminal Matters*[29] provide a similar definition. A 'restorative process' is defined as

> "... any process in which the victim, the offender and/or any other individuals or community members affected by a crime actively participate together in the resolution of matters arising from the crime, often with the help of a fair and impartial third party. Examples of restorative justice process include mediation, conferencing and sentencing circles (Article I (3))."

Restorative justice fosters the equal participation of the stakeholders and focuses on their emotional and social rehabilitation while respecting their human rights.[30] It puts the stakeholders – the victim, the offender and the relevant community – at the center of the decision making process, thereby empowering them to take an active role in repairing the harm that resulted from the crime. The recurring notions of empowerment, active participation and non-domination apply to all participants.

Proponents of restorative justice often regard it not merely as an instrument of diversion from the criminal justice process, but rather as a holistic approach which can be applied in almost every aspect of our daily lives, such as in school

---

University, Canberra 2006. http://thesis.anu.edu.au/public/adt-ANU20061114.100521/index.html (accessed 24 January 2009).

[25] *H. Zehr*, Changing Lenses: A New Focus for Criminal Justice, Scottsdale 1990; *H. Strang*, Repair or Revenge: Victims and Restorative Justice, Oxford 2002, p. 43.

[26] *H. Zehr*, Changing Lenses: A New Focus for Criminal Justice, Scottsdale 1990, p. 181.

[27] *T. F. Marshall*, Restorative Justice: An Overview, Technical Report, Home Office, London 1999, p. 5.

[28] *J. Braithwaite*, Restorative Justice: Assessing Optimistic and Pessimistic Accounts, Crime and Justice 25 (1999), p. 1 (6).

[29] *United Nations*, Principles on the Use of Restorative Justice Programmes in Criminal Matters, Economic and Social Council Resolution 2002/12.

[30] *J. Braithwaite*, Principles of Restorative Justice, in: A. Von-Hirsch/J. V. Roberts/A. Bottoms (eds.), Restorative Justice and Criminal Justice: Competing or Reconcilable Paradigms, Oregon 2003, pp. 1 ff.

bullying,[31] white collar crime,[32] families,[33] as well as in international disputes and terrorism.[34] It is therefore possible to treat restorative justice not only as a mechanism to solve criminal disputes, but to use its values as an alternative approach in the understanding and implementation of human rights.

A restorative approach to human rights can be found in the CRC itself. The Convention articulates a comprehensive, interrelated network of children's rights, reflecting a multidimensional understanding of rights. The Convention's guiding principles of equality, best interests, participation, and the right to life, survival and development are indivisible and should be read into each one of the Convention's other provisions.[35] This interlinking method offers a broad, flexible and yet powerful network of rights which extends beyond the protection-autonomy dichotomy. In other words, the integrated use of the four guiding principles provides a tool for resolving internal dilemmas and ostensibly conflicting priorities in the application of children's rights. To put it in another way, the Convention, when read through a restorative lense, creates a utopian framework in which the worlds surrounding children are being fitted according to the children's special needs, allowing them to be active participants in them. At the same time, this approach acknowledges the centrality of the child's family, relatives, culture and nationality.[36]

A restorative approach to human rights is similar to *Martha Minow*'s relational approach: *Minow*[37] argues against the liberal-based capacity threshold. She contends that to argue that children are different from adults because they lack power, obscures the fact that it is the *relationship* that creates the power differences, and these can be changed. Autonomy, she argues, is not a precondition for having rights. Rather, being a rights holder depends on a community willing for the individual to make claims and participate in the ongoing definitions of personal and social boundaries. Self determination rights therefore express the interconnections between the right holders and others who have obligations towards them.

---

[31] *B. Morrison*, Bullying and Victimization in Schools: A Restorative Justice Approach, Trends and Issues in Crime and Criminal Justice 219 (2002), pp. 1 ff.

[32] *J. Braithwaite*, Markets in Vice, Market in Virtue, Sydney and New York, Federation Press and Oxford University Press 2005.

[33] *J. Pennel/G. Burford*, Family Group decision making: Protecting Children and Women, Child Welfare 79 (2000), no. 2, pp. 131 ff.

[34] *J. Braithwaite*, Pre-Empting Terrorism, Current Issues in Crime and Criminal Justice 17 (2005), no. 1, pp. 96 ff.

[35] *R. Hodgkin/P. Newell*, Implementation Handbook for the Convention on the Rights of the Child, New York 2002.

[36] *T. Gal*, Victims to Partners: Child Victims and Restorative Justice, Australian National University, Canberra 2006. http://thesis.anu.edu.au/public/adt-ANU20061114.100521/index.html (accessed 24 January 2009), p. 48.

[37] *M. Minow*, What Ever Happened to Children's Rights?, Minnesota Law Review 80 (1995), p. 267 (299 ff.).

Similarly, a restorative approach to human rights sees autonomy and rationality not as a capacity threshold to enter the circle of decision makers, but as developmental rights and needs of children (as well as all other individuals) that are promoted through opportunities to take part in shared decision making processes. In other words, a restorative reading of the Convention leads to an inclusive attitude toward children. The Convention requires society to make the needed adjustments to *include* children in public discourse while addressing their vulnerabilities, instead of excluding them from the adult world due to their limited experience and lack of maturity. Specifically, the CRC stipulates that children should be encouraged to develop their evolving capacities, receive any aids they need to overcome disabilities and take part in decision making processes according to their capabilities. Indeed, in restorative settings such as FGC (discussed below), respectful listening and empowering support allows for even the most disempowered to present their standpoints, experiences and wishes in an effective way, thus enabling the listeners to take the "perspective of the other", in *Minow*'s words.

VI. Family Group Conferencing: A Restorative Approach in Practice

One restorative mechanism being used in the child protection context is Family Group Conferencing. FGC typically involves the child, parents, family members and relatives, and existing communities of support such as friends, teachers, spiritual leaders or others who have significant relationships with them. A facilitator arranges an agreed-upon setting and leads the discussion, but otherwise leaves as much of the discussion as possible to the participants to work out for themselves. Other professionals may also be present to provide information. The objective, however, is that the decisions be made by family members, not the professionals. In some programs, professionals and non-family participants leave the room during "family private time", and the child (if possible) and his or her family remain to decide on a plan. After an agreement is reached, the other participants are invited in and the plan then needs to be approved by the participants.

Child protection conferencing is being used in North America, Europe (especially the UK), Australia, New Zealand (where it was initiated) and Israel (in a limited way).[38] Evaluation studies indicate the potential of FGCs as a child-inclusive decision making process and in reaching effective outcomes: children

[38] *J. D. Siepert/J. Hudson/Y. Unrau*, Family Group Conferencing in Child Welfare: Lessons from a Demonstration Project, Families in Society 81 (2000), no. 4, pp. 382 ff.; *L. Brown*, Mainstream or Margin? The Current Use of Family Group Conferences in Child Welfare Practice in the UK, Child and Family Social Work 8 (2003), pp. 331 ff.

are present in the vast majority of conferences, including children as young as five;[39] children aged 11 or 12 and over are regularly present at conferences, and their presence was generally described as 'painful but appropriate'.[40] Indeed, more children attend and participate in conferences compared with other child protection decision making processes. Most conferences ended with a positive agreement to a plan,[41] sometimes with surprisingly creative solutions.[42] Participants show high levels of satisfaction and children benefit from the process.[43] However, there are some indications that implementation is not always satisfactory,[44] although it has been suggested that other child protection procedures do not generate higher implementation rates.[45]

Naturally, the practice of FGC is not without challenges. Perhaps the most serious concerns relate to the involvement of young children.[46] In a recent international survey of child protection FGCs conducted by *Nixon et al.*,[47] children's participation varied. Most programs had restrictions on children's participation, typically due to the nature of the discussion or the child's age and understanding. Children's safety was a major concern.[48] Only in very few programs were children asked whether they wanted to participate. It was also clear that procedures regarding the participation of children were not regulated but more in the hands of practitioners.[49] The authors concluded, however, that with

---

[39] *J. Robertson*, Research on Family Group Conferences in Child Welfare in New Zealand, in: J. Hudson/A. Morris/G. Maxwell/B. Galaway (eds.), Family Group Conferences: Perspectives on Policy and Practice, Leichhardt 1996, pp. 49ff.

[40] *P. Marsh/G. Crow*, Family Group Conferences in Child Welfare, Malden 1998, p. 93, 103.

[41] *J. Robertson*, Research on Family Group Conferences in Child Welfare in New Zealand, in: J. Hudson/A. Morris/G. Maxwell/B. Galaway (eds.), Family Group Conferences: Perspectives on Policy and Practice, Leichhardt 1996, pp. 49ff.; *S. Fraser/J. Norton*, Family Group Conferencing in New Zealand Child Protection Work, in: J. Hudson/A. Morris/G. Maxwell/ B. Galaway (eds.), Family Group Conferences: Perspectives on Policy and Practice, Leichhardt 1996, pp. 37ff.

[42] *P. Marsh/G. Crow*, Family Group Conferences in Child Welfare, Malden 1998, p. 145.

[43] *P. Marsh/G. Crow*, Family Group Conferences in Child Welfare, Malden 1998, p. 120.

[44] *J. Robertson*, Research on Family Group Conferences in Child Welfare in New Zealand, in: J. Hudson/A. Morris/G. Maxwell/B. Galaway (eds.), Family Group Conferences: Perspectives on Policy and Practice, Leichhardt 1996, pp. 49ff.; *P. Marsh/G. Crow*, Family Group Conferences in Child Welfare, Malden 1998, p. 146.

[45] *P. Marsh/G. Crow*, Family Group Conferences in Child Welfare, Malden 1998, p. 148.

[46] *P. Nixon/G. Burford/A. Quinn/J. Edelbaum*, A Survey of International Practises, Policy and Research on Family Group Conferencing and Related Practises (2005). http://frg.ord.uk/pdfs/Family%20Group%20practises%20report.pdf (accessed 24 January2009), p. 34.

[47] *P. Nixon/G. Burford/A. Quinn/J. Edelbaum*, A Survey of International Practises, Policy and Research on Family Group Conferencing and Related Practises (2005). http://frg.ord.uk/pdfs/Family%20Group%20practises%20report.pdf (accessed 24 January 2009).

[48] *P. Nixon/G. Burford/A. Quinn/J. Edelbaum*, A Survey of International Practises, Policy and Research on Family Group Conferencing and Related Practises (2005). http://frg.ord.uk/pdfs/Family%20Group%20practises%20report.pdf (accessed 24 January 2009), p. 36.

[49] *P. Nixon/G. Burford/A. Quinn/J. Edelbaum*, A Survey of International Practises, Poli-

good preparation, adequate planning and sometimes a support person or an advocate, children 'can experience good levels of participation in conferences'.[50]

Indeed, considering children's limited experience and evolving communication skills, a child-inclusive reform needs to find ways of enhancing children's ability to have meaningful participation in the process with maximum protection for their wellbeing. Adults also need to develop their ability to listen to children and understand their messages. The flexible and informal nature of restorative mechanisms allow for such accommodations to occur. The findings regarding FGCs suggest that even in these sensitive and complex matters, children, parents, relatives and professionals can sit together and reach an agreement. Indeed, the conclusions of most reviews of existing studies are positive regarding the operation of FGCs[51].

VII. Conclusion: Conceptualizing the Differences

Three principal differences emerge between the liberal and restorative approaches as reflected in the two case studies presented here, which directly affect the status of the stakeholders. These are demonstrated in *Figure 1.*

The first concerns the *level* of participation of stakeholders in the process. While a liberal reform invites stakeholders to have their say in the process through rules safeguarding their presence, opportunities to speak and receive information, to appeal and so on, a restorative approach transforms stakeholders from invited guests to equal partners in the process. Stakeholders are able to make decisions, not only to affect governmental decisions.

The second difference is the *breadth* of participation. If a liberal reform in child protection strengthens the status of at-risk children and their parents, a restorative reform goes beyond the nuclear family and regards significant others as stakeholders whose contribution to the decision making process is central.

The third difference concerns the *threshold* for meaningful participation in the decision making process. A liberal reform requires some capacity test in order to adhere to the assumption of rationality on which it is based. Children, therefore, are "usual suspects" in this model and even when included in the process, their views are considered with reservations. A restorative reform, on

---

cy and Research on Family Group Conferencing and Related Practises (2005). http://frg.ord.uk/pdfs/Family%20Group%20practises%20report.pdf (accessed January 24 2009), p. 37.

[50] *P. Nixon/G. Burford/A. Quinn/J. Edelbaum*, A Survey of International Practises, Policy and Research on Family Group Conferencing and Related Practises (2005). http://frg.ord.uk/pdfs/Family%20Group%20practises%20report.pdf (accessed 24 January 2009), p. 35.

[51] *C. Lupton/P. Nixon*, Empowering Practice? A Critical Appraisal of the Family Group Conference Approach, Bristol 1999, p. 100.

the other hand, acknowledges the unique experience and perspective of each of the stakeholders and regards every standpoint as relevant. The informality of the process allows for all styles of communication to flow and affect the outcome.

	Liberal Reform	*Restorative reform*
Level of participation:	Invited guests	Equal partners
Breadth of participation:	Children and parents	Other supporters are included
Threshold for participation:	Capacity & best interests test	All stakeholders are welcome

Figure 1: Restorative and Liberal Approaches to Human Rights in Child Protection Reforms

An optimistic account of the Israeli child protection reform can consider it as a positive development in child protection administration. It specifically refers to the CRC and the right of children to participate, to receive age-appropriate information, and to be represented. However, the positioning of the reform within a liberal framework reveals its inability to move the status of children from being guests in the process to equal partners. Additionally, meaningful acquaintances and relatives of the child and the family are excluded from the process, thus failing to acknowledge the interdependencies between the child, the parents, and the community around them. Furthermore, a liberal framework rests on assumptions of capabilities, independence and rationality, thus presenting unique challenges when the "customers" are children. Can a formal process accept the wishes and claims of a young child, even when supported by a representative, when they contradict the opinions of other participants? The answer is, at best, that this is definitely a challenge.

The contrast between the liberal and restorative approaches is not as clear-cut as it is in theory. In fact, many of the articles of the Israeli reform adhere to a restorative approach, such as the plea for partnership with children and families, an emphasis on providing information, and the right of children and parents to invite someone meaningful to the committee. It is therefore possible that the coming years will mark a significant shift in professionals' attitudes toward the inclusion of children and their parents in Decision Committees' discussions. Still, taking the democratic values of equality, freedom and a voice with regard to children seriously requires a step forward to a redistribution of power between professionals, families and children, from the initial stage of choosing the process to the actual treatment plan. The Family Group Conferencing is an example in which families, with the support of professionals and the active involvement of their communities of support, are the decision makers. A restorative bureaucracy utilizes FGC or similar mechanisms as the default option for most children; only in those cases where a restorative process has failed to secure the safety of the child, can child protection professionals assert their decision making power and intervene in the least intrusive way.

Report on the Discussions

Human Rights Traditions and Perspectives

Discussions during the Symposium

Kristina Kühl

Israeli and German participants used the symposium to argue animatedly with one another without regard to nationality- and status-boundaries. Diverse perspectives on the international human rights debate were discussed and interesting research results as well as questions to be explored further presented. The following article highlights the main focus points of the discussions.[1]

I. The Cultural and Local Imprint on the Universal Idea of Human Rights

The idea of human rights is a universal one. Thus the 1948 Universal Declaration of Human Rights states that the "recognition of the inherent dignity and of the equal and inalienable rights of *all* members of the human family" shall be promoted and protected. The discussion of the lectures by *Daniel Bogner* (Max-Weber-Kolleg Erfurt) and *Markus-Michael Müller* (Freie Universität Berlin) focused on the confrontation of this idea with the particular circumstances in the various countries. Both speakers emphasized that when analyzing the human rights situation in a specific country, the cultural embeddedness needs to be taken into account. *Bogner* highlighted especially the important link between historical experiences and the present validity of human rights and stated that experiences are very significant for the normative as well as the factual validity of a norm. *Müller* deepened this point, using the example of the paradoxical history of human rights implementation in Mexico. In looking at the "written" history of the country, it can be seen that, on the one hand, human rights ideas emerged progressively early in Mexico's declarations; but, on the other hand, the history of their concrete implementation has been one with many dark chapters. For instance, Mexico has always clearly emphasized the

[1] Most, but not all of the papers mentioned in this article are inclosed in this book.

social and economic rights more than the liberal rights of opposition to the state, which are more traditional in Europe[2]. But the resulting more active role of the state was not taken seriously, so that the local population did not develop a positive and affirmative image of legal subjectivity and awareness of human rights.

Müller underlined that one shouldn't take one's own Western experiences as a criterion when analyzing the present situation. There were different facets of modernity in the process of closing the gap between the abstract idea and the concrete implementation of human rights. Existing structures should always be seen as a product of dynamic processes. Moreover, *Bogner* said, a thoughtful handling of experiences also bears possibilities for effectively implementing strategies, and this should not be neglected when seeking to contribute towards the acceptance of the idea of human rights. Therefore, promotion strategies need to be tailored exactly according to the particular context[3].

II. Fertile Ground: Awareness of Human Rights and Knowledge of their Violation

The idea of the universal validity of human rights needs the fertile ground of acceptance in the population in order to prosper. Therefore *Michael Bongardt* (Freie Universität Berlin) spoke of a "two-way-approach". He believes that international human rights organizations need to take a look at local contexts so as to adjust their promotion strategies accordingly. At the same time, awareness of human rights within the population needs to be strengthened so that there is enough backup "from below". To achieve this goal, the specific cultural foundations of human rights and the political experiences again need to be taken into account. For example, in a country like Mexico, one must take into consideration that there was no trust in the enforcement of human rights and that social rights played an important role. *Claudia Mahler* (Menschenrechtszentrum der Universität Potsdam) dealt with education as regards human rights, a goal to

[2] In this regard, there were interesting results to a study in Guatemala by *B. Kieselbach* (Menschenrechte in Guatemala: Einstellungen, Einsatzbereitschaft und psychologische Einflussvariablen, Marburg 2004, unpublished diploma thesis, quoted by: *J. Stellmacher/G. Sommer/E. Brähler*, Menschenrechte – Paradoxien einer bahnrechenden Idee, Wissenschaft und Frieden 2006, no. 1, pp. 40 (41)): When asked, 61% of the people spontaneously named the right to education while the right to religious freedom was named a lot less (11%).

[3] Critical regarding this point concerning the European Union's promotion strategies, *T.A. Börzel/T. Risse*, One Size fits All! EU Policies for the Promotion of Human Rights, Democracy and the Rule of Law, Paper prepared for the workshop on Democracy Promotion, 4–5 October 2004, Center for Development, Democracy and the Rule of Law, Stanford University, October 2004; http://iis-db.stanford.edu/pubs/20747/Risse-Borzel-stanford_final.pdf (accessed 25 January 2009).

which the United Nations gave top priority over the last few years. But as *Mahler* said, even at the end of the "United Nations Decade for Human Rights Education"[4] and during the "World Programme for Human Rights Education"[5], there were still big deficits to be filled in so that people worldwide could address their problems as human rights violations and stand up for their rights in an appropriate way. Access to information is the decisive factor and needs to be increased throughout the world – and by the way, this problem exists not only in developing countries but also, for example, in Germany[6]. In addition, teachers and other professionals working in the field of education need to be trained in human rights questions. The other participants in the discussion agreed that political declarations of intent are not enough; the practical effects are decisive. In this field, goals can only be achieved in the long term.

In addition to the awareness of human rights and their importance, knowledge of human rights violations is also necessary in order to get rid of such deficits. *Hadas Eyal* (Hebrew University of Jerusalem) highlighted the role that new media such as the internet, camcorders or notebooks can play in this regard. She emphasized the particular importance of the connection between new and old mass media for the recognition of human rights violations by the public. Mass media all over the world could sharpen their audience's attentiveness to human rights violations by using multimedia-based and unfiltered "eyewitness-accounts". One should remember the Iranian or Chinese oppositional bloggers whose disappearance and imprisonment attracted attention throughout the world. *Eyal* also described various cases from Israel's more recent past: Videos showing Israeli soldiers dealing violently with Palestinians without an identifiable reason gave rise to a lot of discussions among the public. The videos were made by residents of the Gaza strip. The camcorders had been distributed by members of the Israeli human rights organization *Betzelem*, which in doing so used a new way of campaigning for human rights issues. A controversial discussion followed on whether or not it was possible to speak of progress in practical human rights work. After all, the Israeli military had called these incidents "sad individual cases" and they were not discussed in the media for very long. Others argued that the accumulation of cases like these in traditional media would pull

---

[4] For further information on the United Nations Decade for Human Rights Education (1995–2004), see the homepage of the Office for the High Commissioner of Human Rights of the United Nations, http://www.unhchr.ch/html/menu6/1/edudec.htm (accessed 10 February 2009).

[5] For further information on the World Programme for Human Rights Education (2005-ongoing), see the homepage of the Office for the High Commissioner of Human Rights of the United Nations, http://www2.ohchr.org/english/issues/education/training/programme.htm (accessed 10 February 2009).

[6] Cf. *J. Stellmacher/G. Sommer/E. Brähler*, Menschenrechte – Paradoxien einer bahnbrechenden Idee, Wissenschaft und Frieden 2006, no. 1, pp. 40ff.

the rug out from under the feet of these appeasement theories and bring about changes in the long run.

III. Need for Implementation on an International Level

In various panel discussions, the thesis came up that effective human rights protection can only be assured on an international level.

1. Transboundary Problems

One reason for this lies in the specific theme of some human rights constellations. For instance, *Avinoam Cohen* (Tel Aviv University) presented his view on the democratization of migration processes. The background to his thoughts is the assumption that (co-)determining the rules that determine your own life is a fundamental element of democratic societies. But in reality, this normative ideal has failed completely. Given the increasing globalization, there have been ambitions over the past few years to regulate migration processes in cooperation with non-state actors without looking at national boundaries. But these attempts still lack sufficient options for the participation of migrants. Those who took part in the discussion argued that the individual state as a sovereign entity still needs to be the starting point for regulations. But phenomena like the transnational labor mobility of employees or migration streams over several countries would demand state-overlapping solutions. So long as the right to vote is connected to citizenship rather than residence even for people who have lived in a country for several years – as in Germany – it is still a long way until migrants are granted full political participation.

Kristina Roepstorff (Freie Universität Berlin) raised another topic which by its nature needs to be solved internationally: In her lecture she dealt with the justiciability of the human rights layed down in the 1976 International Covenant on Economic, Social and Cultural Rights (ICESCR) and focused especially on the right to food, which is anchored in Art. 11 ICESCR and requires special attention during a world food crisis. *Roepstorff* argued against the common notion that the rights of the ICESCR were already structurally different to political rights as layed down in the International Covenant on Civil and Political Rights (ICCPR). The less attention and importance given to social rights is not the consequence of their vague wording or unrealistic promises, but the result of insufficient steps taken towards implementing them, such as organizing an individual complaint procedure, *Roepstorff* argued. Confronted with the critique that social rights would also interfere with the separation of powers because the financial costs would impair the latitude of the legislative branch, she replied that political rights are also not for free; people need empowerment to use their rights: An exact division of social and political rights is not possible. Only the synopsis of social and political rights would draw a complete picture of human rights. In 2008, the protection of the ICESCR-rights made decisive progress: With the adoption of the Optional Protocol to the ICESCR by the United Nations Assembly in December of that year, the way for an individual complaint procedure has been paved. This is an important step towards equality with the ICCPR-rights and for the right to food, which can only be solved on a global level.

2. *Structural Deficits*

Another reason which could make implementation on an international level necessary is a structural one: Many lectures touched on the fact that on the national level, there are often not the right institutions and sometimes not the corresponding will to enforce human rights.

The absence of adequate institutions and rules can sometimes be due to the fact that a country is already in a complicated peace process. In her presentation, *Sarah Wittkopp* (Freie Universität Berlin) spoke about the enforcement of participation rights of women in such situations. She examined the obligation imposed on states by international human rights agreements to let women participate in peace processes. In her lecture, she focused especially on Art. 7 and 8 of the Convention on the Elimination of All Forms of Discrimination against Women (CEDAW). She spoke of the peace processes in Northern Ireland and Uganda as examples and advocated a comprehensive and early inclusion of women in peace processes. In fragile post-conflict settings, no cutbacks are possible. This is the only way to establish a non-discriminatory, safe society. It is even harder to include single groups later in the process. Therefore, *Wittkopp* stated, the argument that one should first think about peace before wasting time over the luxury of participation rights is not convincing.

The lecture given by *Felicitas Chen* (Freie Universität Berlin) focused on two institutions which from the start have acted transnationally. She presented her thoughts on the correlation between the enforcement of human rights and the loan policy of the Worldbank and the European Bank for Reconstruction and Development (EBRD). *Chen* first explained the different conceptions of both banks: While the Worldbank is explicitly not allowed to engage in political activities but only focuses on economic actions, the EBRD also pursues political policies and was founded in 1991 to pave the way for a liberal economy in the new democratic countries of the former Eastern Bloc. But in practice, the differences are not so big. The reason for this is that the member states of the Worldbank themselves have signed many human rights treaties. For both banks, *Chen* discovered more hesitation as regards the enforcement of social and ecological rights than of political rights. This probably goes back to the different ideologies behind both, as well as the member states of the banks. It is only possible to see the single state as one among others, which, as the case may be, does not promote human rights sufficiently, on an international level.

The idea of a necessary international approach is also important in the repressive arena of international criminal law. The right institutions to prosecute these crimes often may not exist, and frequently the necessary will is also missing. *Julia Volkmann-Benkert* (Freie Universität Berlin) and *Alona Hagay-Frey* (Tel Aviv University) highlighted this problem in their lectures on the protection of women in armed conflicts. They demonstrated the history of the punishability of sexual assaults. *Hagay-Frey* explained that after an "era of silence", there came a time when rape was considered a crime against honor ("era of honor"). Finally, both analyzed the present rules of the 1998 Rome-Statute, the legal foundation of the International Criminal Court (ICC) in The Hague. *Volkmann-Benkert* pointed out Art. 17 and Art. 124 of the Statute. Art. 17 deals with the legitimacy of a case before the ICC. Sufficient "gravity of the crime" is needed. She pleaded for a new interpretation of this term in rape cases, which would do justice to the vulnerability of the victims – independently of their gender. Cases which do not meet the criteria of systematic crimes should also be covered. *Hagay-Frey* stated particularly clearly that the present rules are not sufficient. The particularity of sexual assaults, of the attack on a human being as a *woman* should be stated more clearly. Offenders should be convicted for both: crimes against human beings as *enemies* (murder, torture) and crimes against human beings as *women* (rape). The particular importance of a comprehensive punishability at the international level was also explained with the missing (enforcement of the) punishability at the national level.

IV. Division of Responsibility between State and Society

A point that was touched on in many lectures was the division of responsibility between the state and society when implementing comprehensive human rights protection.

The courts at state level are one suitable instrument of enforcement in individual cases. *Aharon Barak*, who was President of the Supreme Court of Israel until 2006, spoke impressively in the opening session of the symposium about a judge's responsibility in society[7]. He believes that the duties of a judge can be summed up in two elemental points for society. First, the judge must protect the constitution; secondly, he or she must close the gap between law and society. In doing so, he or she must always aim at maintaining the necessary balance between the law's flexibility and its stability. Law must respond to social change

[7] Cf. *Aharon Barak*, The Judge in a Democracy, Princeton 2006.

and must be democratic; at the same time, it must not lose itself in the process. The values of society should be taken into account, but a judge should not decide blindly like the majority wants. Also, he or she needs to be aware of his and her own preconceptions.

On the international level, there are courts and other state-owned institutions as well, which advance the protection of human rights. In her lecture, *Sigrid Boysen* (Freie Universität Berlin) presented the system of human rights protection within the supranational entity of the European Union. She highlighted especially the relationship of the European Court of Justice (ECJ) and the Federal Constitutional Court (*Bundesverfassungsgericht*) in Germany, starting with the famous Solange I-decision (1975), by way of Solange II (1986), up to the decision on the "Bananenmarktordnung" (2000)[8], in which the Federal Constitutional Court stated once again that it would not touch the jurisdiction of the ECJ so long as the protection of general fundamental rights was assured. *Boysen* also spoke about the complicated relationship between the ECJ and the European Court of Human Rights and explained the Bosphorus-decision. She further dealt with the relationship between human rights jurisprudence in the European Union and international law under the United Nations.

When speaking about comprehensive human rights protection, non-state actors cannot be left out of the picture. *Ferry Bühring* (Freie Universität Berlin) approached this question theoretically and took a closer look on the relationship between international human rights law and non-state actors. Aiming to involve those better in international human rights protection, he expressed his thoughts on how to adjust the traditional legal state-centered conception of international law. *Ofer Sitbon* (Tel Aviv University) was concerned with concrete possibilities for involving private companies in the enforcement of human rights. Based on the assumption that the numerous self-regulations in private business have so far not achieved much (except in the field of child labor) and have helped the companies more to improve their image than to enforce human rights, *Sitbon* took a look at a state's attempt to transform these self-commitments into legal rules – as Britain did with the Britain Companies Act in 2006. Section 172 of the Companies Act states now, that in making his or her decisions, the director of a company must consider "the impact of the company's operations on the community and the environment" and "the desirability of the company maintaining a reputation for high standards of business conduct". Even though so far there are no measurable results from this new regulation, *Sitbon* concluded that already the legislative work had benefited the promotion of human rights: The topic was brought onto the public agenda and the dialogue between internationally active companies and human rights organizations was advanced. The discussion circled around the advantages and disadvantages of different regulative

[8] BVerfG, 2 BvL 1/97 from 7 June 2000.

and deregulative approaches. Some argued in favor of bringing both approaches into a productive dialogue in terms of "responsive regulation"[9].

Avishai Benish (Hebrew University of Jerusalem) channeled the discussion towards a specific problem concerning the inclusion of private actors in the transformation of social rights, the privatization of social welfare programs. Looking at more recent developments in Israel and Wisconsin (USA), *Benish* examined the advantages and disadvantages of the changes made under the keyword "new governance": modifications in administration towards more flexibility and decentralized organization as well as the shift in the distribution of welfare benefits to private actors. He was especially skeptical when speaking about the shift of discretionary decisions to decentralized levels or even private actors. Furthermore, where private actors are concerned, the apropriate democratic legitimation is questionable. Also, alluding to the principles of the free market is only possible to a limited extent; the customer has no real choice. Many participants in the discussion viewed especially the privatization of necessary services of general interest – as for example the supply of water[10] – with skepticism.

In speaking about the inclusion of private actors, interest was again focused on the media. After all, the media have been called the "fourth branch" in a democracy. Their high impact should be utilized when seeking to increase the knowledge of human rights violations (see the lecture by *Eyal*) and to put pressure on other actors. So, as *Cohen* suggested, bringing the discussion into the media and thereby putting pressure on national states to make changes, could be a way of strengthening migrants' rights to participation. *Yael Ronen* (Hebrew University of Jerusalem) addressed the problem that the media can on the other hand also activate human rights violations. Using the example of the so-called "media case", in which the head of a radio station was convicted for incitement to genocide in Rwanda on the grounds of "superior responsibility", *Ronen* took a look at the much discussed question of "command responsibility" in international criminal law with regard to the exceptional constellation of private actors. In addition to the fact that there was no military acquisition, she also highlighted the fact that the victims of this crime were not individually identifiable. The case is also so interesting because of the media's special possibility as an instrument of incitement. Therefore, special care should be taken in how they are handled. *Ronen* reasoned that one needs to take into account that private companies are less rigorously structured than the military. The pressure on employees to obey orders is not as high. Therefore one needs to be careful when adopting criteria.

---

[9] Cf. *I. Ayres/J. Braithwaite*, Responsive Regulation: Transcending the Deregulation Debate, Oxford University Press, New York 1992.

[10] Cf. *Klaus Lederer*, Strukturwandel bei kommunalen Wasserdienstleistungen: eine Untersuchung aus verwaltungswissenschaftlicher Perspektive, Berlin 2004.

V. Human Rights as a Protective Fig Leaf?

In various panel discussions, the question was raised, whether human rights were not being used in some contexts more as a nice label to polish the image than as a serious commitment. This problem was addressed in connection with the inclusion of companies in the protection of human rights. Around this topic, there was a controversial discussion of whether the fact that companies always also look to their profit when cooperating in a social project would dilute the idea of human rights and therefore not bring it to a "real realization". In order to evaluate this, the question regarding the criteria of implementation would first of all have to be clarified. Less skeptical participants in the discussion said that it could not do any harm if companies put part of their profits into social projects and cared about aspects of human rights when producing their goods, even if their only motive had to do with image. This approach could be added to other strategies for implementing human rights.

Image reasons are also interesting for states in a globally networked world. Thus, states gladly refer to the constant improvement of human rights in their country when they apply for money at the international community of states (see *Chen*'s lecture) or when they are clearly seeking to strengthen their trade connections. *Müller* explained that the desire to be accepted as a modern and democratic state in the international community is a strong driving force for Mexico. Incidentally, the enforcement of human rights is itself now a highly competitive market. *Müller* said further that in the direct work of local actors, dependence on international sponsors and competition between the different NGO's to get the approval of a financially strong one, plays an important role.

VI. Balancing Different Human Rights Interests

When enforcing human rights concretely in an individual case, one consistently comes up against conflicting human rights interests that need to be addressed. This was obvious in various panel discussions. For instance, *Tali Gal* (Hebrew University of Jerusalem) focused in her presentation on one of the strongest interventions concerning the right to parenthood. She talked about the possibilities of placing a child outside its family when the wellbeing of the child is no longer assured within the family. The children, whose rights are stipulated in the United Nations Convention on the Rights of the Child, are especially affected by such actions. Starting with the present Israeli rules, *Gal* described a reform which was recently introduced by the Israeli Ministry of Welfare. This reform is supposed to strengthen the role children and parents play in the procedure, giving them the right to be present or at least adequately represented at all meetings and to propose their own plan of treatment. *Gal* presented an alternative reform, which tries to support the human rights of children and families through cooperation. Parents and children should be involved in the proceedings as much as possible in order to find individual solutions which take into consideration the concrete interaction between all family members. Instead of having a professionally-controlled process, shared decisions should be made. The so-called "Family Group Conferencing" could be a possible approach. In this method, families try to find their own solutions with the support of a professional. Of course, it must be assured that the negotiators are treated adequately, irrespective of their strong or weak position within the family's interaction; therefore the mediation of experienced professionals is needed.

Tammy Harel Ben-Shahar (Hebrew University of Jerusalem) also spoke about an intervention into the right to parenthood. She highlighted the organization of public education in a multicultural liberal society and took a close look at the separation into public and private schools. *Harel Ben-Shahar* argued for a system of public schools in a broad, institutional sense, in which schools are not only publicly funded, but their core subjects are also publicly organized. At the same time, this system should ensure that the interests of the different cultural and religious groups living in the same society are taken into consideration. Therefore, the system also needs a certain separation, so that public goals like the development of responsible members of society and private goals like that of obedient believers can be combined, and in so doing can reconcile concerns on both sides. The discussion of *Harel Ben-Shahar's* theses showed on the one hand how similar social discussions can be throughout the world. Thus, an intense discussion is going on in Berlin about the role of ethics courses and on the establishment of private schools in the socially very heterogeneous area of Berlin-Kreuzberg[11]. At the same time, the discussion showed how much the local context shapes the way things are seen. The Israeli participants in the discussion emphasized the special role religion plays in their society, where some students do not even get teaching in mathematics because they already feel their rights are being injured through their exposure to public schooling.

Hadas Tagari (Bar Ilan University) deepened the aspect of religion and human rights in her lecture when speaking about family law. First she stated that strictly religious understandings of marriage and family often come into conflict with the exercise of human rights. As an example, *Tagari* referred to the difficulties of interreligious or same sex marriages, the problem of divorce and in general the equality of both genders in a marriage. At the same time, she emphasized that freedom of religion and protection of minorities demands respect for religious understandings. Conflicts are particularly dramatic in personal

[11] Cf. *K. Schaar*, Die Flucht ins Private – In den Großstädten schrecken immer mehr Eltern vor den staatlichen Grundschulen zurück, in: Süddeutsche Zeitung, 2 February 2009, No. 26, p. 40.

status systems within family law, when citizens belonging to different religions are subject to different legal standards and/or jurisdictions in the area of family law, for example in India. In these countries, reforms are frequently very hard to implement – often due to a colonial past reinforced by contemporary religious sentiment and identity politics. *Tagari* concluded that when it is not possible to abolish these systems, they should, if possible, at least be changed and made compatible with human rights. Many participants in the discussion felt that it would be difficult to publicly acknowledge such religious marriages without the required equality of both genders. The problem was discussed, whether a person can really decide freely to enter into such a marriage. It should at least be guaranteed that a person has the possibility of leaving these marriages, even if this goes against the religious rules. In countries where the state and religious law coexist side by side in normative pluralism, there need to be regulations to deal with conflict situations.[12]

Tali Marcus (Hebrew University of Jerusalem) presented a topic from the area of intersection between religious concepts of morality, different views on the wellbeing of a child and the exercise of the human right of parenthood. For her, the right to be a parent consists of two components: the right to procreate and the right to raise a child as a parent, with all rights and duties. According to *Marcus*, there are at present elements in both areas that do not receive enough legal attention. For example, regarding the right to procreate there are different aspects that need further discussion: the use of sperm or ovum donations and the service of a surrogate mother. Concerning the right to raise a child, *Marcus* highlighted the under-exposed situation of the legal acceptance of social parents, meaning one parent's new partner – irrespective of gender – who cares for the child, but does not have the same rights. Those rights can no longer be ignored, even if in recognizing such rights, there must also be a focus on the wellbeing of the child and the rights of the biological parent. It could also be imagined that the right to be a parent be given to more than two persons. The discussion showed how different Israeli and German family law are. While Israel does not have civil marriage, the German model is exactly that. Therefore solutions need to be applied differently. Connecting with existing facts – like that one cares for a child – could lead to good results.

The situation before the ICC could also be seen as a conflict between different human rights. On the one hand, the ICC has the task of following up on severe human rights violations. *Salif Nimaga* (Freie Universität Berlin) concluded in his lecture that the prosecution of crimes against humanity was already an important part of the international protection of human rights because the non-

[12] Cf. M. Kötter/G.F. Schuppert (eds.), Normative Pluralität ordnen: Rechtsbegriffe, Normenkollisionen und Rule of Law in Kontexten dies- und jenseits des Staates, Baden-Baden 2009 (forthcoming).

prosecution would itself be a violation of human rights. In response to this, the discussion raised the question whether or not there can be a right to prosecution and with it, finally, a right to retribution for harm suffered. While strong opposition against the idea of retribution was expressed by some[13], *Nimaga* had fewer reservations. Focusing on the idea of prevention, he has so far come to disappointing results in his study: a) the system is simply too slow to be efficient in reacting to offences that are still in an early stage but that have the potential to expand; b) as regards a preventive effect in general, there are empirical methodological problems; but research so far has not led to the conclusion that state leaders could be kept from committing human rights violations. c) For various reasons including isolating one element, it is also hard to analyze the significance of international criminal law in helping to implement the idea of justice in peace processes.

On the one hand, the human rights of the victims are discussed before the ICC; but on the other hand, the human rights of the offenders must also be preserved. *Birte Brodkorb* and *Elisa Hoven* (both of the Freie Universität Berlin) talked about the present arrangements for proceeding at the ICC. *Hoven* centered on the importance of a fair trial for the accused. In their presentations, both speakers touched on the problem of gathering evidence because of the great distance between the Court and the site of the crime and because the involved states are not always willing to cooperate. *Hoven* emphasized that the equality of arms between the prosecution and the defense is not always guaranteed. She critized especially the role of the chief prosecutor, which is the result of a compromise in the battle around the best criminal procedure, and she argued for an adoption of the Continental-European, more inquisitorial procedure[14] and therefore for a neutral position of the chief prosecutor. The discussion showed the hard front between the continental ("inquisitorial") and the Anglo-American ("adversarial") view; the Israeli system, finally, is very marked by Anglo-American influences. Just as the ICC already combines various elements,[15] others argued that the third way was the right way, thereby referring to the European Union, which also had to find its own, third way. *Hoven* urged not to sacrifice the efficiency of the system to political compromises.

[13] Also critical on this point, cf. *K. Ambos/Ch. Steiner*, Vom Sinn des Strafens auf innerstaatlicher und supranationaler Ebene, Juristische Schulung 2001, p. 9 (12).

[14] On the history of the terminology see *K. Ambos*, Zum heutigen Verständnis von Akkusationsprinzip und -verfahren aus historischer Sicht, Jura 2008, pp. 586 ff.

[15] *K. Ambos* (The structure of International Criminal Procedure: 'Adversial', 'Inquisitorial' or 'Mixed'?, in: M. Bohlander (ed.), International Criminal Justice: A critical analysis of institutions and procedures, London 2007, p. 429, 503) characterizes the present system as a combination of the adversial with the inquisitorial system.

VII. Conclusion

The symposium showed how multi-faceted the protection of human rights is. There is a rich field of topics to be worked on, starting with the reasons for the idea of human rights and its different forms right up to the various strategies for implementing them. On the one hand, the symposium's international and interdisciplinary character made more explanations necessary in order to understand one another; but on the other hand, this also made for a very rich and inspiring experience. The event was a successful prelude to a more intense future cooperation between the Freie Universität Berlin and the Hebrew University of Jerusalem as part of a structured PhD program.

Authors

Aharon Barak, Prof./President of the Supreme Court of Israel (retired) Interdisciplinary Center Herzliya

Daniel Bogner, Dr. theol. Max-Weber-Kolleg Erfurt

Sigrid Boysen, Dr. iur. Freie Universität Berlin, Faculty of Law

Birte Brodkorb Freie Universität Berlin, Faculty of Law

Ferry Bühring Freie Universität Berlin, Faculty of Law

Felicitas Chen Freie Universität Berlin, Faculty of Law

Hadas Eyal Hebrew University of Jerusalem, Department of Communications and Journalism

Tali Gal, Dr. iur. Hebrew University of Jerusalem, School of Public Policy and Government / Institute of Criminology

Alona Hagay-Frey Tel Aviv University, Faculty of Law

Klaus Hoffmann-Holland, Prof. Dr. Freie Universität Berlin, Faculty of Law

Elisa Hoven Freie Universität Berlin, Faculty of Law

Kristina Kühl Freie Universität Berlin, Faculty of Law

Claudia Mahler, Dr. iur. Menschenrechtszentrum der Universität Potsdam

Markus-Michael Müller Freie Universtität Berlin, Institute for Latin American Studies

Salif Nimaga Freie Universität Berlin, Faculty of Law

Kristina Roepstorff Freie Universität Berlin, Department of Philosophy

Julia Volkmann-Benkert Freie Universität Berlin, Faculty of Law

Sarah Wittkopp Freie Universität Berlin, Faculty of Law